James Drummond

Philo Judaeus

The Jewish-Alexandrian philosophy in its development and completion - Vol. 2

James Drummond

Philo Judaeus
The Jewish-Alexandrian philosophy in its development and completion - Vol. 2

ISBN/EAN: 9783337092368

Printed in Europe, USA, Canada, Australia, Japan

Cover: Foto ©Thomas Meinert / pixelio.de

More available books at **www.hansebooks.com**

PHILO JUDAEUS;

OR,

THE JEWISH-ALEXANDRIAN PHILOSOPHY

IN ITS

DEVELOPMENT AND COMPLETION.

BY

JAMES DRUMMOND, LL.D.,

PRINCIPAL OF MANCHESTER NEW COLLEGE, LONDON.

Σπούδασον οὖν, ὦ ψυχή, θεοῦ οἶκος γενέσθαι.

PHILO, DE SOMNIIS, I. 23.

IN TWO VOLUMES.
VOL. II.

WILLIAMS AND NORGATE,
14, HENRIETTA STREET, COVENT GARDEN, LONDON;
AND 20, SOUTH FREDERICK STREET, EDINBURGH.
1888.

[*All Rights reserved.*]

LONDON:
G. NORMAN AND SON, PRINTERS, HART STREET,
COVENT GARDEN.

CONTENTS.

VOL. II.

BOOK III. (*continued*).

CHAPTER IV.
The existence and nature of God .   1— 64

CHAPTER V.
The Divine Powers   65—155

CHAPTER VI.
The Logos . .   156—273

CHAPTER VII.
The higher Anthropology .   274—324

INDEX I. Subjects and Names . . . 325—341

INDEX II. References to passages in Philo . 342—353

INDEX III. References to passages in the Old Testament cited by Philo . 354—355

PHILO JUDAEUS.

BOOK III.

(CONTINUED.)

CHAPTER IV.

THE EXISTENCE AND NATURE OF GOD.

HAVING now inquired into the nature of man, and contemplated the scene amid which he is placed, we must proceed to the profounder questions which are suggested by our survey. In considering both the cosmos and man we came across traces of dependence which seemed to involve the action of an external cause; and in the human soul the faculties of reason and preferential choice, though not without the limitations of dependent being, yet pointed to a supramundane source, and introduced us to a world of ideas transcending the world of sense. We must examine the validity of these intimations, and endeavour to unfold their contents in the order of consecutive thought.

In inquiries about God, says Philo, there are two supreme topics which exercise the intelligence of the genuine philosopher; first, whether the Divine exists; and secondly, what it is in its essence.* This division of the subject affords a convenient arrangement for our own exposition of his views. We proceed, then, first to the evidence of the existence of God.

In constructing a philosophical system it was no more possible for Philo than it is for ourselves to take the existence of God for granted. He was met by atheistic theories more

* Monarch., I. 4 (II. 216).

or less pronounced, and was obliged to justify his faith upon rational grounds. Some, whom he characterizes as atheists, were content with an attitude of doubt; but others went further, and boldly asserted that there was no God at all, and that he was merely said to exist by men who had overshadowed the truth with mythical inventions.* The latter were under the necessity of offering a theory antagonistic to theism, and accordingly maintained that nothing existed but the perceptible and visible universe, which had never come into being and would never perish, but was unbegotten and incorruptible, without a guardian, a pilot, or a protector.† Since there was thus no invisible and intelligible cause outside of perceptible things,‡ it was assumed that everything in the cosmos was borne along by spontaneous motion, and that arts and studies, laws and customs, were due to the activity of the human mind alone.§ Others, who are described as Chaldæans, embraced a pantheistic theory. They too maintained that the phenomenal world was the only existence; but they declared either that it was itself God, or that it included God within itself as the soul of the universe. Apart from phenomena there was no cause, but the periods of the sun and moon and the other heavenly bodies determined the distribution of good and ill, and thus everything was handed over to the dominion of fate and necessity.‖ To these speculations Philo opposed the doctrine of Moses, "the beholder of the invisible nature, and seer of God,"¶ according to which the Divine exists, and the supreme God** is neither the cosmos nor the soul of the cosmos, nor are the heavenly bodies the prime causes †† of human events.‡‡

The arguments for the existence of God fall into two

* Mundi Op., 61 (I. 41); Praem. et Poen., 7 (II. 414).
† Somn., II. 48 (I. 696). ‡ Dec. Orac., 13 (II. 190).
§ Leg. All., III. 9 (I. 93).
‖ Migrat. Abr., 32 (I. 464); Cong. erud. gr. 9 (I. 526); Abr., 15 (II. 11).
¶ Mutat. Nom., 2 (I. 579). ** Ὁ πρῶτος θεός. †† Τὰ πρεσβύτατα αἴτια.
‡‡ Mund. Op., 61 (I. 41); Migrat. Abr., l.c.

divisions, those drawn from nature and those furnished by the intuitions of the soul.

The analogy between the macrocosm and the microcosm lies at the root of the evidence afforded by the contemplation of nature. The invisible mind in man occupies the same position in him as is filled by God in the universe;* and having this example in ourselves we may easily arrive at the knowledge of God. For has not the mind in us been appointed a sovereign, whom the whole community of the body obeys and each of the senses follows? And are we to suppose that the cosmos, the fairest and vastest and most perfect work, of which all other things are only parts, is without a king who holds it together and governs it justly? And if he is invisible, what wonder? For our mind, too, is unseen. If anyone will consider these things, he will know from himself and his surroundings that the cosmos is not the supreme God, but the work of the Supreme.† Appeal is also made to the analogy of human art. Things fabricated are always tokens by which the artificers are known. For who can see statues or pictures without immediately thinking of a sculptor or a painter? Who, when he sees clothes or ships or houses, does not form a conception of a weaver and shipwright and builder? And when one has entered a well-governed city, in which political affairs are most admirably arranged, what will he suppose but that this city is under the presidency of good rulers? When, therefore, one has arrived at the real Megalopolis, the cosmos, and has seen the firm-set earth, with its mountains and plains, filled with trees and fruits and animals of every kind, and flowing over it seas and lakes and rivers, both the perennial and those derived from wintry floods, and the pleasant temperature of winds and air, and the harmonious changes of the seasons, and, over all, the sun and moon, the

---

* Mundi Op., 23 (I. 16).
† Abr., 16 (II. 12). See also Migrat. Abr., 33 (I. 465).

sovereigns of day and night, the planets and fixed stars, and the entire heaven revolving in ranks with its own army, a veritable cosmos within the cosmos, must he not be struck with admiration, and reasonably, or rather necessarily conceive the notion of the Father and Creator, and conclude that beauties so great and of such surpassing order have not sprung spontaneously into being, but have been made by a world-forming artificer, and are ruled by a providence? The cosmos is most completely a work of art, and must, therefore, have been fabricated by some one who is excellent and most perfect in knowledge. In this way we have received our thought of the divine existence, proceeding from below upwards, and endeavouring to reach the Creator by just reasoning from his works as by a heavenly ladder.*

Intermediate between the two methods of approaching the Divine is an argument founded on the axiom of causality. In this argument we have to rely both on the observation of nature and on a mental intuition. We have already seen that the material universe fails in the marks of eternity and of efficiency.† Hence we are compelled by an intellectual law to seek, outside the visible world, for a first cause,‡ and for an efficient cause.§ Philo unhesitatingly discovers this cause in mind.‖ He does not martial his reasons for coming to this conclusion; but we can readily detect them in the views which we have previously unfolded. In rejecting the possibility of an eternal and efficient causality in matter, the only alternative was to have recourse to mind, which was the only other known entity, an entity moreover where the ideas of eternity and

---

* Monarch., I. 4 (II. 216-17); Praem. et Poen., 7 (II. 414-15).
† See Vol. I. p. 291 sq. and 297 sqq.
‡ Πρῶτον αἴτιον, τὸ πρεσβύτατον αἴτιον or τῶν αἰτίων. Conf. Ling., 25 (I. 423); Somn., I. 33 (I. 649); § 41, p. 656; Fort., 7 (II. 381); τὸ ἀνωτάτω αἴτιον, Fort., l.c.; De Nobilitate 5 (II. 442).
§ Τὸ ἐραστήριον αἴτιον, Mundi Op., 2 (I. 2); τὸ ἱρῶν αἴτιον, not said, however, of God, Prof., 24 (I. 565); τὸ πεποιηκὸς αἴτιον, Conf. Ling., 21 (I. 419); τὸ κινοῦν αἴτιον, Prof., 2 (I. 547).
‖ Ὁ τῶν ὅλων νοῦς, Mundi Op., l.c.

efficiency found a natural home. Again, the marks of causality in the universe were all of an intellectual order. The operation which produced the cosmos consisted of the impression of intellectual forms upon shapeless matter, and therefore the flow of cosmical change suggested the action, not of blind force, but of providential reason. And, lastly, within human experience mind alone possessed a self-determining power, and therefore could alone furnish a key to the ultimate mystery of being. Philo was thus led to the belief in a supreme Mind as the original cause of the universe.

He did not, however, believe that this was the highest mode of apprehending the Divine. It had been sanctioned, indeed, by philosophers of the highest repute, who supposed that our apprehension of the Cause must be derived from the cosmos and its parts and their inherent powers. Those who reasoned thus perceived God through a shadow, the artificer through his works. But there was a more perfect and purified mind, initiated into the great mysteries, which did not know the Cause from what had been made, as one might know the abiding substance from its shadow, but, having overstepped the begotten, received a clear manifestation of the Unbegotten, so as to apprehend him from himself. This might be illustrated by a familiar comparison. The visible sun was seen by the aid of nothing but the sun itself; and in the same way God, being his own light, was seen through himself alone, and nothing in heaven or earth co-operated or was able to co-operate in furnishing the pure apprehension of his being. Those who strove to see God from the creation were confined to conjecture; but those pursued the truth who perceived God by means of God, light by means of light.* This faculty of spiritual discernment is the peculiar perogative of our race, and is due to the divine nature of the mind. The thought of the Creator is the limit of blessedness; and, in order that man might not be without this, God breathed

* Leg. All., III. 82-3 (I. 107); Praem. et Pcen., 7 (II. 415).

from above of his own divinity, and it invisibly imprinted its own forms on the invisible soul, which thus received no longer mortal, but immortal thoughts.* We have before treated generally of the soul's power of intuition; we have only to add that this power culminates in the apprehension of God, and as the eyes, which are compacted of corruptible matter, are able to run up from the region of earth to the vast and distant heaven, so the eyes of the soul pursue their sublime course, and, winged with great desire of beholding real Being, pass the limits of the entire cosmos, and press on to the Unbegotten.†

This high faculty, however, though represented as inherent in the very nature of the soul, is far from being invariable in its action; and if we would enjoy its revelations, we must conform to its conditions. It was after Abraham had left "his land and his kindred and his father's house," that is the body, sensible perception, and speech, that God appeared to him; and this shows that God is clearly manifested only to him who has put off mortal things and had recourse to the incorporeal soul. For this reason, also, Moses took his tent and pitched it outside the camp, and removed far from the bodily encampment, hoping thus alone to become a perfect suppliant and servant of God.‡ This detachment from bodily things is naturally sought in that solitude which has always been dear to the devout. Abraham was sent into the trackless wilderness, from which ordinary men would desire to flee, as they would think it silly to choose, for the sake of obscure benefits, acknowledged ills. Yet such is the ordinance of nature: the sweetest life is that remote from the crowd, and those who seek and desire to find God love the solitude which is dear to him, striving in this first to resemble the happy and blessed nature.§ Retirement is favourable to that serenity which is another condition of spiritual discernment. So long as men

---

* Quod det. pot. ins., 24 (I. 208).   † Plantat. Noe., 5 (I. 333).
‡ Quod det. pot. ins., 44 (I. 221).   § Abr., 18 (II. 14).

are immersed in distracting affairs, and, like ships in a wintry storm, are tossed to and fro upon the waves of desire, they are naturally far from Him who is ever still, and draw near to the changeful flow of phenomenal existence. The unchangeable soul alone has access to the unchangeable God, and truly takes its stand near the divine power.* Since it is thus impossible for one who is still moved by the senses rather than the intellect to come to the investigation of real Being, and it is necessary to close the eyes and stop the ears and spend one's time in solitude and darkness, in order that the eye of the soul, by which intelligible things are seen, may not be overshadowed by anything perceptible, he who desires to see God will turn to the consideration of himself and his constitution ; and from that knowledge of himself which is symbolized in Greek by Socrates, in Hebrew by Tharrha (the father of Abraham), he will prepare a way to the knowledge of the universal Father, who is so difficult to reach by our guesses and conjectures. This knowledge is attained by our perception of the mingled analogy and contrast between ourselves and the cosmos, on which we have already touched. But Philo just mentions a deeper thought which brings this condition of self-knowledge under our present head. When Abraham most knew, he then most despaired of himself, that he might come to an accurate knowledge of Him who truly is. And the case is naturally so. For he who has fully apprehended has fully despaired of himself, having clearly learned the nothingness in everything created; and he who has despaired of himself knows the Self-existent.†

From the conditional nature of the higher knowledge it follows that it must appear in varying proportions in different persons, and in the same person at different times. In reference to this subject we may distinguish three stages in the experience of the soul. First, it is profitable, if not for the

* Post. Cain., 7-9 (I. 230-1).
† Migrat. Abr., 34-5 (I. 466-7); Somn., I. 10 (I. 629-30) ; Abr., 16 (II. 12).

acquisition of perfect virtue, at least with a view to civic life, to be trained up in primeval opinions, and to pursue the ancient report of noble deeds which historians and poets have recorded. But this inherited belief is lower than our intuitive perceptions. " When without our foresight or expectation a sudden light of self-taught wisdom flashes upon us, which, opening the closed eye of the soul, makes us seers instead of hearers of knowledge, putting in the understanding the swiftest of the senses, vision, instead of the slower hearing, it is vain to exercise the ears with words." It is God who causes these young shoots of intuition to spring up in the soul, and then the things derived from mere instruction slip away of themselves and are cancelled; for the acquaintance or disciple of God, or whatever name we are to call him, cannot possibly put up with mortal guidance.* And yet this apprehension is not necessarily the highest. The soul which continues in what is good is competent to perceive self-taught wisdom, but may not yet be able to see God, the sovereign of wisdom.† And even if it has attained to this supreme vision, it may still be subject to lower and higher moods. The understanding which is engaged in self-discipline is liable to irregular movements towards fruitfulness and the contrary, and is continually, as it were, going up and down. When it is fruitful and exalted, "it is illumined by the archetypal and incorporeal beams of the rational fountain of God who brings things to their completion; but when it descends and is barren, by the images of these, immortal words, which it is customary to call angels." In other words, when the rays of God, through which are produced the clearest apprehensions of things, leave the soul, the secondary and weaker light of words, no longer of things, rises, just as in this lower world the moon, which bears the second rank, sheds, after sunset, its dimmer light upon the earth.‡ We shall have to recur to

* SS. Ab. et Cain., 22-3 (I. 178). † Quod det. pot. ins., 9 (I. 197).
‡ Somn., I. 19 (I. 638).

these different grades of spiritual discernment; at present it is sufficient to mark their existence, in order to gain some insight into Philo's theological method.

The highest intuition is repeatedly described as seeing God; and the attainment of this vision is the ultimate goal of philosophy. This has been symbolized in ancient story through the change of name with which Jacob was honoured. Jacob is the name of learning and progress, which are dependent upon hearing; but Israel is the name of perfection, for it signifies the vision of God,* and what excellence could be more perfect than seeing that which really is?† Hearing is deceitful, for it is open to falsehood as well as truth; but vision, by which realities are perceived, cannot lie; and therefore Israel, the seer of God, is higher than Ishmael, the hearer.‡ The knowledge of God is the end of that royal way which those who have been endowed with sight desire to tread §; to see him is the most valuable of all possessions, and the firmest support of virtue and goodness.|| We must add, however, that there is no guarantee that we shall ever gain this glorious prize. Whether in seeking we shall find God is uncertain; for to many he did not make himself known, but their toil was ineffectual to the last. Yet the mere search for what is beautiful is adequate of itself to give us a share of good things, and to bring us joy; and those will obtain pity whose mental eye has been blinded, not by their voluntary choice, but by the inexorable power of necessity.¶

The above account is wanting in clearness and precision,

---

* "Ορασις θεοῦ: elsewhere, ὁρῶν θεόν.   † Ebriet., 20 (I. 369).
‡ Prof., 38 (I. 577).   § Quod Deus immut., 30 (I. 294).
|| Leg. ad Cai., 1 (II. 546). See also Leg. All., III. 66 (I. 124); Conf. Ling., 20 (I. 418); Quis rer. div. her., 15 (I. 483); Cong. erud. gr., 10 (I. 526); Mutat. Nom., 12 (I. 590); Somn., II. 26 (I. 681); Abr., 12 (II. 9). See too the expressions, ὄψιν θεοῦ and φαντασιώσῃ τὸν ἀγέννητον, Quod det. pot. ins., 43 (I. 221); φιλοθεάμων ψυχή, Quis rer. div. her., 15 (I. 484); ἡ ὁρατικὴ ψυχή, Prof., 25 (I. 566).
¶ Leg. All., III. 15 (I. 96); Post. Cain., 2 (I. 227); § 6, p. 230.

and does not satisfy the requirements of a rigorous argument; but I have thought it better to retain Philo's own vagueness of treatment than to ascribe to him a severity of reasoning which he nowhere attempts. We may gather with sufficient distinctness that he based his belief in the existence of God upon the evidences of dependence and of rational order presented by the cosmos; upon our intellectual intuition of cause, which he identified with mind; and upon moral and spiritual intuitions, which depended upon variable conditions, and consequently appeared in very different measures in different persons, or in the same person at different times. It is, then, from these sources that philosophy must derive her further knowledge of God. She will see his nature reflected in the order of creation, but will find him with much greater clearness amid the relations of thought and in the ideals which reveal themselves in the purified soul. The laws of our intelligence bear the impress of ontological facts, and things eternal and divine are not seen by the eye, but apprehended by the reason alone.

In entering on an examination of the nature of God as conceived by Philo it will be convenient first to notice the limitations which we must observe in applying the human analogy to the Divine Being. We have seen that the argument for the existence of God is partly founded upon this analogy: the presence of a mind in man guarantees the reality of a universal mind. If we accept this analogy, it is obvious that our knowledge of God must be drawn principally from ourselves. We can know nothing of mind except what is revealed in our self-consciousness, and even the philosopher must be tempted simply to select, enlarge, and spiritualize the human attributes, and fancy that in this way he can form an adequate conception of God. Philo was quite aware that we were thus confined within the limits of our own faculties, that our idea of God was coloured by our mode of apprehension, and that the difference between God and man was not only infinite in scale, but profound in character. We must notice the principal passages in which this view is enforced.

The fundamental failure of analogy between the microcosm and the macrocosm is thus stated: "Our mind has not fabricated the body, but is the work of another; wherefore also it is contained in the body as in a vessel. But the mind of the universe has generated the whole; and that which has made is better than that which is produced, so that it would not be carried in that which is inferior, to say nothing of the fact that it is not suitable for the father to be contained in the son, but for the son to grow up under the care of the father."* This obvious distinction, that man is derived, and is placed amid a scene which he has not created, while God is the underived fountain of all being, will be found to have far-reaching consequences. It secures, as is here intimated, the transcendence of God; and, as will be explained farther on, it reverses the relation in which the finite and the infinite minds stand to what in modern phraseology we may call their common attributes. We must return to these points; but at present it is sufficient to notice the fundamental and infinite difference between God and man.

So deeply was Philo impressed with the magnitude of this difference that he recurs to it again and again. Nevertheless, in speaking of God we are shut up within our own faculties, and are obliged to use language respecting him which cannot be philosophically justified. We are not able, says Philo, to get out of ourselves, but receive our apprehension of the Unbegotten from what happens to ourselves.† It is owing to this limitation, which is inevitably narrower in the uninstructed than in the cultured, that so many things are said in Scripture which it is impossible for the educated reason to accept. Philo's treatment of this subject throws so much light, not only on his exegesis, but on his philosophy,

---

* Migrat. Abr., 35 (I. 466). † Conf. Ling., 21 (I. 419).

that we must produce the substance of two illustrative passages.

When it is said that God swears (as in Ex. xiii. 11) we have to consider whether this is declared as in reality attaching to him, since it has seemed to very many to be inappropriate. For an oath suggests a testimony about something that is disputable, but to God nothing is obscure or disputable, and he requires no witness—indeed he could have none, for there is no other God equal to himself, to say nothing of the fact that he who bears testimony is, to that extent, superior to him to whom testimony is borne, a supposition inadmissible in the case of God. Men, when they are disbelieved, have recourse to an oath in order to obtain credit; but God, when he speaks, is worthy of credit, so that even his words, so far as security is concerned, differ in no respect from oaths. And, indeed, while our judgment is accredited by an oath, the oath itself is accredited by God; for it is not on account of an oath that God is to be believed, but on account of him that the oath is sure. Why, then, did the Hierophant [Moses] think proper to introduce him as swearing? In order that he might at the same time confute and console our weakness. For we cannot constantly store up in our soul that verse, so worthy of the Cause, "God is not as man,"* so as to escape all anthropomorphic expressions; but generally participating in the mortal, and unable to think of anything apart from ourselves, or to escape from our own destinies, sunk in the mortal like snails, or wrapt in a ball, like hedgehogs, round ourselves, we form our thoughts both about the Blessed and Incorruptible and about ourselves, shrinking from the absurdity of statement, that the Divine is in the human shape, but setting up again the impiety in fact, that he is subject to human passions. Therefore we attribute to him hands, feet, ingress, egress, enmities, alienations, wrath—parts and passions inappropriate to the Cause. Among these is included the oath, an aid to our weakness. [A little farther on Philo remarks that] Nature has given us innumerable things attaching to mankind, in none of which does it itself participate; for instance birth, being itself unborn; nourishment, though not requiring nourishment; growth, while it remains unaltered; periods of life, though receiving neither diminution nor addition; an organic body which it is unable to assume. Some one might say that these things are indifferent, but that nature must be in possession of what is confessedly good. Well then, among things that are really good let us examine those that are most admired among us, which we pray to obtain and are considered most happy when we have obtained. Who does not know that a happy old age and a happy death are the greatest of human blessings, in neither

---

* Numb. xxiii. 19.

of which has nature any share, since it is exempt from age and death? We must remove, then, everything begotten, mortal, mutable, profane, from our thought of God, the unbegotten, and incorruptible, and unchangeable, and holy, and only blessed.*

The second passage contains some important statements to which we must attend in another connection; meanwhile we may select the portions which bear upon our present subject. The narrative is under consideration where it is said that God took it to heart or was angry† that he had made man.

Some persons [says Philo], when they have heard these words, suppose that the self-existent Being‡ indulges in anger and wrath. But this Being is not susceptible of any passion whatever; for to be disquieted is peculiar to human weakness, but to God neither the irrational passions of the soul nor the parts and members of the body are at all appropriate. Nevertheless such things are said by the Legislator for the sake of admonishing those who cannot otherwise be brought to a sober frame of mind. For the two highest statements of the Law concerning the Cause are, first, that "God is not as man," second, that he is "as man."§ But the first is guaranteed by the most certain truth; the second is introduced for the instruction of the mass of mankind, and not because God is such in his real nature. For some men are friends of the soul, others of the body. The former being able to associate with intelligible and incorporeal natures, do not compare the self-existent Being to any kind of created thing; but the latter, being unable to divest themselves of their fleshly covering, and to look upon simple and uncompounded nature, have thoughts about the Cause of all which are similar to those that they entertain about themselves, not reflecting that he who is made up of an aggregation of many powers must require many parts for the service of his several necessities. Now God, as being unbegotten and the producer of all else, required none of the attributes of created things. Can we suppose that he has feet wherewith to advance? Whither will he go, since he has filled all things? And to whom, when he has no equal? And for the sake of what, as he is not anxious about health like us? Has he hands for receiving and giving? He receives nothing from anyone; for besides having no necessities, he holds all things as possessions. And he gives by using his Logos as the minister of his gifts. He required no eyes; for eyes have no perception without sensible light, and sensible light is created; but God saw before creation, using himself as light. It is needless to speak of the organs of nutrition, implying, as they do, successive satiety and want. These

* SS. Ab. et Cain., 28-30 (I. 181-3).   † 'Ενεθυμήθην.
‡ Τὸ ὄν.   § Deut. i. 31.

are the mythical creations of impious men, who introduce the Divine, nominally in the form, in reality with the passions, of a man. Why, then, does Moses ascribe feet, hands, ingress, egress, to the Unbegotten? Why does he arm him against his enemies? Why, moreover, does he attribute to him jealousy, anger, wrath, and similar affections? The answer is, that in framing the best legislation it is necessary to keep one end in view, the benefit of all who read. Those, then, who have received a happily constituted nature and an education in all respects faultless, finding the subsequent path of life passable and straight, take truth as their companion, and being initiated by her into the true mysteries of the Self-existent, they attribute to him nothing that characterizes creation. To them the most suitable of the oracles is the verse that "God is not as man,"—but neither is he as the heaven or the cosmos, for these, too, come under sensible perception. But those of duller nature, who have been badly educated and are unable to see sharply, require legislators to act as physicians, and devise for the present malady its suitable cure. To ill-bred and foolish servants a stern master is useful; for dreading his threats they are admonished against their will by their fear. Let all such, therefore, learn the falsehoods by which they will be benefited, if they cannot be brought to a sober state of mind by means of truth. The most honest physicians avoid telling the truth to their patients, knowing that they would thereby dishearten them, and prevent the cure of the disease. Similarly the Legislator, the best physician of the passions of the soul, proposed to himself one end, to eradicate the diseases of the understanding; and he hoped that he would accomplish his purpose, if he represented the Cause as using threats, and indignation, and inexorable wrath, and moreover weapons for attacks upon evil doers—for thus only is the fool admonished. Accordingly, with the two above-mentioned statements, that God is as man, and is not as man, there appear to be woven two other kindred things, fear and love; for all the commandments tend towards either the love or the fear of the Self-existent. To those who do not in thought ascribe to the self-existent Being either part or passion of man, but, in a manner worthy of God, honour it on account of itself alone, love is most appropriate; but to all others fear.*

We arrive, then, at the following results. Our language respecting God is inadequate, and our conceptions injuriously coloured, because we cannot avoid viewing him through the medium of our own nature. Nevertheless, we can to a large

---

* Quod Deus immut, 11-14 (I. 280-3). See also Conf. Ling., 27 (I. 425); Somn., I. 40 (I. 655-6); Post. Cain., 1, 2 (I. 226-7); Qu. et Sol. in Gen., I. 55 (Fragm., II. 669 sq.); II. 54, with the Greek in Harris, Fragm., p. 23.

extent escape from this defect by means of philosophical reflection, and come to regard as useful figures of speech many statements in Scripture which are accepted literally by the uneducated. The fundamental rule is to refuse to ascribe to God anything that can seem characteristic of created being. Hence Philo rejects as impious both anthropomorphism and anthropopathism; that is, he denies to God the possession, not only of a body, but of the irrational affections of the soul. This rule, however, did not apply to the spiritual and invisible man within, the reason and self-determining power which, as we have seen, appeared to give man a unique position in the world, and to be in their nature divine. Here, accordingly, we reach the conception of God which is implied in the very inquiry after his existence. He is free, self-determining Mind. That he is the Mind or Reason of the universe is everywhere assumed.* That the power of free volition properly belongs to him we have learned when considering the question of free-will in man; and so far is the ascription of this power to him from lowering him in the direction of anything created that it marks one of the characteristic distinctions between him and creation.† Even his beneficence is distinctly ascribed, not to any incapacity for ill, but to his preference for the good.‡ It thus appears that Philo accepted without reserve the Jewish doctrine of the personality of God; but instead of conceding that this imposed restrictions upon the divine Being, or dragged him down towards our finite nature, he believed that our personality lifted us above creation, and drew us up towards the infinite perfection of God. It was not that human thought blindly created a

---

* Ὁ τῶν ὅλων or τοῦ παντὸς νοῦς, Mundi Op., 2 (I. 2); Leg. All., III. 9 (I. 93); Gigant., 10 (I. 268); Migrat. Abr., 1 (I. 437); § 33, p. 465; § 35, p. 466; ὁ ὑπὲρ ἡμᾶς, Quis rer. div. her., 48 (I. 506).

† See Vol. I. p. 346; also τὸ αὐτεξούσιον τὸ θεοῦ κράτος, Plantat. Noe., 12 (I. 336); ὁ μὲν θεὸς ἑκούσιον, ἀνάγκῃ δὲ ἡ οὐσία, Somn., II. 38 (I. 692).

‡ Plantat. Noe., 20 (I. 342), ἄμφω δύναται, καὶ εὖ καὶ κακῶς ποιεῖν . . . . θάττερον μόνον βούλεται . . . . ἐκ τοῦ προαιρετικῶς εἶναι φιλόδωρον.

god after its own image, but that the reason and will which dwelt in men bore their own witness that they belonged essentially to the infinite and eternal realm.

In proving the existence of God from the phenomena of the cosmos we arrived at the same fundamental idea. We there recognised God as rational cause; and this is only another expression for self-determining mind. This conception places God in distinct antithesis to creation; for "efficiency,* which it is not allowable to ascribe to what is begotten, is the property of God,† while susceptibility‡ is the property of the begotten."§ As burning is the property of fire, and chilling of snow, so also is efficiency of God, and all the more because he is the source of activity to all others.‖ It follows that he is not simply the First Cause, the former Creator of a universe that now goes without him on its appointed course, but he exercises a continual causality, and is the ontological ground of every phenomenon, without whom the cosmos would vanish. He never pauses in his creative activity,¶ but both fashioned the world long ago without labour, and now and for ever ceases not to hold it together.** Being by nature efficient he never refrains from making the most beautiful things; and if he rests, his rest is not inactivity, but the most unwearied energy, exerted with perfect ease and without distress.†† Thus by our primary conception of him he is placed in contrast with the universe, and is recognised as unlike even the best of natural objects.‡‡

If we remember what Philo has said about the essence of the human mind, we shall not be surprised that he denies, in the most unqualified way, the possibility of knowing the divine essence. In deciding that the mind of man consisted of divine Spirit he clearly marked its place among the finite objects which are open to examination, but he only pushed

---

* Τὸ ποιεῖν. † Ἴδιον θεοῦ. ‡ Τὸ πάσχειν.
§ Cherub., 24 (I. 153). ‖ Leg. All., I. 3 (I. 44). ¶ Ib.
** SS. Ab. et Caini, 8 (I. 109). †† Cherub., 26 (I. 155). ‡‡ Gigant., 10 (I. 268).

the inquiry into its essence back to a prior stage. There we enter a region so exalted that we encounter impenetrable mystery, and the second of the two supreme questions respecting God is pronounced to be "not only difficult, but perhaps impossible" to solve.* This, however, is not owing to any obscurity in God himself, but to the feebleness of our mental vision—a doctrine which is clearly set forth in the following passage:

> "The divine region is truly untrodden and unapproachable, not even the purest understanding being able to ascend so great a height as only to touch it. It is impossible for human nature to see the face of the Self-existent." Face is a figurative expression to denote the purest idea of the Self-existent, for a man is chiefly known by his face. Observe, God does not say, "I am not visible by nature"—for who can be more visible than he who has rendered all other things visible?—but, "Being naturally such as to be seen, I am seen by none of mankind." The reason is found in the infirmity of the created. To speak briefly, one must first become God—which is impossible—in order to be able to comprehend God. If one will die to the mortal life, and live the immortal, he will perhaps see what he has never seen. But even the sharpest vision will be unable to see the Uncreated, for it will first be blinded by the piercing splendour and the rushing torrent of rays, just as fire affords light to those who stand at a proper distance, but burns up those who come near.†

Nor is it wonderful that we possess no faculty by which we can form to ourselves a representation of the self-existent Being, when the mind in each is unknown to us; and if we cannot know the essence of our own soul, it is mere simplicity to inquire into that of the universal soul.‡ In one passage Philo emphasizes the uncertainty of this subject with an absoluteness which goes beyond his accustomed thought:

> God [he declares] has shown his nature to none, and who can say either that the Cause is body or that it is incorporeal, or that it is of a certain kind, or that it is destitute of kind,† or in general express

---

* Monarch., I. 4 (II. 216). † Fragm., II. 654.
‡ Mutat. Nom., 2 (I. 579); Leg. All., I. 29 (I. 62). § Ἄποιον.

himself with certainty about his essence, or quality, or habit, or motion?*

He is usually content with the position that we cannot know what God *is*, though he is quite clear that there are certain things which he is *not*.

The inscrutability of the divine essence is sometimes brought into contrast with our assurance of the divine existence. This is done, for instance, in commenting on a verse in the song of Moses, where God is represented as saying, "Behold that I am"†:

> To speak of the self-existent Being as visible [says Philo] is not a strict use, but a misapplication of language. Accordingly, in the present passage he does not say, "Behold me,"—for it is impossible for God in his essential being to be at all understood by what is created—but, "Behold that I am," that is, see my existence; for it is sufficient for human reason to attain the knowledge that there is and exists something as the Cause of the universe; but to press beyond this, and inquire into essence or quality, is superlative folly.‡

Men of spiritual mind, accordingly, not only refrain from imposing a shape upon God, but are content to think of him simply as being, and to apprehend his existence as free from distinctive impress.§

The doctrine which we are considering is frequently illustrated by a reference to that remarkable passage in Exodus‖ where it is related that Moses prayed for a vision of the divine glory, and the Lord promised to make all his goodness pass before him, and yet could permit him to see only his back parts, and not his face. The most elaborate and suggestive comment upon this passage must be reserved till we come

---

* Leg. All., III. 73 (I. 128).
† Ἴδετε, ἴδετε, ὅτι ἐγώ εἰμι, Deut. xxxii. 39.   ‡ Post. Caini, 48 (I. 258).
§ Τὸ ψιλὴν ἄνευ χαρακτῆρος τὴν ὕπαρξιν καταλαμβάνεσθαι ... τὴν κατὰ τὸ εἶναι μόνον φαντασίαν ἐνεδέξαντο, μὴ μορφώσαντες αὐτό, Quod Deus immut., 11 (I. 281). The doctrine is completely summed up in the statement, ὁ δ' ἄρα οὐδὲ τῷ νῷ καταληπτός, ὅτι μὴ κατὰ τὸ εἶναι μόνον· ὕπαρξις γάρ ἐστι ὃ καταλαμβάνομεν αὐτοῦ, τὸ δὲ χωρὶς ὑπάρξεως οὐδέν. Ib., § 13, p. 282.
‖ xxxiii. 12, sqq.

to the doctrine of the divine powers; meanwhile the following may suffice:—

Moses, the beholder of the invisible nature—for the oracles say that "he entered into the thick darkness,"* intimating thereby the unseen essence—having searched everything else, sought to see clearly Him who is thrice-desirable and alone. But when he found nothing, not even a form resembling what he hoped for, he fled in his despair to the very Being whom he sought, and implored him, "show me thyself, that with knowledge I may see thee." Nevertheless, he was disappointed of his purpose, since a knowledge of the bodies and things which come after the Self-existent was considered an amply sufficient gift for the mortal race at its best; for it is said, "Thou shalt see my back parts, but my face shall not be seen by thee."†

God, then, is apprehensible, not by a front and direct gaze, for this would explain what his nature is, but from the powers which follow him, for these disclose, not his essence, but his being, by means of their effects.‡

The same doctrine is taught in the life of Abraham. The oracles that were delivered to him fanned into a flame his desire of knowing the self-existent Being, and under their guidance he left the land of the Chaldæans, and entered earnestly on his search for the one God; nor did he desist before he received clearer representations, not of his essence, for this is impossible, but of his being and providence. Hence he is said to have been the first to believe God, since he was the first to have a firm persuasion that there exists one supreme Cause, who provides for the cosmos and its contents.§ But his failure to penetrate the divine essence is intimated in the passage where it is said, "He came into the place

---

* Ex. xx. 21.

† Mutat. Nom., 2 (I. 579). We may use this as a comment on the shorter statement in the Vita Mosis, I. 28 (II. 106), in which Philo, wishing to exalt Moses to the utmost, uses these words—"he is said to have entered into the darkness where God was, that is, into the unseen and invisible and incorporeal essence that serves as the pattern of things, perceiving with the mind what cannot be observed by mortal nature."

‡ Post. Cain., 48 (I. 258); see also § 5, p. 229; Quod Deus immut., 24 (I. 289); Prof., 20 (I. 570); Monarch., I. 6 (II. 218-19). § Nobil., 5 (II. 442).

of which God had told him; and having lifted up his eyes he saw the place afar off."*

It sounds like a contradiction to say that he saw the place afar off after he had come into it, and therefore the one word must signify two different things, namely, the divine Logos, and God, who is before the Logos. The Logos is called place [for reasons which will be explained hereafter]. God is called place because he contains all things, but is contained by none. I and all other objects are not place, but in place, for the thing contained differs from that which contains; but the Divine, being contained by nothing, is necessarily its own place. Our passage, then, means that he who has been conducted by wisdom as far as the divine Logos, has not yet reached God in his essential being, but sees him afar off; or rather, he is not competent even to behold him from a distance, but sees only that God is at a distance from everything created, and that the apprehension of him is very far removed from all human understanding. Perhaps, however, place is not here an allegory for the Cause; and if not, we may understand the passage thus—Abraham saw that the place into which he had come was far from the nameless and unspeakable and incomprehensible God.†

Thus everywhere we meet the same conclusion, that the God-loving soul can attain only this as the supreme benefit of its search, to comprehend that God in his essential being is absolutely incomprehensible, and to see that he is not to be seen.‡

Immediately connected with this doctrine is that of the namelessness of God. When Moses inquired what answer he should give to those who questioned him about the name of the Being who sent him, the divine answer was, "I am He who is,"§ which was equivalent to, "It is my nature to be, not to be named."‖ From this answer the Israelites learned the difference between being and not being, and were taught that no name in the strict sense could be applied to him to whom alone being belongs. But since, owing to the feebleness of our mortal race, some mode of addressing the

---

* Gen. xxii. 3, 4.
† Somn., I. 11 (I. 630).
‡ Post. Cain., 4-6 (I. 228-9).
§ Ἐγώ εἰμι ὁ ὤν, Ex. iii. 14.
‖ Εἶναι πέφυκα, οὐ λέγεσθαι.

supremely Good is required, Moses was allowed to call God the God of Abraham, of Isaac, and of Jacob, that is, the God of the three natures or mental characters which seek for wisdom and goodness from instruction, from nature, and from self-discipline. This, however, is not properly speaking a name; and accordingly the Scripture adds, "this is a temporal name,"* as being found in our time,† not in that which is before time; and "a memorial," not that which is placed beyond memory and reflection; and again "to generations," not to unbegotten natures. So unspeakable is the self-existent Being that not even the ministering powers tell us their proper name. For after the wrestling in which Jacob engaged for the acquisition of virtue, he said to the invisible chief, "Tell me thy name;" but he said, "Why dost thou ask my name?" and did not tell it to him. For names are symbols of what is begotten, and are not to be sought amongst incorruptible natures.‡ It might seem to be a contradiction of this doctrine that Philo himself applies a rich variety of names to the Supreme Being. But the contradiction is only apparent. These names are nothing more than modes of reference adapted to the imperfection of our faculties, and do not really express the divine nature. A name, in the full sense which Philo evidently attributes to it, is that which describes and exhausts the essence of the object to which it is applied. The term triangle, for instance, is a complete expression for the figure which it represents. But no equivalent title can be applied to the Divine Being, because his essence is unknown; and accordingly even such terms as God and Lord, so far as they are significant of ideas, and not mere ciphers to denote

---

* Ὄνομα αἰώνιον. The unusual meaning of αἰώνιος is fixed by the context.
† Αἰῶνι.
‡ Mutat. Nom., 2 (I. 580); Vita Mos., I. 14 (II. 92-3); Somn., I. 39-40 (I. 655); Abr., 10-11 (II. 8-9). In § 24, p. 19 of the last-named treatise he says that God is called in Scripture κυρίῳ ὀνόματι ὁ Ὤν, by which he probably means a name devoted to him alone, but not one which is really exhaustive in its significance.

the unknown Cause, express, not the fulness of the divine essence, but only one of its aspects.* The same remark will readily apply to other appellations. The sacred tetragrammaton, however, presented a real exception, which Philo was unable to explain away, and did not attempt to reconcile with his philosophy. His reluctance to admit the consequences which, as he must have perceived, flowed from this undeniable violation of his rule, is apparent in his throwing upon others the responsibility of making the four letters indicative of the divine name, as though a doubt lingered in his own mind whether this could really be the case.† At all events the name was one which only those whose ears and tongue had been purified by wisdom might hear and speak in holy places, and no one else might utter anywhere. The theologian, Moses, says that the name consisted of four letters, perhaps regarding them as symbols of the first four numbers; for the number four contains all things—point, and line, and surface, and solid, which are the measures of all things— and likewise the best musical harmonies.‡ Beyond this vague surmise Philo does not attempt to determine the significance of this mysterious name, and in accordance with his philosophical principles must have viewed it as incomprehensible; the word was revealed to the prophet, but its meaning was not for us. It was agreeable to its awful character that he who unseasonably uttered the name of the Lord of men and gods should suffer the penalty of death. Respectful children keep in reverent silence the proper names of their parents, though they are only mortal, and use instead the terms which express their natural relation, father and mother, intimating thereby the surpassing benefits received from them, and their own thankful disposition. Shall they, then, be deemed worthy of forgiveness who indulge in unseasonable mockery, and make

---

* This statement will be fully illustrated farther on.
† Ἐξ ὧν ὄνομα τοῦ ὄντος φασὶ μηνύεσθαι. Vita Mos. III. 14 (II. 155).
‡ Ib. § 11, p. 152.

the most holy and divine name a mere expletive in their talk?*

The incomprehensibility of God is immediately connected with the doctrine that he is without qualities.† We must pay careful attention to this doctrine, because it is generally supposed that Philo here becomes involved in insoluble contradictions, his speculative conclusions standing in opposition to his religious necessities. A God without attributes, and known only to exist, is not one whom we can worship or love. Philo, accordingly, having, it is said, denied all attributes to God, nevertheless freely ascribes them to him, and thus vacillates between a negative and a positive description of the Divine in a manner which defies reconciliation. There is undoubtedly a certain amount of verbal contradiction; but I venture to think that Philo was perfectly aware of this, and that a considerable portion of his philosophy is devoted to its solution.

The proposition that God is without qualities, though not stated very frequently, is laid down with clearness and emphasis. It is great absurdity, says Philo, to suppose that God breathed through a mouth or nostrils; "for God is not only without qualities, but not even in the human form."‡ He who thinks that God has quality injures himself, and not God; for it is necessary to suppose him to be without quality, and incorruptible and unchangeable.§ And again, in a passage before referred to it is said, the companions of the soul, who are able to associate with intelligible and incorporeal natures, do not compare the self-existent Being to any form ‖ of created things, but divest him of all quality, and apprehend his existence as free from distinctive impress.¶ These statements are sufficiently explicit, and are in perfect agreement with all that we have hitherto said regarding the divine

---

* Vita Mos., III. 26, p. 166. † Ἄποιος.
‡ Leg. All., I. 13 (I. 50). § Ib., § 15, p. 53.
‖ Or *kind, ἰδέα*. ¶ Quod Deus immut., 11 (I. 281).

essence. That essence is inscrutable and nameless, because it is destitute of all the qualities which we recognize in things around us, and is absolutely *sui generis*. Thus the same negative predicate is applied to both God and matter. These stand over against one another, possessing natures entirely different, and each perfectly unique. They constitute the two poles of the universe, the one being the unknown essence which forms the substratum of all material things, the other the equally unknown essence which impresses upon matter its variety, and shapes it into a cosmos. Matter is without qualities because it is beneath them, being intrinsically motionless and dead, and waiting for something higher to differentiate its dull mass; God is without qualities because he is above them, owing nothing to them, but being himself the living source from which they emanate.

That we may clearly understand this doctrine, let us fix in our minds the meaning of the expression "without qualities." It denotes strictly that which does not belong to a class, but is *sui generis*. Philo uses it in this, its proper logical meaning. "Quality"* is that the possession of which makes you a member of a class; and when any quality is ascribed to you, you are to that extent placed on a level with a number of other individuals. This is explained by Philo in illustrating the categories. "I partake of substance," he says, having borrowed from each of the four elements what suffices for my composition; "I partake also of quality, by virtue of which I am a man."† It is evident from this that "quality" must be denied to anything that lies beyond the reach of classification. But it does not follow that that which stands by itself is destitute of properties or characteristic features; for even in a class each single object has its "property" ‡ as well as the "qualities" which bring it under a common name.§ It is a necessary consequence

---

* Ποιότης.   † Dec. Orac., 8 (II. 185).
‡ Ἰδιότης.   § Agr. Noe, 3 (I. 302).

that everything belonging to a class,*. is compound, because it has a share in a quality in which others, equally with itself, participate. It is thus dependent on something more comprehensive than itself, and, since compounds are liable to dissolution, it is destined to come to an end. Accordingly Philo says expressly that it is the nature of things belonging to a class to admit genesis and corruption, although the ideas by virtue of which they are enrolled in a class are incorruptible. For instance, "virginity" is always the same, but a "virgin" is changeable and mortal.† Music, the "habit"‡ by sharing which a man is a musician, is better than the musician, and the medical art is better than the medical man, because the "habit" is eternal, efficient, perfect, but the member of the class is mortal, susceptible, imperfect.§ The belonging to a class, then, involves notions which are quite inconsistent with any worthy conception of God, and nothing remains but to regard him as "without qualities," or unclassified, a Being alone in his infinite perfection, and dependent on nothing more comprehensive than himself.

This result, however, does not involve a denial of all properties, or, in other words, of all but negative predicates to God. It is only necessary that the attributes which are ascribed to him should be regarded as "properties," ‖ and not as "qualities." ¶ Thus matter, although it is "without qualities," may be described as extended and impenetrable;

---

* Ποιός. † Cherub., 15 (I. 148). ‡ Ἕξις. § Mutat. Nom., 21 (I. 597).

‖ Ἰδιότητες. For the meaning of ἴδιον see Aristotle's definition,—"Ἴδιον δ' ἐστὶν ὃ μὴ δηλοῖ μὲν τὸ τί ἦν εἶναι, μόνῳ δ' ὑπάρχει καὶ ἀντικατηγορεῖται τοῦ πράγματος, οἷον ἴδιον ἀνθρώπου τὸ γραμματικῆς εἶναι δεκτικόν· εἰ γὰρ ἄνθρωπός ἐστι, γραμματικῆς δεκτικός ἐστι, καὶ εἰ γραμματικῆς δεκτικός ἐστιν, ἄνθρωπός ἐστιν. οὐθεὶς γὰρ ἴδιον λέγει τὸ ἐνδεχόμενον ἄλλῳ ὑπάρχειν, οἷον τὸ καθεύδειν ἀνθρώπῳ. Organon, Top. I. v. 4. I quote this familiar definition that the reader may perceive clearly the force of Philo's language.

¶ This is illustrated by the phrase ἄποιον ὕδωρ, "pure water," which cannot be intended to deny all properties to water, but denotes that which is simply and absolutely water, and not water of a particular kind, such as salt or muddy. This example shows that the phrase may be applied without regard to the

for these predicates do not place it in a class along with other things which are not matter. They may indeed be applied to an indefinite number of particular objects, which are thus grouped into a class; but when they are so applied, they do not set these objects beside matter as members of the same genus, so that you could affirm that matter and certain other things are extended and impenetrable, but they only class them under matter and declare them to be material. The same reasoning will apply to the spiritual essence of God. He is "without qualities," and nevertheless we may affirm that he is eternal, self-existent, omnipotent, omniscient, perfect; for these predicates belong to himself alone, and place him outside of every genus. If the first two might be applied to matter, we must remember that Philo never does so apply them. If he believed in the eternity of matter, he regarded it as merely a negative reflection of the eternity of God; and so far was he from thinking of matter as self-existent, that he regarded it rather as the non-existent. The attributes which I have mentioned are by their very nature incommunicable. They lie outside of our experience, and are discovered only by an exercise of thought. But there are other attributes which fall within our experience, which distinguish man among the animal creation, which make him a member of a class, and nevertheless are ascribed to God. God is efficient, free, and self-determining. Does he,

---

higher genus under which the object may be included. Water in itself is a species of matter, but the water in question is ἄποιον because it is not a species of water. Much more is the expression applicable to God, who is not only not a species of God, but is not a species of anything. Philo himself uses the word in a similar way. Moses was desired to make a serpent. Why, then, did he make a bronze serpent, when he received no command περὶ ποιότητος? Perhaps because the favours of God are immaterial, ideas, and ἄποιοι, but those of mortals are seen conjoined with matter: Leg. All., II. 20 (I. 80-1). Of course, a serpent can be classified as animal or reptile; but a serpent in the abstract cannot be classified as a particular kind of serpent. So also man in the abstract is still a γένος without species, and it is only the concrete human being that becomes μετέχων ποιότητος, being man or woman: Mundi Op., 46 (I. 32).

then, belong in this respect to the same genus as man? Not at all; for volitional power is, as we have seen, a property of God.* If therefore we find volitional power in man, it only proves that the human mind has a share of the divine essence; and we thus discover the connection between the latter doctrine and Philo's theology. His belief in the divinity of the human mind was necessary in order to reconcile with his doctrine that God is without qualities his ascription to him of those attributes which are demanded by the religious affections. In assigning the same predicates to God and man, he may seem at first sight to class them together, as each participating in the same essence which is more comprehensive than either; but he really means that man has a finite share in an essence which God exhausts and transcends. We shall dwell farther on upon the predicates of God in detail; meanwhile we may observe that Philo does not hesitate to admit such epithets as munificent, propitious, merciful, good. But these do not draw God down from his solitary perfection. They are different aspects of his infinite fulness, archetypal ideas, which, borrowing all from him, lay the impress of quality only on derived existences.

In order to understand the above reasoning it is necessary to bear in mind that the notion of an attribute in the philosophy which we are considering was very different from that with which we are familiar. We may illustrate the difference by a change which has taken place more recently in physical theory. It was formerly supposed that electricity and heat were subtle fluids distributed among the particles of ordinary bodies, and when an object was electrified, or hot, or cold, it was thought that there was an excess or deficiency of these fluids. Here, then, we have an instance in which the predicate denoted, not, as it does to our present scientific apprehension, a certain condition of the object itself, but the

* Ἴδιον θεοῦ.

presence or absence of a substance completely different from the object. Now, if we could imagine, in connection with this hypothesis, that electricity and heat were ultimately the same substance, and were differentiated only through the modes of its manifestation, we could not properly class this substance with hot or electrical bodies; and if we ever spoke of it as hot or electrical, we should obviously use these words in a sense different from that in which they are applicable to glass and iron. The latter would have a share in heat and electricity; the former would be heat and electricity, or rather would be the unknown substance which comprised them both. This furnishes, I think, a strict analogy to Philo's conception of attributes. These were not conditions affecting the minds of which they might be predicated, but were essences in which individual minds had their finite and transient share; but they were all included within God, and were summed up in the unity of his infinite being. We noticed the former of these doctrines in our remarks upon the human powers; the latter must await its full development till we treat of the divine powers and the doctrine of ideas.

We must now direct our attention to those passages by which, as I believe, the above exposition is established. First of all, Philo expressly places God in a genus by himself. It is not allowable, he says, to suppose that anything is better than the Cause, since nothing is even equal, or even a little inferior to him, "but everything after God is found to have descended by a whole genus."* According to this statement God is the highest genus, and may therefore be properly described as the most generic. This is done in a passage where Philo speaks of the supply of water and manna furnished to the Israelites in the wilderness. The rock cut away at the top † is the wisdom of God, which he cut as topmost ‡

---

* SS. Ab. et Cain., 28 (I. 181).

† Ἡ ἀκρότομος πέτρα. I render it in this way, in order to preserve the play upon the words. ‡ Ἄκραν ἔτεμεν.

and first of all from his own powers, and from which he gives drink to God-loving souls. Now when they have received drink they are filled also with manna, which is the most generic thing, for manna is called "what," which is the universal genus. The allusion here is to Exodus xvi. 15, where it is related that, when the Israelites saw the manna, they said to one another, "What is this?"* Philo proceeds: "the most generic thing† is God, and second is the Word‡ of God, but all other things exist in word only,§ and in reality are equivalent to the non-existent."‖ It seems clear that these statements cannot be accepted in their ordinary logical sense. According to this, God would be the term which included the largest number of species and individuals, which denoted more and connoted less than any other term; and he would be "without qualities" only by being turned into an empty abstraction. That this is not Philo's meaning is apparent from the fact that the word God is not, in its highest sense, a generic term at all, but is always limited to one single being. We must therefore understand the above expressions in an ontological rather than in a logical sense. God is the most generic, not on account of his logical emptiness, but on account of his real fulness. He is the Being who includes all else within his own solitary perfection, and who alone imparts meaning and reality to all beneath. As Philo strongly expresses it, " God is full of himself and sufficient to himself, filling and containing all other things, which are deficient and desert and empty, but himself being contained by nothing else, as being himself one and the whole."¶ If, then, we pass from God to the good, the beautiful, the true, it is not by an ascent of thought and by introducing greater richness of meaning into a more abstract notion, but by a descent and by a resolution of the perfect

---

* Τί ἐστι τοῦτο; as it stands in the LXX.   † Τὸ γενικώτατον.
‡ Λόγος.   § Λόγῳ μόνον.   ‖ Leg. All., II. 21 (I. 82).
¶ Εἷς καὶ τὸ πᾶν, Leg. All., I. 14 (I. 52).

unity into lower and less significant conceptions. The latter are unified and exhausted in God; and it would therefore be more correct to say that the good is divine than to say that God is good.* It is for this reason that God is described as "the good," or "the first good,"† and the source of all that may be characterized by that epithet. He is, says Philo, "alone blessed and happy, unparticipant of all evil,‡ and full of perfect good,§ or rather, if one is to speak the truth, being himself the good, who showered on heaven and earth the individual things that are good."‖ Again, he is the most self-sufficing, and in need of nothing created, "the first good, the most perfect, the ever-flowing fountain of prudence and righteousness and all excellence."¶ Similarly he is called "the first and most perfect good, from whom, like a fountain, the cosmos and its contents are watered with the several things that are good."**

The description of God as "the good"†† might seem to determine his essence; but this is far from Philo's intention. God is indeed "the good," but he is much more; and we may therefore legitimately speak of his goodness.‡‡ This, instead of exhausting his being, is only "the oldest of the graces,"— the epithet oldest denoting, as often in Philo, that which is prior or superior in thought. It is eternal, and its exercise belongs to the divine nature.§§ The transcendence of God above goodness and every other property which we, in our limited experience, can ascribe to him is expressed several times in remarkable language. In the account of the embassy to Caius, Philo speaks of the Uncreated and Divine as "the first good and beautiful and blessed and happy, or, if one is to

---

* Compare the statement, οὐδὲν γάρ ἐστι τῶν καλῶν ὃ μὴ θεοῦ τε καὶ θεῖον, SS. Ab. et Cain., 17 (I. 174).
† Τὸ ἀγαθόν, or τὸ πρῶτον ἀγαθόν.
‡ So Tisch., Philon., p. 20, instead of "evils."
§ 'Αγαθῶν.   ‖ Τὰ κατὰ μέρος ἀγαθά. De Septenario 5 (II. 280).
¶ Sacrificant., 4 (II. 254).   ** Τὰ ἐπὶ μέρους ἀγαθά. Dec. Orac., 16 (II. 194).
†† Τὸ ἀγαθόν.   ‡‡ 'Αγαθότης.   §§ Quod. Deus immut., 23 (I. 288-9).

speak the truth, that which is better than the good, and more beautiful than the beautiful, and happier than the happy, and more blessed than blessedness itself, and whatever is more perfect than these. For speech* is not able to ascend to the intangible God, but sinks back, incapable of using proper names as a ladder to the manifestation, I do not say of the Self-existent—for not even the whole heaven becoming articulate voice would be rich in exact and well-aimed words for this purpose,—but of his attendant powers, creative, and regal, and providential."† This might be taken as a mere flight of rhetoric, to convey the most exalted idea of the divine perfection; but precisely similar language is used in calm philosophical exposition. In pointing out the necessity for both a susceptible and efficient cause in the creation of the cosmos, Philo describes the latter as most pure and unmixed mind, "better than virtue, and better than knowledge, and better than the good itself and the beautiful itself."‡ And again, while insisting that though it is possible for us to know God's existence, we cannot know his essence, he says, "for that which is better than the good, and older than the unit, and purer than one, cannot possibly be discerned by any other, because it is right that he should be apprehended by himself alone."§ The meaning of these expressions is at once apparent, if our previous exposition has been correct. God is superior to all our descriptive epithets, because he includes within himself the archetypal good and beautiful and blessed; and if we could know his name, we should find it comprehensive of all these and more. Our reason falters before this central unity. We can, nay must, believe in its existence; but we can see it only through the multiplying medium of our own imperfection, through those powers or ideas in which we are allowed to participate,

---

* Ὁ λόγος. † Leg. ad Cai., 1 (II. 546), slightly abridged.
‡ Mundi Op., 2 (I. 2). § Praem. et Poen., 6 (II. 414).

and we can hold its essence neither in conception nor in speech.

We are fortunately not left without particular examples which serve to illustrate and confirm the above explanation. First we may notice a passage relating, not to God himself, but to his Logos, which shows that Philo does not hesitate to use predicates which are the best available approximation to the truth at the very moment when he contends that they fall short of the truth. In speaking of the rational soul in man, which had the divine Logos for its archetype, he says, "it is necessary that the imitation of an all-beautiful pattern should be all-beautiful. But the Logos of God is better even than beauty itself, that which is beauty in nature,* since it is not adorned with beauty, but is itself, to speak truly, beauty's most becoming adornment."† Similar language is used of God. "He is full of unmixed blessedness. His nature is most perfect, or rather God is himself the summit and end and boundary of blessedness, participating in nothing else for his improvement, but having communicated his own to all individuals from the fountain of the beautiful, himself. For the beautiful things in the cosmos would never have become such if they had not been made like the truly beautiful, the Unbegotten and Blessed and Incorruptible, as an archetype."‡ Hence it is justly said, "There is nothing beautiful which is not of God and divine."§ The statement that God is older than the unit receives an explanation which

---

* Mangey, at the suggestion of Christophorson, reads ἐν τῇ φύσει αἰσθητῷ, which is not very intelligible. Dähne, assuming that αἰσθητῷ must be retained, places it after κάλλει, thus emptying the passage of its real significance [I. p. 262, Anm. 264]. Müller points out that the word is a mere gloss, and is not supported by any old authority [p. 370-1]. Nevertheless it must be confessed that its omission does not remove every difficulty, for the clause ὅπερ ἐστὶν ἐν τῇ φύσει κάλλος seems quite superfluous, unless it is intended to limit in some way the previous αὐτοῦ κάλλους, and this it cannot do if φύσει is to be understood, with Müller, in quite a general sense, and not merely of perceptible nature.

† Mundi Op., 48 (I. 33). ‡ Cherub., 25 (I. 154).
§ SS. Ab. et Cain., 17 (I. 174).

is verbally different, but involves a similar conception. Having demonstrated the unity of God, Philo draws his conclusion thus,—" God, then, has been ranked according to the one and the unit; or rather even the unit has been ranked according to the one God, for all number, like time, is younger than the cosmos, while God is older than the cosmos and its creator."* This shows that God is not one because he participates in unity, but because the eternal simplicity of his own nature is the archetype of unity. All these illustrations may be summed up in what Philo says of the rationality of God; for the rational is with him "the best genus,"† and what is said of its subordinate relation to the Divine must apply *a fortiori* to inferior genera. God, then, is before and above the Logos, and is superior to all rational nature.‡ His relation to the rational is defined in a passage where the difference which I have endeavoured to explain between the predicates of the uncreated and of created beings is exhibited with unmistakable clearness. Each of us, it is said, is two beings, animal and man. To each of these has been assigned a kindred power, to the one the vital, by virtue of which we live, to the other the rational, by virtue of which we have become rational. "In the vital, then, the irrational animals also participate; but the rational, God does not indeed participate in, but rules, being the fountain of the most ancient Logos," and the "archetype of rational nature."§ According to this statement God is rational because, as I have before expressed it, he exhausts and transcends rationality, and is the only source from which it ultimately flows, whereas man is rational because he has received a finite share of rationality, which

---

* Leg. All., II. 1 (I. 67).
† Τὸ λογικόν, ὅπερ ἄριστον τῶν ὄντων γένος ἐστί, Quod Deus immut., 4 (I. 275).
‡ Fragm., II. 625, answering to Qu. et Sol. in Gen. II. 62.
§ Quod det. pot. ins., 22, 23 (I. 207). We may compare the clear statement of Origen:—Ἀλλ οὐδ᾽ οὐσίας μετέχει ὁ θεός. Μετέχεται γὰρ μᾶλλον ἢ μετέχει καὶ μετέχεται ὑπὸ τῶν ἐχόντων πνεῦμα θεοῦ. Καὶ ὁ σωτὴρ ἡμῶν οὐ μετέχει μὲν δικαιοσύνης· δικαιοσύνη δὲ ὢν μετέχεται ὑπὸ τῶν δικαίων. Cont. Cels., VI. 64.

transcends him, and can communicate itself with unexhausted fulness to innumerable multitudes. Rationality is but one expression of God's eternal and infinite essence; and since it reveals itself in our intelligence, it stands, as it were, between God and man, deriving from the former all its store, and imparting a tiny portion to each human soul, or rather impressing each soul with its own form. We may sum up the discussion in words which have been preserved in the Armenian:—"If you wish to speak properly, those things which are justice and truth among men, are similitudes and forms; but those which are so with God are original principles and prototypes or ideas."* We thus see that the doctrine of intermediate powers or ideas, instead of being an artificial resource to reconcile discordant thoughts, grows out of the very roots of Philo's theology. But we must reserve this subject for future treatment, and be content for the present with having determined the force of the statement that God is without qualities, and the general nature of what in modern times we should call the divine attributes. The mode of thought is far removed from our own; but I hope I have succeeded not only in making it clear, but in showing how it was possible for rational men to adopt it. If the foregoing interpretation be correct, the serious and unphilosophical contradiction with which Philo is charged has been resolved; the strictest speculative thought ministers to religious aspiration; God, instead of being an empty abstraction, contains in his infinite fulness the eternal essence of all perfect things; and, though he is too full and too perfect for us to know him as he is, he gives us, in the ideals that impress our souls, side-lights and broken gleams, which are worthy of the implicit trust and devout homage so gladly yielded by the religious heart of Philo.

Having thus determined the general character of the divine

* Qu. et Sol. in Gen. IV. 115.

HIS ETERNITY. 37

attributes, we must now endeavour, though at ... omy* that the repetition, to bring under one view, and exhibit ... with me." predicates which are actually applied to God by Ph... ...ason; must remember that in the philosophy under consideration God is primarily revealed as self-determining Mind, the Cause of the universe. It follows that he must be eternal;* for the belief in something eternal is a necessity of human thought, and if God were not eternal he would depend on something older and greater than himself; in other words, he would not be God, the first and supreme Cause. We find, accordingly, that eternity is with Philo the most indispensable mark of Deity, the want of which deprives all originated gods of every just title to the name; † and eternity and causality are naturally brought into combination in references to the Supreme Being. He is "the unbegotten and eternal and the Cause of all things,"‡ the "oldest and generator and maker of all things, ... who is alone eternal, and Father of everything else, intelligible and perceptible."§ He is "the Father of the universe, the unbegotten God, and generator of all things."|| His eternity is further emphasized by resolving it into the two notions of without beginning and without end: he is "the unbegotten and incorruptible and eternal."¶ This reiteration (and other passages might be cited) shows how fundamental with Philo is the conception of God's eternity. The ascription to him, however, of eternal causality, far from endowing him with qualities and bringing him into a class, differentiates him in the most absolute way from everything else. All other things, however contrasted, have at least the fellowship of origination; but God is not like even the best of natural objects, for the latter have come into being and are destined

* Ἀΐδιος.
† Human., 2 (II. 386), γενητὸς γὰρ οὐδεὶς ἀληθείᾳ θεός, ... τὸ ἀναγκαιότατον ἀφῃρημένος, ἀϊδιότητα.
‡ Dec. Orac., 14 (II. 191). § Nobil., 5 (II. 442).
|| Cherub., 13 (I. 147).
¶ Ὁ ἀγένητος καὶ ἄφθαρτος καὶ ἀΐδιος, Dec. Orac., 10 (II. 187).

3 *

transcends him, it God is unbegotten and always active,* and fulness to inn he requires none of the properties of created expression

From this primary attribute another distinctive mark of the Divine was easily deduced. We have seen in another connection that change was a characteristic of creation, and betokened both an actual beginning and a natural liability to dissolution. The Eternal, therefore, must be incapable of change. He who supposes that God is not unbegotten and incorruptible, or not immutable, injures himself and not God; for it is necessary to regard him as both incorruptible and immutable, and he who does not think so fills his soul with false and godless opinion.‡ Accordingly God and creation (all at least beneath man) are separated from one another by this irremovable difference. Everything generated is necessarily mutable, for this is its property,§ as it is the property of God to be immutable.|| To this antithesis, however, there are some exceptions. The cosmos, which as a whole remains ever self-identical, reflects and guarantees the stability of its maker.¶ Among minor objects not only does the divine covenant share the unchangeableness of its author, but the same privilege is extended to the perfect man, who, by virtue of this exalted gift, occupies an intermediate position between man and God.** The reason for the last two exceptions is found in the system of allegorical interpretation. The immutability of God was taught in Scripture by the words "I *stand* here before thee,"†† standing implying an immovable permanence. The same term is applied to the covenant with Noah, "I will make my covenant to stand";‡‡ and we are told in Genesis§§ that Abraham was

* Gigant., 10 (I. 268). † Quod Deus immut., 12 (I. 281).
‡ Leg. All., I. 15 (I. 53). § Ἴδιον.
|| Leg. All., II. 9 (I. 72); § 22, p. 82; Cherub., 6 (I. 142), τὸ μὲν θεῖον ἄτρεπτον, τὸ δὲ γινόμενον φύσει μεταβλητόν. ¶ Somn., II. 32 (I. 687).
** Ib. sqq.; Post. Cain., 9 (I. 231); Quod Deus immut., 6 (I. 276); Mutat. Nom., 13 (I. 591). †† Ex. xvii. 6. ‡‡ Gen. ix. 11. §§ xviii. 22.

standing before the Lord, and in Deuteronomy* that the commandment came to Moses, "stand thou here with me." In the case of man we may find also a philosophical reason; for "only an immutable soul has access to the immutable God."† These exceptions do not violate the doctrine that immutability is the property of God alone; they only furnish an extreme instance of what we have already learned, that God can communicate to created beings some share of his own most elevated attributes.

With the unchangeableness and incorruptibility of God are closely connected his unity and simplicity. That Philo on every suitable opportunity insists on the unity of God in opposition to polytheism is only what we should expect, and it will be sufficient to notice here two or three passages in which an argument is advanced.

There is [he says], one Ruler and King, to whom alone it belongs to preside over and administer all things; for the Homeric saying, "the government by many is not good, let there be one governor, one king,"‡ is not more applicable to cities and men than to the cosmos and God; for of one cosmos there must of necessity be one Maker and Father and Lord.§

Not only is there but one God in contradistinction from several, one with whom nothing existed prior to creation, and who since the creation of the cosmos still remains in solitary supremacy, but he is himself absolutely one and indivisible, the archetypal unity.

He is "alone and one, not a compound, a simple nature." All other things involve plurality. For instance, man consists of soul and body. The soul has its irrational and rational parts, and the body includes the hot, the cold, the heavy, the light, the dry, the moist. "But God is not a compound, nor composed of many ingredients, but unmixed with all else. For whatsoever might be united to God is either superior or inferior or equal to him. But there is neither an equal nor a superior to

* v. 31. † Post. Cain., 9 (I. 231).
‡ Aristotle ends the eleventh book of his Metaphysics with the same quotation, introduced for the same purpose,—τὰ δὲ ὄντα οὐ βούλεται πολιτεύεσθαι κακῶς. οὐκ ἀγαθὸν πολυκοιρανίη· εἷς κοίρανος ἔστω. § Conf. Ling., 33 (I. 431).

God, and nothing inferior is united to him; otherwise he himself too will become inferior, and in this case he will be also corruptible, which it is not allowable to suppose. God therefore has been ranked in conformity with one and the unit; or rather even the unit is ranked in conformity with the one God: for all number, like time, is younger than the cosmos, while God is older than the cosmos, and its Creator."*

Elsewhere Philo insists that God is altogether without parts, because our parts and members have been formed by nature to serve our necessities; but God is in need of nothing, and therefore could derive no benefit from the possession of parts, and cannot be supposed to have them. He is a "whole, not a part," an expression which must denote that totality belongs to his very essence, and it is impossible to think of him piecemeal.† The stringency of this doctrine of the divine unity must be borne in mind when we have to treat of the manifoldness of divine manifestations.

We have already learned that God is invisible. This may be inferred from the attributes which we have just noticed. There is indeed a sense in which the Lord of the universe may be seen; but it is not with the eyes of the body, for these see only perceptible things,‡ and perceptible things are compound and full of corruption, while the Divine is uncompounded and incorruptible. He is seen, then, only with the eye of the soul. Again, there is this difference: the eyes see only with the co-operation of light, which is distinct both from the thing seen and from the person seeing; but what the soul discerns, it discerns without the assistance of anything else, for noümena are a light to themselves.§ This statement is in complete accordance with the prevailing tone of Philo's philosophy. God belongs absolutely to a realm cognizable only by reason, and to imagine him visible to the bodily eye would be to degrade him into the category of created, compound, and corruptible things. Nevertheless there is one passage in

* Leg. All., II. 1 (I. 66-7).
† 'Ο δὲ υἱὸς ὅλον, οὐ μέρος. Post. Cain., 1 (I. 226-7). ‡ Τὰ αἰσθητά.
§ Mutat. Nom., 1 (I. 578-9).

which another view is presented, and God is regarded as invisible, not by his intrinsic nature, but by his own choice. "He did not think proper," says Philo, "to be apprehended by the eyes of the body, perhaps because it was not consistent with holiness for the mortal to touch the Eternal, but perhaps also on account of the weakness of our sight; for it would not contain the beams poured from the Self-existent, since it is not able to look even at the rays of the sun."* These words certainly place God among objects which are by their nature perceptible, though removed beyond the reach of our imperfect vision. In doing so they contradict a fundamental distinction in Philo's philosophy. I have no explanation to offer, and can only suppose that the passage was written in careless haste.

In this connection we may notice the statement that God is light, which is carefully explained in such a way as to remove him absolutely from the cognizance of the senses. "The eye of the Self-existent," it is said, "requires no other light for apprehension, but being itself an archetypal radiance shoots forth innumerable beams, of which none is perceptible, but all are intelligible."† It follows that, when we hear in Scripture that God was seen by man, we must understand that this was done without perceptible light, for the intelligible can be apprehended only by intelligence; but God is a fountain of the purest radiance, so that, whenever he manifests himself to the soul, he causes the beams to arise that are without shadow and shine on every side.‡ Philo even goes so far as to call God the sun of the sun, the intelligible pattern of our perceptible luminary, supplying visible splendours from his invisible fountains.§ He makes it clear, however, in other passages that he does not wish this to be understood too literally, as though he was speculating on the unknowable essence of God. Intellectual illumination finds its nearest analogy in the reveal-

* Abr., 16 (II. 12). † Cherub., 28 (I. 156).
‡ Mutat. Nom., 1 (I. 579). § Sacrificant., 4 (II. 254).

ing power of light; and Philo's language is founded upon this
analogy, and not on any real resemblance which he supposed
to exist between the divine nature and the light which shines
upon the world of sense. "For as, when the sun has risen,
the darkness disappears and all things are filled with light, in
the same manner whenever God, the intelligible sun, rises and
shines upon the soul, the darkness of the vices and passions is
dispersed, and the most pure and lovable species of the most
radiant virtue becomes manifest."* It is only in conformity
with the rules of allegory that the sun is represented as like
the Father and Sovereign of the universe, for "nothing is
really like God." The resemblance is found, first, in the fact
that God is light, as is said in the Psalms, "The Lord is my
light and my saviour";† "and he is not only light but also the
archetype of all other light, or rather older and higher than
the archetype." The latter words show that the light-giving
power of God is simply one of his attributes, in the sense
already explained: behind it lies the unknown essence. Further to remove all ambiguity Philo reiterates, "he himself is
like nothing created." Another point of resemblance is found
in the fact that "as the sun separates day and night, so Moses
says that God divided light and darkness." And lastly, "as
the sun, when it has risen, displays the hidden things of corporeal nature, so God, when he generated all things, not only
brought them into manifestation, but also made what before
was not, being himself not only an artificer, but also a
creator."‡ These concluding words prove yet again that God
was regarded as more than light, and as having a fulness of
power of which that intelligible light which illumined the soul
was only a partial expression. We are dealing only with
analogies needed by the human understanding, and are not
warranted in the conclusion that Philo conceived of God as a

* Human., 22 (II. 403).
† xxvi. 1, where Philo reads φῶς instead of the LXX φωτισμός.
‡ Somn., I. 13 (I. 631-2).

"light-nature,"* that is, I presume, as one whose essence was light, even though the statement be guarded with the condition that the light was not of a corporeal, but an intellectual kind.†

We come now to certain views which seem necessarily involved in the conception of God as cause. We have already learned that, as the Creator of the universe, he must be transcendent above it, or, as Philo repeatedly puts it, he contains, but is not contained.‡ Nevertheless, though he is outside the universe, he is also within it; for, as the cause of all things, he must permeate all things. And lastly, since he is omnipresent, it is impossible to apply to him any terms which depend on the notion of place; for this, by implying a *here* and a *there*, involves limitation and a relation of parts to one another. This line of thought is connectedly expressed in a passage where Philo comments on the statement that "The Lord came down to see the city and the tower."§

This statement [he says] is certainly to be understood in a figurative sense; for it is the most surpassing impiety‖ to suppose that the Divine is present or absent, or comes down or the reverse, or is in any way affected with the same habits and motions as individual living beings.¶ These things are said by the Legislator concerning the non-anthropomorphic God in accordance with human analogy, with a view to our instruction. For who does not know that he who comes down must necessarily leave one place, and occupy another? But all things have been filled by God, who contains, but is not contained, to whom alone it belongs to be both everywhere and nowhere: nowhere, because he generated place along with the bodies which occupy it, and we may not assert that that which has made is contained in any of the things produced; everywhere, because having stretched his powers through earth and water, air and heaven, he has left no part of the cosmos desert, but, having collected all things together, compressed them with invisible bonds, that they might never be dissolved. To God in his essence, therefore, all terms of motion involving change of place are inapplicable.**

The allusion to the divine powers extended through creation

* Lichtnatur.   † Gfrörer, I. p. 120.
‡ Περιέχων, οὐ περιεχόμενος.   § Gen. xi. 5.·
‖ Ὑπερωκεάνιος καὶ μετακόσμιος, ὡς ἔπος εἰπεῖν, ἐστὶν ἀσέβεια.
¶ Τοῖς κατὰ μέρος ζώοις.   ** Conf. Ling., 27 (I. 425).

suggests questions as to the mode of God's omnipresence which we are not yet prepared to answer; but we may notice a few passages by which the other thoughts which are here combined are illustrated or confirmed. It would be impious and silly, we are told, to imagine that God really planted a paradise, as though he wanted luxurious resting-places, for not even the entire cosmos would be a worthy dwelling for God, the universal Ruler; for he is his own place, and we cannot suppose that the cause is contained in the effect.* It is for this, among other reasons, to show that the efficient cause is not in the thing produced, that Scripture compares the perceptible cosmos to the footstool of God.†

The transcendent solitude of God, however, did not cut him off from the world which he had made. "Though existing outside of the creation, he has none the less filled the cosmos with himself."‡ "He has reached everywhere, he looks to the ends, he has filled the universe, and of him not even the smallest thing is desert."§ From him, therefore, who has thus filled and permeated all things, and left nothing empty of himself, it is impossible to escape or to hide ; for what place can one occupy in which God is not?|| But precisely because he is thus everywhere, we cannot locate him; for place is that which contains, and therefore he who himself contains the universe, and is contained by nothing, cannot, like created things, be said to be in a place, but is his own place. This was taught in Scripture when God said to Adam, "Thou art some-

---

* Leg. All., I. 14 (I. 52); Plantat. Noe., 8 (I. 334).

† Conf. Ling., 21 (I. 419). The unique expression, τὸν σωτῆρα, τὸν ἐν τῷ κόσμῳ θεόν, which is found in Mangey's text of Septen., 23 (II. 296), could only mean that God, as the Saviour who supplies the bountiful provisions of nature, for ever works within the Cosmos, besides existing in his infinite perfection beyond it. In place of this reading, however, Tischendorf's improved text gives τὸν γενέτην καὶ πατέρα καὶ σωτῆρα τοῦ τε κόσμου καὶ τῶν ἐν κόσμῳ θεόν (Philon., p. 64, 1. 1, sq.).

‡ Post. Cain., 5 (I. 229).   § Quod det. pot. ins., 42 (I. 220).

|| Leg. All., III. 2 (I. 88); SS. Ab. et Cain., 18 (I. 175); Post. Cain., 2 (I. 227), § 9, p. 231.

where,"* implying that he himself was not somewhere, not walking in Paradise, and contained by it, as Adam had supposed.† We must therefore understand the language figuratively when Noah prays that God will dwell in the houses of Shem.‡ God is said to dwell in a house, not as in a place, but as exercising a peculiar providence and care over that spot; for every owner has a necessary regard for his house.§ This illustration may help to explain a passage where Philo expresses himself more philosophically. God, he says, is both here and there at the same time, not moving by transposition, so as to occupy one place and leave another, but using an intensive motion.‖ The meaning seems to be that, though God remains immovable in his omnipresence, yet his power may be manifested with varying intensity in different places, just as he is said to dwell in the purified soul as in a house, because his watchful providence is most conspicuous there.

In the foregoing exposition the influence of Stoical language and conceptions is apparent, though Philo differed from the Stoics in maintaining the transcendence and immateriality of God. The question may be raised whether he succeeded in borrowing only so much of the Stoical thought as suited the organizing principle of his own system, and in emancipating himself from materialism so completely as he supposed. The argument that God cannot be in a place because he contains, but is not contained, is not valid except on the supposition that he is an extended substance, vaster than all this visible universe. This notion is still more strongly suggested when it is said that God contains all things "in a circle,"¶ and that he is the boundary of the heaven,

* Gen. iii. 9, που εἶ, understanding που not in its interrogative but declaratory sense.
† Leg. All., III. 17 (I. 97); Somn., I. 11 (I. 630). ‡ Gen. ix. 27.
§ Sobriet., 13 (I. 402).
‖ SS. Ab. et Cain., 18 (I. 175-6). So, I think, we must understand τονικῇ χρώμενος τῇ κινήσει, assigning to τονικῇ the sense, not of extension, but of strain; for the former implies local movement, which is here expressly denied.
¶ Somn., I. 31 (I. 648).

which is indeed thus *contained*, but not by empty space, nor by any material substance* either equal in magnitude to itself or infinite.† This brings before the mind the idea of an essence extended through space, and so participating in one of the properties of matter; or, to borrow the simile which Augustine applies to his own immature thought, it likens God to an infinite sea, enclosing and permeating the universe as though the latter were a huge sponge.‡ Yet I believe that Philo was well aware that his language did not correspond with the reality, but only reflected those forms of the imagination which we so naturally employ when we think of the incomprehensible Cause. In the latter of the two passages just referred to, when he speaks of God as the boundary of the heaven, he calls him in the same line its "charioteer and pilot," words which are obviously figurative; and as he asserts that the heaven is infinitely great, he cannot have conceived of it as literally contained or circumscribed.§ In the former passage he proceeds to explain, in opposition to those who assign a place to God either within or without the cosmos, on the ground that everything in existence occupies some place, that in the opinion of others (evidently including himself) the Unbegotten is not like anything created, but absolutely transcends it, and leaves even the swiftest thought far behind; but for this very reason it is impossible to apprehend the intelligible cosmos except by transference from the perceptible, or to think of the immaterial except by starting from the material. If the "unchangeable beauty" of the higher world can thus be discerned only by an ascent from our lower perception into "some unspeakable and inexplicable vision," I think we may be justified in referring Philo's language respecting the all-containing nature of God,

---

* Σῶμα.   † Quis rer. div. her., 47 (I. 505).   ‡ Confess., VII. 5.
§ Cf. Quaest. et Sol. in Ex. II. 40, " Post autem mundum non est locus, sed Deus," which certainly suggests a meaning not strictly reducible to terms of space.

not to his dimensions in space, but solely to his transcendence as cause. It is not that he literally contains the cosmos as the circumambient air contains the earth, but that as the sole Cause he necessarily comprises within his own Being every visible effect, which remains as it were enfolded in everlasting dependence on his creative will. This view alone is in accordance with Philo's clearly defined doctrine of the divine unity ; for the notion of possible division is inseparable from that of extended substance. We may, therefore, conclude with some degree of confidence that, in Philo's opinion, not only was God incapable of being confined within the limits of any locality, but he was altogether exempt from the conditions of space.

If God is above the conditions of place, he is equally above time.* This subject is fully unfolded in connection with the unchangeableness of God.

Our sentiments [it is said] are inevitably liable to change, because it is impossible for us to foresee either the contingencies of the future or the sentiments of other people. But to God everything is manifest, for he penetrates even to the recesses of the soul, and sees clearly what is invisible to all others, and, making use of his own peculiar excellences, forethought and providence, he suffers nothing to escape his apprehension, since not even the obscurity of the future affects him, for nothing is either obscure or future to God. Future events are shaded by coming time ; but God is the Creator even of time, for he is the Father of its father, the cosmos being the father of time, having generated it through its own movement ; so that time has to God the relation of a grandson.† For the perceptible cosmos is the younger son of God, the

* Post. Cain., 5 (I. 228-9).

† It is, I think, interesting to compare the similar figure, applied to a different subject, in Dante :—

"Filosofia, mi disse, a chi l'attende,
  Nota non pure in una sola parte,
  Come Natura lo suo corso prende
  Dal divino Intelletto e da sua arte:
  E se tu ben la tua Fisica note,
  Tu troverai non dopo molte carte,
  Che l'arte vostra quella, quanto puote,
  Segue, come il maestro fa il discente,
  Sì che vostr' arte a Dio quasi è nipote."
                  Inferno, Canto xi., 97-105.

ideal world being the elder. Time, therefore, having sprung from the movements of this younger son, cannot affect the conditions of the divine existence, and nothing is future with God; for his life is not time,* but eternity,† the archetype of time, and in eternity nothing is either past or future, but only present.‡

This statement helps to confirm our criticism in regard to space; for it is obvious that Philo elevates God absolutely above the conditions of time. Eternity is not, in his view, equivalent to infinite duration, of which time is a finite portion; for such duration necessarily involves past, present, and future. The essence of time consists in succession; for, according to Philo, our idea of it is derived from moving bodies.§ But phenomenal succession is precisely what is denied in eternity. To God the totality of existence is immovably present, and the coming and going of events, which pass in an ever-flowing stream across the limited field of our consciousness, cannot ruffle the stability of his infinite Being. Eternity is the archetype of time, not by communicating to it its own unalterable now, but because it bears to real being, that is to God, the same relation that time bears to phenomenal existence.‖

God's independence of time and space establishes his omniscience. As we have seen in the passage which we have been just considering, no remoteness of time can conceal anything from him to whom time exists not. The same consideration applies to space. No man can hide himself from God, who has filled the universe, and of whom not even the smallest thing is desert. And what wonder, when one cannot emerge even from the material elements, but in flying from one necessarily enters another? Nor can one escape from the cosmos, for there is nothing outside it, the whole of the four elements having been expended in its composition. Since, then, it is impracticable to flee from the work of God, how is

---

* Χρόνος.
† Αἰών.
‡ Quod Deus immut., 6 (I, 276-7).
§ Somn., I. 32 (I. 649).
‖ See Vol. I. pp. 294 sq.

it not rather impossible to run away from its Maker and Governor?* The doctrine of the divine omniscience is brought forward chiefly in its relation to the secrets of the human soul. The impure and impenitent man need not draw near to worship; "for he shall never escape the observation of him who sees the things in the recesses of the understanding, and walks about in its inmost sanctuaries."† Those who revile the deaf or put a stumbling-block in the way of the blind think not of him who holds his hand over and shields those who are unable to help themselves; but they cannot shun the notice of God "the overseer and administrator of all things,"‡ even "of the invisible soul."§ What is a terror to the evil is a joy to the good; for he who honours parents, or pities the poor, or benefits friends, or defends his country, or cares for the common rights of all men, is well-pleasing before God, who sees all things with sleepless eye, and calls what is virtuous to himself.||

That God is omnipotent follows immediately from the doctrine that he is the sole efficient Cause, for any resistance to him involves an adverse causality. This is constantly implied, though not frequently asserted in Philo's discussions. We are not, however, without explicit statements that "all things are possible to God."¶

Having now noticed those attributes of God which bear no moral impress, we turn to the consideration of those which are expressive of his character. The treatment of these rests upon the doctrine of the divine perfection, which is an immediate consequence of the views already explained. If God is the sole absolute Cause, exhausting and transcending, as we have said, every ideal that discloses itself in our minds, then he

* Quod det. pot. ins., 42 (I. 220-1).   † Quod Deus immut., 2 (I. 274).
‡ Justit., 10 (II. 368-9).   § Human., 2 (II. 384).
|| Mutat. Nom., 5 (I. 584).
¶ Mundi Op., 14 (I. 10); Joseph., 40 (II. 75); Vita Mos., I. 31 (II. 108); Qu. et Sol. in Gen. IV. 130.

must be complete in himself, and contain within his own being the sum of all conceivable good. His solitary independence is asserted in the strongest manner by Philo. In commenting on the words "I am thy God"* he says :

> They are employed with a misapplication, and not strictly; for the self-existent Being, regarded simply as self-existent, does not come under the category of relation;† for it is full of itself, and sufficient to itself, equally both before and after the creation of the universe; for it is unchangeable, requiring nothing else at all, so that all things belong to it, but it, strictly speaking, to nothing.‡

In order to understand this passage we must carefully observe the limitation "regarded simply as self-existent," and not hastily conclude that Philo places God beyond the reach of every relation. His statement rests upon the logic of correlative terms, and is well illustrated by the examples in the Organon. To take one of these—man is not the correlative of slave; for though a man may possess a slave, yet he does so not *qua* man, but *qua* master.§ So the conception of pure being is complete in itself, and does not carry the thought to anything beyond; but the moment we speak of God as Creator we are obliged to think also of things created, or when we describe him as Cause we thereby put him in relation to things that are caused. We must not suppose, however, that Philo is drawing a merely logical distinction, for with him logical distinctions are an evidence of reality. God, in the totality of his being, is elevated above all relation; he is absolutely complete in himself, and nothing can add to his fulness and perfection. Accordingly, when we ascribe to him titles which are descriptive of relation, we refer only to certain aspects of his being, certain "powers" which, because they are directed towards objects, are "*quasi* relative."‖ The limitation *quasi* is not used, I think, in order to evade a difficulty. It seems to imply that the dependence of

---

* According to the LXX. rendering of Gen. xvii. 1.
† Τὸ γὰρ ὄν, ᾗ ὄν ἐστιν, οὐχὶ τῶν πρός τι.   ‡ Mutat. Nom., 4 (I. 582).
§ Arist., Org., Cat., vii. 6 sqq.   ‖ Ὡσανεὶ πρός τι.

the correlative terms is not mutual, but is all on one side, and that not the divine side. The powers of the Self-existent are put forth into exercise without experiencing any alteration in their intrinsic character through the reaction of the objects to which they are applied; so that, although their names involve a relation, it would be truer to say that their objects are relative to them than that they are relative to their objects.

The fulness of the divine perfection which gives rise to this kind of one-sided relation, if I may so describe it, is clearly set forth in a passage where Philo alludes to the offerings that were presented in the festivals.

By the institution of festivals for himself God laid down a dogma which is most necessary for the votaries of philosophy. "Now the dogma is this: God alone truly feasts. For he alone rejoices, and alone is glad, and alone has good cheer, and to him alone does it belong to keep peace unmixed with war. He is without pain, and without fear, and unparticipant of evils, unyielding, unharmed, unwearied, full of pure blessedness. His nature is most perfect, or rather God is himself the summit and end and boundary of blessedness, sharing in nothing else with a view to his improvement, but communicating what is peculiarly his own* to all individual beings† from the fountain of the beautiful, himself. For the beautiful things in the cosmos would never have become such if they had not been modelled after the really beautiful, the unbegotten and happy and incorruptible, as an archetype."‡

The thought of the exhaustive completeness of God, which we meet in the above passages, is repeated again and again in various forms. "The full God"§ is in need of nothing, and cannot be benefited by human service.|| He is "full of himself and sufficient to himself."¶ Nothing "takes rank with him; for he needs nothing at all."** God cannot literally swear, because there is none competent to be his witness; for "he is all the most precious things to himself, kindred, relation, friend, virtue, blessedness, happiness, knowledge, understanding, beginning, end, whole, all, judge,

* Τὸ ἴδιον.
‡ Cherub., 25 (I. 154). Cf. Septen. 5 (II. 280).
|| Quod det. pot. ins., 16 (I. 202).
** Leg. All., II. 1 (I. 66).

† Τοῖς ἐν μέρει.
§ Ὁ πλήρης θεός.
¶ Leg. All., I. 14 (I. 52).

opinion, counsel, law, action, sovereignty."* "God is not a salesman, lowering the price of his own possessions, but the bestower of all things, pouring forth the ever flowing fountains of favours, not desiring a recompense; for neither is he in need himself, nor is any created thing competent to bestow a gift in return."† In fine God, "the most self-sufficing, is in need of nothing else," being "the first and most perfect good," "the ever flowing fountain of prudence and righteousness and every virtue."‡

It is a part of God's perfection that he has no participation in evil;§ and it follows from this that he cannot be the source of evil. "It is," says Philo, "a fault difficult or impossible to cure to say that the Divine is the cause of evils." With God are the treasures of good alone.‖ All his gifts are entire and complete.¶ He is "the cause only of good things, and of no evil at all, since he was himself both the oldest of beings and most perfect good."** This doctrine, on which we need not dwell further at present, has important consequences in connection with the problem of evil, which will be considered in its proper place.††

We must notice here a doctrine on which we have already

---

* Leg. All., III. 73 (I. 128). † Cherub., 34 (I. 161).
‡ Dec. Orac., 16 (II. 194); Sacrificant, 4 (II. 254). For the doctrine that God is without wants see also Leg. All., III. 63 (I. 123); Cherub., 13 (I. 147); Post. Cain., 1 (I. 227); Dec. Orac., 10 (II. 187); Fort., 3 (II. 377).
§ See the passages quoted on the last page from Cherub. and Septen., and also Mundi Op., 52 (I. 36).
‖ Prof., 15 (I. 557-8.) ¶ SS. Ab. et Cain., 14 (I. 173).
** Conf. Ling., 36 (I. 432). See also Qu. et Sol. in Gen. I., 100, with the Greek in Harris, Fragments, p. 19, ὡς γὰρ ἀμέτοχος κακίας, οὕτω καὶ ἀναίτιος.
†† One passage, however, expressly contradicts the above doctrine:—δύο φύσεις εὕρομεν γινομένας καὶ πλαττομένας καὶ ἄκρως τετορευμένας ὑπὸ θεοῦ, τὴν μὲν ἐξ ἑαυτῆς βλαβερὰν καὶ ἐπίληπτον καὶ κατάρατον, τὴν δὲ ὠφέλιμον καὶ ἐπαινετήν, καὶ ἔχουσαν τὴν μὲν κίβδηλον, τὴν δὲ δόκιμον χαρακτῆρα .... Εἰσὶ γὰρ ὥσπερ ἀγαθῶν, οὕτω καὶ κακῶν παρὰ τῷ θεῷ θησαυροί: Leg. All., III. 34 (I. 108). If we attempt to reconcile this statement with Philo's habitual teaching, we can only do so by saying that the evil nature is not so absolutely, but only in relation to the moral life of man, in which the lower always becomes evil in presence of a higher.

touched, but which belongs to the idea of the divine perfection. The nature of God is free from pain and fear and every passion.* This follows directly from the fundamental conception of God as cause. As efficiency is his property, so susceptibility is the property of that which is created; and, therefore, as the passions express our susceptibility in relation to certain objects, they cannot affect the supreme causal nature. The same conclusion follows from moral considerations; for whatever we do on account of wrath or fear or pain or pleasure or any other passion is confessedly blameworthy, but whatever we do with right reason and knowledge is laudable.† Nevertheless Philo does not hesitate, in a very serious passage, to speak of the "wrath of God‡" as a thing to be carefully shunned.§ But in doing so there can be no doubt that he consciously used language which did not correspond with his philosophical thought, and that he meant only to express that passionless opposition to sin which we may reasonably ascribe to the Divine; for, as we have seen, he believed that the use of this kind of inadequate or erroneous language was necessary, and in regard to this very passion of anger, he says elsewhere that it is properly predicated of men, but only figuratively of the Self-existent.‖

From the reasonableness of God, thus wholly undisturbed by passion, it follows that he is sinless. This is, of course, everywhere implied, and in one passage it is distinctly asserted. "Not to commit any sin at all is the property of God,¶ and perhaps, also, of a divine man."** This statement derives its chief interest from the added words, which show that Philo did not regard the attribute of sinlessness as absolutely incommunicable. A divine man was conceivable in whom this element of the supreme perfection might dwell. We need not suppose that this concession is inconsistent with the belief that

---

* Abr., 36 (II. 29).   † Quod Deus immut., 15 (I. 283).   ‡ 'Οργὴ θεοῦ.
§ Somn., II. 26 (I. 682).   ‖ Quod Deus immut., l. c.   ¶ Ἴδιον θεοῦ.
** De Poenitentia, 1 (II. 405).

sinlessness is in the strictest sense the property of God; for it does not cease to be so by being lent out, as it were, for the enjoyment of others, and the sinless man could become so only by sharing in this high gift, and incorporating what was really divine.

A parallel to this communication of the Divine occurs in connection with the happiness of God. We have recently cited a remarkable passage in which Philo insists on the divine joyousness. The thought is one which is often repeated in his writings. "The divine blessedness,"* "the blessed and happy nature of God,"† are expressions which he uses when nothing in the context particularly suggests them. Elsewhere he says that "the nature of God alone participates in perfect blessedness and happiness."‡ Here the word "participates"§ is not philosophically accurate; for it implies that happiness is something external to God, of which he is only a sharer. This cannot be intended, unless we have already gone fatally astray in our interpretation; and we may recognize in this example the ease with which language is used in relation to God which is strictly applicable only in the case of lower beings. A little farther on Philo adds, more philosophically, that the genus of joy belongs to no other than the Father of the universe. But notwithstanding this exclusiveness of possession, joy is not wholly unknown to the human race. Though he possesses it, God does not grudge its use to the worthy. He bestows as much as the capacity of the recipient will allow; but joy mingled with pain is all that human imperfection will receive, even as the pure light of heaven is seen by us commingled with our dusky air.

It is a part of the divine happiness to enjoy perfect rest and peace.

Hence [we are told] the Sabbath, which means rest, is repeatedly said by Moses to be the Sabbath of God, not of men; for the one

* Cherub., 6 (I. 142). † Special. leg., IV. 8 (II. 343).
‡ Abr., 36 (II. 29). § Μετέχουσα.

entity that rests is God. But by rest is meant "not inactivity—since the Cause of all is by nature efficient, never ceasing from making the most beautiful things—but the most unlaboured energy, without distress, with ample ease." On the other hand, even the sublimest objects in nature, the sun and moon and entire heaven and cosmos, are distressed by continual movements which are not at their own disposal, and the changing seasons give the plainest evidence of their weariness. But God changes not, and has no weakness, and is therefore unwearied, and, though he makes all things, will never cease to rest.*

The same idea is brought out in an allegory of unusual beauty.

The city of God is called by the Hebrews Jerusalem, a name which signifies the vision of peace.† Wherefore we must not seek for the city of the Self-existent in the regions of earth—for it is not built of wood and stone—but in a soul unwarlike and keen-sighted, which has preferred the contemplative and peaceful life. For what more venerable and holy house could one find for God than an understanding devoted to contemplation, eager to see all things, and not even in a dream desiring sedition or confusion? For the "Spirit which is accustomed to associate with me unseen" testifies that "God alone is the most absolute and real peace, but begotten and corruptible matter is all continual war; for God is volition,‡ but matter is necessity.§ Whosoever, then, is able to leave war, and necessity, and genesis, and corruption, and to go over to the Unbegotten, to the incorruptible, to the volitional, to peace, would justly be said to be a dwelling-place and city of God. Let it, then, make no difference to thee to name the same subject either vision of peace or vision of God; for of the many-named powers of the Self-existent peace is not only a member, but even a leader."||

In these passages the weariness and struggle of nature are ascribed to the necessity under which it labours. The connection of strife and fatigue with necessity is not immediately apparent; but it is probably inferred from the analogy of man, who, when he labours under compulsion, soon grows tired, and inwardly wages war against the demands of his situation. The human experience is easily transferred to the heavenly bodies, which were also supposed to be intelligent beings, and from them to the entire cosmos. We cannot help remembering St. Paul's description of the whole creation as

* Cherub., 26 (I. 154-5).   † Taking the word from רָאָה and שָׁלוֹם.
‡ 'Εκούσιον.   § 'Ανάγκη. || Somn., II. 38 (I. 691-2).

groaning and travailing, waiting to be delivered from the *bondage* of corruption into the *liberty* of the glory of the children of God.* In opposition to the toil and trouble of material nature is the peace of God, which, as we can readily understand, is the immediate result of unrestricted volitional energy. Where the same high purpose flows on undisturbed and unimpeded, the sense of effort and confusion must disappear, and leave behind an eternal rest and peace.

If, before the creation of the universe, God was so perfect, so sufficient to himself, so blissful, why did he make things which he could not need? To this question Philo returns the answer which Plato had given before him †: "Because he was good and munificent,"‡ and did not grudge to matter, which of itself had nothing beautiful, a share of his own best nature.§ And as the goodness of the Self-existent was the reason for creation, so he continued to bestow abundant blessings both on the universe and on its parts, not because he judged anything to be worthy of favour, but having regard to his eternal goodness, the oldest of his graces, and supposing that it belonged to his happy and blessed nature to do good.‖ Philo insists upon this goodness so repeatedly and in such varied terms that we must devote a little space to the survey of its activity.

In the first place, then, God was, by virtue of his goodness, the Cause, the Maker, the Generator of the universe.¶ In connection with creation several questions of the highest importance will arise, but at present we must be content to fix

---

* Romans viii. 19, sqq.   † See Timaeus 29 E.   ‡ Mutat. Nom., 5 (I. 585).
§ Mundi Op., 5 (I. 5). J. G. Müller well points out that Philo imports into the meaning of τὸ ἀγαθόν the Hebrew conception of God's loving-kindness which does not belong to it in Plato [Des Juden Philo Buch von der Weltschöpfung. Herausgegeben und erklärt von J. G. Müller, Berlin, 1841; p. 156].
‖ Quod Deus immut., 23 (I. 288-9). For the reason of creation see also Cherub., 35 (I. 162); Leg. All., III. 24 (I. 102).
¶ It is sufficient to refer to Mundi Op., 2 (I. 2); § 61, p. 42; Cherub., 13 (I. 147); § 35, p. 162; Animal. sacr. idon. 6 (II. 242); Nobil., 5 (II. 442).

firmly in our memory the fact that, whatever agents or methods he may employ, God is regarded as the sole source of creative causality, and as having acted, not under the suggestion of any advocate, but from himself alone.*

In the second place, God must exercise providence over the cosmos, caring both for the whole and for the parts. The doctrine of providence is involved in the very conception of a benevolent Creator, "for it is necessary by the laws and ordinances of nature that that which has made should always care for what has been generated, even as parents provide for children."† Hence God is the "saviour and benefactor" of the world.‡ "Arrayed in sovereignty, he holds the reins of the cosmos by an autocratic law and right, providing not only for those who are more worthy of preference, but also for those who seem to be more obscure."§ He is the one leader and sovereign and king, to whom alone it rightfully pertains to preside over and administer all things,"|| "the Archon of the great city, the general of the invincible host, the pilot who always manages the universe with saving care."¶

In the exercise of his providence God's goodness is poured forth with unrestricted prodigality. Being munificent, he graciously bestows good things upon all, even upon the imperfect, provoking them to the acquisition and zealous pursuit of virtue, and showing at the same time that his superabundant wealth is sufficient even for those who will not be greatly benefited. He displays this very evidently in the case of inanimate nature. For whenever he rains in

---

* Οὐδενὶ δὲ παρακλήτῳ—τίς γὰρ ἦν ἕτερος;—μόνῳ δὲ ἑαυτῷ χρησάμενος. Mundi Op., 6 (I. 5).

† Mundi Op., 61 (I. 41). See also § 3, p. 2; Special. leg., III. 34 (II. 331); Praem. et poen., 7 (II. 415).

‡ Animal. sacr. idon., 6 (II. 242). Σωτήρ also Quod Deus immut., 34 (I. 296); Migrat. Abr., 5 (I. 440); § 22, p. 455; Quis rer. div. her., 12 (I. 481); Abr., 27 (II. 21); Septen., 23 (II. 296); Praem. et Poen., 19 (II. 427); Exsecrat., 8 (II. 435); Fragm., II. 677 (Qu. et Sol. in Ex. II., 2); Tisch., Philon., p. 43, l. 3.   § Migrat. Abr., 33 (I. 465). || Conf. Ling., 33 (I. 431).

¶ Dec. Orac., 12 (II. 189).

the sea, and showers down fountains in the most desert places, and waters the thin and rough and barren soil, making rivers gush forth in floods, does he not display the excess of his riches and goodness?* In accordance with this rule he tempers judgment with mercy, and exercises pity for the benefit even of the unworthy; "and he not only pities after he has judged, but he judges after he has pitied; for with him pity is older than judgment."† In varied figures Philo speaks of "the abundant riches of the graces‡ of God," which are awarded without stint to the worthy.§ They issue from ever flowing fountains, themselves perennial, unceasing, and without intermission.|| Again, they are personified, and become the virgin and immortal daughters of God, whom an immovable law of nature binds in inseparable unison.¶ The kindness of God is described by many predicates. He is munificent,** giver of wealth,†† kind and lover of man,‡‡ benevolent,§§ propitious.|||| He manifests equity and kindness,¶¶ and "his goodness and propitious power are the harmony of all things."***

In speaking of the unrestricted prodigality of the divine beneficence, we refer only to its own intrinsic character, for it is in fact restricted by the limited capacity of those who experience it. The graces of God are uncircumscribed, but

---

* Leg. All., I. 13 (I. 50).   † Quod Deus immut., 16 (I. 284).
‡ Or favours, χάριτες.   § Leg. All., III. 56 (I. 119).
|| Mundi Op., 60 (I. 41); Cherub., 34 (I. 161); Sacrificant, 5 (II. 254).
¶ Post. Cain., 10 (I. 232); Migrat. Abr., 7 (I. 441); Vit. Mos., II. 1 (II. 135).
** Φιλόδωρος. See, besides the passages already cited, Cherub., 6 (I. 142); § 9, p. 144; Post. Cain., 8 (I. 231); Quis rer. div. her., 7 (I. 477); Plantat. Noe, 20 (I. 342); 21 (I. 343); Migrat. Abr., 6 (I. 441); Prof., 13 (I. 556); Praem. et Poen., 20 (II. 428).
†† Πλουτοδότης, Post. Cain., 10 (I. 232).
‡‡ Χρηστὸς καὶ φιλάνθρωπος, Abr., 36 (II. 29).
§§ Εὐμενής, Vita Mos., II. 1 (II. 135); III. § 31, p. 171.
|||| Ἵλεως, Vit. Mos., II. 1; Special. leg., II. 5 (II. 274); De Parentibus colendis, § 9, p. 28, of Mai's edition, this treatise not being in Mangey; Fort., 7 (II. 382); and several other places.
¶¶ Exsecrat., 9 (II. 436).   *** Vit. Mos., III. 14 (II. 155).

not so the faculties of their recipients; for it is not the nature of that which is created to receive benefits, as it is the nature of God to confer them, since his powers are infinite, but the created, being too weak to receive their vastness, would faint unless the lot of each were measured out in due proportion.* If the stream of mercies came with its own inexhaustible flood, the plain would be like a lake and a marsh instead of fruitful soil.† Or we may take an example from the sun, whose flame we cannot look upon unmixed, for the sight would be extinguished by the brilliance of its rays; yet the sun is only a single work of God, a mere aggregate of ether, and how, then, can we view unmixed those unbegotten powers which, round about him, flash forth the most splendid light? Thus no mortal, not even the whole heaven and cosmos, could receive in their purity the knowledge and wisdom and prudence and righteousness, or any of the other virtues of God. The Creator, therefore, in condescension to our natural weakness, is not willing either to benefit or punish as he can, but only in proportion to the capacity which he sees in those who are to be affected.‡ Similarly, he does not deliver oracles conformably to the greatness of his own eloquence, for who could contain the force of the divine words? For this reason the Israelites said to Moses, " Speak thou to us, and let not God speak to us, lest we die."§ For if God wished to display his riches, not even the whole world would hold them; but wishing us to derive benefit from what he bestows, he alternates his gifts, so that the continual enjoyment of the same favours may not produce satiety and harm. If creation were ever without the divine graces, it would utterly perish; but it cannot bear their excessive and unsparing rush, and therefore its strength is the measure of their flow.‖

* Mundi Op., 6 (I. 5).
† Quis rer. div. her., 7 (I. 477). ‡ Quod Deus immut., 17 (I. 284-5).
§ Ex. xx. 19.
‖ Post. Cain., 43 (I. 253-4). See also Ebriet., 9 (I. 302) ; Somn., I, 22 (I. 642); Monarch., I. 6 (II. 218).

While Philo thus retained an assured faith in providence, he was quite aware of the objections which were brought against it. These objections are discussed at great length in two treatises "On Providence," which have been preserved in an Armenian version, and from the second of which Eusebius quotes considerable portions in his Praeparatio Evangelii. There is little that is original in the line of argument, and what is most remarkable in these essays is their purely philosophical and Hellenic character, which broadly distinguishes them from the expository and Judaic colouring of most of Philo's writings. The first is open to suspicion, and cannot be safely appealed to in evidence of Philo's opinions.* It would not greatly advance our knowledge of the Alexandrian philosophy, and it would occupy a disproportionate space, to give an analysis of the contents even of the second treatise, and it must suffice to notice a few of the more salient points.

The constantly recurring arguments against providence are mainly of two kinds. First, the existence of pain, which is inflicted by various natural agents, appears inconsistent with the supreme control of benevolent design. The violence of winds and rain, hail and snow, lightning, earthquakes and pestilence, wild beasts and noxious reptiles, inflict the most terrible calamities on mankind.† In reply to this, several considerations are urged. First, in regard to the whole question of providence, it must be remembered that the doctrine does not imply that God is the cause of everything. Of what is really evil, or what lies outside the course of nature, God is no more the cause, than the beneficent law by which a virtuous state is administered is the cause of the violence and rapine which spring from the wickedness of the inhabitants.‡ Secondly, of those natural agencies which are occasionally attended by calamitous results, some, like wind and rain, were

---

* See Vol. I. p. 306, Note.   † Prov. II. §§ 87-97.   ‡ Prov. II. § 82.

not intended for the ruin of sailors and farmers, but for the benefit of the whole human race, for they purify the earth and air, and so contribute to the support of animals and plants; and if a few suffer, it is no wonder, for they are an insignificant portion of that entire class of men for whose benefit providence is exercised.* Again, some infliction of pain may be necessary to ensure the safety of the entire system. The man who takes a just view will rejoice at whatever is done without moral evil, even if it do not conduce to pleasure, and will regard it as designed for the preservation of the universe. A physician sometimes in dangerous diseases amputates parts of the body in order to procure health for the remainder, and a pilot, when storms assail him, casts over the cargo in order to save the passengers, and no blame, but, on the contrary, praise, attaches to these actions. In the same way we must always admire the nature of the universe, and be pleased with everything that is done apart from voluntary ill, considering, not whether anything conduces to pleasure, but whether the cosmos is directed safely, like a well-governed city.† Another consideration is that some destructive agencies are only accidental consequences of the primary design. We can easily find illustrations of this in human affairs. Often through the showy liberality of the master of a gymnasium some of the vulgar wash in oil instead of water, and so make the ground slippery; but no one will ascribe the slipperiness to the providence of the master. In cities you may observe the porches generally inclining towards the south, so that those who walk in them may be warm in winter, and enjoy the breeze in summer. A consequence follows which was not intended by the builders: the shadows thrown by the supports indicate the hours. So again, fire is an essential work of nature, but smoke is its consequence. Nevertheless, even smoke is sometimes valuable, by betraying the advance of

---

* II. § 99; Fragments, II. 642.   † Praem. et poen., 5 (II. 413).

an enemy when fire is invisible owing to the brightness of the sunshine. Thus, in the realm of nature, the rainbow and halo and similar phenomena are merely accompaniments of her primary works. Eclipses are consequences of the divine natures of the sun and moon; but they serve also as indications either of the death of kings or the destruction of cities. In the same manner earthquakes, pestilences, thunderbolts, and similar things, though said to be sent by God, are not really so; for God is the cause of no evil whatever. The changes in the elements produce these things, not as primary works of nature, but as consequences which follow the necessary and primary works.* And lastly, just as states support executioners, not through respect for their sentiments, but for the utility of their services, so he who cares for that great city the cosmos, appoints tyrants as public executioners over those states in which he perceives violence, injustice, impiety, and other evils; and often, without employing such subordinates, he inflicts the needed punishment through his own agency, and sends famine, pestilence, or earthquake, by which crowds are every day destroyed, and a great part of the habitable world is desolated out of regard for virtue.† There is some contradiction between these last two explanations, so far as earthquakes and pestilence are concerned; but in regard to such causes of suffering they may be accepted as alternative hypotheses.

The suggestion of a moral purpose in pain leads to the second difficulty. If the world is righteously governed, why is pain distributed with such a startling neglect of moral considerations? Why have the wicked an abundance of all good things, riches, fame, honours, health, beauty, strength, while those who pursue wisdom and virtue are almost all poor, obscure, in a low position, without the means of support, weak in their whole body, dull in their senses, languid,

---

* Prov. II. §§ 99-102; Fragments, II. 643-4.
† Prov. II. §§ 31-2; Fragments, II. 642.

diseased, dyspeptic? Why have a Polycrates and a Dionysius everything that heart can wish, while a Socrates is done to death by the plots of a worthless wretch?* Why are the just subject to the fear of death when a battle is imminent, and the righteous and wicked overwhelmed with death at the same time and place when a ship founders at sea?† The first answer is an attempt to limit the extent of the problem. It does not follow that if certain persons are esteemed good by us, they are really so, for the means of judgment possessed by God are more accurate than those enjoyed by the human mind. We have no tribunal which is competent to distinguish between the righteous and the wicked, and secret sins may have been committed by those who are apparently just.‡ Then we must remember that providence takes a comprehensive view, and that the righteous could not be exempt from suffering without altering the whole constitution of things, or suspending the laws of nature for individual benefit. Having mortal bodies we are necessarily exposed to human troubles. Bad men may plot against the good. If we are in pestilential air, we must suffer from disease. If the wise man is exposed to the rain he will be wet; in the north wind he will shiver; in summer he will be hot. Those who live in places where crime abounds must submit to the penalty; and all who brave the wintry seas accept an equality of risk.§ The good man readily acquiesces in this condition, for the things which the wicked prize are not the highest objects of human pursuit, or the sources of real blessedness. If you have made your own divinity, your mind, the slave of innumerable masters, desire, pleasure, fear, pain, folly, intemperance, cowardice, injustice, it never can be blessed; and no one could ever suppose that it would be so who was once

---

* Prov. II. §§ 3-14.
† (I. § 59).
‡ Prov. (I. § 60); II. § 102; Frag., II. 644.
§ Prov. II., §§ 24 and 102; Frag., II. 638 and 644.

smitten with admiration of the God-like good and beautiful. The wise man desires not wealth and glory, but the acquisition of virtue, and to penetrate to the audience-chamber of royal reason.*

The foregoing sketch, in which, for the sake of clearness, I have followed an order of my own, may suffice to show that Philo was provided with reasons which appeared to justify the ways of God, and how largely he followed Greek models in the discussion of this difficult question.

We ought not to leave this subject without noticing the fact that, in speaking of the providential arrangements of the world, Philo sometimes substitutes nature for God. It will be sufficient to illustrate this usage by a few examples. He says that "all-provident nature"† assigned the face as the most suitable locality for the senses.‡ "Nature" appointed man the ruler of plants and animals.§ Though there are co-operating causes in the production of plants and animals, yet nature is the highest and elder and real cause; and it is the fountain and root and foundation of the arts and sciences, and, unless nature be first laid down as a basis, everything is imperfect.‖ Of these passages the last is peculiarly important, because it is the writer's object to show why first-fruits were dedicated to God, and at the same time it is apparent that nature is not used as synonymous with God, but to denote the divine constitution of things, brought about by the divine agency within them.¶

After the foregoing exposition, we shall not think that Philo has fallen into a feeble and unphilosophical contradiction when, having denied that God has any name, he yet speaks of the

---

* Prov., II. §§ 16 sqq.; Frag., II. 635 sqq.
† Ἡ πάντα προμηθουμένη φύσις. ‡ Leg. All., I. 11 (I. 49).
§ Agr. Noe, 2 (I. 301). ‖ Quis rer. div. her., 23 (I. 489).
¶ See also Special. Leg., III. 36 (II. 332), ἐπεκτήνατο ἡ φύσις δεόντως: Human., 9 (II. 390); Exsecrat., 7 (II. 434), ὧν [ἀνθρώπων] μία μήτηρ ἡ κοινὴ φύσις.

"many-titled name of God,"* and himself applies to him, besides the customary term "God," quite an extraordinary number of appellations.† There was no name which could express his essence, and be regarded as the spoken equivalent of his incomprehensible being; yet there were many names by which he might be referred to for the purposes of intelligent communication, though they denoted only some of his modes of operation or some partial aspects of his full and inexhaustible perfection. How the transition was conceived between unity

---

* Dec. Orac., 19 (II. 196), τῷ τοῦ θεοῦ πολυωνύμῳ .. ὀνόματι.

† The following list, though probably far from complete, will convey a fair impression of Philo's usage. There are, no doubt, many passages which I have failed to note, as I did not originally intend to make an exhaustive list; but the numbers attached to each epithet, representing the number of times that I have actually made a note of the expression, will probably give a pretty correct notion of the proportional use of the various terms. Ὁ ὤν occurs perhaps 29 times; but 18 times the gender is doubtful owing to the case; τὸ ὄν, 38 times; τὸ ὄντως ὄν, 3; τὸ πρὸς ἀλήθειαν ὄν, 3; and ὁ ὄντως ὤν very frequently. Τοῦ ἑνός (gender doubtful) occurs once; τὸ μόνον once; τοῦ ἀϊδίου (gender doubtful), once. Ὁ ἀγένvητος is found 4 times; τὸ θεῖον, 12; τὸ αἴτιον, 23; ὁ αἴτιος, 1; τοῦ πάντων αἰτίου καὶ πατρός, 1; τὸ τῶν ὅλων αἴτιον, 2; ὁ τῶν ὅλων νοῦς, 4; ὁ νοῦς τῶν ὅλων, 1; ὁ τοῦ παντὸς νοῦς, 1; ἡ τῶν ὅλων ψυχή, 1; ἡ τοῦ παντὸς ψυχή, 1; ὁ δημιουργός, 6; ὁ ποιητής, 4; ὁ ποιητὴς τῶν ὅλων, 4; ὁ κοσμοποιός, 1; ὁ ἡγεμών, 2; ὁ πατήρ, 15; ὁ θεὸς ὁ πατήρ, 1; ὁ πάντων πατήρ, 1; ὁ τοῦ παντὸς πατήρ, 1; ὁ πατὴρ τοῦ παντός, 2; ὁ πατὴρ τῶν ὅλων, 11; ὁ τῶν ὅλων πατήρ, ὁ ἀγέννητος θεός, καὶ τὰ σύμπαντα γεννῶν, 2; ὁ τοῦ κόσμου πατήρ, 1; ὁ τὰ ὅλα γεννήσας πατήρ, 1; ὁ ἀγένητος καὶ πάντων πατήρ, 1; ὁ πρισβύτερος ἄρχων καὶ ἡγεμών, 1; ὁ πατήρ, ὁ ὅλων θεός, 1; ὁ γεννήσας αὐτοὺς [τοὺς ἀπλανεῖς] πατήρ, 1; ὁ τῶν ὄντων πατήρ, 1; ὁ πατὴρ καὶ ἡγεμὼν τῶν συμπάντων, 2 . . . . τοῦ κόσμου, 1 . . . . τοῦ παντός, 1; ὁ τοῦ παντὸς ἡγεμὼν καὶ πατήρ, 1; ὁ κτίστης καὶ πατὴρ τοῦ παντός, 1; τῶν ὅλων κτίστης καὶ ἡγεμών, 1; ὁ ποιητὴς καὶ πατήρ, 2; ὁ πατὴρ καὶ ποιητής, 1; ὁ ποιητὴς καὶ πατὴρ τῶν ὅλων, 3 . . . . τοῦ παντός, 1; ὁ πατὴρ καὶ ποιητὴς τῶν ὅλων, 1; πατὴρ καὶ ποιητὴς τοῦ κόσμου, 2; ὁ ἀγένητος καὶ ποιητής, 1; ὁ πατὴρ καὶ βασιλεὺς τῶν ὅλων, 1; γεννητὴς τῶν ὅλων, 1; ὁ ἡγεμὼν τοῦ παντός, 1; ὁ τῶν ὅλων ἡγεμών, 5; ὁ πανηγεμών, 1; ὁ πανηγεμὼν θεός, 1; ὁ τοῦ παντὸς ἡγεμών, 3; ὁ θεῶν καὶ ἀνθρώπων ἡγεμών, 1; ὁ πάντων ἡγεμών, 3; ὁ ποιητὴς καὶ ἡγεμὼν τοῦδε τοῦ παντός, 1; ὁ δεσπότης ἁπάντων, 1; ὁ παμπρύτανις, 1; ὁ σωτήρ, 4; ὁ σωτὴρ τοῦ παντός, 1; ὁ σωτὴρ θεός, 4; ὁ σωτὴρ καὶ ἵλεως θεός, 1; ὁ μόνος σωτήρ, 1; ὁ μόνος σοφός, 7; ὑέπτιάτωρ θεός, 1.

The above list, to one who attempts to penetrate its religious and theological significance, will not be without instruction.

and manifoldness, between the absolute simplicity of the supreme Mind and the endless variety of his tokens in the cosmos, between the stillness and peace of an eternal and immutable nature and the stir and rush of the phenomenal world, must be the subject of our consideration in the following chapter.

CHAPTER V.

The Divine Powers.

In referring to the questions with which philosophy concerns itself, we saw that one of these related to the powers by which the universe was held together.* The reason for this inquiry is sufficiently obvious. Detached heaps of unrelated phenomena would not constitute a cosmos. But the human intellect already clearly perceived that the universe was one vast system, in which the remotest parts had certain definite relations to the whole and to one another, and the incessant changes which were observed proceeded according to some fixed sequence or law. Thus was indicated the presence of some mysterious and pervasive power which constrained the multiplicity of phenomena into a cosmical unity. An analogy for this is found in that smaller system which lies so near to our consciousness, the human organism, with its central soul and its extended energy pervading every limb. Such thoughts seem to have been in Philo's mind when, alluding to the journeys of Abraham, he wrote, " Travel through the greatest and most perfect man, this cosmos, and consider how the parts are disjoined by places, but united by powers, and what is this invisible bond of symmetry and unity for all things."† A further reason for inquiry is found in the fact that force is the characteristic mark of a cosmos as distinguished from

---

* Spec. Leg., III. 34 (II. 331); δυνάμεις αἷς συνέχεται καὶ πότερον αὗται σώματα ἢ ἀσώματοι.

† Migrat. Abr. 30 (I. 471).

amorphous matter. Whenever matter assumes a distinctive form, the change must be due to a force impressing itself on the susceptible material. So long as that form remains, the presence of the force is still indicated; for without it matter would necessarily sink back into a condition destitute of quality, and thus we see that form and force are, if not identical, at least coincident. Now, the visible universe presents an endless variety of forms, which stand to one another in certain logical relations; and accordingly, though our notion of force is one, and is justly expressed by a singular noun, we are compelled to speak of forces, such as the habitual or conservative, the organic, the vital, the rational, and countless others, arranged "according to species and genera."*

We see, then, that the contemplation of the world around us opens an inquiry into the nature of cosmical forces. We must now connect this result with positions which we have already attained. Since God is the Creator of the cosmos, and ultimately the sole efficient Cause, it is evident that he is the one fountain of power, and the cosmical forces must be at the same time divine forces. In treating of the nature of God we met with divine powers, into the precise character and functions of which we did not then pause to inquire. Some of these, like the creative and providential, evidently bring God into connection with the universe, and take their place among the forces of the cosmos. Thus, whichever way our thought travels, whether from the universe to God or from God to the universe, we still meet with divine powers as the connecting link. To determine the nature of these powers, and their relation to the world and to God, is the task which must next engage our attention.

Before entering on our exposition, we must observe that there is no part of Philo's philosophy that presents greater perplexities or has received more divergent interpretations.

* Leg. All., II. 7 (I. 71). The line of thought here sketched will be justified and developed as we proceed.

Our difficulties arise from various sources. The character of ancient thought differs widely in some important respects from our own, and what from our point of view appear to be contradictory doctrines, derived from opposing systems, and placed in unreconciled juxtaposition, might wear a more harmonious aspect if we could transport ourselves into the old-world circle of ideas; and this we can do only through an exercise of philosophical imagination. Again, it is, as we have seen, fully admitted by Philo himself that our language about God is necessarily inadequate, and that statements may be used for purposes of instruction which will not bear the scrutiny of rigorous thought. Connected with this is Philo's rhetorical style, and copious use of figurative language. To make the due allowance for popular or poetical expression requires a delicate employment of critical skill. Allegorical interpretation gives rise to further difficulties; for Philo's terminology is repeatedly influenced by the passage on which he is commenting, and it is not always easy to decide whether some particular word is to be understood strictly or as the passing symbol of some higher spiritual truth. Lastly, there are passages which are so far inconsistent with one another that, if they stood alone, we should deduce from them incompatible doctrines; how are we to deal with these passages? The easiest and most obvious plan is to accept the inconsistency, and say that Philo, according to the varying exigencies of his system, adopted now this doctrine and now that, and never perceived that they were in absolute contradiction to one another. In regard to some subordinate points, we may readily admit that the mind of so unsystematic a writer might be exposed to this kind of oblivion; but in regard to a vital and central doctrine of his philosophy we can hardly help surmising that the fault lies in the interpreters rather than the author, and we cannot acquiesce in this easy riddance of difficulties unless the fair laws of exegesis leave us no other alternative. It seems a truer plan to select among these passages the statements which are least ambiguous, and, taking them as our clue, to seek the higher conception in which the inconsistencies will disappear; then, if this cannot be found, to consider whether opposing statements may not be explained as figurative, or even as a temporary conformity to views which had no serious and permanent hold upon Philo's mind; and only in the last resort to admit that our author did not know his own thoughts, or was incapable of comparing them. For the execution of this plan we cannot lay down any rules: everything depends on thoroughness of examination, and candour and insight of philosophical judgment.

Throughout the following discussion we must bear in mind what has been previously said respecting the analogy between the divine and the human, and the differences by which they are contrasted.* The human genus is, says Philo, "the counterpart of the powers of God, a manifest image of the invisible nature, a created image of the eternal."† These words form a compendium of the view which we have fully unfolded elsewhere. The powers of the human soul fall under our experience, and thereby furnish us with the only key by which we can unlock the mysteries that lie beyond our experience; but, in applying this key, we must always remember the infinite distinction between the created and the uncreated.

Addressing ourselves now to the question proposed at the opening of this chapter, and starting from the point most accessible to our experience, we observe that the world is full of forces, which combine its multifarious parts into a cosmos. "This universe," we are told, "is held together by invisible powers, which the Fabricator stretched from the extremities of earth to the ends of heaven, making excellent provision that the things bound should not be loosened; for the powers are bonds of the universe that cannot be broken."‡ God has

---

* Vol. II. pp. 3 and 10 sqq. † Vita Mos., II. 12 (II. 144).
‡ Migrat. Abr., 32 (I. 464).

extended his powers through earth and water, air and heaven, leaving no part of the cosmos desert; through them he has collected and bound all things indissolubly, and thus his power has embosomed and permeated the universe.* Hence the powers are properly described as "unifying";† for, being fastened around the universe, they prevent it from being dissolved and corrupted into its component parts.‡ Owing to this function they are most frequently compared to bonds; but they are also likened to pillars which sustain the whole cosmos as a house.§

These powers, so far as they affect the material world, correspond with what we designate as physical forces, although both the philosophical and the scientific conception of them in Philo may be different from ours. Thus it is said that the nature or organism which distinguishes plants is composed of several powers, those of nutrition, change, and growth.‖ There are "powers in bodies" which affect the senses according to certain properties.¶ We apprehend the Cause "from the cosmos and its parts and the powers existing in these."** The language deviates more widely from our own when the four elements are described as powers,†† and when it is stated that God bestows some of his benefits "through earth, water, air, sun, moon, heaven, other incorporeal powers."‡‡ This inclusion of natural objects among the powers hardly receives adequate explanation from Keferstein's suggestion§§ that "Philo regards them as the dwelling-place of the divine powers." In accordance with our previous exposition, we must rather suppose that the powers constitute the sole reality of natural objects by differentiating them from otherwise indistinguishable matter. The sun, moon, and other bodies are

* Conf. Ling., 27 (I. 425).
‡ Conf. Ling., 32 (I. 430).
‖ Quod Deus immut., 8 (I. 278).
** Leg. All., III. 32 (I. 107).
‡‡ Mutat. Nom., 8 (I. 587).
† 'Ενωτικαί, Plantat. Noe, 20 (I. 342).
§ Frag., II. 655.
¶ Conf. Ling., 13 (I. 412).
†† Quis rer. div. her., 57 (I. 513).
§§ P. 188.

not independent entities which divine powers may inhabit or may leave, but they are sun, moon, and so forth simply from the presence and action of solar, lunar, and other forces, and therefore it is at least as correct to say that they are powers as to say that they are material. Withdraw from them all force and they must lapse into the desert ground of unreality, as if some noble statue, on which the sculptor had impressed his skill, were to lose its informing idea, and sink back into the shapeless block from which it was hewn.

It is a legitimate inference from what we have hitherto learned of Philo's anthropology, that the mental faculties belong to the same great category of divine powers; for though they are not expressly so described, we have seen that they are eternal essences, and their divine character is further proved by the derivation of the rational soul from the very substance of God, " God having breathed in as much of his own power as a mortal nature could receive."* Whether, then, we turn to the world of matter or of mind, we are everywhere confronted by a system of powers, which abide through all the changes of phenomena, give form and reality to the objects of nature, and carry the soul aloft to the primal fount of being.

Before entering on the more difficult questions connected with the powers, we may notice their more obvious predicates, negative and positive. In the first place, they are not independent causes. This follows from the previously established doctrine of the sole ultimate causality of God;† but it is also expressly asserted:—

<blockquote>The sun, moon, and stars were said to have been created on the fourth day, after the earth had produced its herbage, because God foresaw that men would regard the revolutions of the heavenly bodies as the causes of the earth's annual produce, and he wished to teach them that the first causes‡ were not to be ascribed to anything created, and that he himself</blockquote>

---

* Nobil., 3 (II. 440). † See Vol. II. pp. 4 sq. and 54 sq.
‡ Τὰς πρώτας αἰτίας.

did not require the aid of those luminaries, " to which indeed he has given powers, but not autocratic" powers; for, as a charioteer or a pilot, " he leads everything as he will, according to law and right, requiring the aid of nothing else,—for all things are possible to God."*

So it is said elsewhere that

When our mind entertained the Chaldæan opinion, it used to ride round the efficient powers as causes ;† but when it departed from this view, it knew that the cosmos was governed by a Ruler, of whose sovereignty it received a mental representation.‡

The last words will receive their full explanation hereafter; at present it is sufficient to observe that, according to the passages just cited, the powers owe their efficiency to God, and in no way interfere with his independent and absolute sway.

But though the powers are thus subordinated to God, they partake of his mystery and greatness. Our language is unable to describe, not only the Self-existent, but even the powers which act as his body-guard.§ The latter, belonging as they do to the invisible and intelligible God, are themselves absolutely invisible and intelligible. They are intelligible, moreover, not in the sense of being actually apprehended by the mind, but because, if they could be apprehended, it would not be perception, but only the purest mind that could apprehend them. They are, in fact, inapprehensible in essence, and reveal only the effects of their energy.∥ So when Jacob wrestled with an invisible antagonist, one of the "ministering powers," he asked in vain for his name; for the powers, like the Self-existent, are unspeakable, and names, those symbols of the begotten, must not be sought with incorruptible natures.¶ It follows that the powers are immaterial,** and they are accordingly so described.†† If this seems inconsistent with the inclusion of the elements and other bodies among the powers, we must remember the explanation lately

* Mundi Op., 14 (I. 10).   † Τὰς δραστηρίους δυνάμεις ὡς αἰτίας.
‡ Mutat. Nom., 3 (I. 581).   § Leg. ad. Cai., 1 (II. 546).
∥ Monarch., I. 6 (II. 218).   ¶ Mutat. Nom., 2 (I. 580).   ** Ἀσώματοι.
†† Somn., I. 11 (I. 630); Sacrificant., 13 (II. 261).

given. Every object, so far as it differs from primitive matter, does so through the presence of an immaterial force; and when it is itself ranked among the powers, the reference must be, not to its material side, which it possesses in common with every object of perception, but to the intelligible force which alone renders it capable of distinction and classification.

It is but one step further to say that the powers are uncircumscribed and infinite as God himself,* independent of time,† and unbegotten.‡ It follows that they are not exhausted in the world of nature. God uses them unmixed in relation to himself, but tempers them towards creation, for it is impossible for a mortal nature to contain them in their purity. We cannot look upon the flame of the sun unmixed, for our sight would be quenched by the splendour of its beams, though the sun is but a single work of God; and are we to suppose that we can fully understand, in their unblended perfection, those unbegotten powers which, round about him, flash most brilliant light? The heat of the sun is subdued by the frigid air, and so the divine powers are tempered to the natural weakness of created things.§ We have only to add that they are "most holy,"|| and incapable of error.¶ In the application of the above predicates to powers which primarily reveal themselves through their energy as cosmical forces, Philo does not explicitly state the reasons which guided his judgment; but they followed from his inevitable recognition of the powers as divine; and their subtle, invisible, and immeasurable action in nature, if it would not immediately suggest, would at least confirm an opinion reached by the theological path.

We are now prepared to look more narrowly at what we may call the rational function of the cosmical powers. They

---

* SS. Ab. et Cain., 15 (I. 173), ἀπερίγραφος γάρ ὁ θεός, ἀπερίγραφοι καὶ αἱ δυνάμεις αὐτοῦ: Mundi Op., 6 (I. 5), where the statement is made immediately of God's χάριτες, but the context shows that these are equivalent to the powers.
† "Ἄχρονοι, SS. Ab. et Cain., 19 (I. 176).   ‡ Quod Deus immut., 17 (I. 284).
§ Ib. || Frag., II. 655.   ¶ Conf. Ling., 23 (I. 422).

introduce into matter and preserve the distinctions to which the various kinds of objects are due. Withdraw all force, and matter must immediately lose all distinctive marks, and sink into the dead level of what, so far as knowledge is concerned, is tantamount to the non-existent. If this be so, we must recognise the presence of power wherever we discover objects that are capable of being distinguished and classified; in other words it is the powers that determine the characteristics of the various orders of phenomenal existence. This is clearly brought out in a passage in which Philo comments on Abraham's sacrifice of the heifer, she-goat, ram, turtle-dove, and pigeon.* Abraham divided the animals, except the birds, and "laid each piece one against another." After sunset lamps of fire† passed through the midst of the pieces.

"The lamps of fire which were borne," says Philo, "are the decisions‡ of the torch-bearer God, which are brilliant and translucent, whose habit it is to continue in the midst of the pieces, I mean the antitheses, out of which the whole cosmos is composed. For it is said, 'Lamps of fire which passed through the midst of the pieces,' that thou mayest know that the divine powers, going through the midst both of affairs and of bodies, corrupt nothing—for the pieces remain unaffected [that is to say, we are not told that the lamps consumed the parts of the victims]—but very beautifully separate and distinguish their several natures." [In consesequence of this office they are described as] God's "cutters."§

We see, therefore, that the process of differentiation which we observed in noticing the phenomena of the cosmos is due to the action of divine powers, which assign its distinctive nature to each class of objects.

Since the function here ascribed to the powers is that which belongs to the Platonic ideas, we cannot be surprised when Philo explicitly identifies the former with the latter. The principal passage in which he does so is one where he represents God as returning a philosophical reply to the

* Gen. xv. † Λαμπάδες πυρός, LXX.
‡ Κρίσεις,=the separating judgments.
§ Τομεῖς. Quis rer. div. her. 61-2 (I. 518).

entreaty of Moses that, as he could not reveal himself, he would at least grant a vision of his glory,* that is, of the powers which acted as his body-guard. The reply, having explained that the powers were, like God himself, inapprehensible in essence, proceeds—

"As, among you, seals, whenever wax or any similar material is applied to them, make innumerable impressions, not suffering the loss of any part, but remaining as they were, such you must suppose the powers around me to be, applying qualities to things without quality, and forms to the formless, while they experience no change or diminution in their eternal nature. But some among you call them very appropriately ideas,† since they give ideal form‡ to each thing, arranging the unarranged, and communicating determinate limits and definition and shape to the indeterminate and indefinite and shapeless, and, in a word, altering the worse into the better."§

Precisely the same function is elsewhere attributed to God and his powers: it was God who called order out of disorder, quality out of things without quality, and so forth; for it is the constant care of himself and his beneficent powers to reform the discord of the worse substance, and bring it into harmony with the better.|| Again, we hear of "the seal of the universe, the archetypal idea, by which all things, being without ideal form¶ and quality, were marked and impressed."** It can only be in this, their ideal sense, that the powers are spoken of as measures,†† that is, as the standard rules in conformity with which specific objects were made.‡‡ The character thus discovered in them brings them nearer to the realm of thought, and proves them to be amenable to its laws; and so we are introduced to a new and fruitful field of speculation.

We cannot find a better introduction to this subject than

* Δόξα. † Ἰδέας.
‡ Εἰδοποιοῦσι, which we must prefer to the reading ἰδιοποιοῦσι.
§ Monarch., I. 6 (II. 218-19). || Justit., 7 (II. 367).
¶ Or without species, ἀνείδεα.
** Mutat. Nom., 23 (I. 598). Cf. Somn., II. 6 (I. 665). †† Μέτρα.
‡‡ SS. Ab. et Cain., 15 (I. 178). Cf. Qu. et Sol in Gen., IV. 8. See also Mundi Op., 9 (I. 7); § 44, p. 31.

the oft quoted passage in which Philo bases his whole theory upon the analogy of human thought and action. Having stated that the first day in the account of creation relates to the intelligible cosmos, he proceeds to unfold his meaning as follows:—

"For God, as being God, anticipating that there could never be a beautiful imitation without a beautiful pattern, or any perceptible thing faultless which was not modelled in conformity with an archetypal and intelligible idea, when he wished to fabricate this visible cosmos, first shaped forth the intelligible, in order that, using an immaterial and most God-like pattern, he might work out the material cosmos, a more recent copy of an older one, destined to contain as many perceptible genera as there were intelligible in the other. But it is not to be said or supposed that the cosmos which consists of the ideas is in any place; but in what way it subsists we shall know by following up an example of what takes place among ourselves. Whenever a city is founded to gratify the high ambition of some king or emperor, claiming autocratic authority, and at the same time brilliant in thought, adding splendour to his good fortune, sometimes a trained architect having offered his services, and inspected the suitability of the place, describes first within himself almost all the parts of the city that is to be erected, temples, gymnasia, town-halls, market-places, harbours, docks, lanes, equipment of walls, foundations of houses and other public edifices. Then, having received the forms of each in his own soul, as in wax, he bears the figure of an intelligible city, and having stirred up the images of this in his memory, and, still more, having sealed there its characters, looking, like a good workman, to the pattern, he begins to prepare the well proportioned mixture made of stones and timber,* making the material substances like each of the immaterial ideas. Similarly, then, we must think about God, who, when he purposed founding† the great city, first devised its forms, out of which, having composed an intelligible cosmos, he completes the perceptible, using the former as a pattern. As, then, the city which was first formed within the architect had no exterior place, but had been sealed in the artist's soul, in the same way not even the cosmos that consists of the ideas could have any other place than the divine Logos which disposed these things into a cosmos. For what other place could there be for his powers which would be adequate to receive and contain, I do not say all, but any one unmixed?"‡

* I follow Müller's text. † Κτίζειν, as before of the literal city.
‡ Mundi Op., 4-5 (I. 4). Compare the account of the ideal tabernacle revealed to the soul of Moses as the pattern of the material one: Vita Mos., III. 3 (II. 146).

This passage affords a succinct view of Philo's theory; but its more important propositions are selected for separate treatment in different places, and it will be convenient to refer to these in their order.

In the first place, the reality of the ideas and their influential action upon matter are asserted in the strongest way in the following passage:—

> It is only one of the forms of error maintained by impious and unholy men to say that the immaterial ideas are an empty name without participation in real fact. Those who affirm this, remove from things the most necessary substance,* which is the archetypal pattern of all the qualities of substance,† in accordance with which everything is ideally formed and measured. Thus, the opinion which destroys ideas confounds all things, and reduces them to that formlessness which was prior to the elements. Now, what could be more absurd than this? For God generated everything out of matter, not touching it himself, for it was not fitting for the Wise and Blessed to touch indefinite and confused matter, but he made use of the immaterial powers, whose real name is ideas, in order that the suitable form might engage each genus. But the opinion in question introduces great disorder and confusion; for by destroying the things through which qualities arise, it destroys at the same time qualities themselves.‡

We must return to this passage when we come to consider the relation between God and his powers; at present we must fix our attention upon the reality and energy of the ideas. In making them not only realities, but the most necessary substance in material things, we may seem to be departing completely from the analogy between God and the architect; but it is not so if we can adapt ourselves to the moulds of ancient thought. The images§ in the architect's mind were also realities, having their permanent seat within; for though they might pass from his consciousness, yet they could be stirred up again by memory, and be viewed as the pattern by which to regulate his work, and so they corresponded, within the spiritual sphere, to the impressions of seals upon the soul,

---

* Οὐσία=immaterial essence. † Οὐσία=matter.
‡ Sacrificant., 13 (II. 261-2). § Εἴδωλα.

and were abiding forms of thought which might be contemplated and utilised at pleasure. But, further, though their seat was within, and as immaterial essences they could not be located in space, yet they reappeared in the visible city, and were that most necessary reality which alone made it a city instead of a chaos of stones and wood. The architect's thought was manifest, and became objective in the stateliness of every temple, in the beauty of every portico, in the dignity or grace of every statue, in the massive strength of the fortifications, and the useful arrangements of the docks. Everywhere was the impress of human genius, that mysterious combination of ideas, that subtle power, which alone differentiated the materials of which the city was composed from the wildness of the forest and the mountain; and we know how these ideas remain through the vicissitudes of matter, speaking to us still from many a crumbling ruin, or rehabilitated in the young splendour of some fresh creation. It is they, then, that are the realities, apparent wherever art has bodied forth its imaginations; and yet, when you ask for their locality, you can find it only in some artist's soul. So it is with the infinite Artist. His ideas are eternal forms of thought; and though they reside only in the absolute Reason, yet their impress is upon the universe, and they reveal their energy through all the orderly arrangements and ideal shapes of the material world.

The honour of this doctrine is of course ascribed to Moses, and the reality of the ideas confirmed by a Scriptural appeal. It is said in Genesis* that man "was formed in accordance with the image of God,"† that is, as Philo understands it, he was made, not like God, but like the image of God. Now if the part (man) was the image of an image, much more must the whole perceptible cosmos be so.‡ The same conclusion follows from the fact that throughout the first chapter of

---

* i. 27. † Κατ' εἰκόνα θεοῦ. ‡ Mundi Op. 6 (I. 5).

Genesis things are said to have been made according to genus, not according to species.* This is most apparent in the case of man; for God first formed the generic man, including male and female, but afterwards the species, Adam.† Lastly, this view is established by the statement‡ that God made "every green herb of the field before it was produced, and all grass of the field before it sprang up." The verdure and the grass which were invisibly there before they grew upon the earth can be nothing but the intelligible ideas which are the seals of perceptible effects. Taking this as a sample of everything else, we must suppose that of all other things which fall under the senses there pre-existed older forms and measures,§ and that nature completes nothing perceptible without an immaterial pattern.‖

As having their seat in pure reason the ideas are invariably regarded as immaterial.¶ Nevertheless, we have seen that they are the most necessary substance or essence in things; and we may therefore venture to define them as an immaterial intelligible essence or force, belonging by its nature to the realm of mind, yet capable of exhibiting through matter a multiform energy, and of maintaining through all corporeal changes the permanence of ideal types. If these conceptions appear at all incompatible, we must remember, in justice to Philo, that the difficulty recurs in every philosophy which is not materialistic. Who can explain how spiritual volition passes into bodily movement, and impresses its lasting effects upon the shapes of matter? Philosophy can only arrive at ultimate facts, which are of necessity ultimate mysteries; and from this law not even materialism can escape. The relation between consciousness and corporeal movements may be

---

* Κατὰ γίνος=ἰδία, and not κατ' εἶδος. † Leg. All., II. 4 (I. 69).
‡ Gen. ii. 5.   § Εἴδη καὶ μέτρα.
‖ Mundi Op., 44 (I. 30-31); Leg. All., I. 9-10 (I. 47-8).
¶ Ἀσώματοι. See Ebriet., 25 (I. 372); § 33, p. 378; Vita Mos., III. 3 (II. 146); cf. Dec. Orac., 21 (II. 198), οὐρανὸς ὁ ἀσώματος. See before, p. 71.

differently conceived, but cannot be denied; and Philo is therefore guilty of no contradiction in suggesting an analogous relation between the forms of the divine Thought and the lasting types of phenomenal existence. The mode in which he endeavoured to make this relation clear to his own mind will be described farther on.

We learned just now that the nature of the ideas is eternal. This thought, which follows from their connection with the eternal Mind, is elaborated in a passage which serves to exhibit at the same time the identity of the ideas with logical genera.

" As, when some man of letters or grammarian has died, the literary and grammatical faculty in the men has perished with them, but the ideas of these remain, and in a manner live as enduring as the cosmos, in accordance with which [ideas] present and future men in everlasting succession will become literary and grammatical ; so also the prudent, or temperate, or manly, or just, or, in a word, the wise in any individual might be destroyed. nevertheless in the nature of the immortal whole, as on a monument, prudence has been inscribed as immortal, and virtue universally as incorruptible, in accordance with which both now there are good men and hereafter there will be—unless we are to say that the death of any individual man has wrought destruction to humanity, in regard to which whether we are to call it genus, or idea, or notion,* or what, those who inquire into the strict use of terms will know." [The passage goes on to say that] as one seal often survives unimpaired the destruction of innumerable impressions, so the virtues, even if all the characters with which they have marked the souls of those who came to them were effaced by evil living or some other cause, would still retain for ever their pure and incorruptible nature.†

These eternal entities, which reveal themselves as archetypal patterns through the visible objects of creation, form collectively, through their orderly combination, an intelligible cosmos,‡ which is the archetype of the perceptible.§ Hence, the intelligible universe is said to be composed or compacted

---

* Ἐννόημα.

† Quod det. pot. ins., 21 (I. 205-6). See also Mutat. Nom., 11 (I. 590) ; Cherub., 2 (I. 139-40) ; Quis rer. div. her. 24 (I. 489), πᾶν γένος ἄφθαρτον.

‡ Κόσμος νοητός.   § Κόσμος αἰσθητός.

out of the invisible and immaterial ideas.* In this connection a passage occurs which seems to make a distinction between the ideas and the powers. "Through these powers," it is said, "the immaterial and intelligible cosmos was compacted, the archetype of this phenomenal one, composed of invisible ideas, as this one is of visible bodies."† According to this statement, it would seems as though the ideas were something used by, and therefore distinct from, the powers, with which we have previously identified them. We might perhaps escape from this difficulty by the supposition that the ideas which compose the intelligible cosmos do not exhaust the totality of the divine powers, and were consequently used by the creative and other powers which were not included in them. It is, however, an objection to such an explanation that Philo nowhere else draws this distinction, and that he expressly describes the intelligible cosmos as "the idea of the ideas, the Logos of God,"‡ which is with him always the supreme term next to the Self-existent himself; and moreover, no power could enter into the thought of man without being itself a part of the world of ideas.§ We must, accordingly, suppose that there is some confusion owing to the two aspects under which the powers may be regarded, as efficient, and as forms of thought; and the meaning will then be that through the agency which belonged to them as divine they formed themselves into an orderly and ideal world. It is well to notice this seeming contradiction, because the passage, to which we shall have to return, is not in other respects free from difficulty and confusion.

* Somn., I. 32. (I. 648); Vita Mos., III. 13. (II. 154); cf. Gigant., 13 (I. 271).
† Conf. Ling., 34 (I. 431).
‡ Mundi Op., 6 (I. 5).
§ I refer here to the extant Greek works. In the Qu. et Sol. in Ex. II. 68 (Greek in Harris, Fragments, pp. 66 sqq.) the intelligible cosmos is represented as distinct from and inferior to the principal divine powers. Either this may be an earlier and less consistent view, or both here and in the Conf. Ling. the intelligible world may be spoken of in a limited sense, and not include the human race.

Since the intelligible cosmos is immaterial, it is exempt from the conditions of space, and has no locality except the divine Logos, or Thought. The meaning of this statement, which is laid down in the passage placed at the beginning of our present discussion, must be more fully considered farther on; but we may observe here that Philo locates the ideas not only in the Logos, but in God himself, just as we might ascribe the design of a city indifferently to the architect or to the mind of the architect. Not only does he say that before the origin of individual perceptible things the generic perceptible belonged to the forethought of the Creator,* but he describes God as the "immaterial place of immaterial ideas."† From this the transition is easy to the conception of God as himself the supreme archetype, from whom the ideas flow into the perceptible cosmos. He is the archetypal beauty, from whose fount the beautiful things of earth derive their share.‡ He is the archetypal beam, who sends forth countless intelligible rays.§ He is the archetypal pattern of laws, and of the perceptible sun the sun that is intelligible, affording from the invisible fountains visible lights to that which is seen.‖ Since he is incomprehensible, he caused, as it were, a certain splendour to gleam from himself, which we justly call form, scattering around the entire mind immaterial rays, and filling it with supercelestial light; guided by which the intellect is brought through the mediation of form to the archetype.¶ These passages exhibit to us in figures that which is not clearly presentable in thought. The fountain diffusing its waters through various channels, still more the light, which seems so akin to the immaterial, with its silent velocity, its impalpable pervasiveness, and its power of kindling new expression in every object on which it falls, fitly symbolized the flow of the

---

* ’Ην τὸ γενικὸν αἰσθητὸν προμηθείᾳ τοῦ πεποιηκότος, Leg. All., I. 10. (I. 48).
† Cherub., 14 (I. 148). ‡ Cherub., 25 (I. 154).
§ Ib., 28 (I. 156). ‖ Sacrificant., 4 (II. 254).
¶ Qu. et Sol. in Gen., IV. 1.

divine Thought, and the wakening of chaotic matter into beauty and order under the transfiguring touch of the ideas. But Philo did not forget that even the loftiest ideas could not exhaust the essence of God. He was the archetype of light, but he was more, and it was truer to say that he was older and higher than the archetype, and was himself like nothing created.* If we infer from this that the ideas were only partial expressions of the infinite fulness of God, we shall bring the doctrine of ideas into coincidence with that of the divine attributes which we have previously established. As the supremely beautiful and the only source whence beauty could flow, he might be called the archetype of beauty; but, in truth, the archetypal idea was only one mode of the eternal Thought, and included with other ideas in that supernal unity which is inapprehensible by the human mind. This relation is expressed as that of father and son. The idea, the intelligible cosmos, as being the offspring of the divine intelligence, is called the son of God,† and the epithet older is prefixed to distinguish it from its counterpart, the perceptible cosmos, which is named God's younger son.‡ The parallelism which is thus drawn between the two worlds shows that the higher, like the lower, although it has no outward existence, is not regarded as identical with the divine Mind, but only as an expression of its activity. God himself is higher than his mental creations, and folds them within the embrace of his mysterious essence.

Since the powers are identical with the ideas, we might reasonably expect them to be arranged in a logical hierarchy, approaching, as they ascended, nearer to the full reality of God. This conception was certainly entertained by Philo, though he does not attempt any elaborate classification. He recognises a few powers, of universal or nearly universal sweep, as standing closest to the Self-existent; but the countless multitude below these he leaves without arrangement, and with

---

* Somn., I. 13 (I. 632).   † Υἱὸς θεοῦ.   ‡ Quod Deus immut., 6 (I. 277).

only the most casual description or allusion. The fullest account of the descending scale is contained in a passage which gives an allegorical explanation of the cities of refuge.

These are six in number, and correspond with six divine powers. The oldest and best, acting as the metropolis, is the divine Logos. The other five, powers of him who speaks (the word or Logos), are, as it were, colonies. Foremost is the Creative,* by virture of which the Creator fabricated the cosmos by a word.† Second is the Regal,‡ by virtue of which he who has made rules what has been made. Third is the Propitious,§ through which the Artificer compassionates and pities his own work. The remaining two are the two divisions of the Legislative,‖ namely, the Preceptive and the Prohibitive.¶ These are suited to the varying nature and strength of those involved in involuntary faults. The swiftest runner must urge his breathless course to the highest, divine Logos, the fountain of wisdom, that he may draw thence, instead of death, eternal life. He who is not so swift must fly to the Creative power, which Moses calls Deity, since through it all things were *d*eposited** and arranged into a cosmos—for he who has apprehended that the universe has come into being has a valuable possession, the knowledge of him who created it, which immediately induces love towards him. He who is less ready must seek the Regal power—for even if the offspring is not admonished by love of a father, the subject is so by fear of a ruler. But if the aforesaid boundaries are too distant, we must have recourse to the other three. For he who has anticipated that the Divinity is not inexorable, but kind and gentle, even if he has sinned before, again repents, through hope of an amnesty; and he who reflects that God is a legislator will be blessed in obeying all that he commands; but the last shall find the last refuge, the averting of evil, if not participation in good. Of five of these powers there are imitations in the sanctuary; of Precept and Prohibition, the laws in the Ark; of the Propitious power, the lid of the Ark, called the mercy-seat; of the Creative and Regal, the cherubim. But the divine Logos above these did not enter into visible form, as resembling nothing perceptible, but being the image of God, the oldest of all intelligible things. One more distinction remains. The six powers are divided into two classes. For of the cities of refuge three are beyond, that is, at a distance from, the human race. These are the first three powers, to which the heaven and the entire cosmos belong. But the other three enter into closer relations with our perishable race; for what need is there of Prohibition for those who will do no wrong, and what need of Precept for

* Ἡ ποιητική.   † Λόγῳ.   ‡ Ἡ βασιλική.
§ Ἡ ἵλεως.   ‖ Ἡ νομοθετική.
¶ The text is defective; but the meaning is apparent from what follows.
** Θεός, . . . ἐτέθη. I have attempted to preserve the similarity of sound.

those who are not naturally liable to fall, and what of the Propitious power for those who will be absolutely without sin? But mankind are in need of these, because they are naturally prone both to voluntary and to involuntary sins.*

We must observe that the last three powers, which we may reduce to two, the propitious and the legislative, are only subordinate varieties of the two immediately above them; for the legislative naturally belongs to the regal; and it will be apparent that the propitious comes under the creative when we remember that the latter has for its fountain the truly good.† The lower powers, therefore, in the above scale differ from the higher, not in their essence, but in their range.

Since the highest powers next to the Logos (the consideration of which must be postponed) may thus be combined into a pair, it is not surprising that Philo repeatedly dwells, not on an extended list, but on two superlative powers, especially as this classification (on which he evidently prides himself) was suited to the language of the LXX and to the allegorical interpretation of more than one passage. He affirms that

Meditation on the cherubim who were stationed, with a flaming sword, at the entrance of Paradise, revealed to his soul the important secret that in the one‡ really existing God the highest and first powers are two, Goodness and Authority,§ and that by Goodness he generated the universe, and by Authority he rules that which was generated, but that a third, uniting the two, is Thought, or Logos, for by Logos God is both ruler and good. The cherubim, then, are symbols of Sovereignty|| and Goodness, the two powers; but the flaming sword, of Thought. These pure powers meet and mingle, the dignity arising from Sovereignty being manifest in the things wherein God is good, and Goodness being manifest in that wherein he is sovereign.¶

* Prof., 18-19 (I. 560-1). In Qu. et Sol. in Ex., II. 68 (the Greek in Harris, Fragments, pp. 66 sqq.), in an explanation of the Ark and its appurtenances, we find a septenary arrangement. First is the supreme Being himself. Then comes his Logos, the seminal essence of things. Next, from the Logos branch off the two powers, creative and regal. From these come others: from the creative, the propitious or beneficent; from the regal, the legislative or punitive. Under these is the Ark, which is a symbol of the intelligible cosmos.

† Mundi Op., 5 (I. 4-5).   ‡ Κατὰ τὸν ἕνα.
§ 'Αγαθότης and 'Εξουσία. || 'Αρχή.
¶ Cherub., 9 (I. 143-4).

They are represented by the two names for God which are so common in the LXX, "Lord" and "God."* Philo makes frequent use of this interpretation, which, it will be seen, results, in principle, from the doctrine of the namelessness of God. Illustrations will occur as we proceed, and we may confine ourselves at present to the passages which suit our immediate purpose.

The appellations which have been mentioned [says Philo] indicate the powers around the self-existent Being,† for that of "Lord" denotes the power according to which he rules, and that of "God" the one according to which he benefits. For which reason the name "God" is adopted throughout the account of the creation by Moses; for it was fitting that the power according to which the Maker, in bringing things into genesis, deposited‡ and arranged them, should be so called. So far, then, as he is sovereign, he has the power both to benefit and to injure; but so far as he is benefactor, he wills only the one, namely, benefit. The phrase, "eternal God," is equivalent to "he who bestows favours, not at odd times, but always and continuously, who benefits without intermission."§

As the source of creation and the regulator of the divine authority, the goodness of the Self-existent is "the oldest of the graces"; ‖ but inasmuch as the powers are really eternal, and therefore "coeval," the epithet "oldest" refers to priority in thought, and not in time.¶

The central thought connected with these two powers may be expressed in other terms, and such are occasionally found. Thus, it is said that

On one occasion Abraham addressed God as "dread Ruler."** This is

* Κύριος and θεός.   † Τὸ ὄν.   ‡ 'Ετίθετο.
§ Plantat. Noe, 20 (I. 342). For the thought of God's will directing his power towards what is good see also Justit. 7 (II. 367).
‖ πρεσβυτάτη τῶν χαρίτων, Quod Deus immut., 23 (I. 288-9).
¶ Qu. et Sol. in Ex., II. 62 (the Greek in Harris, Fragm., p. 63). Compare Aristotle's τιμιώτατον μὲν γὰρ τὸ πρεσβύτατον (Metaph., I. iii. 6), a sentiment which will explain Philo's frequent use of "older," to denote higher and better. Thus he himself says of the things of the soul, οὐ χρόνῳ, ἀλλὰ δυνάμει καὶ ἀξιώματι πρεσβύτερα καὶ πρῶτα ὄντως, Leg. All., III. 68 (I. 125); and of the virtuous man, πρεσβύτερος μὲν οὖν καὶ πρῶτος ἔστω καὶ λεγέσθω ὁ ἀστεῖος, νεώτερος δὲ καὶ ἔσχατος πᾶς ἄφρων, Abr., 46 (II. 39).
** Δεσπότης, Gen. xv. 2.

said to be synonymous with "Lord"; and it is so to this extent, that the words refer to the same subject, but they differ in the ideas which they suggest. "Lord" is suggestive of supreme authority,* which is stable, in opposition to what is unstable and invalid; but "dread Ruler" is connected with fear;† so that it is equivalent, as it were, to "fearful Lord,"‡ not only having the supreme authority and might, but being able to inspire fear and terror; so that Abraham by using this form of address showed that he approached God with fear and trembling, conscious of the terror of his sovereignty.§

From the conception of God's universal sway the idea of punishment easily flows, for it is the part of a ruler to punish the guilty. Accordingly, this power is sometimes described as punitive.|| "Around the self-existent Being," it is said, "the first and greatest of the powers are the beneficent and punitive; and the beneficent is called 'God' .... but the other 'Lord.'"¶ This and similar statements leave no doubt of the identity of the regal and the punitive powers.** But as one idea may comprise several, so one power may include a plurality. We have seen that the legislative is embraced by the regal, and is itself resolvable into the preceptive and prohibitive. Similarly the punitive power may break itself up, and become a set of punitive powers. Thus Philo speaks of the powers of the Self-existent as "the world-creating, and regal, and providential, and the rest, as many as are beneficent and punitive."††
We may infer from this language, what, indeed, is apparent from the whole course of our exposition, that the two first powers are the highest in the scale, not only of being, but of logic, and that Philo regards goodness and authority as general terms under which the multitude of the divine powers may be classed. But he proceeds a step farther. Logically we may conceive of an unrighteous authority, and hence the necessity for distinguishing the two powers; but in God, as we have seen, goodness is the older and controls the exercise of the

* Κύριος from κῦρος. † Δεσπότης from δεσμός, whence δίος.
‡ Φοβερὸς κύριος. § Quis rer. div. her., 6 (I. 476).
|| Κολαστήριος or κολαστική. ¶ Sacrificant., 9 (II. 258).
** See also Quis rer. div. her., 34 (I. 496); Gigant., 11 (I. 269).
†† Εὐεργετιδές τε καὶ κολαστήριοι, Leg. ad Cai., 1 (II. 546).

other, and therefore the question may be raised whether the punitive powers ought not to be ranked among the beneficent, not only because they are "parts of laws" (which are intended for the reward of the good and the punishment of the bad), but because even punishment often admonishes and sobers the sinful, or, if not the sinful, at least their associates, through fear of a similar chastisement.* With greater decision it is said elsewhere that all the powers around God are helpful and preservative of creation, and among these the punitive also are included, for even punishment is not injurious, being a prevention and correction of sins.† Thus the powers, though capable of a dual distribution, tend to concentrate themselves in the divine goodness, which has driven away from itself envy, that hater of virtue and beauty, and generates graces whereby it has brought into genesis things that were not.‡ A power of so large and benign a scope may well be described by many epithets. Besides those which we have already met, the following may be noticed. It is the bounteous,§ the generous,‖ the beneficent;¶ and under it must be ranked propitious and beneficent and munificent powers,** described also as gentle,†† and favourable.‡‡ We have only to add that we casually hear also of God's saving powers;§§ of thought and purpose, most stable powers by which the Creator always surveys his works;‖‖

* Leg. ad Cai., 1 (II. 546).
† Conf. Ling., 34 (I. 431). For the expression κολαστήριοι δυνάμεις, see also Ebriet., 9 (I. 362); Post. Cain., 6 (I. 229).
‡ Migrat. Abr., 32 (I. 464). § Χαριστική.
‖ Δωρητική, Quis rer. div. her., 34 (I. 496); χαριστική also Somn., I. 26 (I. 645).
¶ Εὐεργετική, Mutat. Nom., 4 (I. 592). Here the creative power is distinguished from it, and represented as akin to it and the regal. The distinction is logically correct, beneficent goodness being wider than creative power, and being in truth its fountain: Mundi Op., 5 (I. 4-5).
** "Ἴλεως καὶ εὐεργέτιδας καὶ φιλοδώρους, Conf. Ling., 36 (I. 432): here punishments are viewed as alien to these powers—an apparent inconsistency, which will be better considered farther on.
†† 'Ημέρους, Plantat. Noe, 12 (I. 336). ‡‡ χαριστηρίους, Ebriet., 27 (I. 373).
§§ Σωτήριοι, Fortitud., 8 (II. 383).
‖‖ Ἔννοια and διανόησις, defined as ἡ ἐναποκειμένη νόησις, and ἡ νοήσεως διέξοδος, Quod Deus immut., 7 (I. 277).

of his prescient power;* and of peace, which, "of the many-named powers of the Self-existent, is not only a member but also a leader."†

The terms which we have hitherto noticed, ideas and powers, mark the main lines of Philo's speculation upon this subject. But inasmuch as the powers denote certain excellent properties, they are also denominated virtues; ‡ the word being used, presumably, not in the sense of moral goodness, but as we speak of the virtue of a plant or a drug—a sense not unknown to classical Greek. That the powers are intended is obvious from the application of the term. Thus, we hear of the "divine virtues, the propitious and beneficent;"§ and the divine powers and virtues are coupled in such a way as to show that they stand for the same thing regarded under different aspects.||

It is now time for us to enter upon the most difficult question connected with the divine powers—What was their precise relation to God? Were they attributes, or were they distinct and subordinate persons, or were they neither, at least in the modern sense of these terms? Or had Philo no settled doctrine, and can we escape from our perplexities only by ascribing to him the most palpable contradictions? Our answer to these questions must be decided by a careful examination of a large number of passages; but our arrangement of these passages, and the importance which we attach to them singly, as affording the true key to Philo's thought, must necessarily be governed, not only by such critical tact as we may happen to possess, but by our conception of the philosophy as a whole. Now, in treating of the doctrine of God, we resolved, if we were not mistaken, what has been usually

---

* προγνωστική, Vita Mos., III. 23 (II. 164); Qu. et Sol. in Gen. IV. 22.
† Somn., II. 38 (I. 692). ‡ 'Αρεταί. § Vita Mos., III. 23 (II. 163-4).
|| Τῶν θείων δυνάμεων καὶ ἀρετῶν, Animal. Sacr. idon., 6 (II. 242). For the use of the word see also Fragments, II. 656 and 660. Other passages confirming what has been said about the classification of the powers will be referred to as we proceed.

regarded as a hopeless contradiction, and, in doing so, we saw that the theory of the divine attributes, as intermediate between the eternal essence and the created cosmos, grew out of the very roots of Philo's theology, and was not a mere device to introduce harmony into an unreconciled dualism. Since the powers confessedly correspond in some sense to the divine attributes, we may naturally take the position which we have already gained as the starting-point for our further inquiry, in the hope that we may thence penetrate in safety the obscurity of a rather abstruse subject.

Philo himself was apparently well aware that the doctrine which he represented was open to misconception, and ought to be communicated only to those who were sufficiently advanced in philosophical culture to understand its nice distinctions. He displays his habitual ingenuity in finding a Scriptural justification for the necessary concealment:—

When Sarah was desired to "knead three measures of fine flour and make hiding-cakes,"* the measures referred to God and his two highest powers. It is good that these three measures should be, as it were, kneaded in the soul, "in order that, being convinced of the existence of the highest God, who has passed beyond his powers, being both seen without them and manifested in them, it should receive impressions of his authority and beneficence, and, becoming initiated into the perfect rites, should not tell anyone rashly the divine mysteries, but, treasuring them up, and holding its peace, should keep them in secret. For the Scripture says, 'make hiding-cakes,' because the sacred initiatory word about the Unbegotten and his powers ought to be hidden, since it is not for every one to keep a deposit of divine ceremonies."†

The same warning is repeated farther on in the same treatise, as a preliminary to the statement that, of all the best powers around God, the legislative, though it is one, and of equal honour with the rest, is naturally divided into two, the one directed to the benefit of those who do right, the other to the punishment of those who sin. This is to be kept as a

* Ἐγκρυφίας, sc. ἄρτος, = bread baked under the ashes, and hence hidden, Gen. xviii. 6.
† SS. Ab. et Cain., 15 (I. 173-4).

secret, to be deposited in the ears of older men when those of the younger have been stopped.* Philo does not explain the reasons for this secrecy; but he was probably apprehensive that the vulgar would misunderstand the division of the divine nature into a series of powers, and construe it into something inconsistent with the principles of monotheism.† This supposition is confirmed by a Fragment,‡ in which it is said that sacred words and things must not be communicated to all, and the two leading qualifications for participating in such matters are the complete rejection of idolatry, and purification in body and soul through ancestral laws; and by another Fragment,§ which declares that it is unlawful to utter sacred mysteries to the uninitiated, on the ground that, "being unable to hear or see incorporeal and intelligible nature," they will blame what is not worthy of blame. We learn from this advice not to be too confident that our first impression of any particular passage is the correct one; and especially if it is inconsistent with the fundamental doctrine of Judaism or with Philo's unequivocal statements elsewhere.

In selecting a passage with which to open our discussion, and which must necessarily exercise a controlling influence on our further progress, it seems not unreasonable to prefer one in which Philo states his view with the most unmistakable philosophical precision. Such a passage exists, though it has not always received the attention which its importance demands. It occurs in the treatise on Abraham, and relates to the visit of the three men recorded in Genesis xviii. Philo first deals with the narrative in its literal sense, and in doing so makes use of some expressions to which we must return at a later period of our inquiry, as they are thought to be inconsistent with the purport of the following remarks. At

---

* SS. Ab. et Cain., 39 (I. 189).
† See the account of a similar caution in connection with the Midrash in Siegfried, p. 212.
‡ II. 658 sq. § II. 658.

present we must be content to observe that the allegorical
interpretation ought to be regarded as the true expression of
philosophical belief, because the writer is less shackled by the
words of Scripture, and because the whole object of the
allegorical method is to exalt the literal sense into philosophy.
This, accordingly, Philo proceeds to do.

" The spoken words " [he says], "are symbols of things apprehended
in intelligence alone. Whenever, then, a soul, as it were in mid-day,* has
been illumined on all sides by God, and, being entirely filled with intelligible
light, becomes shadowless with the beams that are shed around it, it
apprehends a triple representation of one subject; of one [of the three]
as actually existing, but of the other two as though they were shadows
cast from this. Something of a similar kind happens, too, in the case of
those who live in perceptible light ; for there often occur two shadows of
bodies at rest or in motion. Let no one suppose, however, that the word
shadows is used strictly in relation to God ; it is merely a misapplication
of the term for the clearer exhibition of the subject which we are
explaining, for the reality is not so. But, as one standing nearest to the
truth would say, the middle one is the Father of the universe, who in the
sacred Scriptures is called by a proper name the Self-existent,† and those
on each side are the oldest and nearest powers of the Self-existent, of
which one is called Creative, and the other Regal. And the Creative is
Deity,‡ for by this he deposited and arranged everything into a cosmos,
and the Regal is Lord, for it is right for that which has made to rule and
hold sway over that which has been produced. The middle one, then,
being attended by each of the two powers as by a body-guard, presents
to the seeing intelligence a representation§ now of one, and now of three;
of one, whenever the soul, being perfectly purified, and having trans-
cended not only the multitudes of numbers, but even the duad which
adjoins unity, presses on to the idea which is unmingled and uncomplicated
and in itself wanting nothing whatever in addition ; but of three, whenever,
not yet initiated into the great mysteries, it still celebrates its rites in the
lesser, and is unable to apprehend the self-existent Being|| from itself
alone without anything different [from pure being], but apprehends it
through the effects as either creating or ruling. This, then, is, as the
proverb runs, ' a second voyage,' but none the less partakes of opinion
dear to God. But the former method does not partake, but is itself the
opinion dear to God, or rather it is truth, which is older than opinion, and
more honourable than all opining." [The passage goes on to state that]
there are three orders of human character, distinguished severally by the

* Alluding to the time of the visit, Gen. xviii. 1.
† 'Ο ῎Ων.   ‡ Θεός.   § Or mental image, φαντασίαν. || Τὸ ὄν.

possession of these three representations. The best has that of the truly Self-existent, whom it serves by himself, without being drawn aside by any other. The remaining two belong to those who are acquainted with the Father through either the beneficent or the regal power. Now, when men perceive that people want to associate with them for their own advantage, they eye them askance and avoid them; but God "gladly calls to himself all who wish to honour him, in accordance with whatever idea they prefer to do so."* The first reward is reserved for those who serve him for his own sake, and that reward is friendship; the second is for those who on their own account hope to obtain advantages or expect to be delivered from punishments, for even if their service is not disinterested, it is nevertheless confined within divine enclosures, and their reward is not indeed friendship, but acceptance as not aliens. For God receives both him who wishes to share his beneficent power in order to participate in good things, and him who through fear propitiates the sovereign and lordly authority in order to avert punishment; for they will be improved through the continual exercise of sincere piety. The manners from which these several characters start are different, but they have one aim and one end, the service of God. Now that the triple representation is virtually that of one subject is evident not only from allegorical speculation, but from the written word; for when the wise Abraham supplicates those who seemed like three wayfarers, he converses with them, not as three, but as one, and addresses them in the singular number, and again the promise is given by one as though he alone were present.†

In this passage we have, not a hasty and casual remark, the full bearing of which the writer might have failed to perceive, but a long and careful statement, in which one leading thought is insisted upon in a variety of ways. Let us bring the several points together into a single view. In the first place, it is asserted in the most explicit manner that God and his two principal powers are in reality one subject, though presenting to the understanding a threefold mental image ; in other words, the distinction which is drawn is due, not to the nature of God, but to the imperfection of our intelligence. Secondly, for this one subject (whose essence, as we have learned else-

* Ἅπαντας τοὺς καθ' ἡντινοῦν ἰδίαν προαιρουμένους τιμᾶν αὐτὸν ἄσμενος προσκαλεῖται.
† Abr., 24-5 (II. 18-20). With this may be compared Qu. et Sol. in Gen., IV. 2.

where, is unknown) we can find no more expressive name than the " Self-existent," eternal and absolute Being. This is the highest, because the simplest idea of him that we are capable of forming ; it is completely *one*, representing no relation, and neither admitting of analysis nor coming under any more comprehensive term ; and in our holiest moods, when we can detach ourselves from the plurality of what he does, and adore him simply for what he is, we contemplate him as the one reality. But there are lower moods in which we regard him only through what he does, and then we see him as creating or ruling. Observe, it is not said that we see powers which are distinct from and beneath him, but that we see himself in certain aspects. So it is said farther on that men honour, not his powers, but God himself under certain ideas. We must use this expression to interpret the words " propitiates the sovereign and lordly authority," for we can hardly suppose that Philo has embedded a contradiction in the very heart of a continuous comment; and thus we learn that this very natural and easy kind of personification is not inconsistent with the doctrine which is set forth in the present passage. Lastly, we must notice the way in which Philo appeals to the written word, as though it might reasonably suggest a different view from that which he has reached by the method of allegory, thus confirming our impression that his deliberate philosophical belief is contained in his allegorical interpretations rather than in his remarks upon the letter of Scripture.

A parallel passage, which compresses the same thought into two or three lines, is more obscure ; but we may justly interpret it in the light of the foregoing exposition. " God," it is said, " being attended by two of the highest powers, Sovereignty and Goodness, being one in the midst,* wrought in the seeing soul triple representations."†

In a passage relating to another subject a similar view is suggested. Philo is commenting on the words " The Lord

* Εἷς ὢν ὁ μέσος.   † SS. Ab. et Cain., 15 (I. 173).

appeared to Abraham,"* and has shown that the self-existent Being is incomprehensible and without a name. He warns us not to conclude from the words of Scripture that the Cause of all shone upon and appeared to Abraham—

"For what human mind would be competent to contain the greatness of the representation?" It was really one of the powers around the Cause, namely, the Regal, that appeared; for "Lord" is an appellation of sovereignty. But when our mind held the Chaldæan opinion, it took the efficient powers for causes; but when it removed from the Chaldæan dogma, it knew that the cosmos was guided and governed by a supreme Ruler, of whose sovereignty it received a representation. Therefore the Scripture says, not "the self-existent Being," but "the Lord" appeared, meaning the King became manifest, being so from the beginning, but not yet known to the soul, which, even if it learned late, did not continue unlearned for ever, but received a representation of the sovereignty and supreme rule in things. But the Ruler having appeared confers a yet greater benefit upon him who hears and sees, by saying, "I am thy God." Of what, then, in all creation is he not God? He speaks now, not about the cosmos, of which the fabricator is certainly also God, but about human souls, which he has not deemed worthy of the same care; for he thinks it right to be called Lord and Despot of the bad, God of the improving, and of the best and most perfect both Lord and God.†

Nothing can be plainer than that the same being is referred to throughout this passage as revealing himself under different aspects. It is only in these aspects that the human mind is competent to know him, for it could not contain the full revelation of him as he is. Still, it may know that amid a plurality of aspects there is real unity, and, instead of thinking with the Chaldæans that the powers are so many independent causes, may satisfy itself that they are only the mental images of the sovereignty and beneficence of the Supreme Ruler. If this interpretation be correct, there could hardly be a more emphatic rejection of the view which treats the powers as a conclave of separate persons. There is one more fact of great importance which we learn from this passage. When Philo says "the Cause of the universe did not appear," he does not mean that there was no manifestation of God; and

* Gen. xvii. 1. † Mutat. Nom., 3 (I. 581).

that some one else was revealed instead, but that God did not appear in that particular character, that that was not the form assumed by the mental representation. By parity of reasoning we are bound, in all Philo's statements respecting God, to consider the form of the subject, and not hastily conclude that what is denied of God under one term is therefore to be denied of him under another. He may not do as absolute Being or universal Cause what nevertheless he does as Benefactor or moral Governor. This is a mode of language with which we are not familiar; and yet, if we knew a man under strongly contrasted characters, we might say of him, without danger of being mistaken, that it was not the philosopher, but the general, that won the battle, meaning that he succeeded in war, not by his philosophical, but by his military abilities.*

One other passage may be quoted in this connection, although the powers are not directly mentioned.

"To souls which are incorporeal and wait upon him, it is likely that God manifests himself as he is, conversing as a friend with friends, but to those that are still in bodies likening himself to angels, not changing his own nature—for he is unalterable—but placing in the souls which receive the representation an opinion of a different shape,† so that they suppose that the image ‡ is not an imitation, but the archetypal form itself." [It is added that] this was done for the benefit of men who were unable to form any higher conception.§

We learn once more from this passage that God, while remaining unchangeable, reveals himself in various aspects adapted to the weakness of our intelligence. These mental images, since they fall far short of the great reality, or even contain something quite erroneous, as when they clothe God

---

* To take an example from a standard writer: Gibbon says, " It is seldom that the antiquarian and the philosopher are so happily blended," where he refers to the abilities of the same man. [Ch. ix., note r.]

† Δόξαν ἐντιθέντα [for Mangey's ἀντιθέντα] ταῖς φαντασιουμέναις ἑτερόμορφον.

‡ Εἰκόνα, which, from the connection, must mean " the mental image."

§ Somn., I. 40 (I. 655). We may compare the expression in § 12, p. 631: " No longer stretching the mental representations from himself, but from the powers after him."

with the organs and passions of a man, are not the archetypal form, the complete and adequate idea which we may conceive to exist in more exalted minds, who see God as he is, but only an imitation or imperfect copy of this lofty idea, serving indeed to represent it to us, but not to be confounded with it. If this be the meaning of the passage, it bears out the doctrine that when we think of the regal or beneficent or other powers of God, we are dealing with images or representative forms of our own finite understanding, and not with real distinctions in the eternal nature.

Now what are we to say to these passages? Are we justified in taking them as the key to our interpretation of Philo's doctrine of the divine powers? In their favour we may plead their length, their careful elaboration, their explicitness, their manifestly philosophical character, and their agreement with the doctrine of the divine attributes. Yet Gfrörer treats the doctrine which they confessedly set forth as "a mere makeshift* occasioned by the necessity of rescuing the unity of the divine essence."† But as he does so, not on the ground of anything in the passages themselves which renders their meaning doubtful, or of anything in the context which might explain their divergence from what is said elsewhere, but solely on account of their alleged inconsistency with other statements and with Philo's philosophy as a whole, we cannot consider such summary dismissal to be anything but arbitrary and unsatisfactory. Simply to pitch overboard whatever interferes with the main course of our exposition is a very easy and comfortable mode of getting rid of a difficulty, but may itself perhaps lie under the suspicion of being a "mere makeshift." We shall see as we proceed that the view which receives so little courtesy is presented in a large number of passages, and we shall not fail to notice carefully those which appear to contradict it.

* Blosser Nothbehelf.   † P. 155.

Before attending to these passages we may allude to a most instructive paragraph relating to the powers of man, which supplies us with a valuable analogy to a subject lying more remote from our apprehension.

Wisdom [it is there said] being an art of arts, seems, indeed, to change with different materials, but its true idea* appears unalterable to those who have keen sight, and are not led astray by the material mass around it, but perceive the character impressed by the art itself. It is told that the celebrated sculptor Pheidias wrought brass, and ivory, and gold, and other materials, and in all displayed one and the same art, so that not only connoisseurs, but also those who were quite uninstructed, could recognize the artist from his works. Perfect art, being an imitation of nature, seals all materials with the same idea.† The same thing is shown by the power in the wise man;‡ for when it is engaged in things relating to the Self-existent, it is called piety and holiness; in things relating to the sky and its objects, natural philosophy;§ meteorological, in matters relating to the air; ethical, with its species, political and economical, in matters pertaining to the rectification of human morals; and, in other aspects, convivial, regal, legislative. For the many-named wise man has contained all these—piety, holiness, natural philosophy, meteorology, ethics, polity, economy, regal, legislative, and innumerable other powers; but in all he will be seen to have one and the same idea.‖

Now, this passage clearly informs us that wisdom, though it is one and unalterable, is capable of a large variety of applications, which may mislead the undiscerning into the belief that it is changing and manifold; and, further, that the wise man has an endless variety of powers, which are all ultimately and in reality the same, being expressions of wisdom, and owing their diversity of name and function, not to the violation of unity in wisdom itself, but to the multiplicity of objects towards which it is directed. Here we have precisely the same doctrine in regard to the wise man which is dismissed so contumeliously when it is asserted in respect to God. We may legitimately try, for the sake of rendering our thoughts more lucid, whether we can easily and naturally extend the analogy a little farther than Philo's immediate purpose required him to do. We might say, without danger of being misunderstood,

* Εἶδος. † Ἰδέαν. ‡ Ἡ ἐν τῷ σοφῷ δύναμις.
§ Φυσιολογία. ‖ Ebrict., 22 (I. 370·1).

that the wise man used his powers, and that he did one thing by one, and something else by another. We might say that he was known through his powers, meaning that his action as a legislator and in other capacities partly revealed him. We might say, further, that we knew him as a natural philosopher or as a politician, but that we did not know himself, meaning that we knew certain aspects of his mind, but that we had not penetrated to that essential wisdom in which all his powers found their unity, and the apprehension of which would include all partial and inferior knowledge. From this point we might go on to say that he was above or before his powers, because he not only determined their application, but in the completeness and unity of his wisdom was larger and fuller than they in the division and partiality of their nature. We shall do well to bear this analogy in mind as we pursue our further way through the doctrine of the divine powers.

We may begin with the remark that the powers are used collectively as equivalent to the nature or essence of God. Thus, it is said that mankind has obtained the sovereignty of all earthly things, "being a copy of the powers of God, a manifest image of the invisible nature, a created image of the eternal."* Here the parallelism of the expressions shows that the powers of God are identical with the invisible, eternal nature. The same conclusion follows from the statement that the powers communicate qualities to things without quality, and shapes to things without shape, suffering no change or diminution in the eternal nature;† for, if they were distinct from the eternal nature, the phrase would be without meaning. The transition is easy to the use of power in the singular to denote the divine essence, just as "the power in the wise man" signifies the essence by virtue of which he is wise. This practice is illustrated by the saying that, "to possess an

* Ἀντίμιμον γεγονὼς θεοῦ δυνάμεων, εἰκὼν τῆς ἀοράτου φύσεως ἐμφανής, ἀϊδίου γενητή, Vita Mos., II. 12 (II. 144).

† Μηδὲν τῆς ἀϊδίου φύσεως μεταλλαττομένας μήτε μειουμένας, Monarch., I. 6 (II. 219).

unalterable intelligence approaches the power of God, since the Divine is unalterable, but the created naturally changeable."* In a parallel passage it is said that "in reality an unalterable soul alone has access to the unalterable God, and the soul disposed in this way truly stands near divine power;" and a little farther on it is added, " The self-existent Being which moves and alters everything else is immovable and unalterable, and communicates of its own nature, stillness, to the virtuous man."† Here the context relieves the passage of any ambiguity that might be thought to attach to the previous statement. The same explanation of the phrase is the simplest that can be given in two other instances. Moses, we are told, " wishes those who go to the service of the Self-existent first to know themselves and their own essence ; for how could he who is ignorant of himself apprehend the supreme and all-surpassing power of God ?"‡ The antithesis seems to fix the meaning of the power of God. As, however, the passage may be thought to contradict what we have learned elsewhere respecting our ignorance, not only of the divine essence, but of our own, we must observe that the reference is to the mean character of our bodily frame, which we must clearly understand in order to appreciate the infinite superiority of God, and approach him with becoming humility. The implication, therefore, is not a knowledge of God's essence in itself, but only in its contrast to the composition of our bodies, and is not inconsistent with Philo's ordinary doctrine. Again, it is asserted of the first man that " God breathed in of his own power as much as mortal nature could receive," for which reason God was his Father, and he was an image of God.§ It might be maintained here that the power of God is the Logos; but the passage makes no allusion to the Logos, and we may be content to assign to it for the present the meaning which it naturally bears. It is hardly necessary to observe that the doctrine

* Cherub., 6 (I. 142).   † Post. Cain., 9 (I. 231).
‡ Sacrificant., 2 (II. 252).   § Nobil., 3 (II. 440).

which we have thus reached precisely coincides with that of the attributes of God, which in their totality are combined in the unknown unity of the divine essence.

It is a not unexpected result of the foregoing view that God and his power or powers are used interchangeably. This occurs in a long and rhetorical account of the preparation which the soul ought to make for the indwelling of God. That the supreme Deity is meant is evident from the language in which he is described, "the Self-existent," "the intelligible God," "the King of kings and Sovereign God of all;" and yet, when all is ready for his reception, we hear only of "the descent of the powers of God," which bring laws from heaven according to the order of their Father, and become table-companions of souls which love virtue.* Does, then, Philo contradict at the close of the passage the statement with which he starts, that God "invisibly enters the region of the soul?" Does God really hold aloof, and send powers which are other than himself to take his place? We need not resort to so harsh a conclusion if we have travelled thus far upon the right road. The doctrine implied seems to be this, that God himself does indeed enter the soul, but does not reveal himself there in the absolute unity of his essence; he comes as the beneficent, the gracious, the propitious, the legislative, and so forth, and it is only through the medium of these powers that our intellect is able to apprehend him. To call God their Father may seem to imply a personal separation between them; but fatherhood is sometimes used to denote identity of essence, and it is not a more violent figure to represent them as children of God than to describe them as table-companions of the soul. Similarly the wise man might be called the father of his meteorological, ethical, and other activities. In another passage a vision of God, a mental representation of the Unbegotten, is promised to him who is freed from the chains of the body. The proof is drawn from the instance of Abraham,

* Cherub., 28-31 (I. 156-8).

who, when he had left his land and kindred and father's house, began "to meet with the powers of the Self-existent"; for the law says that "God* appeared to him," intimating that he manifests himself clearly to him who has put off mortal things.† There is no hint that "God" is used here in the limited sense of the creative power, and "the Unbegotten"‡ must certainly denote the Supreme God. We may therefore adopt the explanation which we have applied to the previous passage. There is one more example. Prayer, it is said, is a request for good things from God, but a great prayer§ is the belief that God himself is the cause of good things from himself, without the co-operation of any other—of earth as fruitful, of rains as contributing to the growth of seeds and plants, of air as able to nourish, and so forth ; for all these things receive changes by the power of God, so as often to produce the opposite of their usual effects.|| Here the power of God cannot denote any being other than himself, or the argument would be incoherent. The meaning evidently is, that as God often reverses the customary effects of natural agents, he cannot be dependent on their co-operation for the blessings which he bestows.

The interchange of God and his powers leads us to notice a number of passages in which the latter are regarded as predicates of the former, and he is spoken of as being or doing what is implied by their several names. The following is the most general statement of this kind:—"The soul which honours the self-existent Being for the sake of the self-existent Being itself, ought not to do so thoughtlessly¶ or ignorantly, but with knowledge and thought.** Now, our thought†† about him receives division and separation according to each of the divine powers and virtues ; for God is good, and

* 'Ο θεός.   † Quod. det. pot. ins., 43-4 (I. 221).   ‡ 'Ο ἀγένητος.
§ Alluding to the vow in Num. vi. 2, where the LXX translate μεγάλως εὔξηται εὐχήν.
|| Quod Deus immut., 19 (I. 285-6).   ¶ 'Αλόγως.
** Λόγῳ.   †† 'Ο λόγος.

maker and producer of the universe, and provident of what he begat, most happy Saviour and Benefactor, and full of all blessedness, each of which is venerable and laudable, whether considered separately by itself or along with those of the same kind."* The predicative character of the powers is here too apparent to require further remark. Similarly, in an allusion to the legislative as one of the powers around God, the parenthetical explanation is immediately subjoined, "for [God] himself is a legislator and fountain of laws," implying that the legislative power exists only because God *is* that which it denotes.† The same relation is suggested when God is spoken of as "the Benevolent and Propitious, who has filled all things with his own beneficent power."‡ Another mode of expression represents the power as that by virtue of which God acts. Thus, in exposing the folly of the man who fancies that he can escape the notice of God, Philo says, "Thou art ignorant of God's power, by virtue of which§ he sees all things and hears all things at the same moment."‖ Clearly the power is not something which hears and sees instead of God, but God's faculty of seeing and hearing. Again, Jacob's words, "This is the house of God,"¶ mean, "This perceptible cosmos is nothing else than the house of God, one of the powers of him who is really God, by virtue of which he was good."** Lastly, there are several passages in which the two highest powers become simply predicates of the Self-existent. We may cite these in the order in which they occur. The saying, "I am the Lord"†† is not only equivalent to "I am the perfect and incorruptible and truly good;" but stands for, "I am the Ruler and the King and Despot."‡‡ Again, Scripture says "that Noah pleased the powers of the Self-existent, 'Lord and God;'§§ but Moses [pleased] him who

* Animal. sacr. idon., 6 (II. 242).   † SS. Ab. et Cain., 39 (I. 189).
‡ Vita Mos., III. 31 (II. 171).   § Καθ' ἥν.
‖ Sacrificant., 4 (II. 254).   ¶ Gen. xxviii. 17.
** Somn., I. 32 (I. 648).   †† Lev. xviii. 6.
‡‡ Gigant., 11 (I. 268-9).   §§ Gen. vi. 8.

is attended by the powers, and apart from them is understood according to being only; for it is said, in the person of God, 'Thou hast found favour with me,'* indicating himself without any other. Thus, then, the Self-existent himself deems the supreme wisdom in Moses worthy of favour through himself alone, but that which is modelled from this, being second and more specific, through the subject powers, by virtue of which he is both Lord and God, both Ruler and Benefactor."† This passage is most instructive, because the powers are so strongly distinguished from the Self-existent. We must return to it farther on, and endeavour to explain the force of this distinction. Meanwhile we must be content with observing that, whatever the distinction may be, it is asserted in almost the same breath that it is the Self-existent himself who *is* both Lord and God. A similar identification takes place in another passage which it is needless to quote at length. The appellations Lord and God signify the powers around the self-existent Being, that by virtue of which he rules, and that by virtue of which he benefits. So far as he *is* Ruler he is able to do good or ill, but so far as he *is* Benefactor he wills only to benefit. "Eternal God" means, Who gives continually, though he is Lord and able to injure. Accordingly Jacob said, "the Lord shall be my God,"‡ meaning, He will no longer show me the despotic action of his rule, but the beneficent action§ of his propitious and saving power. "What soul would suppose this, that the Despot and Sovereign of the universe, making no change in his own nature, but remaining alike, is continually good and unceasingly munificent?"|| It could hardly be made more evident that Lord and God represent the same subject regarded under different aspects. In the final question, "the Despot and Sovereign of the universe" can denote only the supreme God. It is he that is both despotic and beneficent, and wonderfully harmonizes these antithetic characters in his

* Ex., xxxiii. 17.   † Quod Deus immut., 24 (I. 289).   ‡ Gen. xxviii. 21.
§ Τὸ εὐεργετικόν; as before, τὸ δεσποτικόν. || Plantat. Noe, 20, 21 (I. 342-3).

own unchangeable Being. Again, in the interpretation of Jacob's dream it is said that, "the Lord" who stood above the ladder was the self-existent Being.* We thus learn that the name which is strictly limited to one of the divine powers may, as is so repeatedly the case with "God," be used to denote the absolute Being himself, a practice which is not easily understood if "Lord" and "God" denote separate and subordinate persons. The passage, however, instructs us more plainly. He who stood upon the ladder said to Jacob, "I am the Lord God of Abraham thy father and the God of Isaac." It is not without reason that this distinction is made between Abraham and Isaac; for the former, having lived among the Chaldæans, and acquired his wisdom by learning, needed two powers to care for him, sovereignty and beneficence; but the other, being born under happier circumstances, and having what was good by nature, did not require admonishing rule, but only the gracious power. Moved by this, Jacob offered a most admirable prayer, that to him "the Lord might become God," for he wished no longer to fear him as a ruler, but to honour him lovingly as a benefactor.† Comment is unnecessary. In the last passage to be cited under this head, Philo gives his opinion that by the cherubim on the lid of the Ark were indicated the two oldest and highest powers of the Self-existent, the creative and regal. "For," he adds, "being alone truly self-existent, he is both maker in the strictest sense, since he brought into being things that were not, and king by nature, because no one would rule the things that were created more justly than he who has made them."‡ Here, again,

* Τὸ ὄν.

† Somn., I. 25-26 (I. 644-5). Cf. the passage already fully cited, p. 94, from Mutat. Nom., 3 (I. 581).

‡ Vita. Mos., III. 8 (II. 150). We may refer also to Qu. et Sol. in Ex. II. 66, with the Greek in Harris, Fragments, p. 65, the force of which is quite lost in the Latin. Having spoken of "the creative and regal powers," Philo says, in explanation of the fact that the faces of the cherubim on the Ark inclined towards one another, ἐπειδὴ ὁ θεὸς εἷς ὢν καὶ ποιητής ἐστι καὶ βασιλεύς, εἰκότως αἱ διαστᾶσαι δυνάμεις πάλιν ἕνωσιν ἔλαβον. The rest of the passage too is instructive.

comment is needless. From all these passages we learn that it is the Self-existent himself who *is* what the various powers denote, and who presents to the imperfect thought of man these partial and broken glimpses of his own single and unchangeable nature. Accordingly the powers are sometimes spoken of precisely as we should speak of the attributes of God. Thus we are told, that " 'God' is the name of the goodness of the Cause, that thou mayest know that he has made even lifeless things, not by authority, but by goodness." Immediately afterwards this goodness is referred to as a power.* Again, God has given good things, not because he thought anything worthy of favour; but "looking to the eternal goodness, and supposing that it belonged to his own happy and blessed nature to benefit." Hence "the goodness of the Self-existent, the oldest of the graces" supplies the reason for creation.† Once more, the four letters graven on the golden plate on the high-priest's mitre signified, they say, the name of the Self-existent, as it is not possible for anything to subsist without summoning God;‡ "for his goodness and propitious power are the harmony of all things."§

There is one other indication of Philo's belief which is perhaps worth noticing before we quit the line of thought which we have been following. In the passage where the intelligible and the perceptible worlds are described as the elder and the younger sons of God, time is spoken of as his grandson, because the cosmos is the father of time, and God is the father of the cosmos.‖ This seems to show that, whatever colour Philo's language may occasionally afford to later Gnostic speculations, he himself did not suppose that the material world was separated from God by the intervention of the intelligible; for had he thought that the perceptible cosmos was not the immediate creation of God, but had emanated from

* Leg. All., III. 23 (I. 101). † Quod Deus immut., 23 (I. 288-9).
‡ Ἄνευ κατακλήσεως θεοῦ. § Vita Mos., III. 14 (II. 155).
‖ Quod Deus immut., 7 (I. 277).

the intelligible as from a separate group of powers, which themselves were the immediate offspring of the First Cause, he would have represented it, not as a younger son, but as a grandson. By assigning to both the same relationship, he makes them equally direct expressions of the divine causality; and since, nevertheless, the world of sense was created through the powers, it follows that the latter were not regarded as ontologically distinct from God.

The foregoing passages have been cited at such length in order that a due impression may be formed of their number and weight, and we may clearly see how Philo's writings are pervaded by a conception which Gfrörer treats as "a mere makeshift." Zeller frankly admits the frequent identification of the powers with the divine nature, and perceives the importance of this identification in the philosophical system with which it is connected; but he finds himself unable to reconcile with this view the doctrine presented in other passages, and maintains that Philo flatly contradicts himself, and was compelled to do so by the necessities of his theory. In the doctrine of the powers, he observes, two representations cross one another, the religious notion of personal, and the philosophical of impersonal, mediators. Philo combines the two conceptions without noticing their contradiction; indeed he could not notice it, because, had he done so, he would thereby have sacrificed the double nature which is essential to the mediatorial character of the divine powers, by virtue of which they must, on the one hand, be identical with God, in order that through them the finite may be able to participate in the Deity, and, on the other hand, be different from him, in order that the Deity, in spite of this participation, may remain free from all contact with the world. There is here, as elsewhere, simply a contradiction, which the historian may indeed account for, but cannot remove.* When a writer of such extensive learning and such clear discernment makes so positive a state-

* III. ii. pp. 365 sq.

ment, we must proceed with caution. That the idea of personality was not very sharply defined by the ancient thinkers, we have already had occasion to observe; but the charge against Philo is not that he is vague and uncertain in the application of this idea: it is that he predicates of the same object identity with and difference from God in a sense that involves absolute contradiction. We must carefully examine the tendency of thought on which so serious an allegation is based; but, in doing so, instead of considering first the passages which seem most plainly to contradict those that have been hitherto adduced, we must rather follow, if it be possible, the natural order of exposition, and develop the ideas which we have already gained.

The simplest conception of the mediating office of the powers is that which explains through their agency the omnipresence of God. Gfrörer, in rejecting the doctrine which we have hitherto unfolded as not representing Philo's philosophical opinion, but merely a concession to the popular faith, asks, as though his question were conclusive, " To what end separate the Eternal so anxiously from the world, if, through the powers, which according to the latter exposition are nothing else than his mode of operation, he enters again the circle of the finite ?"* An attentive consideration of Philo's language will rather convince us that a primary function of the powers was not to keep God out of the finite, but to bring him into it. It was to remove the difficulty which must arise, not only in Alexandrian Judaism, but in every system of theism. How is it possible for the Eternal Mind, which transcends both space and time, to act within them? To say that he cannot, that therefore he gets someone else to do it for him, is not a philosophical answer, and I do not believe that it is Philo's. The latter may be satisfactory or not, but it is at least a serious attempt to meet a speculative difficulty.

* P. 155.

The first passage which demands our attention is one in which he is commenting on the words, "The Lord came down to see the city and the tower."*

These words must be figurative, because the Divine is not capable of local motion, which involves leaving one place and occupying another. "All things have been filled by God," who alone is everywhere and nowhere. He is nowhere because he generated place and locality with bodies, and we may not say that the Maker is contained in any of the things made; and he is "everywhere, because having stretched his own powers through earth and water, air and heaven, he has left no part of the cosmos desert, but collecting all things together he bound them throughout with invisible bonds, that they should never be loosed, ... for the self-existent Being which is above the powers is conceived to be superabundant, not according to essence only."†

It is perfectly clear from this statement that the powers are not substitutes for God. It is he that is everywhere, and the powers are introduced simply to explain the mode of his omnipresence. He is present, not in the sense in which a body is present, by having certain relations in space; but while the thought of dimension cannot be applied to him, he yet can make his energy operative in space, and is thus omnipresent, not like a universally diffused matter, but through the action of force, in other words, not essentially but dynamically. A similar explanation, it will be remembered, was given of the connection between the human mind and body: the mind, though residing essentially in the head, was diffused dynamically through the entire frame.‡ The analogy of the sun and its beams which was then used is equally applicable to the subject before us. We must interpret in conformity with this unambiguous doctrine the succeeding words, "The self-existent Being which is above the powers." This superiority need not imply separation. Even the human mind, conceived as a complex unity, is above the powers that compose it, and

* Gen. xi. 5.
† Τὸ μὲν γὰρ ὑπεράνω τῶν δυνάμεων ὂν ἐπινοεῖται περιττεύειν, οὐ κατὰ τὸ εἶναι μόνον.
‡ Vol. I. p. 340 sq.

so he who is better than the good, and more beautiful than beauty, must be above the powers which partially represent him to our thought. We must pay strict attention to Philo's language: it is "the self-existent Being,"* God conceived as absolute Being, God in his perfect and unrelated unity, who is above the powers, the forms of his thought and modes of his activity, which belong to the domain of the relative. Bearing this contrast in mind, we can understand Philo's further statement:—"Now, the power of this [Self-existent], which put and ordered all things, has been strictly called God, and has embosomed all things, and permeated the parts of the universe. But the divine and invisible and inapprehensible self-existent Being, which is everywhere,† is in truth visible and apprehensible nowhere..... Therefore, none of the terms of motion which involves change of place is applicable to God in his essential Being."‡

The same doctrine is laid down in another passage, where Philo is remarking on the statement that Moses entered into the darkness where God was: §

The darkness means unseen thoughts about the Self-existent; "for the Cause is not in 'darkness,'|| nor in place at all, but above both place and time. For having yoked all created things beneath himself he is contained by nothing, but has stepped upon all. But having stepped upon, and being outside creation, he has none the less filled the cosmos with himself; for having through power stretched as far as the ends he wove each to each according to the proportions of harmony." ¶

Here the statement that he has filled the cosmos with *himself* is perfectly explicit, and therefore the power whose presence justifies this statement is not distinct from him. A little farther on Philo adds:—

God " being the same, is both very near and far off, touching indeed

* Τὸ ὄν. † Τὸ θεῖον . . . πανταχοῦ ὄν.
‡ Τῷ κατὰ τὸ εἶναι θεῷ. Conf. Ling., 27 (I. 425).
§ Ex. xx. 21.
|| So Tischendorf, in his Philonea, p. 87, retaining the MS. reading γνόφῳ, for which Mangey reads, χρόνῳ.
¶ Διὰ γὰρ δυνάμεως ἄχρι περάτων τείνας ἕκαστον ἑκάστῳ . . . συνύφηνεν.

with the creative and punitive powers, as they are near to each, but having driven the begotten very far from his nature in its essence."*

It is only as expressions of himself that the powers can be thus said to make him near; it is only in his essence—that is, in the complete and absolute unity of his being—that he is said to be far off. This is a most instructive passage, for we cannot suppose that Philo contradicts himself in the same breath. He is quite aware of the seeming contradiction in the statement that the same being is near and far off, and resolves it to his own satisfaction by explaining that he is near dynamically, remote essentially, near through partial manifestations of his thought, remote in the incomprehensible completeness of his nature.

There are one or two other passages which also support the doctrine of God's presence through the powers, but can hardly be said to throw further light upon Philo's meaning. The question, "Will the Lord's hand not suffice?"† signifies "that the powers of the Self-existent reach everywhere ‡ for the benefit, not only of the illustrious, but also of those who seem to be more obscure, on whom he graciously bestows what is fitting, according to the standards and measures of the soul of each, ruling and measuring the just proportion to each by the equality in himself."§ On these words we need only remark that they do not represent God as withdrawn from all interest in the lower world; it is he that gives, it is he that assigns to every man his due. So when we are told that God "has filled all things throughout with his own beneficent power," ‖ we do not naturally think of a substitute for himself, especially as it is he that is represented as acting. These passages, accordingly, if they do not advance our thought, are, at least, consistent with what has been hitherto maintained.¶

That we may fully appreciate the force of the above argument

* Τῆς κατὰ τὸ εἶναι φύσεως. Post. Cain., 5-6 (I. 228-9).
† Num. xi. 23.   ‡ Πάντη .... φθάνειν.
§ Mutat. Nom., 40 (I. 613-14).   ‖ Vita Mos., III. 31 (II. 171).
¶ See also Gigant., 11 (I. 269).

we must refer back to what was said about the divine omnipresence in treating of the attributes of God. It is to him that this high prerogative belongs. Yet we must think of him, not as an extended and therefore material substance, but as one who, though he transcends the conditions of space, can yet make his energy felt wheresoever his sovereign will may direct.

The term which Philo frequently employs to denote the local action of the powers, is quite agreeable to the conception which we have reached. He says that God *stretches* the powers— a word which would have an odd application to personal mediators, but precisely suits the notion of exerting energy either thoughout space or in particular parts of it. "Stretch"* happily combines the ideas of extension and of strain,† and is used characteristically of the direction of force upon certain objects. We have seen it employed to describe the distribution of the human powers to the various organs of the body, and we are thus furnished with an analogy to the diffusion of the divine powers throughout the universe. We may add two further examples. "He who has stretched the energies of his soul to God, and hopes for benefit from him alone," will disclaim the receipt of his blessings from the objects of nature, and accept all things "from the only Wise, since he stretches his own propitious powers everywhere, and benefits through these." ‡ Again, when one is listening quietly and attentively to an address, the mind is said to "stretch itself to the speaker." § These examples are interesting, because they represent the mind as extending its powers, or itself, beyond the bodily circumference. They may satisfy us that we are not to conceive the extension physically, but to regard it as a figure of speech, representing in the least objectionable way,

* Τείνω.
† Cf. Philo's own κατὰ τὴν ἰσχὺν καὶ εὐτονίαν καὶ δύναμιν, in distinguishing πνεῦμα from αὔρα, Leg. All., I. 13 (I. 51).
‡ Ebriet., 27 (I. 373). § Quis rer. div. her., 3 (I. 474).

a spiritual process whose reality is more obvious than its mode. When we remember what Philo says of the inadequacy of human language respecting God, we must admit that this remark will apply still more certainly to the extension of the divine powers. The latter represents the fact that the energy of the Supreme Cause is operative in space, and supplies us with a physical analogy by which we can hold this fact in our imagination, but is not designed to give a literal description of the inscrutable mode in which God puts forth his power.*

From the conception of stretching, that of touching easily follows, for the power must be stretched to some object with which it may be said to be in contact. The two ideas are combined in a passage in which Philo speaks of the inspiration of the human mind:—God stretches the power from himself as far as the mind, that we may receive a thought of him; "for how could the soul think of God, unless he inspired and touched it dynamically,† for the human mind would not dare to run up to such a height as to lay hold of the nature of God, unless God himself drew it up to himself, so far as was possible for a human mind to be drawn up, and stamped it according to the powers that are accessible to thought."‡ Before commenting on this passage, we may quote another which helps to illustrate it:—"Nothing is higher than God; and if anyone has reached him by stretching the eye of the soul, let him pray for permanence and stability. For uphill roads are wearisome and slow, but the rush down, tearing violently along rather than quietly descending, is swift and very easy. Now the things that force us down are many; but they have no effect whenever God, having suspended the

---

* Nearly all the passages where τείνω is used of the divine powers have been already cited in other connections, and it is sufficient merely to refer to them: Leg. All., I. 13 (I. 51); Post. Cain., 5 (I. 229); Conf. Ling., 27 (I. 425); Migrat. Abr., 22 (I. 455), προτείνας; § 32, p. 464, ἀπίτεινε; Mutat. Nom., 4 (I. 582).

† Κατὰ δύναμιν.   ‡ Leg. All., I. 13 (I. 51).

soul from his powers, draws it to himself with a more powerful pull."* It is evident that in these passages, physical imagery is used to express facts which are hyperphysical. What, then, are these facts? First, there is a real connection between the soul and God, which may be expressed under the twofold aspect of a descent of the Divine upon the human, and an ascent of the human to the Divine. Secondly, this connection is effected through the mediation of the powers. If we ask why there is any mediation, the answer is not supplied in the text before us, but may be gathered from what we have learned elsewhere. If it were said without qualification that God himself touched the soul, it would be implied that he made no partial revelation, but impressed upon the mind that one all-containing thought, inaccessible to man, which would convey a complete knowledge of the totality and unity of his essence. Since this is impossible, if not for all finite natures, at least for souls imprisoned in bodies, God can touch the soul only by his power, that is, he makes his energy present to the human consciousness, where it resolves itself into a plurality of powers or ideas representative of the Divine. In this way the mind is taught to lift the spiritual eye to God, and is drawn up to himself so far as mortal weakness will allow; for it can apprehend as divine the powers or thoughts which are impressed upon it, and refer them to the unknown unity of which they are the manifold expression.

We are now prepared to understand a passage which is frequently quoted as proving decisively the separation of the powers from God. Out of matter, it is said, " God generated all things, not touching it himself, for it was not right for the Wise and Blessed to come in contact with indeterminate and mixed matter; but he used the incorporeal powers, whose real name is ideas, that the fitting form might take possession of each genus."† If the powers were employed to do something which it was not suitable for God to do himself, what can be

* Abr., 12 (II. 10). † Sacrificant., 13 (II. 261).

plainer than that they and God are essentially distinct? Dähne relies upon the passages in which a contrast of this kind is drawn as affording conclusive proof that the powers are persons essentially different from God, and declares that if Philo maintained that it would be unworthy of God to interpenetrate the world, but not unworthy of his attributes, though it is only through their combination that God first became God, he talked perfect nonsense, and we must cease to treat him as a philosopher.* This is a summary way of settling a difficult question, and, from our modern point of view, might appear to be unanswerable. The notion, however, that God is made up by a combination of attributes is so exceedingly remote from the thought of Philo, that we may suspect the critic's judgment of being a little at fault. Instead of yielding to the first impulse of common sense, let us look a little more deeply into the matter, even at the risk of talking nonsense. If Philo had said that God himself touched matter, not through his powers but in his essence, what would he have meant? Could he have meant that he retained his transcendence, and made only some feeble and partial revelation of himself through matter? I think not. According to all that we have yet learned, he could only have meant that God impressed his whole being upon matter, that from being transcendent he became immanent, and made through the cosmos a complete revelation of his eternal essence. In that case the cosmos would be obviously one, instead of letting its unity wait upon the inferences of reason from its complex phenomena; the ideal form impressed upon matter would exhibit to the mind a single thought, and that thought would be tantamount to God; his name would be known, and in surveying the universe we should gaze upon him face to face. But such was not the aspect presented by the world. Matter was not adequate to receive the transfiguring touch which would make it an exhaustive expression of the Divine. Instead of one, there

* I. p. 239 sqq.

were impressed on it a multitude of ideal forms, divine thoughts which gave significance to its dull mass; and no combination of these would produce God or adequately represent him, but even when, through an effort of reason, we had bound them together, and grasped the idea of the good, we should still have to pass on to the unknown and transcendent unity, which embraced in its infinite essence all, and more than all, that a cosmos could reveal. It was necessary, therefore, to say that God used the powers or ideas for his cosmic work, and touched the universe only with these, while he kept the begotten far from his essential Being.* In this their cosmical aspect the powers become as it were objective to God, divine thoughts permanently planted out in a material world, and they might very easily be spoken of as independent essences, just as we habitually refer to the physical forces as though they were so many distinct agents, though we may regard them philosophically as modes of the divine activity. But that a real separation from God is quite inadmissible is affirmed by Philo in the most explicit language :—" Nothing of the Divine is cut so as to separate it, but is only extended." † This indeed is said in immediate relation to the human soul, which is invested with a distinct personality; but it is said in connection with those "invisible powers" whereby it outstrips time, and touches the universe and its parts. A focal aggregate of powers may produce a person, but this, instead of suggesting, is rather inconsistent with the ascription of personality to the powers taken one by one. The great source which includes and transcends them is a person, or, rather, he is the one arche-

---

* See the passage quoted on p. 110 from Post. Cain., 6 (I. 229). Perhaps what I conceive to be Philo's fundamental thought may be more clearly expressed as follows:—‘O Ὤν could not impart Himself to matter; for that would mean that matter became partaker of eternal Being. Creation may become *rational;* but for the creation to become that which has not *become,* but always *is,* would be a contradiction. Hence the absolute separation between pure Being and matter.

† Τέμνεται γὰρ οὐδὲν τοῦ θείου κατ' ἀπάρτησιν, ἀλλὰ μόνον ἐκτείνεται, Quod det. pot. ins., 24 (I. 209).

typal person by participation in whom all lower personality subsists; but the powers are modes of his energy, eternally and inseparably dependent upon him, and destined to vanish if he were not, as rays of light vanish when the central luminary is quenched. They appear as ideal forms in matter, and as thoughts in the human mind. By virtue of their origin they are independent of time and space, and hence our thought can transport itself instantaneously to the most distant regions, and hold heaven and earth within its embrace. Thus they are the connection between the universe and God, mediating between them, not because they are different from both, but because they are strictly separable from neither. Withdraw them from the mind, and it becomes a non-entity; withdraw them from the material world, and it ceases to be a cosmos; detach them, if that be conceivable, from God, and they will sink into nothingness. They are really divine, and, wherever it turns, the seeing soul may discern some thought of God; but they are nowhere exhaustive of the divine, and it would be wholly false to say that in their totality they were the equivalent of God. Through them God has indeed left no part of the cosmos empty of himself; but he has not made himself and the cosmos conterminous, and therefore, as soon as we endeavour to apprehend him in the unity of his being, he remains to our thought essentially outside the universe, though acting dynamically within it.* We may agree with this view or not; but at all events it is something better than sheer nonsense. It is a natural development of Philo's philosophy, and seems to me a reasonable interpretation of his language.

---

* We may compare Philo's statement that the sovereign principle in man is in its essence within the body, but in power is in Italy or Sicily when it thinks about these places: Leg. All., I. 18 (I. 55). This is suggestive, though the notion of locality which is here involved is of course inapplicable to God. Most instructive also is Athanasius's remark about the Logos: ὥσπερ ἐν πάσῃ τῇ κτίσει ὤν, ἐκτὸς μέν ἐστι τοῦ παντὸς κατ' οὐσίαν, ἐν πᾶσι δέ ἐστι ταῖς ἑαυτοῦ δυνάμεσι, . . . περιέχων τὰ ὅλα, καὶ μὴ περιεχόμενος, ἀλλ' ἐν μόνῳ τῷ ἑαυτοῦ Πατρὶ ὅλος ὢν κατὰ πάντα. De Incarnat. c. xvii.

On the other hand, to represent God as physically outside the universe, and therefore requiring separate persons inferior to himself to act upon matter for him, makes the whole subject hopelessly incoherent; and if this was what Philo meant, instead of rescuing his claim to be a philosopher, we may rather pronounce it to be the clumsy device of one incapable or impatient of metaphysical thought.

This view makes it an easy figure of speech to represent the powers as standing round about God, and waiting upon him like the retinue of a court. It will be remembered that the same figure was used of the powers of the human mind, so that we need have no scruple in recognizing here a simple personification. God is "the sovereign of all the powers."* With a view to aid us, power sits as a ready helper beside God, and the Sovereign himself draws nearer to benefit those who are worthy."† God is "attended by the powers as by a bodyguard."‡ They are his "followers and attendants,"§ and by their appearance in the cosmos reveal the existence, though not the essence, of the Supreme Cause.‖ "The glory round about" him¶ is none other than the powers which surround him and act as his body-guard;** but these are invisible and intelligible as himself, and are properly named ideas.†† The figurative character of these passages is apparent, and no comment is needed.‡‡

It is hardly necessary to refer to a few passages where Philo speaks of " God *and* his powers," for such a distinction in thought need not imply any separation in fact.§§ In only one

---

* Somn., I. 41 (I. 656). † Migrat. Abr., 10 (I. 444-5).
‡ Δορυφορουμένῳ πρὸς τῶν δυνάμεων, Quod Deus immut., 24 (I. 289).
§ Ἑπομένων καὶ ἀκολούθων. ‖ Post. Cain., 48 (I. 258).
¶ Τὴν περὶ σε δόξαν. ** Τὰς σε δορυφορούσας δυνάμεις, . . . τὰς περὶ ἐμέ.
†† Monarch., I. 6 (II. 218-19).
‡‡ For the use of the phrase " around God " in connection with the powers see also Quod Deus immut., 17 (I. 284); Plantat. Noe, 20 (I. 342); Mutat. Nom., 3 (I. 581); Sacrificant., 9 (II. 258).
§§ See Quod Deus immut., 1 (I. 273), " The wise man sees God and his powers;" Migrat. Abr., 14 (I. 448), " Inquiries about God and his most sacred powers."

of them is there any appearance of attributing personality to the powers:—"It is always the care of himself and his beneficent powers to change the discord of the worse substance."* The personification, however, belongs to the most familiar figures of speech; and the distinction only calls attention to the benevolent nature of the divine purpose as a whole, and the realisation of this benevolence in the various directions prescribed to the different powers. Thus we might say of some one, without danger of being misunderstood, that the attainment of truth was the object of his mind and its several faculties, and the addition of the latter words would impart strength and comprehensiveness to the meaning of the sentence.

Still less can we attach any importance to the statement that God *used* his powers, for this is in complete agreement with our ordinary modes of speech. One or two examples will suffice. The Maker of the universe possessing thought and purpose as most stable powers, and "always using these, surveys his works."† Again, it is said that "God uses the powers unmixed towards himself, but mixed towards creation, for it is impossible for a mortal nature to contain them unmingled." This is illustrated by the tempering of the solar beams, which reach us through the chill medium of the air.‡ It is impossible in these passages to convert the powers into personal agents, and the statement that God uses them no more suggests real separation than is implied when we say of ourselves that we use our intelligence or skill.§ That which we use may be naturally spoken of as an instrument *through* which we effect our purpose. Thus we may be said to do one thing through our mechanical aptitude, another through our scientific knowledge, a third through our political insight.

* Justit., 7 (II. 367).   † Quod Deus immut., 7 (I. 277).
‡ Ib. § 17, p. 284.
§ See also Gigant., 11 (I. 269); Sacrificant., 13 (II. 261); Qu. et Sol. in Gen. I. 54; cf. Mundi Op., 4 (I. 4), where God is said to have used the intelligible cosmos as a pattern.

Similarly God is said to confer benefits through his gracious powers,* to have placed all things through the creative power,† and to "confer by his own power unstinted abundance of good things on all parts of the universe."‡ Such language may, no doubt, be used of personal agents, but there is not even an apparent implication of personal agency in the above quotations.

We come now to the passages most relied upon by those who maintain the personality of the powers, some of which undoubtedly present considerable difficulties to an interpreter who takes a different view. We will treat them in groups, beginning with those which most easily harmonize with our previous exposition.

First, God is sometimes spoken of as above the powers. This is no more than we should expect, when even the human mind is described as a king attended by powers as its body-guards and messengers,§ and this though Philo looked upon the powers as independent of the mind in whom they were manifested. How much more is the Self-existent superior to those powers which are forms of his thought and modes of his energy, and are absolutely dependent on his will. This is stated in a passage in which the leading object is to show the equality and proportion which prevailed throughout the divisions of the universe. The rule applies even to the highest realm. "The two first powers of the Self-existent, the gracious, by virtue of which he formed the cosmos, whereby he has been called God, and the punitive, by virtue of which he rules and presides over creation, whereby he is named Lord, are separated by him standing above in the midst, for he says, 'I will speak to thee from above the mercy-seat between the two cherubim,'|| in order to show that the highest powers of the

---

* Ebriet., 27 (I. 373).
† Mutat. Nom., 4 (I. 583); Abr., 24 (II. 19), with the dative instead of διά.
‡ Leg. ad Cai., 16 (II. 562), dative.   § See Vol. I. p. 342.
|| Ex. xxv. 22.

Self-existent, the donative and the punitive, are equal, using him as a divider."* The former part of this sentence precludes the notion of any real separation between God and his powers, for they are simply his predicates; and, therefore, the description in the latter part must be figurative, and refer to a distinction in thought. The object is simply to point out the even balancing of God's gracious and punitive agency; and the figure, which is not a harsh one in itself, is obviously governed by the quotation from Scripture on which the doctrine is avowedly based. Again, the statement in Genesis,† that "the Lord departed when he ceased speaking with Abraham, and Abraham returned into his place," is explained as meaning that God who is before all things‡ no longer stretches the representations from himself, but those from the powers after him.§ The reference is clearly to higher and lower spiritual moods. In the higher the mind seems to rise above all phenomenal manifestation, and to commune with God as *one*, the eternal and absolute Being; but when it sinks back to its ordinary condition, it can think of him only in his manifold activity, as Creator, Ruler, Benefactor, and so forth. All these modifications of his power are justly said to be "after" him whose nature they partially express. Lastly, in a passage previously quoted,|| it is said that the highest God¶ "has passed beyond his powers, being both seen without them and manifested in them."** This might well appear at first sight to be one of the most invincible evidences of the essential distinction between God and his powers; yet perhaps a little reflection will show us that it is really a neat compendium of the philosophy which has thus far spoken to us. The passage tells us that it is good for the soul to have within itself the three measures of the universe, the supreme Sovereign himself,

* Quis rer. div. her., 34 (I. 496).   † xviii. 33.   ‡ Ὁ πρὸ τῶν ὅλων θεός.
§ Τὰς [φαντασίας] ἀπὸ τῶν μετ' αὐτὸν ἑυνάμεων.   Somn., I. 12 (I. 631).
|| P. 89.   ¶ Τὸν ἀνωτάτω . . θεόν.
** Ὑπερκέκυφε τὰς ἑυνάμεις αὐτοῦ καὶ χωρὶς αὐτῶν ὁρώμενος καὶ ἐν ταύταις ἐμφαινόμενος. SS. Ab. et Cain., 15 (I. 173).

who measures all things, and his goodness and authority, which are the measures respectively of good and of subject things. Each of these three measures is itself immeasurable and incapable of being circumscribed.* Now if Philo was about to represent the powers as separate persons, it is strange, to say the least, that he should begin by calling them God's goodness and authority, and making them infinite as God himself. So understood the passage involves us in hopeless perplexity. But all becomes clear if we remember that God was above the powers as the unknown unity which comprehended them all, and that he revealed himself in two different ways. The mind may think of him simply as Being, the mysterious source of all that is, and, refraining from all attempts at analysis, may regard him as One, possessing an indivisible essence which it is impossible to know. Thus he is seen without the powers. But the mind is also led by the phenomena of creation and providence to ascribe certain things to God, and to see through broken and coloured gleams that light whose unviolated purity it cannot behold. It is taught by the ideal forces which pervade the universe to recognize God as Creator and Ruler; and thus the Self-existent is manifested in the powers, which partly express his essence, but, owing to the inability of our thought to combine them into a single idea, are unable wholly to reveal it.†

We have already had occasion to notice the distinction between God in his essential being and God conceived under the partial aspect of the powers. We may refer here to two more passages where this distinction is drawn. The statement in the Law that "God is in heaven above and on earth beneath," ‡ does not mean that God is so in his essence,§ for the self-existent Being contains, but is not contained. The

* Ἑκάστῃ μεμέτρηται μὲν οὐδαμῶς—ἀπερίγραφος γὰρ ὁ Θεός, ἀπερίγραφοι καὶ αἱ δυνάμεις αὐτοῦ.

† One other passage in which the self-existent Being is said to be above the powers has been fully dealt with in treating of the omnipresence of God, pp. 108 sq.

‡ Josh. ii. 11. § Κατὰ τὸ εἶναι.

words point to his power by virtue of which * he ordered all things. This is strictly goodness, the generator of graces whereby it brought into existence things that were not. The self-existent Being, as represented in the mind,† appears in opinion everywhere, but in truth nowhere.‡ This passage seems to assert most explicitly that that may be predicated of one of the powers which it would be wrong to predicate of the Self-existent; what, then, it may be asked, can be plainer than that Philo regarded one as essentially different from the other? We may reply by asking, what can be plainer than that Philo is here dealing with a difference in our conception of God himself? Else why is he so careful to speak of God in his essence, and to describe him by the most abstract term? Why not simply say that Scripture refers, not to the real and supreme God, but to a subordinate agent who is frequently, though improperly, called God? This would have clearly and adequately expressed the suggested meaning; and as it is quite different from what Philo actually says, we may fairly conclude that that is not his meaning. What, then, does he intend to teach? The verse in question declares that God is in heaven, and therefore, at first sight, seems to imply that he is immanent in the universe, subject to the conditions of space, and with no reserve of causality above that which is manifested in creation. This, as we know, would be opposed to a fundamental doctrine of Philo's; for, according to him, God is transcendent above the universe, and is not amenable to the limitations of place. Scripture, therefore, cannot have referred to God in his essential being, but to his goodness, which, though it is infinite when regarded simply as an effluence of the divine nature, yet, when viewed as an exercise of creative power, is necessarily co-extensive with creation. Thus the passage naturally allies itself with the rest of our exposition. Similar remarks will apply to a comment on the

---

* Καθ' ἥν.   † Φαντασιαζόμενον.   ‡ Migrat. Abr., 32 (I. 464).

statement in Exodus xxiv. 16, that "the glory of God came down upon Mount Sinai."* This, says Philo, puts to shame those who, whether from impiety or simplicity, suppose that there are local movements in the Divine. For it says plainly, not that the essential God, who is thought of according to being only,† came down, but that his glory did so. Δόξα,‡ being an ambiguous word, admits of two explanations. It either denotes the presence of the powers, as the military power of a king is called his δόξα, or implies merely an opinion about him, so that the representation of the coming of God was wrought in the minds of those present.§ Here again, the careful way in which Philo guards his language shows that he is referring, not to a distinction between God and some one else, but between two aspects under which God may be regarded, between God in his unknown and transcendent essence, and God as manifested through the display of his power.

In the remaining passages the powers appear more or less distinctly as persons, and the question will arise whether we are to understand the language literally or figuratively. In order to form a judgment upon this point, we must be acquainted with the style of our author; and it will be convenient to illustrate here by some examples his peculiar fondness for personification. In passages already cited we may have observed his tendency to describe things under the terms of human relationship, so that even time becomes with him a grandson of God; and, what belongs more closely to our present purpose, we have seen how the powers of the human mind are turned into its body-guards and messengers.|| Similarly, we hear of the "offspring of the understanding which act as its body-guards and shieldbearers," ¶ and find the voice

* Κατέβη ἡ δόξα τοῦ θεοῦ.
† Τὸν οὐσιώδη θεόν, τὸν κατὰ τὸ εἶναι μόνον ἐπινοούμενον.
‡ Meaning either "opinion" or "glory."
§ The Hebrew, כְּבוֹד־יְהֹוָה, might have removed the doubt. Fragm., II. 679 (Qu. et Sol. in Ex. II. 45).
|| Or angels. ¶ Somn., II. 14 (I. 671).

described as having "the rank of herald or interpreter to the suggesting mind." * The impulses of the passions have "sown" superfluous natures in us, and folly is "the evil husbandman of the soul."† In the self-examination which befits the sabbath day, we should take account of our words and deeds "in the council-chamber of the soul, the laws taking their seats with us in the council and joining in the examination." ‡ As the laws are presumably the laws of Moses, and not the powers of nature, there can be no question of their real personality. Conscience § is "a weighty accuser," ‖ and regarded as the power which convicts us of sin ¶ it is finely personified. "Dwelling and growing up along with each soul, accustomed to accept nothing that is under accusation, using always a nature that hates evil and loves virtue, being at once accuser and judge, when stirred up as an accuser it charges, accuses, puts to shame; and again as a judge it teaches, admonishes, advises to be converted; and if it succeeds in persuading, it is joyfully reconciled, but if it fails it wages war without a truce, not desisting either by day or by night, but inflicting incurable pricks and wounds, until it snaps the miserable and accursed life." ** The two principles which contend for the mastery of the human soul are personified throughout a passage which is far too long for complete quotation. "With each of us dwell two women who are hostile and ill-disposed to one another, and fill the mental house with the contentions of jealousy. Of these we love the one, supposing her to be manageable and tame and most dear and appropriate to ourselves; and she is called pleasure. But we hate the other, thinking her untamable, savage, wild, most hostile; and her name is virtue." The former comes to us tricked out with every meretricious ornament, and attended by "craft, rashness, flattery, quackery, fraud, false speech, false opinion,

---

* Somn., I. 5 (I. 625). † Sacrificant., 9 (II. 258).
‡ Dec. Orac., 20 (II. 197). § Τὸ συνειδός.
‖ Quod Deus immut., 27 (I. 291). ¶ Ἔλεγχος. ** Dec. Orac., 17 (II. 195).

impiety, injustice, intemperance;" and standing in the midst of these as the chorus which she leads, she addresses the mind, setting forth the various charms of a voluptuous life, and promising to bestow them without stint if the mind will live with her. Virtue was in concealment hard by, and heard this wheedling speech; and fearing that the mind might be unwittingly captivated, she suddenly presents herself, with quiet step and sober mien, attended by piety, holiness, truth, and a long train of other virtues, which, standing on each side, acted as her body-guard. She then addresses the mind, and exposes the false pretensions of her rival.* After this we need not be startled to hear that "all the virtues are virgins, but she who is piety and righteousness, having received the leadership as in a chorus, is the most beautiful." † But, perhaps, nothing exhibits Philo's fondness for personification more strikingly than its introduction into a plain historical narrative. In his account of the troubles in Judæa he says that Petronius was uncertain how to act, and, "having called together, as in a council, all the thoughts of the soul, he examined the opinion of each, and found them all unanimous in sentiment." ‡ Passing from the domain of the human mind, we find wealth described as the "the spear-bearer of the body." § Noble birth is endowed with speech that she may deliver her sentiments. "I think," says Philo, "that noble birth,|| if God stamped her in the human form, would speak thus to rebellious descendants;" and then follows an address in which she contrasts her own opinion with theirs.¶ The Israelites who ultimately return from the dispersion shall have "three advocates** of reconciliation with the Father:" one, the equity and kindness of God,

---

* De Mercede Meretricis, 2-4 (II. 265-9). The same figure occurs, with less elaboration, in SS. Ab. et Caini, 5 (I. 167).
† Praem. et Poen., 9 (II. 416).   ‡ Leg. ad Cai., 31 (II. 577).
§ Δορυφόρος, which I have generally rendered "body-guard." Fortitud., 3 (II. 376).
|| Εὐγένεια.   ¶ Nobil., 2 (II. 438-9).
** Παρακλήτοις.

who always prefers forgiveness to punishment; secondly, the holiness of the founders of the nation, because, with souls freed from bodies and rendering a genuine service to the Ruler, they make effectual supplications for their sons and daughters; and, thirdly, that which especially moves the kindness of the aforesaid, namely, the improvement * of those who are returning to the way that ends with pleasing God.† Even if it be thought that the equity and kindness of God are distinct persons, we can hardly extend the same notion to the "holiness" of the patriarchs and the "improvement" of the dispersed. Again, we are told that mankind, in their various grades of fortune, are nevertheless akin, since they have "one mother, the common nature of all men." ‡ Sciences and virtues are "the daughters of right reason." § Lastly, we may notice a few personifications in connection with God, which are so similar to the foregoing that we can have no hesitation in accepting them as figurative. God "rains down his virgin and immortal graces." || These graces are "his virgin daughters." ¶ God is "the husband of the virtue-loving intelligence," and laughter is "his ideal son."** "Truth is an attendant of God,"†† and "the overseer and guardian" of the "really vivified and living polity."‡‡

These examples will suffice to show us how easily Philo falls into the language of personification, and ought to make us pause before we insist on throwing his whole philosophy into confusion by too strict an interpretation of his words. At the same time we must remember that we are bound to satisfy the essential meaning of each passage, and not to fritter it away into figures of speech. With this caution we proceed to the personification of the powers.

We are told in Genesis §§ [says Philo] that "Noah pleased the powers

* Βελτίωσις.   † Exsecrat., 9 (II. 436).   ‡ Dec. Orac., 10 (II. 187).
§ Gigant., 4 (I. 265). || Post. Cain., 10 (I. 232).
¶ Migrat. Abr., 7 (I. 441).   ** Ὁ ἐνδιάθετος υἱὸς θεοῦ, Mutat. Nom., 23 (I. 598).
†† Ὀπαδὸς θεοῦ. Vita Mos., III. 21 (II. 162).   ‡‡ Nobil., 5 (II. 443
§§ vi. 8, Νῶε δὲ εὗρε χάριν ἐναντίον κυρίου τοῦ θεοῦ.

of the Self-existent, both Lord and God, but Moses pleased him who is attended by the powers as a body-guard, and apart from them is understood according to being only; for it is said, in the person of God, 'thou hast found favour with me,'* indicating himself apart from every other.† Thus the Self-existent himself deemed the supreme wisdom in Moses worthy of favour through himself alone, but that which was copied from this, as being second and more specific, through the subject powers, by virtue of which he is both Lord and God, Ruler and Benefactor.‡

Now we might reasonably maintain that whatever personality is here ascribed to the powers must be figurative, because the power named God has been immediately before represented as "the goodness of the Self-existent," and been obviously identified with "his happy and blessed nature," and in the closing words of the quotation, if we regard the powers as distinct agents, God is made dependent on his own subjects for his primary and most essential attributes. To this mode of argument, however, Zeller replies fairly enough that if Philo treats the powers in the same connection sometimes as personal beings, sometimes as ideas or divine powers and attributes, he cannot have been aware how irreconcilable were these two modes of presentation.§ The conception of personality is, no doubt, frequently left vague and uncertain by ancient thinkers; but the examples to which Zeller appeals ‖ do not appear to me to illustrate the confusion of thought which is attributed to Philo. The Platonic world with its soul, the deity of the Stoics, the stars in Plato, Aristotle, and the Stoics, are all distinct beings of some sort, and the only uncertainty is whether they are self-conscious or possessed only of an impersonal reason. This was precisely the point which was not determined, whether the enjoyment of reason involved the possession of individual self-consciousness; and an unsteadiness of thought upon this subject is quite intelligible. But the case is very different with Philo's powers. If it was agreed that they were

---

* Ex. xxxiii. 17. † Ἄνευ παντὸς ἑτέρου. ‡ Quod Deus immut., 24 (I. 289).
§ III. ii. p. 366, Anm. 3 of the previous page. ‖ III. ii. p. 365, Anm. 2.

distinct rational beings, and the only question was whether, being so, they were self-conscious or not, we should have an exact parallel. But the question is really the preliminary one, whether they are distinct beings at all, and not simply the partial expression of the divine nature as distributed and classified for the apprehension of our finite intelligence. That Philo was blind to this distinction is not easy to believe, and we must test his language rigorously before we can admit it.

What, then, is the leading thought in the passage before us? Is it not that Noah had a less full and satisfying apprehension of God than Moses? The latter, having wisdom in the unity of its genus, rose above the analytical understanding, and apprehended God in his unity, as eternal Being: the former, possessing wisdom only in the lower form of its different species, naturally was obliged to distribute his ideas, and could view the divine nature only under the double aspect of its goodness and power. The personification corresponds with the distinction which is thus drawn, and is suggested by the language of Scripture. When it is said that Noah pleased the powers, this is only an interpretation of the text, "Noah found favour with the Lord God," and the figure is certainly not so violent as some of those we have met with above. But the figure having been once introduced, what more natural than that it should be carried through, and the powers be represented as the body-guards and subjects of the Self-existent? When we have got so far, the latter may without violence be referred to as "alone" and "apart from every other," when we regard his nature in its unity and without analysis; and Philo may well have thought that he guarded against all misapprehension when he wound up with the statement that, after all, it is the Self-existent himself who is both Lord and God. This interpretation appears to me to give the genuine sense of the passage, and, without constraint, to reconcile its seeming contradictions.

The correctness of this explanation is confirmed by

the unquestionably figurative character of the succeeding passage :—

In contrast with Noah and Moses, Joseph is introduced as the " body-loving and passion-loving mind, ' sold to the chief cook,' the pleasure of our compound being." He finds favour with the chief keeper of the prison. Now prisoners are strictly, not those who are condemned in courts of justice, but those who are full of intemperance and cowardice and injustice and impiety and innumerable other plagues ; and " the keeper and steward of these, ' the governor of the prison,' is a compound and heap of crowded and various vices woven together into one species, to please whom is the greatest penalty." Some, not seeing this, go to him very joyfully, and act as his body-guard. Then the soul is exhorted to strive with all its might not to be pleasing to the chief keepers of the prison, but to the Cause, and, if it cannot please the Cause on account of the greatness of the dignity, to go straight to his powers, and become their suppliant, until they, having received continual and genuine service, place it in the rank of those who have pleased them.

Reduced to plain prose the passage is tantamount to this : do not be subject to your passions and bodily pleasures, but serve God; and if the highest conception of him be too pure and abstract, then serve him under those lower conceptions which appeal most readily to your understanding and your heart. This is surely more reasonable than insisting on a literal interpretation, with the strange result of supposing that Philo deliberately exhorts men to depart from their monotheistic worship and transfer their homage to a crowd of inferior beings, who are divine only by courtesy.

In another passage it is said that Moses prayed to " the self-determination, the might of God himself, and the propitious and gentle powers." The prayer on which this statement is founded is immediately quoted,* and God is throughout addressed in the singular number, and, in order to mark, as Philo himself says, his supremacy and superiority to all need, he is called the Eternal King.† In the commentary which follows, the being to whom the prayer was offered is treated as the supreme God, and there is no allusion to his

---

* Ex. xv. 17, 18.   † Βασιλεύων τῶν αἰώνων κ.τ.λ.

powers except that the hands of God, which are mentioned, but not invoked in the prayer, are explained as "his world-making powers."* It is apparent, then, that when Philo spoke of praying to the propitious powers he had no thought of personal beings other than God himself.

Lastly, under this head, we must notice a passage in which judicial right, or Δίκη, is not only personified, but separated from and, indeed, contrasted with God. It is true that Δίκη is not spoken of as one of the powers; but that is clearly the category to which she belongs, and we must not evade the force of the argument under this plea.

It befitted the nature of God [we are told] to deliver the Ten Commandments, which were summaries of the specific laws, in his own person, but the more detailed laws through the most perfect of the prophets, whom he chose to be their interpreter. It is for this reason that the Decalogue is a collection of simple commandments and prohibitions without the customary provision of penalties. The author was God, the cause of good only, and of nothing evil. He conceived, then, that it was most appropriate to his nature to issue his salutary orders unmixed with punishment, in order that one might not choose the best unwillingly, but with deliberate judgment. In doing so he did not offer inviolability to those who do wrong, but knew that his assessor Δίκη, the overseer of human affairs, would not keep quiet, as being naturally a hater of evil, and likely to accept as a congenial task the duty of defence against the sinning. For it is becoming for the ministers and lieutenants of God, as for generals in war, to use defensive weapons against deserters, but for the great King to attend to the common safety of the whole, maintaining peace, and continually supplying all the blessings of peace richly to all men everywhere. For in reality God is the president of peace, but his under-servants are governors of wars.†

In the latter part of this passage, and especially the last clause, there is no evidence that Philo is speaking of the highest powers; at least I am not aware of any other place in which they are spoken of as God's under-servants;‡ and it is certainly possible that, having referred to Δίκη, he is led on to

---

* Plantat. Noe, 12 (I. 330-7).   † Dec. Orac., 33 (II. 208-9).
‡ Ὑποδιάκονοι.

speak more generally of subordinate agents, whether human or not, as in the beginning he had spoken of Moses as the proper mediator for the communication of specific laws. In regard to Δίκη herself, however, the case is different. She must be admitted to be one of the powers; and yet she is personified, and has a function assigned to her which makes it unnecessary for God to attach penalties to the violation of the Ten Commandments. The mere personification we may at once dismiss, for no one can imagine that Philo literally placed an assessor beside God. But how shall we explain the function which seems to give her an objective existence apart from God? I believe we can easily do so in conformity with the doctrine which we have laid down. According to that doctrine Δίκη can be nothing less than a permanent mode of divine operation, established in the universe as one of its persistent laws, and therefore representing in its manifold activity a single divine thought and volition. In this aspect it is exceedingly natural to speak of it as though it were a distinct force, an objective thought embodied in the constitution of the world, though we know all the time, as philosophers, that it has no existence apart from the supreme will. Now, the passage tells us that, when God graciously gave the Ten Commandments in his own person, he wished to secure for them a perfectly voluntary obedience, and therefore would not introduce any deterrent ills which might be inconsistent with the benignity of his nature. Instead of enacting separate penalties, which would represent so many distinct volitions, and make him appear harsh and stern, he preferred relying on the universal law of retributive justice established in the providential order of the world,—a law which was of wider scope, and, as we have seen, beneficent in design. It became him, instead of continually forming fresh plans, and stepping upon the scene with new punishments, to act through those vast purposes which he had, as it were, projected upon matter, and wrought as unchangeable laws into the constitution of things. It seems to me that in this way Philo's language may be adequately explained in entire consistency with the views hitherto ascribed to him.

We may consider in this connection another passage in the same treatise, in which reference is made to the divine voice through which the Ten Commandments were proclaimed from Sinai.*

> Are we to suppose [it is asked] that God himself spoke in the manner of a voice? Such a thought must not enter our mind; for God is not as a man, requiring a mouth and tongue, but, thinks Philo,† he wrought at that time a very sacred and wonderful thing, "having ordered an invisible noise to be fabricated in the air, fitted with perfect harmonies more wonderfully than all instruments, not lifeless,‡ but neither consisting of body and soul like an animal, but a rational soul§ full of clearness and distinctness, which, having shaped and strained the air and changed it to a flaming fire, sounded forth, as breath through a trumpet, so great an articulate voice that those who were farthest off seemed to hear as well as those who were nearest." For the voices of men naturally grow weak with distance. "But God's power breathing on the newly created voice raised and kindled it, and shedding it everywhere rendered the end clearer than the beginning, putting in the souls of each a different sort of hearing [from the sensible], far superior to that which comes through the ears. For the sensation, being slower, keeps quiet until, struck by the air, it is aroused; but the [hearing] of the inspired understanding hastens with keenest swiftness to meet the words that are spoken."∥

The only argument for the personality of the powers which can be derived from this passage is founded on the apparent identity of the "soul" which produced the voice with "God's power" to which the same office is ascribed. There are some circumstances, however, which render this argument more than precarious. In the first place, there is no good reason for asserting the supposed identity. The soul created for a momentary purpose, and presumably dissipated again as soon as the purpose was fulfilled, would of course be an expression of, and inspired by, divine power, but cannot be synonymous

---

* Ex. xix. and xx.   † 'Εμοὶ δοκεῖ.   ‡ Ἄψυχον.
§ Ψυχήν, for which Mangey suggests ἠχήν.   ∥ Dec. Orac., 9 (II. 185-6).

with it. The latter is used here in its largest and vaguest meaning, and no allusion is made to its mediatorial function; on the other hand, the soul is fabricated for the special object of acting in a single instance as the divine organ. Secondly, it is by no means certain that a "rational soul" made and employed in the way described would be regarded by Philo as a person. Thirdly, Mangey would read $ἠχήν$, "sound," instead of $ψυχήν$, "soul." In favour of this change we might plead that the lines in which $ψυχήν$ occurs require, in any case, some emendation; that the epithets applied to it are more suitable to $ἠχή$; and that it is strangely harsh to say that an invisible noise was a rational soul. With this change of reading the argument would fall. Fourthly, it is far from clear that Philo is not mixing up a literal with an allegorical interpretation. Literally a voice was fabricated in the air; but at the end of the passage it turns out that this voice was not really a noise in the air at all, but was apprehended only by the inspired understanding. Hence it is said in Scripture* that "all the people *saw* the voice"; for "all the things that God says are not words, but deeds, which eyes distinguish rather than ears."† For these reasons I am unable to admit that this passage affords the least support to the doctrine of the personality of the powers.

We must now return to that long passage about the visitors to Abraham from which we borrowed, as the key to our interpretation, a considerable extract in which the triple appearance of God is ascribed to the imperfection of the human understanding. In the earlier part of this passage the three visitors, who had seemed like men, are said, after they communicated the divine promise, to have conveyed a more sublime impression, that "of either prophets or angels, changing from spiritual and mental substance into the human form."‡ Philo himself regards them as angels, "sacred and divine natures, under-servants and lieutenants of the first God,

---

* Ex. xx. 18.   † § 11, p. 188.   ‡ Abr., 22 (II. 17).

through whom, as ambassadors, he announces as many things as he wishes to foretell to our race." In entering Abraham's tent they presumed that he was "kindred and a fellow-slave of the same master."* Nothing can be plainer; and Gfrörer appeals to this passage as a decisive proof of the personality of the powers.† We must observe, however, that Philo is here giving the literal sense of the Scripture narrative; and he makes no allusion to the powers till, in the next section, he expressly enters on the symbolical interpretation; and surely it is most unwarrantable, when Philo says that literally the three men are three angels in the form of men, figuratively they are nothing of the kind, to force these two statements together, as though they belonged to the same comment, and cry, Behold! a contradiction. If we act thus, let us at least be consistent, and press the contradiction a little farther. Almost within the limits of a single page we learn that all three were angels, fellow-slaves with Abraham of the same master, and that one of them was "the Father of the universe," "the Self-existent." Was the Self-existent, then, an angel, and his own slave, and was Philo quite unconscious of any incompatibility between these notions? This may convince us that we are not justified in mixing together two systems of interpretation which the writer himself broadly separates.

A later portion of the same passage occasions greater difficulty, because Philo himself is no longer so careful, but apparently blurs the two lines of exegesis. He devotes three sections‡ to the destruction of Sodom and the surrounding country, considered as an actual historical event, and then in the succeeding section proceeds to the allegorical interpretation.§ Contrary to what we should expect, he omits the powers from the latter, and introduces them into the former, where, according to his previous treatment of the

* Ib. § 23.   † Pp. 155, sq.   ‡ 26-28.   § 29-31.

history, we ought to meet only with angels. This temporary confusion occurs in an intermediate section* between the history of the destruction of Sodom and the symbolical interpretation of the Pentapolis, and from its position may naturally give a stronger appearance of personal separation between God and his powers than was really in Philo's thoughts. The general meaning, however, does not seem to me inconsistent with the results of previous investigation. Let us observe in the first place, that in the preceding section† Philo says, without any qualification, that it was God who punished the Sodomites by ordering the air to rain down fire upon them; and therefore if he afterwards says that it was not the Self-existent who punished, but only his powers, we properly fall back upon the distinction so often drawn between God in his absolute being and God as partially and analytically apprehended by men. Let us see, however, what the passage says. Philo states that his object in relating the dreadful calamities of Sodom has been to show that of the three who appeared as men to Abraham only two, according to the Scripture, came to punish the inhabitants, while the third did not think it right to come. The latter was, in Philo's opinion, the really Self-existent,‡ and supposed it to be fitting to confer good things in personal presence through himself, but to execute the opposite of good by the ministration§ of the powers, "that he may be antecedently thought to be the Cause of good things only, and of nothing evil. Those kings also who imitate the divine nature appear to me to act thus, extending favours through themselves, but confirming punishments through others. But since of the two powers one is beneficent, and the other punitive, each, as we might expect, appears on the land of the Sodomites, because of the five best cities in it four were to be burnt, and one to be left unaffected and secure from all evil. For the destruction ought to take

* 28. † 27. ‡ Κατὰ τὴν ἐμὴν ἔννοιαν ἦν ὁ πρὸς ἀλήθειαν ὤν.
§ Καθ' ὑπηρεσίαν.

place through the punitive power, and salvation through the beneficent. But since even the part that was saved had not entire and perfect virtues, it was benefited by the power of the Self-existent, but was antecedently thought unworthy to obtain the representation of the latter." Now, if this passage stood alone, we should certainly believe that God and the powers were quite distinct from one another; and if we are bound to take the words as a literal expression of Philo's thought, we must admit that he contradicts himself, and that at least in this one passage his doctrine of the powers becomes a mere jumble of heterogeneous elements. But there are some considerations, besides those already noticed, which must make us pause before we conclude that the fault is not in the expression rather than the thought. This is a continuation of the passage in which Philo lays it down with so much precision that God and his powers are in reality one subject, and that the triple representation in our minds is due solely to the imperfection of our spiritual vision. He thereby shows that he is aware of the difference between the conceptions of one God capable of manifesting himself in various modes, and of one God presiding over a number of persons separate from himself. It is not likely that within a few pages he entirely confounds these two conceptions, and announces that what was declared to be really one subject, though apparently three, was, after all, three both apparently and really. But there is within the passage itself a statement which compels us to give it a very liberal interpretation. It is said that the Self-existent "supposed it to be fitting to confer the good things in personal presence* through himself." This refers of course to the visit to Abraham's tent; and therefore we learn that, in Philo's opinion, the supreme and eternal Cause did really come down, and enter the tent of a man, and talk and eat with him. Is any interpreter of Philo prepared to admit this? One can almost see the scorn with which our philosopher would

* Παρών.

desire such a one to "get away," and not to be so silly as to impute to him this enormous impiety. We are, then, compelled to allow that the language of the passage does not strictly represent its thought, and that Philo was led through some cause to confuse ideas which he knew would not really blend. The cause, I believe, is that which has been already pointed out, that he mixes the literal and the allegorical interpretations. Literally the three men or angels were three distinct persons; and in the progress of the story they separate from one another, and only two of them repair to Sodom. Why did the story assume this form? "In order that [the Self-existent] may be thought* to be the cause of good things only, and of nothing evil." The intention, then, was not to draw a real distinction between God and his powers, but to affect the thoughts of men. Men are apt to look upon punishments as evils, and therefore God, in order that they may not misconceive his nature, often sends punishments through subordinate agents, or even, as in the present narrative, allows them to look upon the punitive force of nature as an agent distinct from himself. Philo accepted the doctrine that God was the cause only of good, but he had another way of escaping the difficulty connected with providential punishments: these were not evils, but blessings in disguise, and the punitive power, justly regarded, coalesced with the beneficent.† Another evidence of the correctness of this interpretation is afforded by the statement that the city which was saved was deemed unworthy to retain the representation of the Self-existent, for thus we are expressly thrown back into the domain of mental images. In the allegory the city is vision, the queen of the senses, which alone is able to transport itself to incorruptible natures. If we venture to complete the allegory which Philo has left unfinished, we must say that the eye discerns throughout the cosmos the presence of the divine beneficence, but is too imperfect to look upon God himself;

* Νομίζηται. † See before, p. 87.

and then we shall have a distinction which introduces no new or contradictory thought. But what are we to say to the comparison with kings, who, imitating the divine nature, inflict punishments through others? The reply is perhaps to be found in the more literal part of Philo's description. He says that God ordered the air to rain down fire, and destroy the country. The air, then, is the subordinate agent employed to execute the divine purpose. Now, the air, we must remember, is itself "a power," but it is a power permanently impressed upon matter; and regarded from the other side, as matter under the constraint of divine force, it becomes objective to God, and is properly viewed as a subordinate, though still impersonal, agent. As the destroyer of Sodom it was charged for the time with punitive power, and thus the latter, too, was temporarily planted out, as it were, into distinct objective existence; for being impressed upon matter it fulfilled the one condition which made an objective world possible. In this way, I think, Philo's language may be explained. He cannot indeed be acquitted of some confusion in his manner of presenting his subject; but this confusion may be accounted for, and is very different from a radical contradiction in thought.

We come now to the explanation of a passage in Genesis which evidently occasioned Philo some perplexity, and led him into some confusion of thought and expression. In his remarks upon it we meet with far the strongest evidence that is produced to show that he ascribed distinct personality to the powers. He treats of it in no fewer than four different places, all of which we must consider if we wish to arrive at his real meaning, or to discover whether he had any consistent interpretation to offer; and in arranging them we may advantageously reserve his longest and most elaborate exposition for the last. The passage in question is that in which a plural is used in connection with the creation of the human race: "Let us make man."

One might reasonably doubt [says Philo] why Moses ascribed the creation of man alone not to one fabricator, as he did everything else, but, as it were, to several. For does the Father of the universe, to whom all things are subject, require any one? Or did he need no one to co-operate with him when he made the heaven and the earth and the sea, but prove unable to prepare of himself, without the assistance of others, such a little animal as man? The truest reason for this is necessarily known to God only; but we must not conceal the one that seems probable, and has the merit of a plausible conjecture. It is this. Some things have no participation in either virtue or vice, such as plants and irrational animals, the former because they are without souls,* the latter because they are not endowed with mind and thought, in which moral good and evil reside. Other things participate only in virtue, being entirely free from evil, as the stars. But other things are of mixed nature, as man, who admits the opposites, prudence and folly, sobriety and intemperance, bravery and cowardice, justice and injustice, and, in a word, good and evil, fair and base, virtue and vice. Accordingly it was most appropriate for God, the Father of all, to make what was excellent through himself alone, on account of its relationship to him; and it was not alien to him to make what was indifferent, since it, too, is without the vice that is opposed to him; but in regard to the things of mixed nature it was partly appropriate and partly inappropriate: appropriate, on account of the better idea mixed up in them; inappropriate, on account of that which is the contrary and inferior. Therefore it is only in connection with the creation of man that God said " Let us make man," which signifies the adoption of others as co-operators, in order that God, the sovereign of all, may be ascribed [as author] to the blameless counsels and deeds of man acting uprightly, but others, from among his subjects, to those of a contrary kind; for the father ought not to be the cause of evil to the offspring, and vice and vicious activity are an evil.†

As this passage does not contain a single word about the powers, it may be thought out of place to quote it; but it is interesting in several ways. The general conception is of course borrowed from Plato's Timaeus,‡ where the subordinate divinities are called in to assist in the formation of mortal creatures. Philo's difficulty, however, springs from a different root from Plato's. He feels that the moral contrariety in man's nature betokens a mixed origin, and cannot be traced back to one divine thought. In the present passage he is speaking of the intelligible man, the idea of humanity, as is

* Or sentient life   † Mundi Op., 24 (I. 16 sq.).   ‡ 41 C. sqq.

shown not only by the entire context, but by his concluding remark that, although individual men had not yet taken form, the species were properly distinguished through the statement that "male and female were fabricated," for the species exist within the genus. What we immediately learn, then, from the passage before us is this, that, since the very idea of humanity involves the possibility of moral evil, it is not purely divine, but must be in some way of mixed origin. The stars which were above the reach of sin, the beasts which were below it, might alike be true expressions of the thought of God; but man in departing from God thereby showed his participation in an idea which was alien to the divine nature. Whether Philo had formed any clear view of the origin of this lower idea, or had attempted to reconcile it with his doctrine of the Logos as containing the whole of the ideal world, it is impossible to say. At all events he seems to have carried down the division thus found in the ideal cosmos into the actual, and to have assigned the creation of man in part to other agents than God. This will become apparent as we proceed; but before leaving the present passage we must make one or two further remarks.

The very absence of reference to the powers is itself a fact of some importance, because it helps to show that Philo had no very decided and settled theory as to the nature of the subjects who co-operated with God in the creation of man. Again, Philo broaches his explanation only as a plausible conjecture which may not be coincident with the truth, and does not, like some of his interpreters, represent it as belonging to the very kernel of his philosophy. And, what is most important of all, the formation of man is represented as an exception to the general order of creation, and as alone requiring the presence of mediatorial agents. Has, then, Philo forgotten all that he has previously said about the Logos and the creative power? We have no right to assume this. He could not conceive of creation without their

presence and activity ; and if the helpers who were other*
than God were not other than the most exalted divine
powers, then man was no exception to the universal rule.
Those, therefore, who insist on a strict interpretation of single
passages, apart from their bearing upon other passages, are
bound either to admit that God was the immediate creator
even of the beasts, and to abandon the whole doctrine of
mediatorial creation, and of a separation between God and
the universe, or to regard the subordinate agents in the
creation of man as different from the divine powers in the
highest sense.

This important result, however, is not left to mere inference.
Elsewhere Philo comments as follows on the words " I am
thy God : "†

> The self-existent Being, as such, is not relative ; but some of the powers
> are, as it were, relative ; for instance, the Regal and Beneficent. Akin to
> these is the Creative, called God ; so that " I am thy God " is equivalent to
> "I am maker and fabricator." " Now, it is the greatest gift to obtain the
> architect himself, whom also the whole cosmos obtained. For he did not
> form the soul of the bad, for vice is at enmity with God ; but the middle
> soul he formed not through himself alone, according to the most
> sacred Moses, since, like wax, it was going to receive the difference of fair
> and base, for which reason he says, 'Let us make man according to
> our image,' in order that, if it received a bad form, it might appear to be a
> fabrication of others, but if a good one, of the artificer of things fair and
> good alone. He, therefore, is altogether excellent to whom he says, ' I am
> thy God,' since he has obtained the Maker alone without the assistance of
> others."‡

In this passage, again, we are not told who assisted in the
creation of the bad man ; but it is perfectly clear that it
was not the high power known as the creative, for to have
been framed by this alone was the prerogative of the good
man, as of the universe at large. We must remember, then,
that the subordinate agents in the creation of man are
separated from the highest powers, which we have treated

* "Ετεροι.   † Gen. xvii. 1.   ‡ Mutat. Nom., 4 (I. 582-3).

as predicates of God, not only by inevitable inference from man's exceptional position in the plan of creation, but by Philo's express statement.

In the next passage the powers are introduced, and we shall have to consider whether it contradicts those that have been just referred to or can, without violence, be harmonized with them. It will be better to quote it entire in order that we may have the case fairly before us.

"It is not becoming for God to punish, as he is the first and best legislator, and he punishes through the ministration of others, not through himself; for it is suitable for him to extend favours and gifts and benefits, as being by nature good and munificent, but [to inflict] punishments, not indeed without his own order, since he is king, but through the agency of others who are adapted to such services. Now the self-disciplined [Jacob] bears witness to my statement by his words, 'God who nourishes me from my youth, the angel who rescues me out of all evils'; * for he ascribed to God the older blessings, by which the soul is nourished, but to a servant of God those that were more recent, as many as result from the avoidance of sins. For this reason, too, I suppose, when he gave a philosophical account of creation, while he said that all other things were made by God, he signified that man alone was formed as though with the co-operation of others ; for the words occur, ' God said, Let us make man according to our image,' a multitude being implied by the phrase 'let us make.' The Father of the universe, therefore, converses with his own powers,† to whom he gave the mortal part of our soul to form, by imitating his art when he shaped the rational principle in us, judging it right that the sovereign principle in the soul should be fabricated by the sovereign, but the subject part by subjects. But he made use of the powers after him,‡ not only for the reason which has been mentioned, but because the soul of man alone was to receive thoughts of evil and good, and to use the one if it were not possible to use both. He considered it necessary, therefore, to assign the genesis of evils to other fabricators, but that of good things to himself alone. For this reason, too, though first the phrase is used, 'Let us make man,' as if referring to a multitude, it is added, as if in reference to one, ' God made the man.' For the one only God is fabricator of the real man, who accordingly is purest mind, but the multitude [is the maker] of man who is so called and mixed with

---

* Gen. xlviii. 15, 16.   † Ταῖς ἑαυτοῦ δυνάμεσιν.
‡ Reading μεθ' ἑαυτόν instead of μεθ' ἑαυτοῦ. The latter, however, would also suit the context, as we have above, μετὰ συνεργῶν.

sensation. On this account man in the pre-eminent sense is mentioned with the article—for it is said 'God made the man,'* that invisible and unmixed thought†—but the other, ' man,' without this addition ; for the phrase, 'Let us make man,' signifies him who is woven together out of irrational and rational nature."‡

In dealing with this passage it is very easy to cry out that the question is settled, for here the divine powers are expressly mentioned, and are set over against God as personal agents in the creation of man. This is quite contradictory to the view which regards them as attributes, and therefore it is proved that Philo vacillated illogically and blindly between two irreconcilable tenets. Yet it is the duty of a good critic to consider whether there may not be some view which will harmonize, or at least may have appeared to Philo to harmonize, these contrasts. I am fully aware indeed of the danger which Zeller§ points out, of imposing upon Philo what are only our own inferences from difficulties of which he himself was unconscious ; but we must be equally careful not to ascribe to him contradictions out of which he provides us with a clue. Now, we have one very strong reason for pausing before we commit ourselves to a hasty interpretation of the passage before us. If we insist upon adopting the sense which most easily presents itself, and understanding by the powers the creative and regal and the rest with which we have become familiar as predicates of God, we not only involve Philo in a confusion between the personal and the impersonal (into which he may conceivably have fallen), but we attribute to him a view which contradicts what the most celebrated critics have regarded as the very root and essence of his philosophy. In this passage, no less clearly than in the two previously cited, man is broadly distinguished from the rest of creation, and the distinction consists in this, that, whereas all other parts of the cosmos were made by God himself, the intervention

* Τὸν ἄνθρωπον.   † Λογισμόν.
‡ Prof., 13-14 (I. 550).   § III. ii. p. 365, Anm. 3.

of the powers was required only for the construction of the irrational portion of the human soul. This simply sweeps away the entire doctrine of powers which we have hitherto learned; and if we can find no better interpretation, we can only set the passage aside as lying beyond the limits of Philo's philosophy, and containing views which were temporarily forced upon him by the words of Scripture on which he was commenting. We are not, however, shut up in this harsh alternative; for, notwithstanding Zeller's adverse opinion,* I think Kefersstein† has pointed out the true solvent for our difficulties, although his criticism may require some modification and expansion.

It will be observed that the comment on the phrase, "Let us make man," is suggested by the words of Jacob, who speaks of God as his nourisher, but of an angel as the being who rescued him from evil. May we not, then, reasonably infer that when Philo speaks of personal agents as acting under God in the creation of man he alludes to angels? But if we grant this, it may be immediately urged that the divine powers are thereby identified with angels, and their personality is fully established. In order to form a sound opinion upon this subject we must make a short digression, and notice the more important statements respecting the angelic nature. We will only premise that the relations between angels and the Logoi will be reserved for future treatment.

A considerable part of Philo's doctrine of angels has been already unfolded in treating of the human soul, and we need now only recapitulate the most necessary parts of what was there said. Those whom other philosophers called demons, Moses was accustomed to call angels. Now, they are souls flying in the air, some of whom descend into bodies; "but others did not think fit ever to be united with any of the parts of the earth, whom, being consecrated and

---

* III. ii. p. 365, Anm. 3. † Pp. 195 sq.

taking charge of the service of the Father, the Fabricator is accustomed to use as assistants and ministers for the care of mortals." Souls and demons and angels are, then, different names for one and the same subject. Good angels are ambassadors of men to God and of God to men, inviolable and sacred on account of this blameless and honourable service. Others, on the contrary, are profane and unworthy, and only creep into the name of angels.* To this general description we must add one or two very important statements. The angels were created, and are spoken of as powers. "The Maker," says Philo, "made two genera both in earth and air; in the air the perceptible winged creatures, and other powers† by no means apprehended anywhere by sense. This band consists of incorporeal souls, not disposed in the same ranks"; for some are said to enter mortal bodies, but others, having obtained a more divine constitution, neglect the earth and are next the ether itself. The latter are called by the Greeks heroes, and by Moses angels, as they report good things from the Sovereign to the subjects, and to the King the things which the subjects need.‡ The fact that the angels belonged, not to the eternal, but to the created realm is also casually mentioned in another passage, which furnishes an instructive example of the way in which Philo says what appears to him at the moment appropriate to the words of Scripture on which he is commenting, without taking pains to make a long interpretation consistent in all its parts. He is remarking on the words, "The angel of God said to me in a dream, Jacob; and I said, What is it? And he said to me, Look up, . . . I am the God who appeared to thee in the place of God."§ His first observation is, "You see that the divine word records as God-sent dreams not only those that appear in connection with the oldest of causes, but also those that come through his announcing

---

* Gigant., 2-4 (I. 263-5). See also the brief statement that "angels are an army of God, incorporeal and blessed souls," SS. Ab. et Caini, 2 (I. 164).

† Δυνάμεις ἄλλας.   ‡ Plantat. Noe, 4 (I. 331-2).   § Gen. xxxi. 11-13.

and attendant angels, who have been deemed worthy of a divine and blessed lot by the Father who begat them."* It is apparent from this that Philo at the beginning of his exposition understood by the angel of God one of those subordinate beings whom God made or begat, and who, as we have seen, inhabited the air. Yet this angel says, " I am the God who appeared to thee in the place of God." Only on the previous page Philo has explained, in connection with the " house of God," that God denotes "one of the powers of the real God, by virtue of which he was good." What an admirable opportunity, then, for telling us that this power was an angel, and removing in this way the startling difficulty presented by the fact that the angel of God says, "I am God." Yet he does nothing of the kind ; and we may legitimately infer that he refrains from using this obvious explanation because it never occurred to him to identify the goodness of God with an angel flying in the air. He adopts instead an interpretation which is not very consistent with his opening remark; but as it is given after an interval of a few pages, the inconsistency may the more easily have escaped his notice. In the words, " I am God," he understands God in the supreme sense. He says nothing of the difficulty of putting such language into the mouth of an angel ; but presumably he has this difficulty in his mind when he says that to souls which are still in bodies God appears in the likeness of angels, not changing his own nature, but putting in the minds of those who receive the representation the opinion of another form. Thus our angel, who seemed so literal at the beginning, is spirited away into an erroneous mental impression.† One other passage deserves particular attention. In the great cosmic temple, in which heaven is the sanctuary and the stars the votive offerings, the priests are the angels who are under-

---

* Τοῦ γεννήσαντος. The object is not expressed, but is sufficiently evident from the context.

† Somn., I. 33, 39, 40 (I. 649, 655).

servants of God's powers,* "incorporeal souls, not mixtures of rational and irrational nature, as ours are, but having the irrational element cut out, wholly intelligent throughout, pure thoughts,† like a monad."‡

Such, then, is Philo's doctrine about the angels. Does it follow that he identified them with those high powers which we recognized as predicates of God? If things are distinguished by their attributes, it is not easy to imagine how Philo could have distinguished these two classes more sharply from one another. The powers are unbegotten, the angels are begotten and made. The powers are uncircumscribed as God himself, and stretched through earth and water, air and heaven; the angels are obviously finite and local, for they are souls flying in the air. If, notwithstanding these broad distinctions, we maintain that Philo identified the powers with angels, we ascribe to him not only a want of clearness in his notion of personality, but an absolute incapacity for coherent thought. How little are we justified in doing so in the present instance is apparent from the last passage which we have quoted, where the angels are represented as under-servants of the powers. Zeller must surely have overlooked this passage when he affirmed that Philo nowhere indicates a distinction between the powers and the angels.§ But if we maintain the existence of this distinction, how can we consistently suppose that the powers with whom God conversed at the creation of man were angels? By the very simple reflection that, though the powers were not necessarily angels, the angels were most certainly powers. They are, as we have seen, expressly so called; but then so are earth, water, air, fire, nutrition, growth, improvement; and, in a word, all classes and functions in nature or in man come under this term. If it is applicable to material things because they have been differen-

* Τοὺς ὑποδιακόνους αὐτοῦ τῶν δυνάμεων ἀγγέλους.
† Λογισμούς. ‡ Monarch., II. 1 (II. 222).
§ III. ii. p. 366, Anm. 3 of the previous page.

tiated by the impress of some rational force, how much more is it applicable to immaterial souls, which, in their uncompounded being are nothing but divine power set apart and concentrated into an individual life. We do not in this view distinguish two classes of powers. The same conception of them is everywhere present, and the various names and operations which Philo attributes to them result from the logical unfolding of the same primary thought, that God is the sole rational and efficient Cause. The most that can be said is that we regard them under two different aspects, now in the totality of their essence, as genera which express the modes of the divine activity, and again as partially and locally manifested in species and individuals. Souls, or angels, were one form of divine power, and each angel, being a pure expression of that form, might itself be called a power. As this interpretation not only reconciles apparently conflicting passages, but springs immediately from the roots of Philo's philosophy, it seems entitled to our acceptance.

We have still to examine one long passage, and consider how far it confirms or overthrows the results which we have just obtained. It opens with a reference to the words ascribed to God, "Come, and let us go down, and confound there their tongue."*

Here God appears to be conversing with persons co-operating with him. The same thing occurred before when he said, "Let us make man according to our image," and again, "Adam has become as one of us, to know good and evil."† This, then, must first of all be stated, that nothing in existence is equal in honour to God, but there is one Ruler and Sovereign and King, to whom alone it belongs to preside over and administer all things. This being previously acknowledged we may proceed. "God, being one, has innumerable powers around him, all helping and preservative of what was created, among which the punitive also are included: but even punishment is not injurious, being a prevention and correction of sins. Through these powers, again, the incorporeal and intelligible cosmos was compacted, the archetype of this apparent one, consisting of invisible ideas, as this does of visible bodies.

* Gen. xi. 7. † Gen. iii. 22.

Some people, then, being struck with astonishment at the nature of each of the cosmi, not only deified them as wholes, but also the most beautiful of the parts in them, sun and moon and the whole heaven, which, without any shame, they called gods. And Moses, having observed their thought, says, 'Lord, Lord, King of the gods,'* to show his superiority as a ruler to subjects. But there is also in the air a most sacred band of incorporeal souls, attendant on the heavenly [beings]; for the prophetic word is accustomed to call these souls angels. The whole army, then, of each, having been disposed in suitable ranks, ministers to and serves the Sovereign who disposed it, whom in accordance with right and law it follows as its commander; for the divine army may never be convicted of desertion. Now, it is becoming for a king to associate with his own powers, and use them for services in such things as would not be suitably fixed by God alone. For the Father of the universe is in need of nothing, so as to require service from others if he wished to fabricate; but seeing what is becoming to himself and to the things that are entering into being, he allowed the subject powers to mould some things, without having given even to these an absolutely autocratic knowledge of completing the work, in order that none of the things coming into genesis should be out of harmony." These explanations having been necessarily premised, we return to the creation of man. Beings above and below man are alike free from sin; but man almost alone, having a knowledge of good and ill, often chooses what is worst, and avoids what is worthy of pursuit. For this reason God attached the formation of man to his lieutenants, saying, "Let us make man," in order that the right actions of the mind might be ascribed to him alone, but the sins to others. For it did not seem becoming to the all-ruling God to fabricate through himself the way to evil in the rational soul, for which reason he committed the formation of this part to those who are after† him. For it was necessary for the voluntary also, the antagonist to the involuntary, to be prepared with a view to the completion of the universe. Further, we ought to attend to this consideration, that God is the cause of good things only, and of nothing evil at all, since he was himself both the oldest of beings and the most perfect good. Now, it is most becoming for the best of beings to fabricate the best things, as being appropriate to his own nature, but for punishments inflicted on the wicked to be made secure through the agency of those under him. This is attested by the words of Jacob, " God who nourishes me from my youth, the angel who rescues me out of all my evils." He hereby acknowledges "that genuine good which nourishes virtue-loving souls is attributable to God only as its Cause, whereas the domain of evil, on the contrary, has been committed to angels, though even they have not an autocratic authority to punish, in

---

* The reference is apparently to Deut. x. 17. † Or beneath.

order that his preservative nature may not begin any of the things tending to corruption. Wherefore he says, 'Come, let us go down, and confound.' For the impious were worthy to suffer such a penalty [as this], that his propitious and beneficent and munificent powers should be appropriated to punishments.* Knowing, however, that [punishments] are profitable to mankind, he appointed them through the agency of others, for it was necessary, on the one hand, that mankind should be deemed worthy of correction, and, on the other, that the fountains of his ever-flowing graces should be kept unmixed with evils, not only actual but even supposed."†

I have quoted this passage at such length in order that its full bearing and the connection of its parts may be clearly seen; for in it pre-eminently Philo is supposed to identify the powers with angels. When referring to it in another connection we had occasion to observe that its phraseology was deficient in precision; but a little attention will enable us to trace its line of argument, and to perceive that Philo, so far from confounding the highest powers with angels, draws a very sharp distinction between them. At the opening of the discussion he seems apprehensive that the use of the plural may suggest a polytheistic conception, and he therefore begins by strongly asserting the absolute unity of God. He then passes on to the powers in their largest and most universal sense, taking care to observe that the punitive, with which he is more immediately concerned, were included among these, and were, like the rest, of a beneficent character. He has, I think, various reasons for referring to the powers. He wishes to show that polytheists, though they revered what was intrinsically divine, yet committed an error in breaking up the divine unity and worshipping the partial and subordinate manifestations of God. Again, he would point out that punishment, though it is inflicted through the instrumentality of inferior agents, nevertheless has its source in the depths of the divine benevolence. And, lastly, he traces the descent of

---

* Τοιαύτης ἐπάξιοι δίκης τυγχάνειν, ἵλεως ... δυνάμεις οἰκειοῦσθαι τιμωρίαις.
† Conf. Ling., 33-36 (I. 430-3).

these agents, that they may not be regarded as a hostile force, but recognised as obedient servants of God. The next step, accordingly, is to describe the creation of the world, with special reference to the parts which were deified by men. This is done with the utmost brevity, so as not to interrupt the main purpose of the exposition. We learn, however, what is essential, the universal agency of the powers in the construction of the intelligible cosmos; and I venture to affirm that throughout the entire passage this is the only agency which is ascribed to these superlative powers. If Philo wanted no other agents, why does he go further and introduce the perceptible cosmos and angels, with no other result than confusing the impression and misleading the thought? It seems quite clear that, having mentioned the powers, he has not yet reached the ministers of God of whom he is in search. He proceeds, accordingly, to the visible world, and to the sun, moon, and whole heaven, which men were particularly fond of deifying. Now we know that in Philo's philosophy the celestial bodies were intelligent beings, marching their orderly round, and fulfilling beneficent functions towards the earth beneath. Here, then, it seems to me we have the first part of that army of obedient powers to which Philo presently alludes. This conclusion is perhaps confirmed by comparing with the present passage the language which is used elsewhere about the sun and moon. To these God gave powers, but not autocratic ones, just as here it is said that he did not give the powers in question autocratic knowledge;* and, again, he leads each thing according to law and right, as here the army is said to follow him according to right and statute law.† The heavenly luminaries, then, were actually intermediate agents employed by God for the benefit of mankind. But some freer activity

---

* Δυνάμεις μὲν ἔδωκεν, οὐ μὴν αὐτοκρατεῖς, compared with οὐδὲ ταύταις εἰς ἅπαν αὐτοκράτορα ἴους . . ἐπιστήμην.

† Κατὰ νόμον καὶ δίκην, compared with κατὰ δίκην καὶ θέσμον, Mundi Op., 14 (I. 10).

was needed than was compatible with their stately movements in settled orbits; and hence Philo hastens to tell us that there is also* in the air a band of angels, who form the second part of the divine army. The little word "also" is of great importance, because it clearly distinguishes the angels from the beings hitherto mentioned, and the same distinction is implied by the word "each" in the phrase "the whole army of each." If the allusion is to the powers originally referred to, then the powers in their highest sense are distinguished from the angels, and the fact that the latter are afterwards spoken of as subject powers affords, as we have seen, no reason whatever for their identification. I believe, however, that the reference is to the sun, moon, and stars, which form an ethereal host more remote from man, while the angels are an aerial army, nearer to the earth and more interested in human affairs. These two wings of the divine forces render an obedient service to God, not because he needs them, but because he thinks it becoming to entrust some things to their charge. The application to them of the term "powers" can no longer perplex us; and it is peculiarly suitable here, because an army constitutes the power or forces of a king. That the powers in the supreme sense are not alluded to is obvious from the limitation of their agency, which is as carefully marked here as in the passages previously considered. God permitted them to mould some things.† Are these the all-pervasive powers through which the intelligible cosmos was made? Surely not, as they are thus separated by an absolute difference of function. The section relating to the creation of man throws no further light upon the question. We are simply told that God employed his "lieutenants"‡ and "those after him,"§ but nothing is said to indicate their precise nature. The succeeding section, however, on the confusion of tongues seems to me conclusive. Philo brings in his favourite text about the angel who rescued

* Ἐστι δὲ καί. † Ἐστιν ἃ διαπλάττειν.
‡ Ὕπαρχοι. § Τοῖς μετ' αὐτόν.

Jacob from evil, in order to prove that the duty of punishment was delegated to angels. It was so delegated in order that God's preservative nature* might not begin things tending to corruption, that is, I presume, punishments which, though intended to act beneficially, sometimes involve the destruction of the offender. The succeeding words are of the utmost importance, and have been fully quoted above. What do they mean? Surely this, that the men at Babel were so bad that they deserved to be punished by the immediate action of divine power, seeing even the propitious and beneficent powers of God armed with the terrors of punitive justice. But instead of exercising these powers God employed the agency of others, presumably of angels; and he did so in order that the fountains of his ever flowing graces, that is, the powers just mentioned, the sources of all divine favour, might be kept free from the very suspicion of evil. If this interpretation be correct, the powers, in agreement with Philo's whole philosophy, take their place within the divine nature, and are sacred and inviolable as God himself, and it is only as partially enshrined within some definite personality, which participates in but does not coincide with them, that they act as subordinate agents in the creation of man and the punishment of the wicked.

This exposition would hardly be complete if we did not observe that Philo's admission of a plurality of creators is occasioned solely by the difficulty of interpreting the passage in Genesis, and not by the pressing requirements of his philosophy; for when he speaks of the creation of man apart from this passage, he discards the plurality and is content with the agency of God. This will become apparent when we treat of the creation of the first man.† In such references he is anxious to exalt the prerogatives of the founder of our race, and circumstances which might seem to lower the dignity of his origin are quietly omitted.

* Ἡ σωτήριος αὐτοῦ . . φύσις.
† See Mundi Op., 47 (I. 33); § 49, p. 33; Nobil., 3 (II. 440).

We have thus exhausted, if I am not mistaken, all the passages that can be adduced in favour of the personality of the powers, and have seen that, with no greater latitude of interpretation than must be reasonably allowed to a rhetorical and not always exact writer, they may be reconciled with the philosophical views which were explained in the earlier part of this chapter. These views are stated by Philo with a distinctness and precision which entitle them to a dominant place in his doctrine of the powers, and flow as a logical consequence from his theory of the Divine Nature. We are therefore bound to accept them as representing his permanent belief. That he unconsciously entertained at the same time a totally different order of thought is not proved by any express assertion, but only inferred from passages of which many appear to have been misunderstood, and to be really confirmatory of the opinions to which they are thought to be opposed; others, although if they stood alone they might leave on our minds a contrary impression, are easily reconciled with Philo's weightier utterances; and others, again, exhibit the familiar figure of poetic personification. We are, therefore, no longer shut up in an interpretation which fills the whole theory of the powers with incoherence and confusion, and reduces it to a mere curiosity of incompetent speculation. With its truth or falsehood we are not here concerned; nor can we yet tell whether our researches into the doctrine of the Logos may not compel us partially to reverse our judgment. But thus far we have obtained a self-consistent philosophy, and we can trace the divine powers by logical descent and sub-division from their single home in the unknown essence of God through the intelligible cosmos down to this visible image of the eternal thought, with its vast tissue of genera and species, till we find their impress upon individual forms, the chorus of stars, the angelic host, man with his reason stretching beyond the universe, the bird that wings its way through the air, the flower that blooms in the field. We meet these powers everywhere, for they alone give reality and meaning to all that we see and touch. They are the secret beauty in each humblest thing; they are the mighty bonds which constrain earth and ocean and sky into the harmony of a cosmos; and since they are but the varied expression of the divine energy, it is through them that the universe lies enfolded in the all-pervading immensity of God.

CHAPTER VI.

THE LOGOS.

AMONG the powers we have met with the Logos, and it may have seemed as though we ought to have treated it along with the creative, regal, and other members of the dynamical hierarchy; but on account of the magnitude and complexity of the subject we have been obliged to reserve it for separate discussion. We encounter here once more all the difficulties that beset our way in the consideration of the powers: the same florid and rhetorical style, the same fondness for personification, the same mingling of the literal and the allegorical. Moreover the uncertainty arising from Philo's eclectic method now reaches its highest pitch, and it is increasingly difficult to decide whether the heterogeneous elements of which his doctrine is composed, Platonic, Stoical, and Jewish, lie side by side without organic connection or have been fused together in the moulds of a really philosophical mind. Besides these sources of perplexity, which affect Philo's philosophy in general, the doctrine of the Logos has an ambiguity of its own, springing from the variety of meanings which belong to its principal term. These meanings have been elaborately, if not always quite happily, classified by Grossmann.* No useful purpose would be served here by going through his enormous list of passages; but we may point out very briefly the principal

* Quaest. Philon., II. p. 3 sqq.

senses in which the word is used, apart from the metaphysical doctrine which we are about to investigate. In its highest signification it denotes the mind itself, the rational and sovereign principle in the human soul.* This meaning, however, passes so easily into that of the rational faculty in the mind that Philo is not careful to distinguish them, the exercise of reason being in his view the one characteristic function of mind. We are told accordingly that the sovereign principle† is the place of the inward Logos,‡ and that the latter is "in the understanding,"§ and yet within a few lines it is identified with the understanding.|| From this the transition is made to any kind of relation or condition which can be regarded as an expression of reason. A very few examples will suffice to illustrate this familiar use of the word. We are told that the human mind has in man the logos which the great sovereign has in the entire cosmos.¶ The context proves that the meaning here is "relation"; and we thus see that the term may be used in immediate connection with God and yet have no trace of its metaphysical sense. Again, we meet with the logoi, that is the relations or laws of harmony** and of music,†† and "the unshaken and most stable and really divine logos in numbers,"‡‡ that is, the rational principle or law which underlies them. The term seems to aquire the meaning of character or condition where ὁ σωφροσύνης λόγος or ὁ κατὰ σωφροσύνην λόγος is used as equivalent to the simple σωφροσύνη,§§ and where Jacob, regarded as the representative of a particular state of mind, is described as "the ascetic logos,"|||| which here corresponds with the more usual τρόπος.¶¶ Hence it

---

* See Quod det. pot. ins., 23 (I. 207), "the best species of soul, which has been called νοῦς καὶ λόγος. Abr., 18 (II. 13), where ὁ ἐνδιάθετος, sc. λόγος, is identified with τὸν ἡγεμόνα νοῦν.
† Τὸ ἡγεμονικόν. ‡ Λόγος ἐνδιάθετος, Vit. Mos., III. 13 (II. 154).
§ 'Εν διανοίᾳ. || Migrat. Abr., 13 (I. 447). ¶ Mundi Op., 23 (I. 16).
** Post. Cain., 5 (I. 229). †† Migrat. Abr., 32 (I. 464).
‡‡ Vit. Mos., III. 12 (II. 154). §§ Leg. All., II. 20 (I. 80-1).
|||| Quod Deus immut., 25 (I. 290).
¶¶ See other examples in Grossmann II. p. 24 sqq., under b.

comes to denote the rational contents or meaning of a thing. Thus we read, "the ethical logos [or meaning] is of the following kind,"* and, "it is worth considering fully what λόγον the saying has."† These and cognate significations all rest upon the fundamental idea of reason; and it deserves notice that, under this division, the meaning passes from the personal mind itself through an attribute or function of the mind down to the most abstract and impersonal expression of reason. The second leading sense of the term is speech, language being the offspring of reason, and the thoughts of the human mind naturally shaping themselves into the form of words. As words may be written as well as spoken, logos is applied to any kind of expression of thought through words, such as argument, discourse, treatise, doctrine or system, saying, rumour. This usuage does not require illustration, and we need only refer to Philo's application of the term to Scripture. A Scriptural passage is frequently referred to as logos, and Scripture generally is described as " the sacred," or " divine," or " prophetic logos." I see no reason to suppose that Philo intends by this phrase to represent the universal Logos as speaking through the medium of Scripture. The Old Testament or any part of it was a logos according to the current use of the word, and its sacred character is indicated simply by the qualifying epithets.

This rapid survey may be sufficient to convince us that we must proceed with caution, and not hastily assume that logos always denotes the same subject. Its shades of meaning are so various that we must bear its ambiguity in mind if we would do full justice to the passages which come under investigation. Our difficulty is increased by the fact that we have no corresponding term of equal elasticity in our own language. We are compelled to use several expressions to translate this single Greek word, and we are not only thus in

* Leg. All., II. 6 (I. 69).
† Conf. Ling., 33 (I. 430). See also Migrat. Abr., 27 (I. 459).

danger of giving it greater precision in particular instances than really belongs to it, but we are almost sure to lose some of its finer shades of suggestiveness. Perhaps the nearest parallel which English affords is the word "thought"; for we can apply it not only to the faculty of the mind and the inward products of that faculty, but to their outward embodiment in language, as when we refer, for instance, to Young's "Night Thoughts," or say of any book that it is full of thought. Still the word is far from being co-extensive with logos; and though we may occasionally employ it as the most appropriate translation, we shall be obliged to have recourse to other terms as well. With these preliminary cautions we may now enter on our difficult task.

In order to develop the subject from the point which we have reached we must begin by viewing the Logos in its connection with the powers, regarded first in their ideal and then in their dynamical aspects. We have seen that when we cast our eye around the world every object of contemplation is distinguished from inert matter by the presence of a rational impress or idea. The ideas are only varied forms of the same ultimate reason; and therefore when we survey the cosmos as a whole, and rise to the apprehension of its unity, we cannot but view it as the pictured thought of God. If we perceived nothing but the juxtaposition and succession of material phenomena we could never rise to the discovery of unity and law; but the ideas range themselves by logical necessity under one superlative term, and in the ideal cosmos, accordingly, we detect the unity which our reason demands. This unity is selected by Philo as characteristic of the intelligible world, for he finds in it the explanation of the fact that the first day of creation, which was devoted to the intelligible universe, is called in Genesis not first, but one.* Wherein, then, does the unity consist? Since we are dealing with logical relations, it

* Οὐχὶ πρώτην, ἀλλὰ "μίαν," . . διὰ τὴν τοῦ νοητοῦ κόσμου μόνωσιν μοναδικὴν ἔχοντος φύσιν, Mundi Op., 9 (I. 7).

must be found in the highest genus, which may be predicated of every lower term. Now all the ideas are rational, not indeed in the sense of possessing a personal reason of their own, but as forms and varieties of reason. At their head, therefore, must stand supreme, abstract Reason; or, in other words, the multitudinous thoughts which speak to us from every part of creation may be gathered together into one Thought expressive of the Divine. Philo accordingly tells us that the rational is the best genus of things.* He is not at a loss for Scriptural warrant to confirm this assertion. The miraculous food which was given to the Israelites in the desert was a natural symbol of the divine nourishment which feeds the soul. What this nourishment is Moses himself declares. By an arbitrary apposition Philo obtains the clause : " This bread which the Lord has given you to eat, this word† which the Lord enjoined."‡ The "word" is immediately identified with the "Logos of God," which has many points of resemblance to manna: its pervasiveness, like that of dew; its appearing only on what is desert as regards passions and vices; its rarity, brilliance, and purity. Now manna means "'something,'§ that is, the most generic of things ; and the Logos of God also is above all the cosmos, and oldest and most generic of the things that have come into being."‖ By the latter words, which will demand our attention farther on, Philo wishes to guard himself against the appearance of making the Logos absolutely supreme. We have learned before that God himself is at the head of the logical hierarchy ; and hence it is stated in another passage that "God is the most generic thing, and the Logos of God is second,"¶ that is, Reason or Thought ranks logically beneath Being or the Divine.

* Τὸ λογικόν, ὅπερ ἄριστον τῶν ὄντων γίνος ἐστί, Quod Deus immut., 4 (I. 275).
† 'Ρῆμα. ‡ Ex. xvi. 15, 16.
§ I think Philo understood by τί ἐστι τοῦτο in the LXX. " this is *something*." Others obtain the same sense from " *what*," as I have rendered τί on p. 29.
‖ Leg. All., III. 59-61 (I. 120-1). See also Quod det. pot. ins., 31 (I. 213-14).
¶ Leg. All., II. 21 (I. 82).

The logical superiority of the Logos is not worked out by Philo with any fulness or precision; but there are a few examples from which it receives casual illustration. In a passage cited in another connection we learn that the Logos of God, which is the all-beautiful pattern of the human mind, is better even than beauty itself, such beauty as is in nature, being not adorned with beauty, but being itself beauty's most becoming adornment;* in other words, it takes a higher place in the scale of ideas, and communicates rather than participates in beauty. So in the account of the cities of refuge, which symbolize six divine powers, the Logos is " the oldest and strongest and best mother-city, not merely a city," and to it it is most profitable to fly first. It is "the highest," and to be reached only by the swiftest runners. While the other five powers had their visible resemblances in the sanctuary, the divine Logos—which was above the cherubim, the creative and regal powers of God—did not come into visible form, because it was like nothing perceptible, but was the oldest of all intelligible things. This exalted position is indicated by the words, " I will speak to thee from above the mercy-seat between the two cherubim,"† which show " that the Logos is the driver of the powers, but he who speaks is the rider, giving to the driver the orders which tend to the correct driving of the universe."‡ It is simply due to its logical force that the Logos is thus placed between the powers: it is "the uniter of both," that is, it includes both ideas under itself, " for by reason God is both ruler and good."§

From what has been said, it is apparent that the Logos, or divine Thought, sums up and comprehends the whole intelligible cosmos. This is taught in the most explicit way, and

---

* Mundi Op., 48 (I. 33). † Ex. xxv. 22.
‡ Prof., 18-19 (I. 560-1). For the Rabbinical parallel to this figure see Siegfried, p. 220.
§ Cherub., 9 (I. 144). These passages seem quite decisive against Baur's view that the Logos stands beneath the two principal powers as their common emanation. Die christliche Lehre von der Dreieinigkeit, I. p. 69.

presented in various lights. "The intelligible cosmos," it is said, "is nothing else than the Thought of God when he is already engaged in making a cosmos; for neither is the intelligible city anything else than the reflection* of the architect when he is already purposing to create the perceptible city by the intelligible."† The precise shade of meaning to be attached to the term in this passage will be more suitably considered when we speak of the relation of the Logos to God; at present we simply mark the fact that by virtue of its being the highest genus it includes the whole intelligible cosmos. Hence it may be figuratively spoken of as the place of that cosmos. The ideal world is not subject to the conditions of space; you cannot pick out any particular spot, and say that it is there; it is located only in the divine Thought, just as the intelligible city exists only in the soul of the architect.‡ That the Logos not only contains but coincides with the intelligible universe may be inferred from another passage, where the word "place" in Scripture is represented as being sometimes an allegorical expression for " the divine Logos which God himself has filled entirely§ with immaterial powers."‖ This statement seems to imply that the powers or ideas collectively exhaust the Logos, and that therefore they and the Logos are convertible terms, and the divine Thought is neither more nor less than the sum total and logical equivalent of the divine thoughts. Since God is more generic than the Logos, he of course includes it and its contents, so that there is no inconsistency when, in a single passage, God, and not the Logos, is described as the "immaterial place of immaterial ideas."¶

A place filled with ideas readily lends itself to the notion of a book, and Philo has no difficulty in finding his whole ideal theory in the words, "This is the book of the genesis of heaven and earth, when they were made."** By "book" is

* Λογισμός, evidently used instead of λόγος for the sake of variety.
† Mundi Op., 6 (I. 5). ‡ Ib., 4, 5 (I. 4), and § 10, p. 7.
§ Ὅλον δι' ὅλων. ‖ Somn., I. 11 (I. 630).
¶ Cherub., 14 (I. 148). ** Gen. ii. 4.

denoted "the Logos of God, in which are inscribed and engraved the constitutions* of all other things." The description of the universe as "heaven and earth" leads him to make a broad classification of the intelligible cosmos, heaven indicating symbolically the idea of mind, and earth the idea of sensible perception. He applies this doctrine with much ingenuity to the next verse in Genesis, but we need not dwell upon subtleties of interpretation which give no further insight into his philosophical system.†

If we have been thus far right in our interpretation, the Logos must be itself an idea; and so accordingly it is expressly called. "God," it is said, "gives the soul a seal, an all-beautiful gift, teaching that he shaped the substance of all things when it was unshaped, and stamped it when it was unstamped, and gave it form when it was without quality, and, having finished, he sealed the entire cosmos with an image and idea, his own Logos."‡ Here it is not only characterized as an idea which, like other ideas, is impressed upon matter so as to bring it into rational form, but it is clearly represented as the universal idea, the one supreme and all-embracing thought which brings the multiplicity of qualities into the unity of a cosmos. Substantially the same doctrine is expressed when it is affirmed that the "human mind is God-like, being stamped in conformity to the highest Logos as an archetypal idea."§ The highest Logos can be no other than the crowning idea, which, as we learn from these two passages, lays its impress alike on the macrocosm and the microcosm. In this connection the term may even be dropped, and referred to simply as the "rational idea," as we learn by comparing with the statement last cited the following :—Murder is sacrilege of the most heinous kind, for "nothing among the possessions and treasures in the cosmos is either more sacred or more God-like than man, an all-beautiful impression

* Συστάσεις. † Leg. All., I. 8-10 (I. 47-8).
‡ Somn., II. 6 (I. 665). § Spec. Leg., III. 37 (II. 333).

11 *

of an all-beautiful image, stamped with the pattern of the archetypal, rational idea."* Finally, as the head and sum of the ideal world, it is called the "idea of the ideas."†

We have already learned from these passages that the Logos, since it is an idea, is also an archetype or pattern, and comes under the familiar figure of a seal, and further that it is applicable in this respect to the two worlds of matter and of mind. It may, however, be advantageous to produce a few more illustrations of this doctrine. Having inferred from the particular instance of man that the entire perceptible cosmos was "an imitation of a divine image," Philo proceeds: "It is evident that the archetypal seal also, which we affirm to be the intelligible cosmos, would itself be the archetypal pattern, the idea of the ideas, the Logos of God."‡ Elsewhere he speaks of "the seal of the universe, the archetypal idea, by which all things, when without form and quality, were made significant and stamped."§ The Logos is not mentioned here, but that it is referred to is shown not only by the similarity of the expressions to those used in the previous passage, but by the parallelism of this statement to one recently quoted where the Logos is named, both being founded on an allegorical interpretation of the story of Thamar.‖ Again, we read that "the Thought¶ of the Maker is itself the seal by which each thing has been shaped, in accordance with which also the species** that accompanies created things from the beginning is perfect, as being an impression and image of a perfect thought. For an animal, when produced, is incomplete in quantity, ... but perfect in quality, for the same quality remains, as having been impressed from a divine thought, that remains and in no wise changes."†† We learn very clearly from this passage that the Logos is the genus under which the various

* Spec. Leg., III. 15 (II. 313).
† 'Ιδέα τῶν ἰδεῶν, Mundi Op., 6 (I. 5); Migrat. Abr., 18 (I. 452).
‡ Mundi Op., 6 (I. 5).   § Mutat. Nom., 23 (I. 598).
‖ See Somn., II. 6 (I. 665).   ¶ Λόγος.
** Εἶδος.   †† Prof., 2 (I. 547-8).

ideal types that are observed in the universe are classed, and that the permanence of specific forms, which till modern times was believed to be a fact of experience, is ascribed to their participation in the unchangeableness of creative thought. More particularly the Logos is spoken of as the archetype of light,* and hence it is symbolically called the sun in Scripture, being the pattern of the sun which revolves in the sky.† This selection is no doubt made because of all material things light, from its subtle and revealing energy, bears the nearest analogy to intelligence, and reason is the supreme source of intellectual illumination.‡ Among all the objects of nature, however, man stands supreme, through the possession of self-conscious rational power, and he, therefore, in a pre-eminent degree exhibits the divine impress. "Every man," it is said, "has been made in understanding akin § to divine Reason."|| God used for the preparation of the human soul no other pattern than his own Reason alone,¶ to which mankind is related, and from which, as an archetype, the human mind has been formed;** or, as it is elsewhere expressed, the rational soul or spirit in us, being shaped according to the archetypal idea of the divine image, is itself an image of the divine and invisible, stamped with the seal of God, the impression of which is eternal Reason.††

That which determines the rational forms of the various objects of creation, and maintains the permanence of ideal types, may be regarded as a law which regulates the succession of phenomena, and remains constant amid their changes. We are thus transferred from the Platonic ideas to the Logos of Heraclitus and the Stoics, and led to recognize everywhere the presence of a cosmical power, the apparent counterpart of that

---
* Somn., I. 13 (I. 632); Mundi Op., 8 (I. 6-7). † Somn., I. 15 (I. 633).
‡ See Leg. All., III. 59 (I. 121).
§ 'Οικείωται, taken in connection with συγγένεια. || Mundi Op., 51 (I. 35).
¶ Ib., § 48, p. 33. ** Exsecrat., 8 (II. 435).
†† Animal. Sacr. idon., 3 (II. 239); Plantat. Noe, 5 (I. 332). Cf. also Leg. All., III. 31 (I. 106-7).

reason of which we are conscious in ourselves. To this power we naturally attach the name by which we designate the regulative principle in ourselves; and inasmuch as our individual thought is liable to mistake and perversion, we frequently distinguish the universal force as "right Reason,"* or "the Reason of nature."† A few illustrative passages will give us the necessary insight into this use of the term. "This cosmos," says Philo, "... uses one polity and one law. Now, it is the Logos of nature enjoining what ought to be done, and prohibitive of what ought not to be done."‡ This language implies a plurality of commands, like several statutes included under one code. We hear, accordingly, of "ordinances and laws which God ordained to be immovable in the universe."§ The immobility which characterizes the laws of nature is due to the fact that they are expressions of Reason, which is in its essence unalterable. "That which is truly lawful is thereby eternal, since right Reason, which is law, is not corruptible."‖ The eternity and pervasive power of law are well described in a passage where, according to our present text, the Logos is not mentioned. Eusebius, in quoting this passage, reads "Logos" instead of "Law";¶ but the change is not important, for we have now learned that the law of nature is identical with the Logos. "The everlasting law of the eternal God," says Philo, "is the firmest and most secure support of the universe. This, being stretched from the centre to the ends and from the extremities to the centre, runs the long, unconquerable race of nature, collecting and binding all the parts. For the Father who begat it made it a bond of the universe that cannot be broken."** The idea which was thus manifested as a natural law in the physical world reappeared as a moral law in man. "Since every city which is under law†† has a civic constitution,

* Ὀρθὸς λόγος. † Λόγος φύσεως. ‡ Joseph., 6 (II. 46).
§ Mundi Op., 19 (I. 13). ‖ Ebriet., 35 (I. 379).
¶ Praep. Ev., VII. 13. ** Plantat. Noe, 2 (I. 330-1).
†† Ἔννομος, for which Müller reads εὔνομος, "under good laws."

it was necessarily the case that the citizen of the cosmos used the same civic constitution as the entire cosmos. Now, this is the right Reason of nature, which by a stricter appellation is named ordinance, being a divine law,* in accordance with which the suitable and appropriate things were assigned to each."† The transition is obvious from this doctrine to the Stoical maxim, "Live conformably to nature." Philo establishes this maxim of " the best philosophers " by the statement that "Abraham went as the Lord spoke to him."‡ This shows that the mind, when it has entered the path of virtue, walks in the steps of right Reason§ and follows God, and the works of the wise man are not different from divine words.|| Elsewhere the Scripture says, " Abraham did all my law."¶ "Now, law is nothing but divine Reason** enjoining what is right and forbidding what is wrong," so that in doing the law we do the Logos, and our supreme end is to follow God.†† We must observe how "God" takes the place of "nature" in Philo's mind, and how the notion of something which is *expressed* attaches itself to the word Logos throughout this passage. To illustrate the definition which is here given of the law of nature, we may compare the similar definition of law in general, such as proceeds from a king or legislator, in the treatise "On rewards and punishments." "Law," it is there said, "is nothing else than a logos‡‡ enjoining what is right and forbidding what is wrong."§§ The idea of law easily connects itself with that of a covenant; and so the covenant established with Noah is represented as "law and Logos," and in this sense is said to possess the attribute of stability in a degree second only to that of the Self-existent himself.|||| The reason for another comparison is less evident. The flaming sword which

---

* θεσμός, νόμος θεῖος ὤν.   † Mundi Op., 50 (I. 34).   ‡ Gen. xii. 4.
§ Here the idea of *spoken* reason is clearly present, for thus only can we find a connection between ἐλάλησεν and λόγου.
|| Or uttered thoughts, λόγων.   ¶ Gen. xxvi. 5.   ** Λόγος.
†† Migrat. Abr., 23 (I. 456).   ‡‡ Or rational statement.
§§ Praem. et Poen., 9 (II. 417). |||| Somn., II. 33 and 36 (I. 688 and 690).

guarded the entrance to Paradise symbolized the swift, hot, and fiery Logos. This resemblance would naturally occur to one who was deeply imbued with the Stoical philosophy; but Philo had a further reason for this particular explanation. The cherubim represented the two highest powers, the goodness and sovereignty of God, and therefore the sword between them must be the Logos which combined these powers into one. When Philo adds that this Logos "never ceases to move with all zeal, with a view to the choice of what is good and the avoidance of the contrary," and thus attaches to it the idea of law, he must be guided by a consideration of the office which the sword is said to fulfil in the original story.*

As the pervasive law of the universe, the Logos exercises a function at once logical and dynamical. "Looking to the archetypal patterns" of God himself, "it gave shape to species."† In other words, it is a rational force, which not only determines the character and due subordination of species, as we have already seen, but plants them out upon the field of objective existence. In this capacity it receives a highly characteristic name, "the Cutter."‡ It is the province of reason, both in ourselves and in the universe, though it is itself indivisible, to discriminate and divide innumerable other things. Our mind distributes into endless parts what it receives by the intelligence; and the divine Logos has separated and apportioned all the things in nature. This conception is worked out in great detail in the treatise on "The heir of divine things,"§ and is founded upon the narrative of Abraham's offering,‖ in which, while the other animals were divided, the two birds, representing the archetypal Reason above us and its counterpart in us, were left without division. We noticed this passage when we were considering the classifi-

* See Cherub., 9 (I. 144).
† 'Εμόρφου είδη, Conf. Ling., 14 (I. 414). The Logos is not named in this passage; but that it is referred to is evident from expressions which will be considered farther on.
‡ 'Ο τομεύς.   § Quis rer. div. her. 26 sqq. (I. 491 sqq.).   ‖ Gen. xv.

cation of natural objects; and we need not now dwell upon it farther than to observe that the differentiation which we then noticed is made the basis of a philosophical doctrine, and carries our minds to the height of metaphysical thought. The classification which is interpreted by our receptive reason must be the product of an operative Reason, by which God has cut all the natures of things in accordance with pre-established ideas.* We are carried only one step farther back when it is alleged that the divine Logos not only contained the ideal creation, but disposed it into a cosmos.†

In considering the Logos under the aspect of natural law, we have seen that it was regarded as the pervasive bond of the universe. As this conception, which completes our description of it as the sum-total of the powers, is of great importance, we must allude to some passages in which it is enforced without the mediating notion of law. The Logos is in the universe,‡ where it dwells as an "intelligent and rational nature," like the soul in man.§ We are not, however, to suppose that the universe holds the Logos as the larger contains the smaller, for "as place is inclusive of bodies, and is their refuge, so also the divine Logos includes and has filled the universe."‖ This passage seems to teach the transcendence of the Logos; and no doubt it is transcendent when regarded as the ideal cosmos in the supreme Mind, though when impressed upon matter as the potent Thought of God it must become co-extensive with the visible scene. It is in this latter capacity that it makes the cosmos a temple of God, where it ministers as a high-priest.¶ In the fulfilment of its

---

* For the notion of the "cutting and division of things," see also SS. Ab. et Cain., 24-26 (I. 179 sq.). If the Logos here is itself divided, we must explain the seeming inconsistency by the modification of its meaning: as rational force, everywhere one and the same, it is indivisible; as the most generic idea, it is resolvable into its species.

† Mundi Op., 5 (I. 4). ‡ 'Εν τῷ παντί, Vit. Mos., III. 13 (II. 154).
§ Quis rer. div. her., 48 (I. 505). ‖ Τὰ ὅλα. Fragments, II. 655.
¶ Somn., I. 37 (I. 653).

function it is all-pervasive, for otherwise the permanence of ideal types would disappear: remove the divine Thought from any part of creation, and nothing but formless matter would be left. The Logos, accordingly, is a "nature which, being stretched and poured and having reached everywhere, is entirely full,* having harmoniously woven together all things else."† In figurative language we may say that it "puts on the cosmos as a garment, for it arrays itself in earth and water and air and fire and their products," as the individual soul puts on the body; and it is "the bond of all things, and holds together and binds all the parts, and prevents them from being dissolved and separated."‡ Thus, the order which the Creator brought out of disorder is securely established by his strong lieutenant, the Logos.§ All other things are in themselves prone to dissolution, and wherever there is anything compact, "it is bound by divine Reason, for this is a glue and bond, having completely filled all the things that belong to matter;‖ and, having strung and woven things severally together, it is strictly full of itself, not at all requiring anything different [from itself]."¶ Thus it is that the Logos holds together and administers the universe.**

Thus far, then, we have obtained a clear and self-consistent doctrine. The cosmos to the eye of reason is a tissue of rational forms, ideas, or powers, which are permanently impressed upon formless matter. As these powers find their highest unity in the unknown divine essence, which exhausts and transcends them all, so at a lower stage they are summed up in the Logos, with which in their totality they are co-extensive; for they are all expressions of divine Thought, and of that Thought there can be no expression which is not an ideal

---

* Πλήρης ὅλη δι' ὅλων.
† Τὰ ἄλλα. Quis rer. div. her., 44 (I. 503). That the Logos, though not named, is meant, is proved beyond question by the entire context.
‡ Prof., 20 (I. 562).   § Somn., I. 41 (I. 656).
‖ Τὰ πάντα τῆς οὐσίας.   ¶ Quis rer. div. her., 38 (I. 499).
** Vit. Mos., III. 14 (II. 155).

power. Hence, the Logos is the expressed Thought of God, which takes up into itself all inferior ideas, and combines into one force all the powers of nature. As in some magnificent cathedral we may detach our minds from the multiplicity of detail, and, viewing it as a whole, penetrate to the central thought of the architect, so in the cosmic temple we may group together its multifarious phenomena into one grand impression, till we rise to the conception of a single universe on which is imprinted the Creator's Thought; and henceforth, wherever we turn our gaze, to the lowliest flower by the river's brink or to the majestic heavens with their marshalled host of stars, we still discern the presence of that Thought which alone, by its pervading energy, gives life and meaning to the wondrous all.

We must now inquire into the precise extent of the analogy between the divine and the human Logos; for it is evident that the use of the term was founded on the experience of the microcosm, and some notice of the resemblances and differences in its application to the larger and the smaller world will give us a clearer insight into Philo's meaning. We have seen that Philo was familiar with the Stoical division of the human Logos, into inward and uttered. Did he set the example to the later theology of carrying up this distinction into the divine nature, or did he recognize only a single aspect of the higher Logos, and interpret it by the analogy of only one phase of the Logos in man? To this question opposing answers have been returned, and we must form our judgment by a careful examination of the evidence.

Two facts are equally certain, that Philo acknowledges a distinction of some sort in the universal Logos, and that, for some reason or other, he never expresses this distinction by the terms applied to the Logos in man.* The leading passage upon this subject occurs in the "Life of Moses."† An allegorical interpretation is there given of the high-priest's vestments,

* 'Ενδιάθετος and προφορικός. † Vit. Mos., III. 13 (II. 154).

which collectively and severally represent the cosmos and its various parts. Among these was the breast-plate, called by the LXX "Logeion," and described as twofold. "Logeion," of course, suggests Logos, and we are informed that

"The Logos is double both in the universe and in the nature of man. In the universe there are both that which relates to the immaterial and pattern ideas, out of which the intelligible cosmos was established, and that which relates to the visible objects (which are accordingly imitations and copies of those ideas), out of which this perceptible cosmos was completed. But in man the one is inward and the other uttered, and the one is, as it were, a fountain, but the other sonorous,* flowing from the former." (The passage goes on to interpret the square shape of the breast-plate as an intimation that both the Logos of nature and that of man ought to have gone everywhere, and in no respect to waver.) Two virtues were appropriately assigned to it, declaration and truth;† "for the Logos of nature is true and declarative of all things," and that of the wise man ought to imitate it. But also to the two logoi in each of us, the uttered and the inward, were assigned two suitable virtues—to the uttered, declaration, and to that in the intellect, truth; for it is proper for intellect to receive nothing false, and for interpretation ‡ to offer no impediment to the most exact declaration.

In this account we cannot but be equally struck with the explicit recognition of an analogy between the human and the divine Logos in the possession of a dual nature, and with the failure to describe this common characteristic by the same or similar terms. The words "inward" (or its equivalent "in the understanding") and "uttered" are applied no less than three times to the logos in man, but not once to that in the universe; and, further, the two virtues which are allotted severally to the two forms of the human logos, are attributed to the Logos of nature without reference to any such distinction. This diversity of treatment can hardly be, as Gfrörer supposes,§ accidental, and due to the fact that the distinction in reference to the divine Logos was too well known to require exposition. There is no evidence, except such as may be

---

* Γεγωνός.
† Δήλωσις and ἀλήθεια, as the LXX render Urim and Thummim.
‡ Ἑρμηνείᾳ.   § I. pp. 177-8.

gathered from Philo, that this doctrine had yet been formulated; and the suggestion which ascribes to Alexandrian speculation the familiar Stoical division of the human logos into inner and outer, and traces so "unnatural" a conception to a previously acknowledged distinction in the divine nature, is of course quite untenable. Philo never shrinks from unfolding ideas which had become the common property of the philosophical world; and in the present passage, even if the order of thought had been such as Gfrörer imagines, he would surely have used the accepted terms in stating a well-known doctrine, and would have given some intimation of the mode in which the uttered Logos was derived from the inward Logos in God. But as the words stand, we can only conclude that he wished to carry up the human distinction into the nature of God, but, owing to some perceived failure in the analogy, did not choose to describe it by the same language. We must, then, turn our attention to the exact character of the dual Logos in the universe, and notice the points in which the human analogy breaks down.

The Logos which alone can answer to the "inward" is "that which relates to the immaterial and pattern ideas, out of which the intelligible cosmos was established." But Zeller affirms that this does not answer to the "inward," because the distinction which is drawn does not refer to the question whether the Logos remains within the subject to whom it belongs or issues forth from him, but to the question of the objects with which it is engaged.* This is perfectly true in regard to the mere form of expression, and it is evident that Philo shrank from pressing the human analogy too closely. But, as the objects referred to are "immaterial and pattern ideas," and perceptible "imitations of those ideas," the very division of objects suggests a hidden and a manifested Logos. The Logos, as the uniting thought under which all the ideas

* III. ii. p. 376.

are subsumed, is never represented as objective to the divine Mind. God is himself, as we have seen, the place of immaterial ideas;* and the intelligible cosmos, as being older than the perceptible, was deemed worthy of the privilege of remaining with him, while the younger son alone was sent forth to move through space and mark the intervals of time.† This surely implies that the Logos, regarded as the sum of ideas, and not yet impressed upon matter, is hidden in the mind of God, just as truly as an intelligible city is hidden in the mind of an architect; and I see no reason why Philo should not have applied to it the epithet "inward" except his reluctance to use the correlative "uttered." That he did not consider it unworthy of the divine nature is apparent from his applying it to laughter as the son of God.‡

The same conclusion is established by the passage quoted in another connection, in which Philo himself, at considerable length, compares the action of the Creator to that of an architect, who plans a city in his mind before he proceeds to build it of wood and stone. Before that comparison is introduced, two divine processes are distinguished, which, though one is prior to the other in thought, were in fact simultaneous. These two processes are "ordering" and "purposing."§ I doubt whether we give a sufficient account of these words by making them, with Müller,|| equivalent to the uttered and the inward Logos; indeed I am not sure that this exegesis, without some important qualifications, does not involve the whole subject in

* See before, p. 162. † Quod Deus immut., 6 (I. 277).
‡ 'Ο ἐνδιάθετος υἱὸς θεοῦ, Mutat. Nom. 23 (I. 598). Zeller also dwells upon the fact that while δήλωσις and ἀλήθεια are applied separately to the two λόγοι in man, the λόγος of nature is said to be ἀληθής καὶ δηλωτικὸς πάντων, and this can only be because he did not recognize the same distinction. We ought to observe, however, that the λόγος of the wise man is treated in the same way as that of nature, and the distribution of the two virtues is made subsequently, so that Philo may not have intended to mark in this way the difference between the two cases.
§ Οὐ προστάττοντα μόνον, ἀλλὰ καὶ διανοούμενον. Mundi Op., 3 (I. 3).
|| P. 139.

confusion. According to it the "uttered Logos" could be nothing else than the spoken word or command in obedience to which the visible universe sprang into being, and the "inward Logos" would be only the divine intention to issue such a command. This is entirely different from any meaning which we have hitherto found for the Logos. The words rather express simply the initial and the final process in the work of creation. It is in a divine purpose that everything has its origin; it is in instant response to a divine command that everything springs into objective existence. Thus the purpose extends itself to the complete result. It is, indeed, as Philo himself says, not the thought which is laid up within, but the issuing forth of thought,* and is therefore really more applicable to an uttered than to an inward Logos. Hence we find farther on in the passage that the purpose extends itself to the visible cosmos as its ultimate object,† and is represented as distinct from the inward conception, the formation of which was the first step in the fulfilment of the purpose.‡ This inward conception, which sprang immediately from the creative purpose of God, was the intelligible cosmos, and this again, as we are expressly told, was the Logos. Here, then, for the first time, and not in the purpose, which is logically prior, we meet with the inward Logos. Our passage does not speak of any other Logos; nevertheless, when illuminated by what we have learned elsewhere, it easily betrays the place of the "uttered." Two acts of creation are described : the first, that which we have just considered; the second, that of the perceptible cosmos. The latter was formed by impressing the Logos upon matter, in other words by making it objective, just as the architect stamps his ideas upon marble or timber; and this Logos, planted out, as it were, from God, and everywhere active, through air and earth and sea and sky, this divine

* Ἔννοιαν καὶ διανόησιν, τὴν μὲν ἐναποκειμένην οὖσαν νόησιν, τὴν δὲ νοήσεως διέξοδον, Quod Deus immut., 7 (I. 277).

† Βουληθεὶς τὸν ὁρατὸν τουτονὶ κόσμον δημιουργῆσαι.

‡ Τὴν μεγαλόπολιν κτίζειν διανοηθεὶς ἐνενόησε πρότερον τοὺς τύπους αὐτῆς.

Thought, whose mighty presence can alone convert matter into a cosmos, and which reveals itself in the beauty and harmony of nature, is clearly distinguishable from the same Thought when hidden in the silent depths of God, and known only to his omniscience. This objective Logos corresponds, in a certain sense, with the uttered Logos in man.

In the course of the passage which we are noticing there is some apparent confusion in the references to what, for convenience, we must call the inward Logos. Where it is first introduced it seems equivalent to the faculty of reason. The words are as follows:—"As, then, the city which was first formed within the architect had no exterior place, but had been sealed in the soul of the artist, in the same way not even the cosmos consisting of the ideas would have any other place than the divine Logos which disposed these things into a cosmos." If these words stood alone we should conclude that the Logos, as parallel to the human soul, was not identical with the ideal world, but was rather the rational faculty which produced and retained it; yet within a page or two we are told that it *is* the intelligible cosmos. How are we to explain this contradiction? Probably Philo regarded any particular thought, so long as it was unexpressed, as being in strictness only a mode of the general faculty of thought. Thus, he says that, speaking without figurative language,* "one might affirm that the intelligible cosmos is nothing else than the Logos of God when he is already creating the cosmos; for neither is the intelligible city anything else than the reflection of the architect when he is already purposing to found the perceptible city by the intelligible." This statement seems to imply that the intelligible cosmos is not strictly a product of the divine Reason, but is rather the mode which it assumes in the act of creation. At this point a distinction becomes evident, which, though not expressed, is, I think, implicitly acknowledged by

* Γυμνοτέροις χρήσασθαι τοῖς ὀνόμασιν.

Philo. An architect is capable of planning many cities; and therefore any particular city as conceived in his thought is only one out of many modes which that thought might assume. But there is only one cosmos, and its ideal is exhaustive of the divine Thought. The ideal world, therefore, is not one of many modes which the universal Reason may put on; it is the absolute and unchangeable mode of its existence, without which it cannot be so much as conceived. Remove all ideas, and nothing but a mere potentiality of reason will remain. Hence, in the Supreme Cause, reason and what might seem to be its product become coincident. The ideas are summed up in one superlative term, beyond which there is no further faculty of reason; and, as the idea of the ideas, the intelligible cosmos and the Logos of God become indissolubly identified.

We must now turn to the other aspect of our subject. That Philo recognized some kind of analogy between the divine Logos and the uttered Logos in man is evident from several passages besides the one which was quoted in the earlier part of this discussion. In one of these he says that the "father's house" which was left by Abraham,* denotes the uttered Logos; for the mind is our father, since to it belongs the care of all our parts; and speech is its house, where it disposes and arranges itself and its various conceptions. Similarly God, the mind of the universe, has his own Logos for a house, as may be inferred from Jacob's reference to the "house of God." † The comparison, however, is not worked out, and throws no further light upon the point under consideration. We can only say that the disposal of the ideas in that universal Thought which is stamped upon the visible creation answers to man's disposal of his conceptions in speech, for in each instance the process serves to make the inward notions objective, and to locate them, as it were, in a habitation different from the mind itself. Again, Logos is used as

* Gen. xii. 1. † Migrat. Abr., 1 (I. 436-7). Gen. xxviii. 17.

synonymous with ῥῆμα, a spoken word. We are told, for instance, that the universe was fabricated by the speech or word of the Cause.* It is by his own most brilliant "speech, word," † that God makes both the idea of mind and the idea of perception.‡ This notion of a creative word, prior to the existence of the intelligible cosmos, is very different from anything which we have hitherto met, and can hardly be reconciled with the identification of the ideal world and the Logos. The confusion, however, is a very natural one; for the creation of the ideas could only be regarded as the result of a divine command, and this Philo expresses by the familiar term Logos, adding, however, the explanation ῥῆμα, without perceiving its inconsistency with his more usual doctrine. I cite this passage, not as throwing light on a subject which it only perplexes, but as proving that Philo connected with the divine Logos the sense, not only of rational thought, but of rational speech. Again, the nourishment which God gives the soul is his own word and his own speech.§ This is stated in the course of an allegorical interpretation of the manna in the wilderness.‖ The lesson intended by this incident was "that man shall not live on bread alone, but on every word that issues forth through the mouth of God;"¶ that is, the soul shall be nourished by the whole Logos and by its part, "for the mouth is a symbol of the Logos, and the word is a part of it. Now of the more perfect the soul is nourished by the whole Logos, but we might be content if we were nourished even by a part of it."** The precise way in which the Logos is regarded as the nourisher of the human soul, must be considered farther on; meanwhile we may observe that in one passage the manna is identified not only with the "heavenly Logos of virtue," but with "prophecy,"†† and in another, prophecy is replaced by

* Λόγῳ, parallel with διὰ ῥήματος. SS. Ab. et Cain., 3 (I. 165).
† Λόγῳ, ῥήματι. ‡ Leg. All., I. 9 (I. 47). § 'Ρῆμα and λόγος.
‖ Ex. xvi. 14 sqq. ¶ Deut. viii. 3.
** Leg. All., III. 60-1 (I. 121-2). Cf. Prof., 25 (I. 566).
†† SS. Ab. et Cain., 26 (I. 180).

philosophy. The words in the latter run thus :—" This royal way, which, as true and genuine, we affirm to be philosophy, the Law calls the word and speech of God; for it is written, 'thou shalt not incline from the word which I command thee this day.'"* The connection of prophecy and philosophy with the spoken word is obvious. As declared by human lips they belong to the uttered logos of man; but in their ideal aspect they are identical with the law which is impressed upon the face of nature; and this law, again, is, as we have seen, nothing less than the divine Logos. Therefore we return to the doctrine of the passage from which we started. The Logos in the universe which answers to the uttered logos in man, and may therefore be described as the Word of God, is the impress of the supreme idea upon matter, the rational force which binds the multitude of phenomena into the harmony and unity of a cosmos.

It may seem strange that when Philo so freely speaks of the Word of God he withholds from it the epithet "uttered." The reason is found in the fact that, philosophically considered, the Word of God and the word of man are totally different in kind. The term "uttered" immediately suggested the physical organs through which human speech issued; but God had no such organs, and though his expressed Thought might not inappropriately be compared to a Word, it could hardly be associated with an adjective which at once recalled to the mind a mouth and tongue. The distinction is carefully pointed out by Philo himself. Having quoted the verse "once the Lord spoke, these two things I heard,"† he remarks,

The word "once" is applicable to what is unmixed and a monad or unit, while "twice" refers to what is mixed, and susceptible of composition and dissolution. God, accordingly, speaks unmixed units; for speech ‡ is not for him a sonorous § body of air, since it is mingled with nothing else,

---

* Post. Cain., 30 (I. 244). † Psalm lxi. 11 in the LXX. ‡ 'O λόγος.
§ Reading γεγωνός instead of the unmeaning γεγονώς.

but is incorporeal and naked, not differing from a unit. But we hear by a duality, for the breath, when it is being sent forth from the sovereign principle, is shaped in the mouth by the tongue, and then issuing forth and getting mixed with its kindred air, and striking it, completes the combination of a duality.*

In consequence of this peculiarity the divine voice was seen, and not heard.

It is said in Scripture, "All the people saw the voice," † not heard it, since what took place was not a beating of the air by the organs of mouth and tongue, but a brilliant light of virtue, not differing from a rational fountain. In another passage Scripture distinguishes the audible from the visible by saying, " You heard a voice of words, and you saw, not a resemblance, but a voice."‡ For the voice which is divided into noun and verb and the parts of speech generally, is properly called audible, for it is tested by hearing; but that which does not consist of verbs or nouns, but is the voice of God, is rightly introduced as visible, since it is seen by the eye of the soul. Now observe with what novelty it is said that the voice was visible, though the voice is almost the only thing connected with us which is not visible, except the intellect. It is true, we do not see tastes and smells regarded simply as such, but we see them when regarded as bodies. The voice, however, is not visible, whether we regard it as audible or as a body, supposing it to be a body; but these two things in us are invisible, mind and speech.§ But our faculty of sound has not been made like the divine organ of voice; for ours is mixed with air, and flies to the kindred region of the ears; but the divine consists of pure and unmixed thought,‖ which, on account of its rarity, outstrips hearing, and is seen by pure soul on account of its sharpness of discernment.¶

I have referred to these passages at such length to show that Philo was distinctly and fully aware of a failure in the analogy between divine and human speech. So long as the Word was regarded as simply an expression of thought it might, without irreverence, be attributed to the divine Being; but as soon as it was defined by an epithet which was proper only to spoken and audible language, it ceased to be applicable.

There are still one or two highly suggestive passages which

* Quod Deus immut., 18 (I. 285). † Exod. xx. 18.
‡ Deut. iv. 12. § Λ.'γος. ‖ Λόγου.
¶ Migrat. Abr., 9 (I. 443-4).

will serve to complete our doctrine. Referring once more to the statement that all the people saw the voice, Philo asks why that of man was audible, but that of God visible. The answer is, "Because as many things as God says are not words, but works, which eyes rather than ears distinguish."* Again, referring to the dream of Jacob, he speaks of the "promises made through words" as being confirmed by "works of truth," and adds, "for it is the peculiar attribute of God to speak certainly what will come to pass; yet why do we say this? for his words† differ not from works."‡ It might be supposed that the intention here was only to emphasize the certainty with which the divine promise or prediction must be fulfilled. But I think more than this is implied. To say that God foretells future events seems to separate the world's movements from his sovereign will, and to place him, as it were, in the position of a man who foretells an eclipse; and therefore Philo demurs to the expression which he has just used. God's promises are not spoken words, relating to a course of events which goes on independently of them, but rather the potency by which the future is controlled, as the seed is the promise of the harvest. Thus the word of God, in any particular instance, is really a work; it is the imprinting of a divine idea which realizes itself through the ages. This view is confirmed by the remaining passage. It is there said that even time did not co-operate in the production of the universe, "for God in speaking created simultaneously,§ placing nothing between the two;—but if one ought to set going a truer opinion, the word‖ is his work."¶ In the first statement the word and the deed are represented as different, though contemporaneous. But Philo has a view which he considers truer: the word and the deed are identical; the utterance is the stamping of the divine and cosmical Thought

---

* Dec. Orac., 11 (II. 188). † Λόγοι. ‡ Somn., I. 31 (I. 648).
§ Λέγων ἅμα ἐποίει. ‖ Ὁ λόγος.
¶ SS. Ab. et Cain., 18 (I. 175).

upon matter; and the Logos, the Word, is the finished work, the Thought of God made objective, for the sole creation and the sole reality in this material universe is that Thought which resolves itself into a permeating tissue of ideas, and speaks to our reason as an expression of the Supreme Mind.

It is not wonderful, then, that Philo abstained from applying to the Word of God an epithet which, however convenient it became in the course of time, was too strongly associated in his mind with spoken language to serve as a fitting medium for his doctrine. If it be asked why he did not go farther, and discard the use of "the Word" altogether, various reasons may be given. Not only does it furnish a very natural figure by which to represent the expression of divine Thought, but it was already current in religious and philosophical language. It had the sanction of the Old Testament, and the term Logos with its convenient ambiguity provided an easy transition from the Scriptural "Word of God" to the Stoical "Reason," by which Philo's philosophy was so deeply influenced. His belief in the transcendence of God led inevitably to the distinction which was afterwards denoted by the words "inward" and "uttered"; but it was one thing to adopt and interpret the language of the day, and quite another to introduce for the first time a pair of correlative terms which might suggest a much closer analogy between God and man than he was willing to admit.

From what has been said the relations of the Logos to God and to the cosmos have already become apparent. We must, however, view these subjects separately, and consider how far Philo's language in regard to them is consistent with the doctrine which we have just set forth.

"Neither before creation was anything with God* nor since the creation of the cosmos is anything ranked with him."† In these words Philo asserts the absolute solitude of God. He

---

* Σὺν τῷ θεῷ. † Leg. All., II. 1 (I. 66).

presents them as a possible interpretation of the statement that "it is not good for the man to be alone."* Why is it not good for *man*? Because it is good for the Alone to be alone. This loneliness of God may be interpreted as above; and though Philo himself referred it rather to the simplicity of the divine nature, there is no reason to doubt that he accepted the doctrine contained in the former explanation. Agreeably to this he says elsewhere that God, in determining to create, "used no assistant†—for who else was there ?—but himself alone."‡ We must, then, start by conceiving of God as originally existing not only in the absolute simplicity of his being, but in perfect solitude. There is no Logos distinguishable from himself to share his counsels or to execute his plans. But, as we have seen, the simplicity of his unknown essence resolves itself to our thought into a variety of predicates expressive of his manifestations in the cosmos. These may be summed up in the two statements, he is good, and he is powerful or sovereign, and these two, again, find their unity in the proposition, he is rational. He is, accordingly, the Mind or Reason of the universe. Have we, then, discovered his essence, and when we have said that he is Reason, have we given an exhaustive description of him ? No, for pure Being is a more comprehensive conception than Reason, and includes other predicates. Being, for instance, is eternal and omnipresent, and may have other attributes unknown to us, none of which is necessarily involved in the rational. Reason, therefore, is a mode of the divine essence, but not that essence itself ; and, as in the case of all the powers, God exhausts and transcends it. He may, accordingly, be spoken of as the fountain from which it flows, as the Being who is before it. This view is clearly exhibited in a passage previously quoted,—" God, the fountain of the oldest Reason,§ does not participate in, but rules, the rational power."‖ This, of course, does not mean

---

* Gen. ii. 18.   † Or advocate, παρακλήτῳ.   ‡ Mundi Op., 6 (I. 5).
§ Λόγος.   ‖ Quod det. pot. ins., 22 (I. 207).

that God has none of the rational power, but that he has it all. We participate in it and are dependent upon it for the possession of our reason; but it depends upon God for its very existence. That it belongs to his essence is implied in the comparison of a fountain; and the same conclusion follows from an argument which Philo uses,—"Since God is the fountain of Reason, it is a necessity that he who lives irrationally has been separated from the life of God."*
This argument would not be valid unless reason were involved essentially in the divine life. But that it is not exhaustive of the divine essence is taught in many passages. God, who is before and above the Logos,† is declared to be superior to all rational nature.‡ He who has been conducted by wisdom into the divine Reason does not reach God in his essence,§ but sees him from a distance, or rather is not competent even to behold him from afar off, but sees only that God is far from all creation, and the comprehension of him most widely removed from all human understanding.|| When, therefore, we say that God is the Mind or Reason of the universe, we not only express our own best conception, but assert a truth; yet the truth is inadequate, for above and beyond the immanent Reason of the universe is the transcendent and eternal Being whose it is, and into whose depth and fulness of perfection man, whose highest experience is of reason, can never penetrate.

The view here sketched corresponds precisely with our doctrine of the divine powers; but can we reconcile the notion of a rational power or rational nature with the conception of the Logos as the ideal cosmos? We can do so only in the way already indicated, by supposing that in God the faculty and the product are coincident. We, with

---

* Τῆς θεοῦ ζωῆς. Post. Cain., 20 (I. 238).
† Πρὸ τοῦ λόγου, ὑπὲρ τὸν λόγον.
‡ Κρείσσων ἐστὶν ἢ πᾶσα λογικὴ φύσις. Fragments, II. 625, answering to Qu. et Sol. in Gen., II. 62.
§ Τὸν κατὰ τὸ εἶναι θεόν. || Somn. I. 11 (I. 630).

our imperfect gifts, fling off fugitive ideas which c
considered, either separately or collectively, as constitu
essence of reason. But the divine Reason consists of ͺ
nent ideas and relations, which, though they might seve
be spoken of as its products, yet in their totality represe.
its unchanging essence. Rationality in its highest sense
means the logical array of divine and eternal thoughts;
and if we refer to the Logos now as a power and again as
the collective cosmical idea, we only adapt our language t·
different aspects of the same thing.

As the idea of the ideas, the most generic thought,
Logos is spoken of as the oldest of things, an expres
which probably describes its logical rather than its chron
logical relations, since we have seen that the latter do not
enter into the creative activity of God.* Since it is dependent on the self-existing Cause, and, as a thought, must be
conceived by us as produced, it is represented under the figure
of a son,—a kind of metaphor for which we have already
noticed Philo's predilection; and when this notion is combined with the preceding, it becomes the oldest, or first-born
son.† It is, if I am not mistaken, always in its cosmical
relations, that is, as the Thought of God made objective in
the universe, and capable, therefore, of being conceived apart
from God, that it is described in this way; and Philo's meaning is admirably illustrated by a passage where the figure is
carried still farther, and it is said that the Logos has for its
father God, who is the father of all things as well, and for
its mother Wisdom, through whom the universe came into
being,‡ and that this oldest Logos of the Self-existent puts
on the cosmos as a garment, for it is arrayed in earth and

* See, besides the passage quoted on p. 183 from Quod det. pot. ins. and others to be mentioned presently, Prof. 19 (I. 561); Leg. All., III. 61 (I. 121).

† Agr. Noe, 12 (I. 308), τὸν ὀρθὸν αὐτοῦ λόγον, πρωτόγονον υἱόν: Conf. Ling., 14 (I. 414), πρεσβύτατον υἱὸν . . . πρωτόγονον: § 28, p. 427, τὸν πρωτόγονον αὐτοῦ λόγον: Somn., I. 37 (I. 653), ὁ πρωτόγονος αὐτοῦ θεῖος λόγος.

‡ Εἰς γένεσιν.

THE LOGOS.

d air and fire and their products.* The relation
Logos to Wisdom must be reserved for separate dis-
; at present we will only observe that the Logos
is the son of God is here evidently represented, not
the interior Reason or Thought of God, but as the supreme
idea impressed upon the visible universe.

In its filial or objective relation the Logos is the "image"
of God, and the archetype of the cosmos and of man.
"God," we are told, "gives the soul a seal, an all-beautiful
, teaching it that he shaped the substance of the universe
it was unshaped, ... and sealed the whole cosmos
an image and idea, his own Logos."† Here it is obvious
it the Logos is the all-comprehending divine Thought which,
ike a seal, is stamped upon matter, and gives rational form to
its otherwise formless mass. Similarly, the mortal soul "was
stamped according to the image of the Self-existent; and
Thought,‡ through which the whole cosmos was fabricated,
is an image of God."§ This conception is frequently repeated
in regard to the human soul, or man in the highest sense. Of
the possessions in the cosmos nothing is more God-like than
man, "an all-beautiful impression of an all-beautiful image,
stamped with the pattern of an archetypal rational idea,"‖
"the highest Thought," or Reason.¶ In somewhat varied
phrase, "the rational spirit in us has been shaped according to
an archetypal idea of the divine image."** In one passage the
figure of a seal or a pattern is abandoned in favour of that
of participation: man is related to God by virtue of participation in Reason.†† It thus appears that man and the cosmos
bear the impress of the same supreme Thought, and the great
laws of reason of which we are conscious within are perceived
without. Philo has no direct Scriptural proof of this doctrine;

* Prof., 20 (I. 562). † Somn., II. 6 (I. 665).
‡ Λόγος. § Monarch., II. 5 (II. 225).
‖ Spec. Leg., III. 15 (II. 313). ¶ Τὸν ἀνωτάτω λόγον, ib., § 37, p. 333.
** Animal. Sacr. idon., 3 (II. 239).
†† Κατὰ τὴν πρὸς λόγον κοινωνίαν, Spec. Leg., IV. 4 (II. 338).

but he infers it from the statement that man was formed according to the image of God.* If the part was an image of an image, much more must the whole cosmos be so, and macrocosm and microcosm bear the stamp of the same archetypal seal.† This Scriptural foundation for the doctrine, combined with the fact that reason in us is self-conscious, and therefore lies closer to our knowledge than the rational laws in the cosmos, naturally induces Philo to dwell most frequently on the human mind as a copy of the Logos. Confining our thoughts to this relation, we obtain a descending series of three terms—God, the Logos, the human reason. The undivided birds of Abraham's offering signify the two winged and soaring Logoi, one an archetype above us, the other an imitation existing in us. Now, Moses calls the one above us an image of God, and the one in us an impression of the image; so that the mind in each of us, which is properly and truly man, is a third impress‡ from the Creator, while the intervening one is a pattern of the one and a copy of the other.§ In another, not very clearly expressed, passage, an ideal man seems to be interposed between the Logos and the actual man. "There are," it is said, "two kinds of men, that which has been made according to the image, and that which has been moulded out of earth, for it desires the image. For the image of God is an archetype of other things; and every imitation desires that of which it is an imitation, and is ranked with it."|| Perhaps we may explain this by saying that the compound man, consisting of mind and body, must, like everything else, have an idea,

---

* Κατ' εἰκόνα θεοῦ, Gen. i. 27.   † Mundi Op., 6 (I. 5).   ‡ Τύπος.
§ Quis rer. div. her., 48 (I. 505). See also Quod det. pot. ins., 23 (I. 207), "A divine power which Moses calls by a proper name, 'image,' showing that God is the archetype of rational nature, but man an imitation and copy, not the two-natured animal, but the best species of the soul, which has been called νοῦς καὶ λόγος."
|| Leg. All., II. 2 (I. 67).

in correspondence with which each individual man is framed; and this idea must come below that of the real and inward man, regarded simply as mind. It is this inward man that is a copy of the Logos. What, then, is the philosophical meaning of representing the human mind as third in the scale of being, instead of making it the immediate image of God? Is it not this, that the individual mind may, and does, fall far short of its ideal, and it is not the imperfect reason of Smith and Jones, but perfect and ideal Reason, that is the image of God. So far as our minds are rational, however feeble and perverted, they must bear the impress of their ideal; but beyond that ideal is the infinite Archetype of all. This statement has a sufficiently clear meaning even for our modern conception; but we must remember that the ideal of human reason is not a mere abstraction, gathered by deducting the imperfections of individual minds, but a permanent reality, being the supreme divine Thought,—that which, in the unknown unity of the divine essence, reveals itself to us as reason, and, in the universe, is apprehended as an all-pervading rational force. As the ideal of the human mind, the Logos is even spoken of as "man." This is not done, however, without Scriptural warrant. Zechariah* says, "Behold a man whose name is rising."† What a strange appellation, says Philo, if you think of man composed of body and soul. But the name is most appropriate if you will acknowledge that incorporeal man, not differing from a divine image; for the Father of things caused this oldest son to rise,‡ whom elsewhere he named first-born.§ The same designation is justified by the statement of Joseph's brethren, "We all are sons of one man."|| "If we have not yet become fit to be considered children of God, at least we are children of his eternal image,

---

* vi. 12.
‡ 'Ανέτειλε.
|| Gen. xlii. 11.

† 'Ανατολή, in the LXX.
§ Conf. Ling., 14 (I. 414).

most sacred Thought; for the oldest Thought is an image of God."*

We must now ascertain as nearly as we can what is meant by calling the Logos an image of God. The most significant passage is the one in which the cherubim on the Ark are said to have symbolized the creative and regal powers.

The divine Logos above these had no visible representation, "as it was like nothing perceptible, but was itself an image of God, the oldest of all intelligible things, the nearest model of the only Being that truly is, there being no bordering interval;† for it is said, 'I will speak to thee from above the mercy-seat between the two cherubim,'‡ so that the Logos is the driver of the powers, and he who speaks is the rider."§

From this statement we learn, first, that the Logos which is the image of God is the spoken Word, that is, the objective Thought of God stamped upon the universe; secondly, that the creative and providential activity of God is controlled by this Thought, which is therefore represented as older; and, thirdly, that as the oldest of intelligibles, or the highest genus, it is the one immediate expression of the divine nature, not, of course, an adequate expression, but one which leaves no higher term to mediate between it and God. All other things are an expression of Thought, but Thought is an expression of God alone. It is not unsuitable, then, to call it the image of God; for as a grand poem or a profound treatise is a reflection of the mind of its author, so God can have no nearer resemblance than the Thought which is the direct offspring of his causality, and embraces the entire scheme of things. If we may say so, the cosmical order is a divine poem, and matter is the page whereon it has been inscribed, which, from its blank, unmeaning look, has become replete with rational form; and he who can read the poem sees, not indeed

* Conf. Ling., 28 (I. 427).
† Ὁ ἐγγυτάτω, μηδενὸς ὄντος μεθορίου ϊαστήματος, τοῦ μόνου ὃ ἐστιν ἀψευδῶς ἀφιδρυμένος.
‡ Ex. xxv. 22.   § Prof., 19 (I. 561).

all the depths of eternal Being, but the purpose and the mind of God.

The same idea is brought out by Philo under another figure, that of a shadow. This is done in connection with Beseleël, who was chosen to execute the necessary work in the preparation of the Tabernacle.* Beseleël means, "God is in a shadow."† Now, his Logos, with which as an organ he made the cosmos, is the shadow of God; and this shadow, and, as it were, copy, is an archetype of other things. For as God is a pattern of the image, here called shadow, so the image becomes in its turn a pattern. That the shadow, in this passage, is equivalent to the Thought projected upon matter, is evident from what follows. One way of understanding the Divine, it is said, is from the cosmos and its parts and the powers existing in these. This is to apprehend God through a shadow, to understand the artist through his works. Presently the shadow is explained to mean "both the Logos and this cosmos."‡ The inclusion of the cosmos in a shadow which was previously identified with the Logos, is intelligible if our interpretation thus far has been correct. The cosmos is certainly different from the Logos, because it includes the material condition which is absent from the latter; and yet *qua* cosmos, as a tissue of logical relations, it becomes identical with it, and may be comprised under the same term. It is as though the shadow of God, otherwise invisible, had fallen upon matter, and so revealed a rational form, the substance of which is hidden from our view.

From the foregoing discussion it has become apparent that the Logos stands between God and the material world. Though intimately united with the latter, as the pervasive force which alone gives it reality, it is yet distinct from it, because, being immaterial, it does not fall under the senses, but is apprehended only by the intellect. On the

---

* Ex. xxxi. 1 sqq. † ’Εν σκιᾷ ὁ θεός = בְּצַל אֵל.
‡ Leg. All., III. 31-3 (I. 106-7).

other hand, it is no less closely united with God, because it has flowed directly from his essence; and yet it is different from him, not only as a part from the whole, nor only as our thoughts become different from ourselves when we make them objects of contemplation, but as the force which is rounded off and made permanently objective in the order of the universe. To recur to the oft used analogy, it is as though the artist's thought were not only visible in the form of the statue, but were the enduring power which held its particles together, and prevented it from sinking into undistinguishable dust. In that case the statue would have no reality as a work of art if the constraining thought of the artist were withdrawn; nor would the thought have any reality except as an inseparable expression of the artist's sovereign and causal mind. Thus the thought would mediate between the mind and the marble block, and seem to border on both the ontological and the phenomenal realms. This mediating position is distinctly assigned to the Logos by Philo. To it, he says,

"The Father who generated the universe gave a special gift, that standing on the borders it should separate the created from the Creator ..... And it exults in the gift, and with dignity tells of it, saying, 'And I stood between the Lord and you,'* being neither unbegotten as God nor begotten as you, but in the middle between the extremes, serving as a pledge to both; on the side of him who planted, for a security that the race will never wholly vanish† and depart, having chosen disorder instead of order; and on the side of that which has grown, for a good ground of hope that the propitious God will never overlook his own work."‡

The words which are here ascribed to the Logos, so far as they are a quotation, are said in Scripture to have been spoken by Moses; but Moses is more than once represented as

---

* Deut. v. 5. This is elsewhere applied to "the understanding of the wise man." Somn. II. 34 (I. 689).

† 'Αφανίσαι, apparently in an intransitive sense. Mangey suggests ἀφηνιάσαι.

‡ Quis rer. div. her., 42 (I. 501-2).

a type of the Logos; and in the passage here referred to a reason for treating him as such may have been found in the fact that he proceeds to report the *words** of the Lord, an office which naturally belonged to the interpreting Logos. The general doctrine laid down by Philo in the above sentences has already become sufficiently clear; but we must notice for a moment one or two of its particular expressions. The Logos is not unbegotten as God; for even if we regard the Thought of God as eternal, still it is always logically dependent upon God, and cannot be conceived as self-existent. A thought, even if it be in fact coeval with the mind, must yet be looked upon as the mind's offspring. On the other hand, it is not begotten as man, because it has not been born in time or become a part of the phenomenal universe. The distinction which is here pointed out was afterwards expressed by the words "begotten" and "made"; but Philo, though evidently aware of the distinction, has not introduced a terminology answering to it, and we must not be surprised if, while words are still fluid, and have not yet settled down into permanent moulds, the use of language is occasionally a little inconsistent. The firstborn son of God must have been begotten; but as Philo applies the latter term to everything created, it was necessary to deny its applicability to the Logos, at least in the sense generally intended. Hence, instead of distinguishing the Logos from the Father, as the begotten from the unbegotten, he declares that it was neither, but occupied a position between the two. The twofold pledge, also, which the Logos offers is significant. As the mighty Thought of God, ever linked with the divine Causality, it secures the universe against a relapse into chaos. As a power essentially divine ever active in the sphere of phenomena, it guarantees the lasting continuity of Providence. The cosmos is God's "own work."† The Logos, therefore, is not a demiurge who acts

* Τὰ ῥήματα. † Τὸ ἴδιον ἔργον.

for or instead of God, but is God's own rational energy acting upon matter; and as a material world cannot, like a human work, be finished off and left to itself, this energy is always there, and links the cosmos to the infinite source of power and order.

These remarks may enable us to understand the contradictory predicates which are attributed to the Logos. On the one hand it is eternal and incorruptible. The rational soul in man, it is said, is stamped " with the seal of God, whose character is eternal Reason."* Here the Logos is regarded simply in its aspect of archetypal idea ; and although the imprinting of that idea must have had a beginning, yet the idea itself, as existing in the unchangeable God, must have been eternal. In one other passage the same epithet is applied to the Logos : " If we have not yet become fit to be considered children of God, at least we are children of his eternal image, the most sacred Logos."† Though we have seen that the Logos is the image of God by virtue of its being made objective in the universe, still it is intrinsically the same whether it has become objective or is hidden away in the mystery of the divine essence ; and so the image may be described as eternal, although the eternal and subjective Logos would not in the first instance have been called an image of God. That it is incorruptible follows as a matter of course, and hardly requires remark. " Being a Thought‡ of the Eternal, it is of necessity itself also incorruptible."§ This necessity would not exist unless the Logos were a direct expression of the divine essence ; and thus Philo's inference helps to confirm our past exposition. Again, we read that " the truly lawful is *ipso facto* eternal,|| since right reason, which is law, is not corruptible."¶ Philo has just been speaking of "an immortal law inscribed on the nature of the universe";

---

* 'Αΐδιος λόγος, Plantat. Noe, 5 (I. 332).
† Conf. Ling., 28 (I. 427).
§ Conf. Ling., 11 (I. 411). || Αἰώνιον.
‡ Λόγος.
¶ Ebriet., 35 (I. 379).

and it is evident from the words which we have quoted that right reason is the rational law which regulates the cosmos, and this law, considered in its essence, and not in its application, is eternal. But as soon as we withdraw our attention from its essence, and think only of its application, it takes its place among the objects of creation. The Logos, as the Word or purely objective Thought of God, "is above all the cosmos, and oldest and most generic of all the things that have come into existence."* Its coming into existence can describe only its assumption of the character of "Word," its passing forth to take possession of matter and constrain it to be a vehicle of divine ideas, which else must have dwelt for ever within the solitude of God.

In conformity with the foregoing doctrine, we may distinguish three grades in the knowledge of God. We may have an immediate intuition of the transcendent Cause; we may know him inferentially from the Reason displayed in his works; or, lastly, we may stop short with that Reason, and fail to apprehend the Divinity beyond. The two former are set forth in the passage about Beseleël, to which we lately referred. We there learned that the supreme Artist may be known through his works as through a shadow. "But there is a more perfect and more purified mind, initiated in the great mysteries, which knows the Cause, not from the effects, as it would the permanent substance from a shadow, but, having looked beyond the begotten, receives a clear appearance of the Unbegotten, so as to apprehend from himself him and his shadow, the latter meaning the Logos and this cosmos." This higher mind is represented by Moses, whom God called up, and to whom he spoke mouth to mouth; but a lower mode of apprehension is symbolized by Beseleël, who received the appearance

---

* Τῶν ὅσα γέγονε. Leg. All., III. 61 (I. 121). Compare Migrat. Abr., 1 (I. 437), where, however, there is a comparative instead of a superlative, ὁ πρεσβύτερος τῶν γίνεσιν εἰληφότων. Here also Philo is speaking of the Word, and of its office in creation and providence.

of God, not from the Cause himself, but from the things that were made, as from a shadow, perceiving the artist by a process of inference. We saw just now that the shadow denotes the Logos, and it is of course only as tenanted by the divine Reason that the cosmos is capable of revealing God.* It follows, therefore, that those who under the guidance of wisdom have reached the divine Logos have not necessarily attained to God himself; they only see him afar off, or, rather, that he is far from all genesis.† In more modern phrase, they discern an all-pervading energy and order in nature, which points to a permanent ontological ground, but of this ground itself they discern only that it is mysterious, impenetrable Being. But the same mind may be differently affected at different times. Now it may soar aloft, and be illumined with the archetypal and immaterial rays of the rational fountain of God; and, again, it may descend and meet only images of these; and thus to meet the Logos is a most sufficing gift for those who cannot behold God, who is before the Logos, for they have the benefit of a mingled light when the unmingled has set.‡ With some the latter state of mind is permanent, and indeed, even among philosophers, there is a yet lower stage than this. The companions of knowledge ought to desire to behold the self-existent Being, and if they cannot do this, to see at least his image, the most sacred Logos, and next to this the most perfect of perceptible works, this cosmos; for the accurate discernment of these is the object of philosophy.§ The Levites represent minds of the highest order. The Sovereign of all is their refuge, while others fly at most to the divine Logos; and while the former have as their law the God to whom they are consecrated, the imperfect have the sacred Logos as theirs.‖

It follows that the Logos may be spoken of as a God in

* Leg. All., III. 31-3 (I. 106-8). † Somn., I. 11 (I. 630).
‡ Ib., § 19, p. 638 § Conf. Ling., 20 (I. 419).
‖ SS. Ab. et Cain., 38 (I. 188-9); Prof. 18 (I. 560).

13 *

relation to our inferior perceptions. Philo, however, very rarely avails himself of this privilege, and never without Scriptural warrant. Commenting on the words addressed to Jacob, "I am the God who appeared to thee in the place of God,"* he asks—

Are there really two Gods? For it is said, " I am the God who appeared to thee," not in my place, but " in the place of God," as of another. The solution is the following: The true God is one, but those improperly so called are several. Wherefore the sacred Word has indicated the true God in the present passage by the article, saying ὁ θεός, but the one improperly so named without the article, ἐν τόπῳ, not τοῦ θεοῦ, but simply θεοῦ. The latter is the eldest Logos. This usage is adopted in order to benefit him who cannot yet see the true God ; for as those who are unable to see the sun itself look upon the reflected ray as the sun, so they mentally perceive the image of God, his Logos, as himself.†

In another passage Philo remarks on the words, "I swore by myself, saith the Lord."‡

God alone affirms by himself, since he alone accurately knows his own nature, and those must be considered impious who say that they swear by God, for they cannot discern his nature. We must be content, then, if we can swear by his name, according to the command in Deuteronomy,§ "Thou shalt swear by his name," not by himself; that is, by the interpreting Logos ; for this would be a God to us imperfect men, while of the wise and perfect the first God would be so.||

Here there is no use of the word God in a subordinate sense in the Scripture passages which are appealed to; but the application of the term to the Logos is readily suggested by the context. The object of an oath is to confirm one's words by the highest possible sanction ; and as men are precluded by their ignorance from swearing by the supreme God, the Logos must take for them the place of the Supreme. The name of God is made to denote the Logos because, as a name expresses the thing which it signifies, so the Logos is an expression of the divine nature which it interprets to us. The phrase " the

---

* Gen. xxxi. 13, ὁ θεὸς . . ἐν τόπῳ θεοῦ.
† Somn., I. 39 and 41 (I. 655-6).   ‡ Gen. xxii. 16.   § vi. 13.
|| Leg. All., III. 73 (I. 128).

first God "* receives illustration from its use elsewhere in opposition to those who thought that the cosmos was God: those who consider it closely, says Philo, will know full well that it is not the first God, but the work of the first God.† This language seems to allow by implication a subordinate divinity to the cosmos, and we might think it strange that a monotheist did not disclaim any such meaning. No doubt he would have done so had he supposed that the world was a mere fabric put together by God. But he viewed it as a tissue of divine forces; and therefore those who worshipped it as God held not so much a false as an imperfect view. The Logos, the cosmic principle in the material universe, was really divine, being the rational energy, the formative Thought of God, and consequently it was not by a mere figure of speech that it was spoken of as God. Yet since it represented only the immanence and not the transcendence of God, since it was an expression of the eternal Cause and not that Cause itself, it was necessary to distinguish it from the supreme and infinite Being; and as the latter was called, in opposition to polytheistic and pantheistic schemes, the First God, the Logos, the highest term next to the Supreme, might be termed the second. This appellation is actually used, but only once, and that in a fragment preserved by Eusebius from the "Questions and Answers." Philo asks—

"Why, as though speaking of another God, does he say, 'I made man in the image of God,' but not in his own image?" The answer is that nothing mortal could be made like the supreme Father of all, but only like the second God,‡ the Logos. For the rational impress in the soul of man must be stamped by divine Reason, and cannot have as its archetype God, who is above Reason.§

Here the application of the term "God" to the Logos is rendered necessary by Philo's interpretation of the passage on

* 'Ο πρῶτος θεός. † Abr., 15-16 (II. 11-12).
‡ Τὸν δεύτερον θεόν.
§ Fragments, II. 625, answering to Qu. et Sol. in Gen., II. 62.

which he is commenting. According to his own conception, as expressed in the words before us, the Logos is simply the archetype of the rational principle in man, and this archetype, as we have seen, is the immanent Thought of the universe. Whether in the doctrine that the Logos was a God to the imperfect, whose conceptions could reach no higher, Philo had the Stoics in his mind, I will not undertake to decide. But at all events his language receives an interesting light from the Stoical doctrine, which recognised no God above the all-pervading Logos of the material system. When we remember the philosophical atmosphere of the time and the requirements of allegorical interpretation, we shall not be surprised that Philo three times in his voluminous works speaks of the Logos as a God, nor shall we be disposed to extract from such language a doctrine inconsistent with all that we have hitherto learned of the nature of the Logos and its relation to the eternal Cause.

Little need be added to what has been already said respecting the relation which the Logos bears to the universe; but one or two forms of expression must be more distinctly noticed. From the doctrine hitherto described we should expect Philo to represent the Logos as the instrument of creation and of providence. This indeed has become apparent in some of the passages which we have quoted, and we need only allude to one or two others which possess more than usual interest. Having occasion to explain that God was a cause, and not an instrument, Philo observes that—

> Four things must concur in every act of creation—namely, that by which, that out of which, that by means of which, and that on account of which; or, in other words, the cause, the material, the instrument, and the reason or purpose. Accordingly, the cosmos has for its cause God, by whom it has been produced; for its material the four elements, out of which it was compounded; for an instrument God's Logos,* through which it was prepared; and for its reason the goodness of the Creator.†

* Ὄργανον δὲ λόγον θεοῦ. † Cherub., 35 (I. 161-2).

In what way the Logos is the instrument of creation has been so fully explained that it would be superflous to remark further upon this and similar statements.* Creation and providence naturally go together, and therefore these two agencies of the Logos are sometimes spoken of at the same time. Thus, we are told that the pilot of the universe, holding the Logos as a tiller, steers all things, and when he moulded the cosmos he used this as an instrument for the composition of the things produced;† and, again, he employs "Reason as a minister of his gifts, by which also he made the cosmos."‡ The supremacy of a rational law over the seeming drift of events is alluded to in a remarkable passage. The object of the passage is to show the vanity of mortal affairs, which differ nothing from false dreams.

This is illustrated by the changing fortunes of nations. Once Greece flourished, but the Macedonians took away its strength. Macedonia again had its period of bloom, but was separated and weakened till it was totally extinguished. Before the Macedonians the Persians prospered, but one day destroyed their mighty kingdom. And now the Parthians are more powerful than the Persians, who lately ruled them, and the former subjects are the masters. The welfare of the once brilliant Egypt passed away as a cloud. And so the whole habitable world is tossed up and down like a ship at sea, which now has favourable, and again contrary winds. For the divine Logos, which most men call fortune,§ moves in a circle. In constant stream it acts upon cities and nations, assigning the possessions of one to another, and those of all to all, merely exchanging the property of each by periods, in order that as one city the whole habitable world may have the best of governments, democracy.‖

This passage hints at rather than unfolds some very striking thoughts. First of all, it distinctly recognizes a rational direction in the fate of nations, and sets aside the common belief in chance. Secondly, as reason implies an end in view, it assumes that some end is being worked out by the rise and

---

* See also SS. Ab. et Cain., 3 (I. 165), δι' οὗ καὶ ὁ σύμπας κόσμος ἐδημιουργεῖτο: and Monarch., II. 5 (II. 225), where almost the same expression occurs.
† Migrat. Abr., 1 (I. 437).
‡ Quod Deus immut., 12 (I. 281), where we have ᾧ instead of δι' οὗ.
§ Τύχη.   ‖ Quod Deus immut., 36 (I. 298).

fall of successive empires. This end, in the case of divine Reason, must be good; and Philo conjectures that the ultimate aim must be the good of mankind, the universal distribution of the blessings enjoyed by any, and the universal establishment of that form of government which rests on the equal rights of all. So far as the Logos is concerned, it must, in conformity with previous statements, be simply the instrument through which the divine purpose is carried out. God directs the affairs of men through the operation of that rational law which is bound up in the very constitution of the world. In this capacity the Logos is spoken of not only as "the tiller" held by God, but as itself the "steersman and pilot of the universe."* Thus, the two worlds of nature and of man are ruled by the same divine Reason, and the beneficent purposes of God are being fulfilled, not only through the sublime law which is interfused through every part of the material cosmos, maintaining its majestic and harmonious movements, but through a law no less sublime, though less easily discerned, which underlies the seeming fortuity of our human lot, and directs the vicissitudes of nations. These two laws are one: both alike are the Logos, the supreme idea imprinted upon the world, the rational energy of God acting within the realms of time and space.

Such, then, in its broad outlines, is Philo's doctrine of the Logos, a doctrine which, when taken in connection with the previously established doctrines of the divine attributes and the divine powers, is sufficiently clear and consistent; and were we content to leave without discusion difficulties which Philo himself has not discussed, we might consider the duty of exposition as now discharged. There are, however, some passages, hitherto unnoticed, which raise inevitable questions about the distinct essence and the personality of the Logos, and, having been variously understood by different writers,

---

* Cherub., 11 (I. 145). Cf. SS. Ab. et Cain., 12 (I. 171).

will require our serious attention. But before we enter upon these perplexities, it will be better to examine some peculiarities in Philo's phraseology, which will throw a further light upon his opinions. He speaks not only of the Logos, but of the Wisdom,* of God, and though the relation between these two terms is evidently intimate, its precise character is rather obscure, and has been very differently conceived. They are frequently supposed to be identical in meaning, the former having been introduced under the influence of Greek philosophy, strengthened by the desire to obtain a masculine name for the mediating power, the latter being a survival of the old Hebrew expression. From this view Dähne and Baur diverge in opposite directions. Dähne declares that the divine Wisdom is one of the powers of the divine Logos,† and denotes that capacity for making wise arrangements which must necessarily be postulated in the mediating cause of the world's formation.‡ Baur, on the other hand, places it on the highest stage, in the most intimate union with the supreme Being, and along with it, though subordinate, the two principal powers, goodness and sovereignty, and assigns the Logos to the second stage, where it is the same unity for the divine power operative in the universe as Wisdom (or the supreme God himself, with whom it is one) is upon the highest stage.§ To decide among these conflicting opinions, it is necessary to review the passages on which our judgment must rest.

We will notice first those places in which, notwithstanding some apparent distinctions, Wisdom and the Logos seem on the whole to be identified. In an allegorical interpretation of Eden, Philo says that generic virtue receives its beginnings from Eden, the Wisdom of God, which rejoices in its Father alone, and the four specific virtues are derived from the generic. Presently the former statement is repeated with an

---

* Σοφία.   ‡ Eine Theilkraft desselben.   ‡ I. p. 221.
§ Lehre von der Dreiein., I., p. 70.

addition: generic goodness "goes forth out of Eden, the Wisdom of God. Now this is the Logos of God; for in accordance with this [Logos] generic virtue has been made."* Here, I think, the identity is not, as Gfrörer seems to suppose,† between the Logos and Wisdom, but between the Logos and generic goodness. Eden is Wisdom, and the river is generic goodness or the Logos, which divides itself into the four specific virtues. Thus Wisdom and the Logos are distinguished from one another, and if this passage stood alone, we should not refer to it at present; but when we compare it with corresponding passages, we receive a different impression. We have observed before that Philo's allegorical interpretations follow a pretty regular system. We are accordingly told elsewhere that Scripture "calls the Wisdom of the Self-existent Eden";‡ and yet we are informed in another passage that "Eden is, symbolically, right and divine Reason."§ Farther on in the same treatise, Wisdom and the Logos seem to be used as interchangeable terms. The soul is "watered by the stream of Wisdom."‖ "The Logos of God gives drink to the virtues; for it is the beginning and fountain of beautiful deeds." The virtues "have grown from the divine Logos, as from one root."¶ "Whence is it likely that the understanding thirsting for prudence should be filled except from the Wisdom of God, the unfailing fountain?" Presently we hear again of "Wisdom, the divine fountain," and then of "the stream of Wisdom";** and farther on, "the sacred Logos which waters the sciences is itself the stream."†† It would seem, then, that the distinction drawn in the first passage, whatever it may be, belongs to the thought rather than the terms; for Wisdom and the Logos appear alike under the figures of Eden,

* Leg. All., I. 19 (I. 56).   † I. p. 225.
‡ Somn., II. 37 (I. 690).   § Post. Cain., 10 (I. 232).
‖ § 36.   ¶ § 37.   ** § 41.
†† § 45. The whole passage extends from I. 249 to 255. The argument is not affected by Tischendorf's reading ταυτὸν in the last quotation, instead of Mangey's αὐτός.

of a fountain, of a stream. The words are similarly interchanged when it is said that "in those by whom the life of the soul has been honoured the divine Logos dwells and walks"; and a few lines farther on, "they have a secure and unshaken power, being fattened by the Wisdom which nourishes virtue-loving souls."*

The impression thus received, that the Logos and Wisdom are, at least to a certain extent, convertible terms is strengthened when we find that some of the most striking characteristics of the former are attributed to the latter. Thus, Wisdom is represented as the highest of the divine powers. This is done in a commentary on the passage in Deuteronomy† where Israel is exhorted not to forget the Lord, "who brought forth for thee out of a scarped‡ rock a fountain of water, who fed thee with manna in the desert." So, spiritually, we thirst "until God sends upon us the stream of his own scarped Wisdom, and gives drink to the soul, . . . for the scarped rock is the Wisdom of God, which he cut topmost and absolutely first§ from his own powers, out of which [Wisdom] he gives drink to God-loving souls." This language is evidently governed by the figure under which the thought is presented, and we must not insist on the word "cut," which, if taken strictly, would contradict the doctrine that the powers are stretched, and not severed; but it seems sufficiently clear that Wisdom is regarded as the highest divine power operative in the world. Yet this is precisely the position we have already claimed for the Logos. In the sequel of the passage, however, it might seem as though the Logos were distinguished from Wisdom. When souls have received drink "they are filled also with manna, the most generic thing; . . . . now the most generic thing is God, and the Logos of God is second."|| This distinction is rendered necessary by the allusion in Deuteronomy

* Ib., 35 (I. 249).   † viii. 15, 16
‡ 'Ακροτόμου, "top-cut."   § Ακραν καὶ πρωτίστην ἔτεμεν.
|| Leg. All., II. 21 (I. 81-2).

to food as well as drink; but that it is only verbal is apparent from another passage of very similar import. The nourishment of the soul, it is said, is described by the Legislator as "honey from a rock and oil from a firm rock."* The rock is "the solid and unsevered Wisdom of God," the nurse of those who desire incorruptible food. "The fountain of the divine Wisdom" sometimes comes with gentler flow, and sweetens like honey, sometimes more swiftly, and "becomes, as it were, the oil of mental light." Here there is nothing in the Scriptural words to suggest a distinction between Wisdom and the Logos. But neither is there anything to require their identification. Nevertheless Philo proceeds to identify them in the most express terms. "In another place," he says, "making use of a synonym, he calls this rock manna, the divine Logos which is the oldest of things, and is named the most generic 'something,' from which two cakes, the one of honey and the other of oil, are made."† We need not pursue the explanation farther: it is clear that the rock, the fountain, the manna, Wisdom, and the Logos are one, and differ to the ear rather than to the understanding. Again, God, "the only wise," is "the fountain of Wisdom," just as we have seen that he is the fountain of rational power, and, as such, he delivers the sciences to mankind.‡ He is also "the sovereign of Wisdom," and as we have learned that some may recognise the Logos who cannot rise to the apprehension of the Self-existent, so some may perceive Wisdom who are not yet able to behold its sovereign.§ Wisdom is of course, like every divine power, "older than the creation of the entire cosmos";|| but, more than this, it is, like the Logos, instrumental in the production of the cosmos. God being the Father of the universe, Wisdom or Science¶ is its mother. The details of this not very pleasing metaphor must not, I think, be pressed into the service of Philo's

---

* Deut. xxxii. 13.
‡ SS. Ab. et Cain., 17 (I. 175).
|| Human., 2 (II. 385).

† Quod det. pot. ins., 31 (I. 213-14).
§ Quod det. pot. ins., 9 (I. 197).
¶ Ἐπιστήμη.

philosophy, but be treated as purely figurative. The figure is due to the direction in Deuteronomy, that, if anyone has a disobedient son, the father and mother shall seize him and bring him to the elders of the city.* Now, none could bear the punitive powers of the parents of the universe; but it is good to obey their followers who preside over the soul—namely, as a father, the masculine and perfect and right Reason, and, as a mother, encyclical education.† Here Wisdom first of all takes the place which we have been accustomed to assign to the Logos, being the divine instrument in creation, and then the Logos is introduced as subordinate both to God and to Wisdom. We must presently seek for some explanation of this kind of inconsistency; meanwhile we must not attach too much weight to passages which are written for purposes of edification, and not with a view to unfolding a philosophical doctrine, and especially when the manner of treatment is under the control of an allegory. Wisdom appears again as the medium of creation in connection with the commandment "Honour thy father and mother, that it may be well with thee,"‡ not, observes Philo, with those who receive the honour, but with *thee*. This is the case when we honour "as a father him who begat the cosmos, and as a mother Wisdom, through which the universe was completed; .... for neither the full God nor the highest and perfect Science requires anything," so that in serving them you benefit yourself.§ The same figure of a mother recurs in yet another connection. "The high-priest is not man, but divine Reason, free from participation in all unrighteous deeds, not only voluntary, but even involuntary," for he cannot defile himself either "for father," the mind, or "for mother," sensation,|| because "he had as his portion incorruptible and most pure parents, as a father God, who is also the Father of the universe, and as a mother Wisdom, through which all things came into being." Philo goes on to say, in

* xxi. 18, 19.   † Ebriet., 8-9 (I. 361-2).   ‡ Ex. xx. 12.
§ Quod det. pot. ins., 16 (I. 201-2). || Lev. xxi. 11.

words already quoted, that the "oldest Logos of the Selfexistent puts on the cosmos as a garment," and is the bond of all things.* Here the creative function usually assigned to the Logos is attributed to Wisdom, and yet the pervasive Logos of the universe apparently owns it as a mother. This seeming confusion will be noticed presently. In another passage the cosmos is simply spoken of as "fabricated by divine Wisdom."† In one other place, although the creative action of Wisdom is not mentioned, it is referred to as "the mother of all things." Here, too, a Scriptural passage suggests the metaphor: "A man shall leave his father and mother, and cleave to his wife,"‡ that is, for the sake of sensation the mind leaves "the Father, the God of the universe, and the mother of all things, the Virtue and Wisdom§ of God."‖ The figure is somewhat modified when God is spoken of as " the husband of Wisdom," for here Wisdom is the generic virtue or wisdom of mankind, symbolized by Sarah, which cannot become fruitful unless visited by divine influence;¶ but we may remark that it is not easy to distinguish this wisdom ontologically from the Logos or rational nature in which mankind participate. They are indeed used interchangeably by Philo in a passage which serves in other respects also to identify Wisdom and the Logos. The statement in Genesis** that "God planted a paradise in Eden towards the east" is under consideration. Divine and heavenly Wisdom, we are told, is many-named,†† for Scripture "has called it beginning and image and vision of God." This reminds us at once of the many-named Logos of the Stoics; and it is noticeable that Philo himself elsewhere applies the same epithet to the Logos, and the very first name which he mentions is "Beginning." He also speaks of it as the image of God, and as "Seeing Israel," which is equivalent to "the

* Prof., 20 (I. 562).
‡ Gen. ii. 24.
‖ Leg. All., II. 14 (I. 75).
** ii. 8.

† Quis rer. div. her., 41 (I. 501).
§ Ἀρετὴν καὶ σοφίαν.
¶ Cherub., 13, 14 (I. 147-8).
†† Πολυώνυμος.

vision of God" in the passage before us.* The resemblance becomes still more apparent as we proceed. Earthly wisdom is an imitation of the heavenly as an archetype, a fact which is symbolized by the planting of Paradise; for God plants in the mortal race earthly virtue, an imitation and copy of the heavenly. Now virtue is called metaphorically "Paradise;" and the planting of Paradise is towards the east, "for right Reason does not set and become extinguished, but always according to its nature rises, and as, I think, the sun, when it has risen, fills the darkness of the air with light, so also virtue, when it has risen in the soul, illumines its mist and disperses its great darkness."† It thus appears that Wisdom, Virtue, and right Reason are different names for the same thing, regarded, it is true, now on the earthly, now on the heavenly, side, but not distinguishable from one another in essence. Intellectual perception is associated with light; and hence Wisdom, like the Logos, is brought into connection with "the seeing Israel," and the Wisdom of God is declared to be "the archetypal light of the sun, of which [light] the sun is an imitation and image."‡ We have only to add that even the function of the "Logos the cutter"§ is ascribed to Wisdom, though it is not worked out so as to enable us to institute a detailed comparison. "The fountain of judgment" or separation,|| mentioned in Genesis xiv. 7, is turned into the Wisdom of God, "the judgment¶ of all things, by which all opposites are disunited."**

In some of the foregoing passages we have observed that, though Wisdom and the Logos are identified either expressly or by the possession of the same characteristics, yet they are also, under the pressure of allegorical interpretation, distinguished from one another. A few other places in which a distinction is assumed require notice. Wisdom, "the best dwelling of

* See Conf. Ling., 28 (I. 427). † Leg. All., I. 14 (I. 51-2).
‡ Migrat. Abr., 8 (I. 442). § Λόγος τομεύς.
|| Τῆς κρίσεως. ¶ Or separation. ** Prof., 35 (I. 575).

virtue-loving souls," is said to be the land of sacred Reason. This statement is founded on the commandment given to Jacob,* "Return to the land of thy father."† As the Logos in man takes the place of father, Wisdom was required to represent the land, and it would not be safe to infer from such figures that Philo had in his mind any clear relation between the two terms. If the language of Scripture had led him to do so, I have no doubt that he would without scruple have reversed the order, and represented the Logos as the land of Wisdom. We have an actual instance of this kind of inversion in the comparison of Wisdom and the Logos to a fountain and a stream. Where Eden is made to represent Wisdom, and its river the Logos, we learn that "the divine Logos, like a river, descends from Wisdom, as from a fountain;"‡ and yet, when the first of the cities of refuge does duty for "the highest divine Logos," we are informed, quite gratuitously, that the latter is the "fountain of Wisdom."§ Agreeably to this order of thought, it is said that he who is conducted by Wisdom arrives at the divine Logos,‖ and that all the branches of education and wisdom¶ flow perennially from the "Word of God and divine Logos."** The latter passage is peculiarly instructive, because the Logos, which here stands for the heavenly bread or manna, presently becomes "ethereal Wisdom," which God showers down upon well-disposed minds.

Before we remark on this curious identity, difference, and interchange of Logos and Wisdom, it will be advantageous to notice those passages in which the latter is brought into immediate connection with mankind, but without any expressed relation to the Logos, for we shall thus gain a fuller insight into its nature. "The divine spirit of Wisdom" may abide with men, as it did with the wise Moses.†† This Wisdom is the

* Gen. xxxi. 3.　　　　　† Migrat. Abr., 6 (I. 440).
‡ Somn., II. 37 (I. 690).　§ Prof., 18 (I. 560).　‖ Somn., I. 11 (I. 680).
¶ Παιδείαι καὶ σοφίας.　** Prof., 25 (I. 566).　†† Gigant., 11 (I. 269).

perfect or royal way which leads to God,* and may be spoken of as "the way of wisdom," or "the way of prudence."† Human wisdom, however, is not the same as divine Wisdom, but is related to it as species to genus, or as imitation to archetype,‡ and whereas the universal prudence § which inhabits the Wisdom of God is imperishable, the individual prudence in me perishes with me.|| Accordingly, the branches of human knowledge are the principles or theorems¶ of God's own Wisdom.** Being itself equivalent, as we have seen, to science,†† the divine Wisdom is the fountain from which the individual sciences are watered.‡‡ It concerns not only the sciences, but the arts; and Wisdom, as it appears in the wise man, is described as "the art of arts,"§§ which, preserving its own true species unaltered, exhibits itself in a variety of applications.|||| We have only to add that Philo distinguishes wisdom and prudence by saying that the former relates to the service of God, while the latter is directed to the administration of human life.¶¶

It is apparent from the preceding account that Wisdom does not receive from Philo the elaborate treatment which he bestows upon the Logos and upon the divine powers generally, and that if we were confined to this account the most striking features of his philosophy would become obscure or disappear. Nevertheless, it suggests a few questions to which we must attempt an answer.

We must ask, first of all, how we are to understand the relation between the Logos and Wisdom when they are distinguished from one another. The most obvious reply is that given by Heinze,*** that the Logos or Wisdom regarded as a divine power working upon the world is different from the same power when at rest in God, and that, therefore, either

* Quod Deus immut., 30 (I. 294); § 34, p. 296.   † Plantat. Noe, 22 (I. 343).
‡ Quis rer. div. her., 25 (I. 490).   § Φρόνησις.
|| Leg. All., I. 25 (I. 59).   ¶ Θεωρήματα.
** Quod Deus immut., 20 (I. 286).   †† 'Επιστήμη.
‡‡ Prof., 35 (I. 575).   §§ Τέχνη τεχνῶν.
|||| Ebriet., 22 (I. 370).   ¶¶ Praem. et Poen., 14 (II. 421).   *** P. 253.

may be represented as issuing forth from the other. I doubt, however, whether this is the true solution of the difficulty. There is only one passage which lends itself easily to this interpretation. When Wisdom is represented, apparently, as the mother of the universal cosmical Logos (symbolized by the high-priest), we may fairly take the latter to be the uttered Word, the former the eternal attribute of God. Yet even here it would be hazardous to say that Philo was clearly conscious of this distinction. In his allegory he wanted a mother for the Logos, and none could be found but Wisdom; and if we look a little more closely at the details of the passage we shall find room for a different explanation. The high-priest, though standing for "divine Reason," represents in the main that portion of it which dwells in each man as a judge and rebuking conscience. "The oldest Logos of the Self-existent" is introduced only to point out the universal laws of reason, which necessarily reappear in its particular manifestations. When we are told that this Logos put on the universe as a garment, it is immediately added that the individual soul puts on the body, and the understanding of the wise man the virtues; and when it is said that the Logos of the Self-existent is the bond of all things, it is only to show that the individual soul exercises a similar faculty, and the purified mind of the wise man keeps the virtues unbroken. The death of the high-priest is the departure of "this most sacred Logos" from the soul, and the consequent inroad of sin. I believe, therefore, that the distinction in Philo's mind was not that between the inward and the uttered, but between the universal and the particular, and that what he meant to teach was that the divine principle of righteous law in each one of us was the offspring of that cosmical law which "preserves the stars from wrong." This view is fully borne out by other passages. Human or earthly wisdom or virtue or right reason is related to the divine or heavenly as species to genus, and is a copy or imitation of it. If, therefore, Wisdom and the Logos be identical, you may say with equal propriety that human wisdom flows from the "highest divine Logos" as a fountain, and that human reason flows from the fountain of the divine Wisdom. It is as perennially flowing into God-loving souls, in the form of "words and ordinances,"* that the divine Logos is compared to a river;† and such a stream, distributing itself specifically to individual minds, may be said, indifferently, to come from universal Wisdom or Reason. So, again, the Logos which is the father of the man is that portion of the Logos which belongs to him, and, as such, it owns universal Wisdom as its land. Reversing the terms, he who allows himself to be guided by the share of wisdom which dwells in him reaches the cosmic Reason from which it comes. In the passage where Wisdom is described as the mother of the universe, and the Logos is ranked below it, the latter is the right reason of men, which has received the care of souls, and is classed with encyclical education; in other words, it is the species, and is justly made subordinate to the genus. There is, however, one passage to which this explanation will not apply. It is where Wisdom and the Logos are distinguished as the drink and food of man, for here they stand together in the same relation to man. The distinction is, as we have seen, forced upon Philo by his allegory; but we may also say that Wisdom and the Logos, though identical in God, are distinguishable in human apprehension. Wisdom, being interchangeable with virtue and science,‡ carries with it the notions of moral soundness and acquired knowledge, which are not necessarily present in Logos, the rational principle by which men are separated from the brutes. Thus the apparent inconsistencies in Philo's language may be explained without violating the ultimate identity of the Logos and Wisdom.

We must ask, in the next place, why Philo uses "Wisdom" at all, and is not content with Logos. The explanation given by Gfrörer§ and accepted by Heinze,‖ that he adopts it

---

* Λόγων καὶ δογμάτων. † Post. Cain., 37 (I. 250).
‡ Ἀρετή and ἐπιστήμη. § I., p. 226. ‖ P. 256.

principally when the mediating power is symbolized by some feminine word in the Scriptural passage under consideration, is certainly not sufficient. There are several passages in which the rule is applicable, especially those in which Wisdom is the mother of the universe, but there are also several (I have counted seven) in which no reason of the kind exists, and there are four others in which the rule is distinctly violated. Wisdom is represented by Isaac,* by Paradise,† and by bread,‡ which are all masculine; and, on the other hand, the Logos is signified by a city,§ which is feminine, although it is described as the fountain of Wisdom, and the relation might easily have been reversed.|| We must, therefore, seek for some further explanation. One reason for its adoption is to be found, we can hardly doubt, in its traditional use by Jewish writers, a use sanctioned by the authority of the Old Testament. Philo himself appeals to Proverbs to prove the antiquity of Wisdom, —" God acquired me absolutely first of his works, and founded me before the age."¶ But I think the prevailing reason is to be found in its greater suitability to express certain ideas. Heinze has noticed the fact that it is never represented as the all-penetrating bond of the universe.** But he might have gone further. It is almost invariably used in relation to mankind. It is the divine food and drink of the soul, the dwelling-place of those that love virtue, the perfect way of human life, the fountain from which the sciences are watered; and even in the few passages where it is spoken of as instrumental in the act of creation, it is nearly always brought into connection with men. It is a reasonable inference that it is often used on account of its more distinct personal associations, and because it expresses a source and form of character and attainment

* Quod det. pot. ins., 9 (I. 197).   † Leg. All., I. 14 (I. 51-2).
‡ Ἄρτοι, Prof., 25 (I. 566).   § Πόλις.
|| Prof., 18 (I. 560).
¶ So he renders viii. 22-3, deviating from the text of the LXX. Ebriet. 8 (I. 362).
** P. 255.

which are not so well indicated by the less definite term Logos.

We must ask, then, in conclusion, why Logos is so constantly preferred. One reason is probably to be found in its gender, a point to which Philo undoubtedly attached some importance. This is evident from a curious passage about Wisdom which we have not yet noticed:—

Bethuel, which, being interpreted, means the daughter of God, is a name of Wisdom. Nevertheless, Bethuel is called the father of Rebecca. How can the daughter of God be justly termed a father? Because the name of Wisdom is feminine, but its nature masculine. So all the virtues have the titles of women, but the powers and actions of men; for that which is after God, even though it be older than all other things, is feminine in comparison with that which makes the universe, the male always having the prerogative. Hence Wisdom, the daughter of God, is masculine and a father, generating in souls learning, instruction, science, prudence, beautiful and laudable actions.*

If we may judge from this passage, Philo must have been pleased to find a term of the desired gender which he could conveniently substitute for the traditional "Wisdom," and which, moreover, was not without the sanction of Scriptural usage. It seems probable, however, that he was mainly influenced by the philosophical qualifications of the word. It was more flexible, and could be more easily used, in conformity with human analogy, now for the inward conception, now for the uttered or objective thought; and its established position in the Stoical philosophy must have forced it upon the attention of one who was so strongly attracted as Philo by the moral ideal of that austere system. He must have found it no small advantage to have ready to his hand a theory of the universe which only needed to be removed from its pantheistic basis, and brought into harmony with the doctrine of the transcendence of God, to become a fitting vehicle for his own speculations; and with the theory, however modified, he naturally adopted its characteristic term.

* Prof., 9 (I. 553).

There is another Old Testament term which is used by Philo with less frequency, "the divine Spirit;" and though his treatment of it does not greatly illumine our conceptions of the Logos, we must briefly notice the leading thoughts which he attaches to it. It is curious that, although Philo is unusually careful to furnish us with definitions, this subject has been thrown into confusion by more than one interpreter, from a failure to distinguish two completely different meanings of the Greek word πνεῦμα.* These two meanings are clearly pointed out by our philosopher himself.

"The Spirit of God" [he says] signifies in one sense the air, the third element, and it is used in this sense at the beginning of Genesis, where it is said "the Spirit of God was borne above the water," for air, being light, is borne up, and uses water as its basis. In the other sense, it is the pure wisdom in which every wise man participates.†

Gfrörer quotes this passage, and then adds that πνεῦμα occurs only once more, so far as he is aware, in the physical sense.‡ The place referred to is one in which fresh water is represented as one of the forces by which earth is held together, the other being πνεῦμα.§ The parallelism of spirit with water proves that it here denotes air. Gfrörer, however, might have observed that this article of the Stoical physics occurs elsewhere. We have seen that spirit, in the sense of air, is the source of "habit" in inorganic objects, and of higher qualities in organized beings.|| The term is also used in an enumeration of the elements;¶ and when the question is asked whether the mind is "spirit or blood or body at all,"** we can hardly doubt that the sense of air or breath is intended. We have seen, in dealing with anthropology, that this is its meaning in a fragment where it is represented as the essence of the irrational

---

* Heinze, generally so careful, is particularly unfortunate, p. 242-3. Dähne, also, I. p. 294-5, and Keferstein, p. 102, confound the physical with the metaphysical sense.
† Gigant., 5 (I. 265). ‡ I. p. 230. § Mundi Op., 45 (I. 31).
|| See Vol. I. p. 281. ¶ Ebriet., 27 (I. 373). ** Somn., I. 6 (I. 625).

soul ;* and where, on the contrary, it appears as the essence of the rational, Philo is careful to explain that he does not mean "air in motion."† It is apparent, therefore, that the physical sense was sufficiently familiar, so familiar indeed that, when Philo departed from the Stoical view, he had to guard himself against misapprehension.

Of the metaphysical sense two definitions are given which are intended to be precise. In the passage last cited the term is defined as "a stamp and impress of a divine power which Moses calls by a proper name, 'Image.'" As the "image" has been already identified with the Logos, it follows that the Spirit which forms the essence of man's rational soul is the impress of the Logos; it is the communicated divine idea, the imitation or the share which each man enjoys of the universal Reason. According to this definition, it is the permanent principle of rationality in man, breathed into him by the Creator from his own essential life. According to the other definition, it is the universal Wisdom which manifests itself transiently and mutably in individual men. As we have seen, it is "the pure knowledge of which every wise man partakes."

This [Philo proceeds to say] is shown by the words of Scripture, that "God called up Beseleël and filled him with divine Spirit, wisdom, understanding, knowledge,"‡ "so that what divine Spirit is is defined through these terms."§ Of this kind is the Spirit of Moses also, which came upon the seventy elders; for, though they were elders, they could not have been really superior to others unless they participated in that all-wise Spirit. For it is said, "I will take from the Spirit that is upon thee, and will put it upon the seventy elders."∥ But this taking from the Spirit did not involve cutting and separation, but resembled what occurs in the case of fire, which, though it may kindle innumerable torches, remains in no respect diminished. Such is the nature of knowledge, which, when it

* See Vol. I. pp. 320 sq. † Quod det. pot. ins. 23 (I. 207).
‡ Ex. xxxi. 2-3. The LXX has πνεῦμα θεῖον σοφίας, κ.τ.λ.; Philo reads πνεύματος θείου σοφίας, and evidently regards σοφίας, &c., as in apposition with πνεύματος.
§ Τὸ τί ἐστι πνεῦμα θεῖον ὁρικῶς διὰ τῶν λεχθέντων ὑπογράφεσθαι.
∥ Num. xi. 17.

has rendered all its votaries experienced, is not lessened, but often is even improved. If, then, the spirit of Moses himself, or of any other created being, were to be distributed to such a multitude, it would be divided into so many little pieces, and diminished; "but, as it is, the Spirit on him is the wise, the divine, the indivisible, the inseparable, the excellent,* that which is everywhere entirely filled up," which is not injured by communication, nor lessened in understanding and knowledge and wisdom. Divine Spirit, accordingly, can remain,† but not permanently remain,‡ in the soul, because it is hindered and oppressed by the flesh and other things, as it is said, " My Spirit shall not continue to remain§ in men for ever, because they are flesh."||

It is evident that the Spirit is here identified with Wisdom in its highest generic sense, and is therefore ontologically the same as the Logos. The passage hardly requires comment; but we must pause for a moment upon one expression on account of the singular interpretation which is put upon it by Keferstein¶ and Heinze.** The words which I have rendered, "That which is everywhere entirely filled up,"†† are interpreted by both these writers as "Die Alles erfüllende Kraft," the former translating them "Der Alles durch Alles erfüllende," and explaining that by "Alles" nature and man are to be understood. Thus the Spirit is made into a cosmical power, and then Heinze, ignoring its double meaning, complains of Philo's inconsistency in making it elsewhere the binding force of only one part of the earth. Was ever poor philosopher so badgered? He is not the most precise of writers; but when he is precise his precision affords him no shelter, and even his Greek is mistranslated to prove that he is inconsequent. The meaning ascribed to the phrase in question would be out of place even if it were legitimate to turn a perfect passive participle into a present active one. The notion to be established is that of a uniform, inseparable essence, which does not consist of parts, and is therefore

* Τὸ ἀστεῖον. † Μένειν. ‡ Διαμένειν. § Καταμενεῖ.
|| Gen. vi. 3. Gigant., 5-7 (I. 265-6). See also §§ 11 and 12.
¶ Pp. 161 sq. ** P. 242.
†† Τὸ πάντη δι' ὅλων ἐκπεπληρωμένον.

not lessened by communication, and this is presented under the figure of a substance which has been so completely filled throughout that there are no interstices such as mark a divisible object; you may take from it, as from a flame, and still it remains exactly as it was.

We need not dwell further on the relation of the Spirit to man, or consider its bearing on prophecy, till we treat of the higher anthropology. Sufficient has been said to show that it is ontologically the same as the Logos, though in its higher sense it is used of the Logos only in connection with mankind. The latter term is generally preferred, and Gfrörer points out that πνεῦμα is adopted only where it occurs in the text of Scripture which is under discussion.* We may now pass on to a term of more immediate interest.

Philo, still following the example of the Stoics, frequently speaks, not only of the Logos, but of Logoi. A few instances of the use of the latter term will make it apparent that these Logoi are partial or limited expressions of the universal Logos. The Logos, we are told, is compared to a river, on account of the perennial flow of Logoi and ordinances,† by which God-loving souls are nourished.‡ So the high-priest, who is a recognized symbol of the Logos,§ is said to be "the father of sacred Logoi."|| These figures represent with sufficient clearness the logical dependence of the Logoi on the general principle of Reason. This dependence is further exemplified by the occasional interchange of the singular and plural, the former exhibiting in its unity what the latter resolves into its parts. Thus the deeds of the wise man differ not from divine Logoi, because he walks in the steps of the Logos. If, it is argued, the Law is divine Reason, and the virtuous man keeps the Law, he keeps Reason also; so that the Logoi of God are the actions of the wise man.¶ Here the Logos is used in its ethical relation.

* I. p. 242. † Or opinions, δογμάτων. ‡ Post. Cain., 37 (I. 250).
§ See Migrat. Abr., 18 (I. 452); Prof. 20 (I. 562). || Somn., II. 28 (I. 683).
¶ Migrat. Abr., 23 (I. 456). Cf. § 31, p. 463.

The entire life of the good man is controlled by Reason, but his particular acts correspond to special phases of that Reason, so that the Logoi become, as it were, the special precepts of the one rational code which constitutes the law of nature. Hence the soul is nourished with unearthly and incorruptible Logoi, which God showers from that lofty and pure nature which he has called heaven,* the Logos pregnant with divine lights.† With this close relationship, they may well borrow a characteristic epithet of the Logos, and be described as "the right words of wisdom."‡ They must share the same divine attribute, and therefore, when they ascend and descend through the soul, they do not throw it down, but descend with it, out of humanity and compassion towards our race, "for neither God nor divine Reason is a cause of injury."§ Like the Logos, they are not heard, but seen with the eye of the soul.‖ Like it, too, they come to our knowledge before we rise to the highest apprehension of God. Abraham, the wise man, always desiring to understand the Sovereign of the universe, first converses with divine Logoi.¶ So also Jacob, when he came into Charran, sensible perception, met not God, but the divine Logos; for God, not disdaining to come into sensible perception,** sends his own Logoi to assist the lovers of virtue; and they heal the infirmities of the soul, laying down sacred admonitions as immovable laws. Accordingly, when he has entered into sensible perception, he meets no longer God, but the Logos of God.††

The above statements, while proving the subordination of the Logoi to universal Reason, direct our attention to another point, which will become more striking as we proceed. The

* In allusion to Ex. xvi. 4, "I shower upon you loaves from heaven."
† Leg. All., III. 56 (I. 119), and § 34, p. 108.
‡ Οἱ σοφίας ὀρθοὶ λόγοι, Somn., I. 34 (I. 651). See also Prof., 33 (I. 573), ὀρθοὶ καὶ τροφιμώτατοι λόγοι.
§ Somn. 23 (I. 643).   ‖ Migrat. Abr. 9 (I. 443).   ¶ Post. Cain., 6 (I. 229).
** Οὐ γὰρ ἀπαξιῶν ὁ θεὸς εἰς αἴσθησιν ἔρχεσθαι. The context, as well as Philo's prevailing view, seems to require ἀξιῶν instead of ἀπαξιῶν.
†† Somn. I. 12 (I. 631).

subdivisions of the Logos have hitherto been described as powers or ideas, and with these accordingly the Logoi must be identified. Philo, however, uses the latter term especially to denote the rational and ethical thoughts which present themselves in the mind, and serve to direct the life of man, and we can only appeal to a few passages in which the identity of the Logoi and the powers is immediately apparent. One is that which we last noticed, where converse with the sacred Logoi is attributed to the fact that God imparts mental representations, no longer of himself, but of the powers. A similar interchange takes place in the previous passage about Abraham: the divine Logoi, when referred to in their peculiar relation to God, become "the creative and punitive powers." Again, when the high-priest is described as the father of sacred Logoi, it is added that some of these are overseers and guardians of the affairs of nature, and others are ministers of God, desiring to kindle the heavenly flame. The former of these two classes must be the cosmical powers or ideas, the latter the ethical laws which present themselves in human consciousness.* As the overseers of nature they are equivalent to the "seminal Logoi" of the Stoics; and yet, for some reason, Philo never avails himself of this term. The only place where it occurs is in a speech which is put into the mouth of the Emperor Caius.† There is, however, at least one passage which proves that the notion expressed by it was not foreign to Philo's thought. In speaking of the creation of plants he says that

"The fruits were not only food for animals, but were also preparations for the continual production of their like, containing the seminal substances in which exist, obscure and unseen, the Logoi of the universe, becoming, however, clear and manifest in the revolutions of seasons. For God intended nature to run the long race, immortalizing genera, and giving them a share of eternity."‡

---

* For the reason why Philo gives this interpretation to the children of the high-priest, see Keferstein, p. 141 sqq. As it does not advance our philosophical doctrine, we need not dwell upon it.

† Leg. ad Cai., 8 (II. 553). ‡ Mundi Op., 13 (I. 9).

The Logoi here must be the rational laws in accordance with which everything is evolved, and of which the most striking exemplification is found in the seed; or, in more logical phrase, they are the permanent essences which constitute genera. They are thus the precise equivalents of the powers or ideas. The comparison of natural processes to the long race refers to the way in which nature, as it were, doubles back upon its own course, and returns to its original position. The seed is at once the starting-point and the goal in the life of the plant, so that the same conditions are continually reproduced, and the permanence of the type, idea, or Logos in each thing is secured.

In one other passage the word Logoi seems to be used quite in the Stoical sense, if not indeed in express reference to the Stoics. Philo is speaking of different forms of error.

> Some denied the reality of immaterial ideas, and thereby virtually denied the existence of qualities. Others went farther, and along with ideas rejected the existence of God, declaring that he was only *said* to exist for the sake of benefiting men. A third class took exactly the opposite course, and, although pursuing atheism, nevertheless, owing to their reverence for that which seemed to be everywhere present and to survey all things, introduced a multitude of male and female, older and younger beings, filling the cosmos with a polyarchy of Logoi, in order to cut away the belief in the one really existing God from the understanding of men.*

The parallelism which is here expressed between the ideas or their resulting qualities and the Logoi determines the meaning of the latter: they are the rational principles which, dwelling within material objects, make them what they are; and Philo's objection is not to the philosophical assertion of their existence, but to their elevation into independent, personal powers which superseded in men's worship the one only God.

In other passages where the Logoi are brought into connection with the theory of ideas they describe, not cosmical,

---

* Sacrificant., 13 (II. 261-2).

but human relations. "The wise man .... dwells as in a native land, in intelligible virtues, which God speaks, not differing from divine Logoi."* The Logoi here must be the uttered thoughts, or divinely expressed ideals of virtue, in which the good are able to participate. These, of course, are species of the one supreme virtue or Reason, and hence the number of specific virtues corresponds with that of the Logoi. This notion is worked out in an allegorical interpretation of a passage in Deuteronomy : †

"Ask thy father, and he will report to thee, thy elders, and they will tell thee ; when the Most High divided the nations, when he distributed the sons of Adam, he set boundaries of the nations according to the number of the angels of God,‡ and his people Jacob became the portion of the Lord, Israel the allotment of his inheritance." Father and elders cannot be meant literally, for they know no more than ourselves about the division of the nations. Therefore the reference must be to right Reason, the father of our soul, and to the divine Logoi, our elders, which were before everything earthly. It was these that first fixed the boundaries of virtue, and to these we must go for the necessary information. When God apportioned and walled off the nations of the soul, he made the boundaries of the offspring of virtue equal in number to the angels; "for as many as are the Logoi of God, so many are the nations and species of virtue." The specific virtues belong to the servants, but Israel, the chosen genus, to the sovereign.§

The relation of the Logoi to angels will be considered farther on ; at present we only notice their identification with the divine ethical ideas of which the several species of virtue among men are the counterparts.

As the Logos is the rational law of the universe, so the Logoi, considered as ethical ideas, are the laws, precepts, or admonitions by which the soul ought to be governed. The term is used in this sense very frequently ; but as the passages throw no important light on Philo's philosophy, it will be sufficient to cite a few by way of example, and content ourselves with a bare reference to the remainder. The divine Logoi are the manna, the heavenly food, by which men may be

* Conf. Ling., 17 (I. 417). † xxxii. 7-9.
‡ According to the LXX reading. § Post. Cain., 25-6 (I. 241-2).

nourished,* "the immortal words of science and wisdom."† "In regard to justice and every virtue there is an ancestral law and ancient ordinance. But what else are laws and ordinances than nature's sacred Logoi, possessing firmness and fixity of themselves, so as not to differ from oaths?"‡ Hence, the promise made to Abraham assumed the character of an oath, for "the Logoi of God are oaths and laws of God and most sacred ordinances."§ In this sense the term is strictly applicable to the Ten Commandments. These were Logoi, not only in the ordinary sense according to which all rational statements are Logoi, but as the immediate expression of divine ideas, "the ten generic laws,"∥ or "generic summaries, roots and principles, of the countless individual laws,"¶ spoken by God with that mysterious voice which, unlike the human, pierces with subtle swiftness the ears of the inspired understanding.**

The only remaining question affecting the Logoi is involved in the one which we have reserved in regard to the supreme Logos, namely, whether Philo regarded the latter as a distinct person. This question is not raised by the philosopher himself, and it may be that his conception of personality was not very strictly defined. Zeller's caution†† against judging of this matter from the postulates of our modern thought is

* Congr. erud. gr., 30 (I. 544).   † Migrat. Abr. 14 (I. 448).
‡ Spec. Leg., II. 4 (II. 272).
§ Leg. All., III. 72 (I. 127-8). See also Leg. All., III. 4 (I. 90); SS. Ab. et Cain., 38 (I. 189); Conf. Ling., 13 (I. 413-14); Somn., I. 34 (I. 650-1); Dec. Orac., 3 (II. 182); Praem. et Poen., 14 (II. 421); cf. Prof., 25 (I. 566), where the bread from heaven, the ῥῆμα, is equivalent to ἡ θεία σύνταξις.
∥ Quis. rer. div. her., 35 (I. 496).   ¶ Congr. erud. gr., 21 (I. 536).
** Dec. Orac., 9 (II. 185-6). See also § 29, p. 205; § 33, p. 208; De Circumcisione, 1 (II. 210); Mutat. Nom., 3 (I. 582).

†† III. ii. p. 378 sq. Zeller himself, I cannot but think, falls to some extent under his own rule. He says that people assume either that Philo's Logos is a person outside of God, or that he is only God under a definite relation. His own solution is that "according to Philo's view he is both, but for this very reason neither exclusively." Zeller thus admits that there is no other alternative, and so imposes upon Philo a contradiction of the most glaring kind. According to the exposition which we have given, the modern alternative may

perfectly just; and if we find that Philo habitually united notions which to our minds are totally incompatible, we must only endeavour to escape from our own sharpness of definition into his cloudy and vague speculation. Nevertheless we ought not to thrust this inconsistency upon him unless we are constrained to do so by a faithful exegesis. In this exegesis we have only to estimate the value of single passages and single expressions, and are not driven by the demands of the philosophy itself now to volatilize the Logos into a divine attribute and again to condense it into a person standing between God and man. In this our position differs from Zeller's. According to him the confused changes of meaning belong to the very essence of the philosophy, and he is therefore less ready to admit the plea of poetical personification in particular instances. But according to our view the separate personality of the Logos would be a purely disturbing element, and introduce a quite needless perplexity into an otherwise coherent system, and therefore we shall be inclined to make a large allowance for Philo's bold and figurative style.

When the same question came before us in connection with the divine powers, we noticed Philo's extreme fondness for personification, and we must bear in mind the instances which were then adduced. We may add here a few examples of the personification of the Logos, or, if it be thought by any that it is really regarded as a person, of the ascription to it of a clearly figurative kind of personality. The fool, it is said, casts off "the charioteer and umpire Reason," while a man of the opposite character chooses "divine Reason as his pilot." That these expressions are metaphorical is evident, and that

be dismissed. The Thought of God permanently impressed upon the universe cannot be properly described as God under a definite relation any more than the shape of York Minster can be described as the architect who conceived it; but neither is it a person outside of God, or even possessed of any abiding reality apart from God. This is neither a modern conception nor an illogical mixture of two modern conceptions.

no conception of real personality was attached to them by Philo may be inferred from his presently substituting for Logos "the rational part of the soul" and "rational nature."* In another passage the Logos is symbolized by the river which "makes glad the city of God,"† the soul of the wise man, in which God is said to walk as in a city, for Scripture says, "I will walk in you and will be God in you."‡ "And for a blessed soul holding forth the most sacred goblet, its own reflection,§ who is it that pours the sacred measuring-cups of true good-cheer except Reason, the cupbearer and toastmaster of God? Though it differs not from the drink, but is itself unmixed in brightness, ... the ambrosial potion of good-cheer, that we ourselves, too, may make use of poetical terms."|| The succession of metaphors here is alone sufficient to show how remote is the idea of real personality, though it of course does not exclude it. Again, "the moderator Reason,"¶ arming itself with the virtues and their ordinances, attacks and mightily vanquishes the nine arbitrary governments of the four passions and the five senses.** Elsewhere we learn that "the right Reason of nature has the power at once of a father and of a husband;" and this statement is exemplified by its relations to the soul, in which, among other things, it appears as a "physician."†† By another figure "the right Reason of nature" becomes "a military officer,"‡‡ in whose ranks the good man ought to be enrolled.§§ Even the logos or speech of man does not escape from Philo's tendency to personify: it is not only the defensive armour and panoply of men, but their "spear-bearer" and "champion."||||

This fondness for personification was strengthened by the

* Migrat. Abr., 12 (I. 446). † Ps. xlv. 4; LXX.
‡ Lev. xxvi. 12. Philo reads ἐν ὑμῖν θεός, instead of ὑμῶν θεός.
§ Λογισμός. || Somn., II. 37 (I. 691).
¶ Τὸν σωφρονιστὴν λόγον. ** Abr., 41 (II. 35).
†† Spec. Leg., II. 7 (II. 275). ‡‡ Ταξιάρχης.
§§ Human., 17 (II. 396).
|||| Δορυφόρος, προαγωνιστής. Somn., I. 17 (I. 636).

system of ᴇ   .cal interpretation. The persons of Old Testament h: ry become the symbols of abstract qualities, and consequently the allegory is frequently responsible for the ascription of personal attributes to the general idea. The Logos comes in for its share of this treatment. Abraham is first the representative of "the wise man," and then, by a further abstraction, of the distinctive quality of the wise man, "divine Reason," the parent of laughter and joy, for this is the signification of Isaac. A little farther on in the same passage it is said that, "The Lord begat Isaac." This is the explanation of the words "The Lord made laughter for me."* If we require a rigid consistency, the Logos thus becomes identical with the Lord, but it is very doubtful whether this is intended. "The Lord," in a subordinate sense, stands everywhere else for another power than the Logos, and therefore I believe it is here used in its highest meaning. What proceeds from the Logos proceeds from God, "the Father of the perfect nature." But if we decide that the Logos is the "Lord," this identification results from the language of Scripture, and can no more prove the personality of the Logos than its previous identification with Abraham.†

Again, Melchizedek, the "righteous king" of peace, or Salem, gives injunctions by which men may have a good voyage through life, "being steered by the good artificer and pilot," who is "right Reason." Melchizedek also brings forward wine, and gives drink to souls; "for Reason is a priest, having the Self-existent as his portion, and entertaining high and sublime and magnificent thoughts about him," for this is the meaning of the statement that "he is a priest of the most high God."‡ To entertain thoughts is a characteristic of personality; but it is evident that the personality here is introduced to suit the statement about Melchizedek. Nevertheless, the ascription of thoughts to the Logos must have some sort

* Gen. xxi. 6. † Leg. All., III. 77 (I. 130-1).
‡ Gen. xiv. 18; Leg. All., III. 25-6 (I. 102-3).

of justification in experience, and a conside. of this may throw a clearer light upon our subject. The ;os is known to consciousness as the very essence of our personality; it is by participation in reason that we are persons, and not merely animals or things. Our sublime thoughts about God are expressions of this reason; and wherever right reason holds sway among men, there elevated thoughts about God arise. It is, I think, on this ground that Philo declares that " God has given to his Logos the knowledge of himself as a native land to dwell in."* The Logos, in the connection where these words occur, stands in opposition to him who has committed involuntary manslaughter, and must therefore be viewed in relation to its function in the human mind. The meaning seems to be that whereas a man who has involuntarily committed a crime, owing to the absence of reason,† can attain to the knowledge of God only as an alien flies to a refuge, reason apprehends God by virtue of its birthright, and lives in this superior knowledge as in its native clime. Such are the facts of experience on which Philo might justly rest many statements similar to that which we are considering. But though the Logos assumed personality the moment it appeared in finite individual minds, it does not at all follow that the abstract idea was conceived of as a person. A pantheistic philosophy can represent God as impersonal, and yet as evolved into personality at the various centres of finite consciousness. This mode of conception would suit all that we have hitherto learned of Philo's doctrine of the Logos. Philo, however, avoided pantheism by his belief that God was transcendent above the Logos. From the depths of the divine personality flowed forth the rational energy which pervaded creation, and in this its universal form it had no personality distinct from that of God; but as it passed on and took possession of finite minds, personality once more appeared. Thus we meet with consciousness both at the upper and the lower ends, and the Logos is not a

* Prof., 14 (I. 557). † See § 21, p. 563.

person, but ;   ..n essence of personality derived from God and communi ..ed to man, and constituting the intermediate link of energy by which the infinite person imparts himself to his finite children. This explanation fully satisfies the passage which we are considering; and, if it is not disproved by other passages, it will go far towards reconciling the apparent inconsistencies of language by which interpreters of Philo are so much perplexed.

Another representative of the Logos is Moses. He, like Melchizedek, stands for the Logos, not in its cosmical aspects, but as the common reason of mankind, that higher principle of personality by which we are brought into contact with divine thoughts and precepts. He is "the prophet Logos" which bids us remember the way by which the Lord God has led us.[*] In even less ambiguous phrase, he is "the purest mind,[†] the truly excellent," inspired at once with legislative and prophetic functions, the genus of the Levitical tribe, the adherent of truth.[‡] By such language the general properties of human reason are described, and it is evident that we are moving in the region of abstract ideas. This is still more apparent when we find that Aaron represents the uttered Logos, the faculty of speech in man, which Moses, the mind or understanding, uses as his interpreter.[§] "Moses, the prophetic Logos, says, 'When I go forth from the city,' the soul—for this is the city of the animal, giving laws and customs—'I will spread out my hands'[||] and spread forth and unfold all my actions to God, calling him as witness and overseer of each." Now, all the disturbing voices of the senses cease "when the understanding has gone forth from the city of the soul, and attached its actions and purposes to God." And the hands of Moses are heavy,[¶] because the actions of the wise man are difficult to move or shake, for they are supported by Aaron, the

[*] Congr. erud. gr., 30 (I. 543).
[‡] Ib. § 24, p. 538.
[||] Ex. ix. 29.

[†] Ὁ καθαρώτατος νοῦς.
[§] Migrat. Abr., 14 (I. 448).
[¶] Ex. xvii. 12.

Logos, and Or,* which is light, that is, true ence Aaron, when he comes to an end, that is, is made fect, goes up into Or, which is light,† for the end of Logos [speech] is truth.‡ These instances sufficiently illustrate the strange blending of historical persons with the abstract properties of human reason and speech, which justly induces us to give a very wide latitude to Philo's use of personification.§

From individual men we come to a class. It was the function of the priests to act for men in their divine relations, and therefore they naturally represented reason, the true priest of mankind, while the high-priest, who presided over them all, stood, not only for human reason, but for the universal, cosmical Logos. In reference to the procedure enjoined upon the priest in matters of jealousy,|| it is said that "the priest and prophet Reason has been commanded to set the soul before God."¶ That the high-priesthood signifies something higher than a human office is proved by an injunction connected with the cities of refuge. The involuntary slayer of a man was to remain in his retreat till the death of the high-priest.** This, says Philo, is a most unequal punishment, and therefore it cannot be intended literally. The high-priest is not a man, but divine Reason, which arrays itself in the cosmos as a garment, and lives in the soul as a judge. So long as this most sacred Reason survives in the soul, no involuntary change can enter it; but if it dies, in the sense of being separated from our soul, there is an immediate lapse into voluntary faults.††
In another connection we have seen that the dress of the high-priest symbolized the several constituents of the universe. The high-priest himself is the Logos, the bearer of the powers.

* Ὤρ in the LXX.   † Num. xx. 25.   ‡ Leg. All., III. 14, 15 (I. 95-6).

§ For Moses, θεσμοθέτῃ λόγῳ, see Migrat. Abr., 5 (I. 440); and for Aaron, ὁ γεγωνὸς λόγος προφητεύων διανοίᾳ, one of αἱ τοῦ βασιλεύειν ἀξίου νοῦ δορυφόροι δυνάμεις, ib., § 31, p. 462; also Leg. All., I. 24 (I. 59), compared with Leg. All., III. 33 (I. 108).

|| Num. v. 15 sqq.   ¶ Cherub., 5 (I. 141).
** Num. xxxv. 25.   †† Prof., 20-1 (I. 561-3).

If, says Philo, you examine the high-priest Reason, you will find his raiment variously wrought out of both intelligible and perceptible powers. Two examples will suffice, taken from the two extremes, the head and the feet. On the head is a pure golden plate having the impression of a seal, " holiness to the Lord;" and on the feet, on the extremity of the undergarment are bells and flowered work.* That seal is an idea of ideas, according to which God stamped the cosmos, and is of course incorporeal and intelligible; but the flowered work and the bells are symbols of perceptible qualities, of which seeing and hearing are the criteria.† We must notice here the want of consistency in the figure. The idea of ideas is, as we have learned, the Logos, and it is suitably represented by the seal with which intelligible qualities were stamped. But at the beginning of the comparison the high-priest himself is the Logos, and thus becomes identical with the seal which was impressed upon his golden plate. How evident it is that we are dealing with logical, and not with personal relations. The same universal thought or genus is at once the bearer and the seal of all more partial ideas, bearing them as its species and at the same time impressing them with its essence. We cannot be too careful in distinguishing the serious doctrines of Philo from the strange garb in which they are so often clothed.

We need notice in this connection only one other passage where the cosmical and the human reason are distinguished. "There are two temples of God: one this cosmos, in which also is a high-priest, his first-begotten divine Reason; and the second, rational soul, of which the priest is the true man, whose perceptible imitation is he who offers the ancestral prayers and sacrifices."‡

From this cloud-land of shifting and dissolving imagery, where no one, I presume, will maintain that the limits of poetical personification are transgressed, we pass to the more

* LXX; Ex. xxviii. 30, 32.   † Migrat. Abr., 18 (I. 452).
‡ Somn., I. 37 (I. 653). See also Gig., 11 (I. 269).

serious arguments for the personality of the Logos. Some of these we have anticipated in our own exposition of Philo's doctrine, where we have explained certain terms consistently with the general scheme of thought; and in regard to them I need do little more than refer back to what has been already said. This is the case with the titles "God," "Son of God," "Image of God." Laughter also is the son of God, and we can hardly suppose that Philo looked upon laughter as a person. Moreover, the variety under which the connection is conceived proves that we are dealing only with the figurative relations of thought. God is the husband of Wisdom, and yet Wisdom is the daughter of God, the mother of the Logos, and the father of instruction.

More stress may be laid upon the fact that the Logos is the image of God and the archetype of man; for, if the two extremes be persons, must not the connecting link also be a person? This question demands a fuller consideration, and our reply to it will throw an instructive light upon our previous conclusions. No one, I suppose, ever believed that the number seven was a person, and yet that number is an image of God. Not only does this statement bring it into connection with the Logos, but our fullest information respecting the essence of the Logos is found in its conformity to seven. It is, in fact, "the Logos of seven,"* "the holy Logos according to seven,"† "the perfect Logos moving according to seven."‡ Philo's treatment of the number seven, therefore, may be expected to illustrate his meaning when he speaks of the Logos. We must next observe that by an image need be meant no more than an intellectual conception possessing a property similar to that which distinguishes the object of which it is the image. Thus, the number two is the image of matter, because, like matter, it is divisible. Two is no doubt selected rather than any higher number because it gives us the most elementary notion of

* Mundi Op., 40 (I. 28).   † Leg. All. I. 6 (I. 46).   ‡ Ib. § 8, p. 47.

division. Three is the image of solid body, because the solid has three dimensions.* Seven is the image of God for the following reason. Among the numbers up to ten it alone neither produces nor is produced, that is to say, it is not formed from any other number by multiplication, nor is any other number formed by multiplication from it. It is, therefore, the motherless virgin, who is said to have sprung from the head of Zeus, and remains immovable, for all genesis consists in movement. But the elder Ruler and Sovereign alone neither moves nor is moved, and consequently seven would be properly called his image.† Let us see, then, how this image is impressed upon creation. By the number seven "all things are brought to perfection." It has numerous "ideas" or relations connected with numbers, harmonies, and ratios, on which we need not dwell. "But its nature extends also to the whole visible substance, heaven and earth, the limits of the universe; for what part of the things in the cosmos is not enamoured of seven, being subdued by the love and desire of seven?"‡ This number is "the idea of the planets," as unity is of the fixed sphere. For the immaterial heaven, the pattern of the visible, consists of unity and seven; and so the actual sky has been made out of indivisible and divisible nature. Of the indivisible, "unity is the overseer"; "seven is the guardian" of the divisible, wherein revolve the seven planets.§ But even the fixed sphere is not wholly exempt from the dominion of seven; for the constellations of the Bear and the Pleiades consist each of seven stars. Nor is this sway perceived only in the numbers of the heavenly bodies, but also in the circles by which the parts of the sky are zoned off, the Arctic, Antarctic, Summer tropic, Winter tropic, Equinoctial, Zodiac, and Galaxy. The phases of the moon, moreover, are regulated by weeks, consisting of seven days. This same "Logos of seven, beginning from above,

---

* Leg. All., I. 2 (I. 44). † Mundi Op., 33 (I. 23-4).
‡ Mundi Op., 34 and 38 (I. 24 and 27). § Dec. Orac., 21 (II. 198).

has descended also to us, visiting mortal genera." The part of the soul which is different from the sovereign principle has a sevenfold division. The internal and external organs of the body are each seven. The head has seven most essential parts —two eyes, two ears, two nostrils, and the mouth. The things perceived by the eye are of seven kinds—body, interval, form, size, colour, motion, rest. The modifications of the voice are seven—acute, grave, circumflex, aspirated, smooth, long, and short. There are seven movements—up, down, right, left, forwards, backwards, and in a circle. "The power" of this number has also come to the best of the sciences, grammar and music. The seven-stringed lyre yields the famous harmonies, and is almost the queen of musical instruments. Among the letters in grammar there are seven vowels, and to these pronunciation is due, for they "inspire with their own power" the semi-vowels and consonants, so that what could not otherwise be sounded becomes vocal.* The seventh day, on which God is said to have ceased from his works and to have begun to contemplate what was made, is "a pattern of the duty of philosophising," as the six days are a pattern of the appointed time for our actions. "Let us not, then, pass by such an archetype of the best modes of life, the practical and the contemplative, but, always looking to it, engrave clear images and types on our own understandings, making mortal nature as far as possible like immortal."† We need not now be surprised to learn that this is the great prerogative of seven, that "through it especially the Maker and Father of the universe is manifested; for, as through a mirror, the mind forms to itself a representation of God acting and creating the cosmos and superintending the universe."‡ All this hardly requires comment; it is itself the best comment on Philo's doctrine of the Logos. We now see more plainly how a thought may be an image of God, and how it may be impressed not only on

* Mundi Op., 38 sqq. (I. 27 sqq.); Leg. All., I. 4-5 (I. 45-6).
† Dec. Orac., 20 (II. 197).   ‡ Ib., § 21, p. 198.

the universe, but on the bodily and mental constitution of man, on the sciences which he pursues, and on the life which he ought to lead; and if we cannot recognize a person in the number seven, that image and mirror of God, which meets the eye amid the shining spheres, and looks upon us from the human face, neither ought we to insist on discovering one in that larger Logos which embraces seven and every other rational conception, simply because it is the image of God and the archetype of man.

It may, however, be said that when the Logos, as the image of God, is described as "the mind* above us," of which our mind is a copy,† its personality is necessarily implied. I think it would be truer to say that throughout this passage (the only one, if I am not mistaken, where the highest Logos is described as mind) Philo uses the word "Mind" only as a variation of Logos, and means by it simply that rational quality which we, in our complete personality, possess. It is indeed described as "an intelligent and rational nature," which rather suggests an abstract quality than a concrete person; and if it is said that the mind in each of us "is strictly and truly man," this is founded on the statement that "God made man according to his image," and implies no more than that man is to be distinguished by his characteristic quality, just as we might say, it is the faculty of reason that makes us human. That the term mind‡ is used in this abstract sense may be shown by a few examples. "Intellectual power," it is said, "is peculiar to the mind." This rational or logical faculty is twofold, "that according to which we are rational, participating in mind,§ and that according to which we discourse."|| If "the mind" is to be understood in a concrete sense in the first instance, yet when we are said to participate in it, it is obviously regarded

---

* Νοῦς.
† Quis rer. div. her., 48 (I. 505-6). Νοῦς τε ὁ ἐν ἡμῖν καὶ ὁ ὑπὲρ ἡμᾶς, at the end of the section.
‡ Νοῦς. § Νοῦ μετέχοντες. || Leg. All., II. 7 (I. 71).

as an abstract quality or power. It is, of course, in Philo's philosophy not the less real on that account, but the notion of distinct personality attaching to it becomes evanescent. From this more general signification the word passes on to denote the meaning or purport of a sentence or statement, and it is occasionally thus employed by Philo.* These instances prove that the mere adoption of the term mind as descriptive of the Logos is no guarantee of personality. How little the latter conception entered into Philo's thought in dealing with this subject is further apparent from one or two passages which deserve separate notice. In one the part of the soul which allies us to God is described as " the power which flowed forth from the rational fountain." This had as its essence " a stamp and impression of divine power, which Moses calls by a proper name, ' Image,' intimating that God is the archetype of rational nature, and man an imitation and copy—not the two-natured animal, but the best species of the soul, which has been called mind and reason."† Here mind or reason is regarded as one of the powers of the soul, which bears the stamp of that higher Reason or rational nature which is a divine power. This is the passage, before referred to, where it is said that God does not participate in, but rules the rational power. He is its transcendent source, while man becomes rational by participation, by drawing from the universal stream of reason those rills of mental power which flow down into individual life. The notion of personality becomes still more remote when we discover that Philo carefully distinguishes between "the individual mind,"‡ and "the idea of mind," the latter being the pre-existent archetype and pattern of the former, and that in his view it was the ideal, heavenly, intelligible, incorporeal man that was made according to the image of God.§ Thus

* See SS. Ab. et Cain., 19 (I. 176); 37 (I. 188); Mutat. Nom., 8 (I. 587); Fragm., II. 678; in all four instances, τοιοῦτον ὑποβάλλει νοῦν: Animal. Sacr. idon., 5 (II. 241), μηνύεται δὲ καὶ νοῦς ἕτερος.

† Quod det. pot. ins., 23 (I. 207). ‡ Νοῦν τὸν ἄτομον.

§ Mundi Op., 46 (I. 32); Leg. All., I. 1 (I. 43); § 9, p. 47; § 12, p. 49.

we are completely transported from the realm of concrete persons into the most general conceptions of abstract thought; the Logos, conceived as mind, is simply the rational power of God, from which is copied the generic idea of human reason.

We pass on to another expression which is liable to be misunderstood. We hear a few times of "the suppliant Logos."* It is important to observe that the Greek word denotes, not an intercessor, but one who supplicates on his own behalf, because Keferstein imports into it the notion of intercession,† and thus suggests a mediatorial office for the Logos to which the term does not properly correspond. In the first passage which we shall notice it is evident that no such metaphysical doctrine is contained.

The statement in Scripture that "their cry went up to God,"‡ bears witness to the grace of the Self-existent; "for unless he powerfully called to himself the suppliant word,§ it would not have gone up; that is, it would not have been lifted up, and increased, and begun to go aloft, having escaped the lowness of earthly things." The subsequent words, "Behold, the shouting of the sons of Israel has come to me,"‖ show that the supplication reached as far as God, which it would not have done unless "he who called was kind."¶

Here "the suppliant Logos" is nothing but the cry of the oppressed Israelites. In the next passage the sense is more general, but the reference is still obviously to human supplication, for the Logos in question

Is received " out of the most central and sovereign portion of the soul," as the Levites out of the midst of the sons of Israel, for " the word which has fled to God and become his suppliant is named Levite."**

Elsewhere Moses, who, as we have seen, represents the universal reason of mankind, becomes the suppliant Logos.

The just man contributes abundantly to the benefit of mankind, and what he does not find in his own resources he asks God for; and God opens the heavenly treasure and showers down blessings. "These things

---

* Τὸν ἱκέτην λόγον. † Eine eigentliche fürbittende Intercession, p. 103.
‡ Ex. ii. 23. § Λόγος. ‖ Ex. iii. 9.
¶ Leg. All., III. 76 (I. 130). ** SS. Ab. et Cain., 36 (I. 186).

he is accustomed to give, not turning away from the Logos that supplicates him,* for it is said in another place, when Moses offered supplication, 'I am propitious to them according to thy word.'"†

This use of Logos receives an admirable illustration from a passage to which Keferstein‡ calls attention.

We cannot [it is there said] give genuine thanks to God, as most men suppose, through offerings and sacrifices, but through praises and hymns, not those sung by the voice, but those which the invisible and pure mind accompanies. There is an old story, invented by wise men, and handed down traditionally, to the following effect. When the Creator had finished the whole cosmos, he asked one of his interpreters whether he missed anything in the entire circle of creation. He answered that all things were perfect and full, and he sought only one thing, "their praiser Logos,"§ who should not so much praise as proclaim the exceeding excellence even in what seemed smallest and most obscure; for the declaration of the works of God was their all-sufficient praise. The Father of the universe approved of what was said, and created the musical and hymnful race.||

It is evident that in all these passages we are concerned only with certain functions of human reason and speech, and that to clothe the logos in them with personality would simply make them unintelligible. Do they, however, furnish the key to the remaining passage, in which the Logos appears in its more universal aspect? I think they do. The passage is part of one on which we have already commented at some length,¶ and to which we shall have to return once more at a later stage of our inquiry, where the Logos is described as standing in the midst between God and creation. It is there said that the Logos is a suppliant of the mortal with the incorruptible, and an ambassador** of the sovereign to the subject.†† So far as any literal supplication is intended, it is probable that the function of human reason which we have just described is

---

* Τὸν ἱκέτην ἑαυτοῦ λόγον. Though Keferstein, p. 108, thinks such a construction sehr hart, I think ἑαυτοῦ here is the object; for to make it the possessor of the Logos gives no good sense, and the construction is precisely parallel to ὁ ἱκέτης αὐτοῦ γεγονὼς λόγος in the passage last cited.

† 'Ρῆμα. Num. xiv. 20. Migrat. Abr., 21 (I. 454-5).   ‡ P. 107.

§ Τὸν ἐπαινέτην αὐτῶν λόγον. || Plantat. Noe, 30 (I. 348).

¶ P. 101 sqq.   ** Πρεσβευτής.   †† Quis rer. div. her., 42 (I. 501).

meant. But it is easy to extend the figure to the whole material world. As Paul could hear the groaning and witness the travailing of creation, so to Philo not only man with articulate voice, but the universe, through its struggle into forms of reason, seemed to supplicate God, and to direct towards him the pleadings of a Thought which was conscious of its divine birth. This suppliant Thought, this aspiration of the visible cosmos to realize its ideal, was, as it were, an assurance to the Creator that the genus was imperishable, and would never choose disorder instead of order. On the other hand, the constant flow of Reason from its divine source was a pledge that God would never overlook his own work. To find in this anything but poetical personification, and make the Logos here an individual person, seems to me quite bewildering. Equally strange is Keferstein's conjecture* that in applying the name " Suppliant " to the Logos, Philo is only expressing the opinion of a party in Alexandria, with which he himself did not fully concur, since he describes the function of an ambassador, but gives no explanation of the office of intercessor. The Greek term, however, does not mean an intercessor, and the two functions are sufficiently distinct in the above interpretation. Reason coming from God to man has the character of an ambassador, proclaiming the divine requirements; in ascending from man to God it assumes the guise of a suppliant, praying for fuller light and purer wisdom from the infinite Giver.

Another term of higher interest occurs in Philo—Advocate or Paraclete.† Some of his interpreters believe that he applies this epithet to the Logos; but Keferstein has, I think, shown conclusively that he does not do so.‡ The passage in question is one in which the vestments of the high-priest, when he is engaged in his ministry, are represented as symbolical of the various parts of the cosmos,

"In order that, whenever he goes in to offer the ancestral prayers and sacrifices, all the cosmos may enter with him, through the imitations

* Pp. 102-3. † Παράκλητος. ‡ Pp. 104-5.

which he wears." [Then follows an account of the symbolical meaning of his dress, ending with the breast-plate,* as representing "the Logos which holds together and administers the universe." Then Philo proceeds] "for it was necessary for him who was consecrated to the Father of the cosmos to use as an advocate a son most perfect in virtue, with a view to the amnesty of sins and the supply of most abundant blessings."

It seems pretty clear that the "son" in question is not the Logos, but the cosmos, to which the whole passage refers. This is further apparent from the sequel, in which the Logos is not mentioned.

Another lesson to be learned from the vestments is that the servant of God, if he cannot be worthy of the Maker of the cosmos, should endeavour at least to be worthy of the cosmos, in the imitation of which he is clad ; and bearing its pattern as an image in his understanding, he ought, in a manner, to change from man into conformity with the nature of the cosmos, and to become, if one may say so, a minute cosmos.†

The union of the high-priest with the cosmos, not with the Logos, is evidently the point which is here insisted on. That this interpretation is correct seems placed beyond doubt by a parallel passage. After showing that the sacred robes are "an imitation of the universe," Philo goes on :

"For he wishes the high-priest, first, to have around him a visible image of the universe, that from the continual sight he may make his own life worthy of the nature of the whole ; secondly, that in his ministrations all the cosmos may join with him in the service. And it is most becoming that he who has been consecrated to the Father of the cosmos should bring forward the son also to the service of him who begat it." It follows also that, while the priests of others offer prayers and sacrifices for their own friends and countrymen only, the high-priest of the Jews offers prayers and thanksgiving, not merely for the whole race of men, but also for the several parts of nature, believing the cosmos to be his country.‡

Here there is no mention of the Logos ; it is the cosmos which appears as the son of God, and if it is not called Paraclete, it fulfils the office which is implied by that word, and assists the high-priest in his ministry. But even if the title of

* Τὸ λόγιον. † Vit. Mos., III. 14 (II. 155).
‡ Monarch., II. 6 (II. 227).

"advocate" were given to the Logos, it would not be a proof of personality, for Philo applies the word to that which is certainly not personal. He calls "the conviction* in the soul"† of one who desires to make restitution "an advocate," who accompanies the offender when he goes into the temple to beg for forgiveness.‡ Again, he says that when the scattered Israelites return, under the guidance of a divine vision, they will have "three advocates of reconciliation with the Father": one, "the equity and kindness" of God; secondly, "the holiness of the founders of the nation;" thirdly, their own "improvement."§ These are good examples of Philo's figurative style, and show once more how dangerous it is to infer his belief in the personality of the Logos from mere casual expressions. Our conclusion is that it is more than doubtful whether he ever described the Logos as an "advocate," and certain that if he did it is not thereby proved that he looked upon the Logos as a person.∥

We proceed, finally, to a very important set of passages which are often considered decisive of the question. No fewer than seventeen times the term angel is applied to either the Logos or the Logoi. What, then, can be plainer than that the Logoi are identical with the hierarchy of angels, and are, therefore, persons, with the personal archangel Logos at their head? To those, however, who are familiar with Philo's system of allegorical interpretation, it may happen that this conclusion will not be at once obvious; for possibly the Logos is no more regarded as an angel in reality than Sarah is really virtue or Hagar encyclical education. We cannot come to a decision upon this point without carefully examining the passages; but before we proceed to this task we must make a few general observations.

* Or conscience. † Τὸν κατὰ ψυχὴν ἔλεγχον.
‡ Animal. Sacr. idon., 11 (II. 247). § Exsecrat., 9 (II. 436).
∥ We may here refer once more to the statement, Mundi Op., 6 (I. 5), that God, in determining to create, used no παράκλητος.

It is to be noticed, in the first place, that, with a single exception, Philo never describes the Logos as an angel without the express warrant of some Scriptural passage: the angel, or some equivalent expression, in the text of the Bible is interpreted into the Logos in the same way as Melchizedek, Moses, Aaron, and the high-priest.

Secondly, we must attend to a form of expression which is occasionally used, and is sometimes thought to establish the identity of the Logoi and angels. It is said of the Logos, "Let it be called an angel,"* that is, let it be so called in the passage under consideration. And, again, in relation to the Logoi, it is said, "Whom it is the custom to name† angels."‡ The custom here mentioned refers, I believe, simply and solely to the usage of Scripture, which, in conveying its lessons under a symbolical form, describes as angels the divine words, precepts, laws, or thoughts which visit the human soul. An instructive example of Philo's treatment of Scripture, in this connection, is found in the comment on the statement that the angels of God entered in to the daughters of men.§

The angels enter after the departure of the divine Spirit; for as long as pure rays of wisdom shine in the soul, through which the wise man sees God and his powers, none of those who falsely act as angels enter the reason. But when the light of the understanding is overshadowed, "the companions of darkness" unite with the effeminate passions, which Scripture "has termed daughters of men."‖

It is evident that the angels here are simply the lower thoughts that make the passions fruitful of ill; and no one, I presume, will contend that the passions are persons because Scripture "has termed them daughters."

That this latter mode of speech is agreeable to Philo's practice we may learn from a few other examples. Sometimes

---

* Καλείσθω δὲ ἄγγελος. Vit. Mos., I. 12 (II. 91). † Or to call.

‡ Migrat. Abr., 31 (I. 463), οὓς ὀνομάζειν ἔθος ἀγγέλους: Conf. Ling., 8 (I. 409); Somn., I. 19 (I. 638), οὓς καλεῖν ἔθος ἀγγέλους.

§ So Philo gives the passage, Gen. vi. 4. ‖ Quod Deus immut., 1 (I. 272-3).

he guards his meaning by the insertion of a qualifying word, such as "symbolically." Thus, he says that Scripture "symbolically calls the mind heaven, ... and sensation earth," alluding to the statement that, "the heavens and the earth were finished";* and our "body is called symbolically Hebron."† Again, he speaks of the "Logoi, lovers of prudence and knowledge, whom the Legislator, using a metaphor, calls ransom and first-born," referring to the Levites as the ransom of the first-born.‡ Frequently, however, the qualifying word is left to be supplied by the good sense of the reader. The following are instances. Scripture " has termed § the Logos of God a book," in the statement, " This is the book of genesis of heaven and earth."|| So it "has termed" the idea of mind, or the generic intelligible, "verdure of the field," and it has also "called it 'all.'"¶ Again, it "has termed the mind a fountain of earth, and the senses a face," where it says, " a fountain was going up from the earth, and watering all the face of the earth."** We hear also of "the lofty Logos, pregnant with divine lights, which, accordingly, it has called heaven,"†† where the reference is not immediately apparent in the context. Farther on the allusion is explained in a comment on the passage, " Behold, I shower down for you loaves from heaven,"‡‡ which proves " that the soul is nourished not by earthly and corruptible things, but by Logoi which God rains down from the lofty and pure nature which he has called heaven."|||| In another passage we are told that, " making use

* Gen. ii. 1. Leg. All., I. 1 (I. 43) ; § 9, p. 47, συμβολικῶς, διὰ σημείου.
† Gen. xxxvii. 14. Quod det. pot. ins., 6 (I. 194). See also Leg. All., II. 4 (I. 68), οὐρανὸν δὲ καὶ ἀγρὸν συνωνύμως κέκληκεν, ἀλληγορῶν τὸν νοῦν : Cherub., 18 (I. 150), τμῆμα . . . ὃ κέκληκε προσηγορικῶς μὲν γυναῖκα, ὀνομαστικῶς δὲ Εὔαν, αἰνιττόμενος αἴσθησιν : Ebriet., 25 (I. 372), ἐν τῷ μετὰ σώματος βίῳ, ὃν ἀλληγορῶν καλεῖ στρατόπεδον.
‡ Num. iii. 12. SS. Ab. et Cain., 37 (I. 188).   § Εἴρηκε.
|| Gen. ii. 4. Leg. All., I. 8 (I. 47).
¶ Gen. ii. 5. "Ὁ δὴ καὶ πᾶν κέκληκεν, ib., 9 (I. 47-8).
** Gen. ii. 6. Ib., § 11, pp. 48-9.
†† "Ὃν δὴ κέκληκεν οὐρανόν. Leg. All., III. 34 (I. 108).
‡‡ Ex. xvi. 4.   [''] § 56, p. 119.

of a synonym, he calls this rock manna, the divine Logos, the oldest of things, which is named the most generic 'something.'"* Once more, the human logos, or speech, "which has fled to God and become his suppliant, is named† Levite," in the saying, "Behold, I have taken the Levites from the midst of the sons of Israel."‡ One more example may suffice. In allusion to the statement that " a river goes out from Eden to water the garden," it is said that Scripture "calls the Wisdom of the Self-existent Eden."§ But Philo goes beyond the usage here indicated, and sometimes joins the word Logos immediately to its symbol, and thus combines the literal and allegorical meanings into one presentation. Thus we are told that " the high-priest Logos " is not able to remain always in the holy dwellings,|| and that, if you examine " the high-priest Logos," you will find his dress wrought out of intelligible and perceptible powers.¶ He even goes so far as to make the symbol the direct predicate of the thing symbolized, as when he says, in relation to two forms of character,** that "those sprung from the mother sensation are Ammonites, and those from the father mind are Moabites."†† It is apparent, therefore, that, whether Philo says that the Logos is called an angel, or himself speaks of the angel Logos, the mere form of the expression is not sufficient to identify the two terms,‡‡ and that even their union as subject and predicate may indicate nothing more than an allegorical connection. Before leaving the question of Philo's mode of conveying his thought, we may

* Ex. xvi. 15 and 31. Quod det. pot. ins., 31 (I. 213 sq.).
† 'Ονομάζεται.
‡ Num. iii. 12. SS. Ab. et Cain., 86 (I. 186).
§ Gen. ii. 10. Somn., II. 37 (I. 690). See also the preceding section, τὸν τοῦ Ὄντος λόγον, ὃν διαθήκην ἐκάλεσε.
|| Gigant., 11 (I. 209). ¶ Migrat. Abr., 18 (I. 452).
** Τρόποι. †† Leg. All., III. 25 (I. 103).
‡‡ On the other hand, it does not prevent their identification; for see Conf. Ling., 34 (I. 431), where, speaking of the souls in the air, Philo says, "the oracular Word is accustomed to call these souls angels," and Somn., I. 22 (I. 642), " these [souls] other philosophers are accustomed to call demons, but the sacred Word angels."

remark that the word angel retains in Greek its proper meaning of messenger, and that it is necessary to bear this in mind throughout the following discussion. In our own language it would be no very startling metaphor to say that thought was God's messenger who conveyed to us a knowledge of his will. Philo himself declares that anticipated evil sends forth in advance "alarm and anguish, ill-omened angels."*

Lastly, we must remark that Gfrörer seems to attach great importance to the fact that the narratives in the Pentateuch were believed to be real histories as well as allegories, for he three times calls attention to it.† It is not at once apparent how it follows from this unquestioned fact that the angel who appeared to Hagar was really and literally the Logos, unless it also follows that Hagar herself was really and literally encyclical education. We might even be inclined to suppose that in Philo's conception a personal angel, who could appear and talk to a woman in the wilderness, bore as little resemblance to divine Reason as the woman did to propaedeutical instruction. But as it seems otherwise to Gfrörer, we shall do well, in reviewing the several passages, to bear the literal meaning in mind as well as the allegorical.

We may consider, first, Philo's explanation of the appearance of the angel to Hagar. This subject is introduced at the beginning of the treatise "De Cherubim,"‡ in order to illustrate the statement that God "drove out Adam."§

Why, asks Philo, does the writer now say "drove out" when he had previously said "sent out"?|| The words are carefully chosen; for he who is sent out may return, but he who has been driven out by God incurs an eternal exile. Thus we see that encyclical education Hagar twice went forth from the ruling virtue Sarrha. The first time she returned, for she had run away, and not been banished, and she was brought back to her master's house, "an angel, who is divine Reason, having met her";¶ but the second time she was driven out never to come back. The reason was that in the first instance Abram, "the high father," had not yet changed

* Dec. Orac., 28 (II. 204).
‡ §§ 1-3 (I. 138-140).
|| 'Εξαπέστειλεν, verse 23.
† I. pp. 290, 291, 293.
§ 'Εξέβαλε, Gen. iii. 24.
¶ Gen. xvi. 7 sqq.

16 *

into Abraham, "the elect father of sound," that is, had not ceased to be the natural philosopher and become the wise lover of God, and Sara had not been changed into Sarrha, specific into generic virtue; and therefore Hagar, encyclical education, though she might be eager to run away from the austere life of the virtuous, will return to it again; but when the change takes place, the preliminary branches of instruction called after Hagar will be driven out, and her sophist son, called Ishmael, will be driven out also.* What wonder, then, if, when Adam, the mind, became possessed of folly, an incurable disease, God drove him out for ever from the region of the virtues, when he banished even the sophist and his mother, the teaching of the preliminary branches of education, from wisdom and the wise, whose names he calls Abraham and Sarrha?

This passage does not require much comment. It is evident that all the persons mentioned in it are dissolved into abstract ideas, and that it would be a complete departure from its method, instead of volatilizing the angel into universal Reason, to solidify Reason into a visible angel.

The next passage relating to Hagar is in the "De Profugis," which begins by quoting the narrative of her first flight.

There are three causes of flight : hatred, fear, shame. Hagar fled on account of shame, as is evident from the fact that an "angel, divine Reason, met her, to admonish her what she ought to do." [Presently we are told that] "the friend and counsellor conscience† teaches not only to be ashamed, but also to use courage."‡

Here the angel signifies indifferently divine Reason or conscience, that messenger of God which reminds us of our duty; and it is quite clear that conscience is not literally an external and visible angel. The same interpretation recurs towards the end of the treatise. There it is conscience§ that,

"Speaking to the soul, says to it, 'Whence dost thou come, and whither art thou going?'" And this it does, not because it is in doubt, for an angel may not be ignorant of any of the things connected with us, as is proved by the angel's knowledge of Hagar's condition. "Whence comest thou," then, is said to rebuke the soul which runs away from the better judgment that is its mistress. The conscience says, "Return to thy mistress"; for the presidency of the teaching [soul] is profitable to that which is learning, and bondage with prudence is advantageous to

---

* See Gen. xxi. 10.
† Ἔλεγχος, inward proving, elsewhere identified with the Logos.
‡ § 1 (I. 546-7). § Ὁ ἔλεγχος.

the imperfect [soul]. [And so the allegory proceeds, till we are told that] "the soul which is pregnant with the sophist logos* says to the conscience which speaks to it, 'Thou who lookest upon me art God,' equivalent to, 'Thou art the maker of my purposes and offspring'; and perhaps reasonably; for of free and truly excellent souls He who is free and makes free is the fabricator, but of enslaved [souls] slaves [are the makers], namely angels, ministers of God, supposed to be gods by those involved in labours and bondage"; for the soul sunk in the knowledge of the encyclical preparatory studies cannot thereby see the Cause of knowledge.†

It surely is obvious that throughout these passages Reason or conscience is the allegorical interpretation of the angel in the original story. The only words which can occasion any difficulty are those last quoted. But it will be observed that Philo no longer confines himself to the single angel which appeared to Hagar, but lays down a general rule, which, however, is expressed in words suggested by the narrative under consideration. The less instructed souls are unable to apprehend the infinite Cause, and are therefore shaped by inferior conceptions, those angel thoughts which God sends to admonish them, and which they are apt to mistake for complete mental representations of the Supreme; but souls of higher quality pass beyond these partial and subject thoughts, and are moulded by the sovereign Cause whom they intuitively discern.

We come now to a passage which, as Keferstein‡ attaches to it the greatest weight, we must present at some length, though we may abridge the less important portions. Philo is commenting on the passage in which "the angel of God" says to Jacob "I am the God who appeared to thee in the place of God,"§ where, as we have seen, the subordinate God, distinguished by the absence of the article, is "the oldest Logos." He proceeds in words which we have already quoted and explained,‖ but which must be repeated, as Keferstein's argument is largely founded upon them:—

* Ishmael. † §§ 37-38, pp. 576-7. ‡ Pp. 119 sqq.
§ Gen. xxxi. 11 sqq.   ‖ Pp. 95 sq.

"To souls which are incorporeal and wait upon him, it is likely that God manifests himself as he is, conversing as a friend with friends, but to those that are still in bodies likening himself to angels, not changing his own nature—for he is unalterable—but placing in the souls which receive the representation an opinion of a different shape, so that they suppose that the image is not an imitation, but the archetypal form itself." There is an old story that God went about the cities "likening himself to men," examining their unrighteousness; and this, though not true, is certainly profitable. But the Word,* though always having higher thoughts about the Self-existent, yet desiring at the same time to educate the life of the foolish, likened him to man, though not to any individual man, and ascribed to him a face, hands, feet, anger, and so forth. It did so, not agreeably to the truth, but for the benefit of the learners; for it knew that some natures are so dull that they cannot think of God at all without a body. "And these are almost the only two ways of the whole legislation: one, that inclining towards the truth, through which is constructed 'God is not as man';† but the other, that inclining to the opinions of the more stupid, from which comes the saying, 'The Lord God will educate thee as if a man will educate his son.'‡ Why, then, do we still wonder if God is compared to angels, when he is compared even to men, for the sake of helping those who require it? So that, when it says, 'I am the God who appeared to thee in the place of God,' this is to be understood, that he apparently assumed the place of an angel, though not having altered, in order to benefit him who was not yet able to see the true God. For as those who are not able to behold the sun itself see the reflected ray as the sun, and the changes about the moon as the moon itself, so also they mentally perceive§ the image of God, his angel Logos, as himself. Do you not see encyclical education Hagar, that she says to the angel, 'Thou art the God who lookest upon me?' For she was not yet competent to see the oldest Cause, being by race one of those from Egypt. But now the mind begins to improve, gaining a mental representation of the Sovereign of all the powers; wherefore also he himself says,∥ 'I am the Lord God, whose image thou didst formerly behold as myself, and whose pillar thou didst dedicate, having engraved on it a most sacred inscription. Now, the inscription intimated that I alone stand, and set firm the nature of all things, having brought the [previous] disorder and confusion into order and arrangement, and having propped up the universe, that it may be fixed securely by my strong lieutenant Reason.'"¶

Keferstein begins his comment with the remark that, as the Logos is here expressly identified with the angel, all that is

---

* Logos = Scripture. † Num. xxiii. 19. ‡ Deut. i. 31. § Κατανοοῦσιν.
∥ The words are founded on Gen. xxxi. 13. ¶ Somn., I. 40-41 (I. 655-7).

said of the one naturally holds good of the other. In reply, I can only say that I see nothing in the passage to carry the mind beyond an allegorical identification. The angels who appeared to Hagar and Jacob in the ancient stories, and whom they mistook for God himself, are symbolically the divine Thought, objective in nature, subjective in man, which God sends to minds still engaged in preparatory studies or in ascetic striving towards perfection, and which is the highest manifestation of the Divine that they are yet capable of receiving. This statement is illustrated by the practice of Scripture, which compares God not only to angels, but even to man : it does so in order to convey the best available idea to minds which have not risen high enough to think of God at all apart from a human body. Thus God, remaining unchangeable, graciously allows men to see him, not as he is, but as they can ; and the spiritual perceptions of mankind rise from the grossest anthropomorphism, through the recognition of God as the immanent Reason of the universe and the common Reason of men, up to that faith which apprehends him as the transcendent and infinite Cause, who alone is real and eternal Being.

Such I conceive to be the force of the passage; and Keferstein admits that it is a question whether Philo speaks of a visible appearance of God, of theophanies, or of subjective recognition, of his appearance merely in the thoughts of men. He decides, however, in favour of the former, for two reasons.

The first is that the opening of the passage, where it is said that God appears to disembodied souls in his proper essence, requires in the sequel the antithesis that to man involved in the body he shows himself, objectively and really, merely in the form of an angel. To this argument certain objections immediately present themselves. In the first place, the antithesis alleged by Keferstein, so far from being demanded, is not a true antithesis at all. The spiritual essence of God and bodily form belong to two totally unrelated modes of conception, and the real antithesis must be between a higher and a lower mental apprehension; between perceiving in its essence the all-comprehending unity of Being, which Philo so repeatedly declares to be unknowable by man, and perceiving one or more of the partial manifestations of the unknown Unity. In the second place, the last antithesis is the only one that Philo could possibly have meant; for his proposition is quite universal, and of course he did not believe that God appeared to all men in the visible shape of angels.

Keferstein's second argument is that the expressions in the beginning of the passage can be suitably understood only of a theophany. He appeals especially to the caution which is interposed that God, in likening himself to angels, does not change his own nature. This, he says, would be quite inappropriate if the discussion related only to a subjective apprehension of God; for although Philo connects with this an objective spiritual manifestation of God, yet it would be understood as a matter of course that this did not involve an objective change of the divine essence, but only, as is shown by other expressions of Philo's, an imperfect manifestation of it in certain relations, whereas, if he appeared to man in the shape of an angel, the objection would arise that this could not happen without an alteration of the divine essence. I cannot but think that the real force of the argument lies in the opposite direction. The mere production of a visible shape to guarantee his presence for a temporary purpose would in no way imply a change in the spiritual essence of God, or even in men's conceptions of that essence, though I do not deny that Philo might pause to warn his readers that such was the case. But the notion of change in the divine essence would naturally arise when it was maintained that God revealed himself to the spiritual apprehension of souls in very various aspects. If these were really revelations, how could they be different unless God himself changed from time to time? The answer is that the form of a revelation depends on both the giver and the recipient, and that the various forms of our intuition of God depend, not on any change in the object of the intuition, but on the uncertainty of our imperfect and progressive faculties. We may perhaps use an illustration of our own to make the meaning clear. If several men, on successive days, were to view the same planet through telescopes of different power and finish, and were to compare their impressions, they would probably think at first that they had not been looking at the same object; and when they were assured that it was the same object, they would suppose that it must have been variable, having exhibited a blurred and coloured image on one day, and on the next a clear achromatic definition. It would be only on further reflection that they would ascribe the variation to their own instruments of vision, and admit that the same undisturbed star was revealing itself according to the faculty of the observer. Thus the human soul sees God, now blurred with the semblance of human limbs and coloured with human passions; again as a creative, beneficent, or punitive power; once more as Reason and Wisdom; and only gradually learns that these are nothing more than our various modes of apprehending the same unchanging essence. This thought is not so trite that Philo would think it unnecessary to notice it.

Lastly, Keferstein lays stress on "the weighty words, God shows a differently shaped appearance."* I fear that in his anxiety to support a certain interpretation, he has completely misunderstood the meaning of the Greek. The words in question are, δόξαν ἐντιθέντα ταῖς φαντασιουμέναις ἑτερόμορφον. These Keferstein translates, "Indem er den Schauenden einen anders gestalteten Schein vorhält." A more misleading translation could hardly be given. Ταῖς φαντασιουμέναις does not mean "den Schauenden," by which Keferstein seems to understand "to the *men* who see." The original word, of course, refers to ψυχαῖς, souls, and therefore the allusion must be to something apprehended within the soul, and not to anything discerned by the

---

* Δόξαν ἑτερόμορφον. "Gott zeige einen anders gestalteten Schein."

bodily eye. This is also apparent from the meaning of the word, which is applied to mental representation, and not to physical vision. Again, ἐντιθέντα* is neither "vorhält" nor "zeigt," but "putting into," so that we must seek for something which is put into the soul, and not held before or exhibited to the eye. This at once determines the sense of δόξα, which must be "opinion," and not "Schein"—a conclusion which is confirmed by the use of τὰς νωθεστέρων δόξας farther on, and of ὅσα τῷ δοκεῖν, which refers to what seems so to the mind, and not to visible manifestations.† I believe, therefore, that the notion of a literal theophany is excluded alike by the general tenor of the thought and by a correct interpretation of the Greek terms, and that this passage tends in no way to prove that the Logos was supposed to be a personal angel in whom God appeared visibly upon earth. Indeed, if we have correctly understood Philo, he would rather exclaim, Away with such a thought, and let it not even enter your mind.

From Hagar we pass to Abraham, in connection with whom we hear of Logoi "whom it is customary to name angels," and also of a divine Logos in the capacity of an angel.‡ The thought is illustrated, also, by the history of Moses, and it is necessary briefly to sketch the context, that the figurative character of the passage may be clearly seen.

<small>The mind [it is said], when elevated on high, will not suffer any of the parts of the soul to linger still with mortal things below, but will draw up all with it, as though they were suspended from a string. Wherefore the following oracle was delivered to the wise man: "Go up to the Lord, thou and Aaron and Nadab and Abiud, and seventy of the senate of Israel."§ This means, "'Go up, O soul, to the vision of the Self-existent, harmoniously, rationally, voluntarily, fearlessly, lovingly, in</small>

---

* Mangey has ἀντιθέντα, but the Tauchnitz edition gives, without remark, ἐντιθέντα, which I have no hesitation in preferring, as the other participles are in the present tense.
† The words are used in relation to God's occupying the place of an angel.
‡ Migrat. Abr., 31 (I. 462-3). § Ex. xxiv. 1.

holy and perfect numbers of ten times seven.' For Aaron is called in the Laws the prophet of Moses, the vocal Logos prophesying to intellect. And Nadab means voluntary"; and so on. " These are the spear-bearing powers of the mind worthy to reign, which ought to escort and accompany the king"; for it is dangerous for the soul to ascend alone to the vision of the Self-existent, not knowing the way, but elevated by ignorance and audacity. So "he who follows God necessarily uses as fellow-travellers the Logoi that attend him, whom it is customary to name angels. At any rate, it is said that 'Abraham went with them, escorting them.'"*

A moment's reflection will disclose the reason why Philo introduces here an identification of Logoi and angels. He wishes to prove that the soul can rise to the vision of God only when it is attended by its own higher powers. One argument is found in the history of Abraham, who went along with the angels that visited his tent. These visitors are at first spoken of as men; but their superhuman character is apparent throughout the narrative, and two of them are expressly spoken of as angels farther on.† Now, by the custom of allegorical interpretation, angels meant Logoi, and Abraham the mind, so that the statement in Genesis really signified that the mind went along with those higher thoughts that visit it, and show it the way to God, thoughts which in the earlier part of the passage Philo has treated as "parts of the soul," and "powers of the mind." There is surely nothing here to imply any real identity between the Logoi and personal angels, any more than between the mental faculties and Nadab and Abiud. The passage proceeds to point out that the less advanced mind does not accompany, but only follows its leader towards divine knowledge.

"As long as it has not been made perfect, it uses a divine Logos‡ as leader of the way; for there is an oracle: 'Behold, I send my angel before thy face, to keep thee in the way, in order that he may bring thee into the land which I prepared for thee. Take heed to him, and listen to him, do

---

* Gen. xviii. 16. † Gen. xix. 1.

‡ Λόγῳ θείῳ without the article; and though the article may not be necessary for so familiar a term, which has become almost a proper name, I think the context makes the indefinite meaning preferable. The change from plural to singular is due, I conceive, solely to the singular "angel" in the passage Scripture on which the argument rests.

not disobey him; for he will not shrink from thee, for my name is upon him.'* But whenever it has attained to the height of knowledge, eagerly running up, it equals in speed the former leader of the way. For both will thus become followers of the universal leader God, no one of a different opinion any longer accompanying."

The meaning of this, translated into ordinary language, seems to be that the imperfect mind lingers beneath its own highest thought, the divine messenger that leads it upwards; but when it is perfect, it escapes from every lower consideration, and rises to the height of its purest ideal. At all events, it is clear that the angel of Scripture is allegorized into a Logos; and to argue from this that the Logos was the historical angel who led the Israelites into the Promised Land is totally irrelevant to the scope of Philo's discussion.

In another passage an incident in the life of Abraham is contrasted with a similar event in the history of Jacob.

The names of both patriarchs were changed; but whereas Abraham ever afterwards retained the more honourable appellation, Jacob was not permanently known as Israel. This difference indicates characters whereby virtue which is taught is distinguished from that which is the result of ascetic self-discipline. He who is improved by teaching† lays firm hold of what he has learned, and securely retains it; but the ascetic, when he has exercised himself energetically, again pauses for breath and relaxes his efforts, collecting the strength which has been exhausted by his labours. It was for this reason that the name of Abraham was altered by the unchangeable God, that it might be securely fixed by Him who stands and is ever the same; but an angel, a servant Logos of God,‡ changed the name of Jacob, in order that it may be confessed that nothing after the self-existent Being is a cause of inflexible and unwavering stability.§

Now, the mysterious being who changed the name of Jacob is described in Scripture, not as an angel, but as "a man,"|| and it may be supposed, therefore, that Philo looked upon this man as really the Logos, and called him an angel only because the Logos was one of the angelic hierarchy. I believe,

* Ex. xxiii. 20-21. † Here, as elsewhere, represented by Abraham.
‡ Ἄγγελος, ὑπηρέτης τοῦ θεοῦ λόγος. § Mutat. Nom., 13 (I. 590-1).
|| Gen. xxxii. 24.

however, that the order of thought is the reverse of this. At the beginning of the chapter in Genesis we are told that the angels of God met Jacob; and it was natural to infer that the man who wrestled with him was one of these angels, and therefore, allegorically, a Logos of God. To fancy, with Gfrörer,* that Philo really understood this passage of a literal appearance of the divine Logos to Jacob betrays, to my mind, a singular incapacity for comprehending our philosopher's method. If he accepted the passage literally at all, he accepted it just as it stood; and it is only in his allegorical interpretation that Jacob becomes ascetic self-discipline, and the man or angel represents, not *the*, but *a* Logos of God. It is, however, very questionable whether this is not one of those parts of Genesis which Philo received only in their allegorical meaning; at least, he combines it with a passage which it was impossible for him to regard as literally true. He scornfully repudiates the notion that God bestowed on Abraham and Sarah consonants or vowels or names, and insists that the spiritual meaning is the true one.† So here he is thinking, not of an historical incident, but of permanent principles, not of a man wrestling with a material angel or Logos, but of the inward struggle by which a soul rises from the striving and weary Jacob to the seeing Israel, blest with the beatific vision. This struggle brings no abiding satisfaction, for we are still engaged with what is lower than God; and though we catch a momentary vision of him through some flashing thought or holy precept, some word which expresses the will of God, but is not himself, with which we wrestle till it blesses us, yet we cannot keep the strain of high endeavour, or hold the blessing which we have won. It is only when, with the wise Abraham, we pass from the contemplation of the cosmos to the knowledge of its Maker, that we receive an abiding wisdom, and share the changeless character of the Self-existent on whom our mind reposes.

* I. p. 290. † Mutat. Nom., 9-10 (I. 587-9).

Such I conceive to be, in substance, Philo's meaning; and how little this has to do with the personal agency of the Logos in patriarchal history is sufficiently apparent.

The wrestling of Jacob is briefly referred to in another passage in which Philo is speaking of the prayer that God would "dwell in the houses of Shem."*

The house is the mind, "for what house in creation could be found more appropriate for God than a soul perfectly purified and considering the morally beautiful† alone to be good . . . . . ? But God is said to dwell in a house, not as in a place—for he contains all things, being contained by none—but as pre-eminently exercising providence and care for that place." Let everyone pray that he may have as a dweller the universal Sovereign, who will raise up this little tenement, the mind, aloft from earth, and unite it to the bounds of heaven. According to this view, Shem is," as it were, the root of excellence, and out of this sprang a tree bearing edible fruit, the wise Abraham, of which the self-hearing and self-taught genus, Isaac, was the fruit, from which again the virtues acquired by labours are sown, of which [virtues] Jacob, who has been exercised in wrestling with passions, is an athlete, making use of angels, gymnast-training Logoi."‡

This passage requires no comment after what has been already said. It is apparent that Philo is revelling in allegories, and it deserves notice that Jacob's wrestling is now not with a heavenly visitor, but with the passions, and he is trained to resist them, not by the Logos, but by Logoi, showing how little Philo thought of an individual and personal angelic Logos in connection with that mysterious incident in the patriarch's history.

There are some other passages relating to incidents in the life of Jacob which are of great importance in the present connection. In one of these Philo is speaking of the nourishment of the soul; and having stated that the soul of the more perfect is nourished by the whole Logos, while *we* should be content if we were nourished even by a part of it, he proceeds:

"But Jacob, having looked above even the Logos, says that he is

---

* Gen. ix. 27.   † τὸ καλόν.
‡ Ἀγγέλοις ἀλείπταις λόγοις, Sobriet., 13 (I. 402).

nourished by God himself, and speaks thus, 'The God whom my fathers Abraham and Isaac pleased, the God who nourishes me from my youth until this day, the angel who delivers me out of all evils, bless these children.'* This mode is suitable. He considers God, not a Logos, to be a nourisher, but the angel, who is a Logos, to be as it were a physician of evils. He does so most agreeably to nature; for it is his opinion that the Self-existent himself gives the leading blessings in his own person, but that his angels and Logoi give those that are secondary."†

The context of this passage makes it abundantly clear that the Logoi have nothing personal about them, and that, therefore, "angels" must be understood in a purely figurative sense. Philo has spoken of the soul's nourishment as consisting, not of earthly and corruptible things, but of Logoi which God showers down from the lofty and pure nature, which [in connection with the manna] is called heaven. He was hardly so absurd as to fancy that the soul fed upon a shower of angels. On the contrary, as angels are not mentioned in the narrative about the manna, they do not appear in Philo, and the Logoi are speedily changed into "sciences," "the graces of God," "good things,"‡ "the heavenly sciences,"|| "the Logos of God."¶ Not till the speech of Jacob has been quoted are angels introduced. They are then carefully placed in company with Logoi, which I regard as an explanatory word to warn the reader that literal angels are not intended; and they speedily lapse once more into "sciences."** The general meaning is rendered sufficiently apparent by an apt illustration: "God bestows absolute health, which is not preceded by bodily disease, through himself alone, but through art and medical skill that which arises in escaping from disease. . . . . . Similarly in the case of the soul: the good things, the nourishments, he bestows through himself, but through angels and Logoi all that comprises deliverance from evils."†† The distinction here drawn is that between immediate divine agency and

---

* Gen. xlviii. 15, 16.   † Leg. All., III. 62 (I. 122).
‡ § 56, p. 119. || § 58, p. 120.   ¶ § 59 sqq., p. 120 sq.
** § 63, p. 122.   †† § 62, p. 122.

secondary causes. The latter are represented by angels, who, in maintaining that bodily health which God has originally bestowed, are nothing more than art and medical skill. So the soul is nourished by immediate communion with God; but when it cannot rise so high, it may be kept from evil by the heavenly sciences, words, precepts, or admonitions, which warn it against wrong and guide it to what is right. As it may possibly be thought inconsistent to recognize here an allegorical interpretation, whereas in a former connection, when speaking of the creation of man, we allowed the literal to stand,* we must observe that the former does not exclude the latter. In the actual history an angel waited upon Jacob; but this means allegorically the influence of Logoi on the soul.

We come now to the one passage which presents a serious difficulty, and which, when read without its context, naturally seems decisive of the question:—"The divine place and the sacred country is full of incorporeal Logoi. Now, these Logoi are immortal souls." The immortal souls are afterwards identified with angels.† Nothing can be plainer. Yet, before we proceed to an examination of the passage, we cannot but recollect that even an express statement of this kind does not necessarily guarantee more than an allegorical identification. To the examples already given we may add one from the present treatise. The form of character represented by the precept, "Know thyself," the Hebrews call Tharrha,‡ and the Greeks Socrates; "but the latter was a man, while Tharrha was the very Logos about knowing oneself."‖ Again, in the second book "On dreams," we are told that the censurable logos [of man] "was the Egyptian river."¶ It is apparent, therefore, that our question is not finally disposed of by the few words cited above, and that we must judge from the general course of Philo's exposition in what sense they are to be taken. They occur in the midst of a long interpretation of

* Pp. 142 and 144.   † Somn., I. 21 (I. 640).   ‡ Terah.
‖ § 10, p. 629.   ¶ Somn., II. 39 (I. 693).

Jacob's dream, in which he saw the angels of God ascending and descending on a ladder that reached from earth to heaven.* The account in Genesis begins by saying that Jacob "met with a place."

"Place" here signifies the divine Logos; for God "sends his own Logoi to assist the lovers of virtue; and they treat and completely heal the sicknesses of the soul, giving sacred admonitions as immovable laws, and calling to the exercise of these, and, like trainers of gymnasts, implanting strength and power." Jacob met, no longer God, but God's Logos, because he had come into Charran, sensation.† His mental condition is shown by the words "the sun set," that is, the brilliant light of the invisible God no longer illumined the understanding, but made way for the "second lights of Logoi."‡ For the ascetic understanding is subject to irregular movements, going up and down continually; and whenever it is elevated, it is illumined by the archetypal and incorporeal beams of the rational fountain of the perfect God, but whenever it descends, it is lighted " by the images of these, immortal Logoi, whom it is customary to call angels."||

We may remark here that the notion of the soul's going up and down is clearly derived from the movement of the angels upon the ladder;¶ and that the conception of Logoi, instead of the single Logos which is symbolized by the "place," must also be due to the appearance of angels in the original narrative. These angels, by the usage of allegory, represented Logoi, and, consequently, their appearance to Jacob after the setting of the sun signified the inferior light of divine words or precepts which alone the struggling soul can enjoy when it sinks from its highest contemplation. That this is the meaning is evident from what follows:—

" Whenever the rays of God, through which the apprehensions of things are made most clearly, leave the soul, there rises the second and weaker light of Logoi,** no longer of things.†† . . . And meeting with a place or Logos was an amply sufficing gift for those who were not able to see God, who is before place and Logos, because they had not the soul entirely deprived of light, but when that unmingled light set from their view, they enjoyed the use of the mingled."||

* Gen. xxviii. 11 sqq.   † Somn., I. 11-12 (I. 630-1).
‡ § 13, p. 631. || § 19, p. 638.
¶ See § 23, p. 643, where it is said that ascetics, since they border on the extremes, " often go up and down as on a ladder."
** Words.   †† Λόγων, οὐκέτι πραγμάτων.

It is plain that personal angels form no proper antithesis to "things," and that the recognition of angels when the soul cannot rise to the apprehension of God, answers to no real experience; but when the angels are nothing more than the allegorical expression for Logoi, all becomes clear. Logoi, in the sense of "words," is strictly antithetical to things; and, when we are no longer able to apprehend realities through an immediate divine illumination, we fall back upon the secondary and mingled information which comes through the medium of language.

Passing on to the next clause, "He took of the stones of the place, and put it beside his head, and slept in that place," Philo remarks that "one might admire not only his manner of life and natural science contained in hidden meanings, but also the expressed inducement to the practice of labour and endurance;" in other words, he divides his interpretation into literal and allegorical. He addresses himself first to the former, and obtains a lesson against soft and luxurious living from the fact that the "athlete of honourable pursuits" slept upon the ground, with a stone for his pillow, and afterwards prayed only for food and raiment, nature's wealth, thus becoming "the archetypal pattern of an ascetic soul."* At this point he avowedly turns to the investigation of the allegorical meaning, and begins with the words which were quoted at the opening of this discussion. He goes on to say that—

Jacob, having taken one of these Logoi, selecting the highest in merit, places it near his head, his understanding; for this is in a manner the head of the soul. And he does this ostensibly to sleep, but in reality to rest on a divine Logos,† and place upon that his whole life as a very light burden. But he willingly hearkens, and receives the athlete as one who will be a disciple at first. Then, whenever he has received fitness of nature, he summons him, like a trainer of gymnasts, to exercise, and leaning on him compels him to wrestle, until he has imparted to him irresistible strength, having changed his ears into eyes, and called him Israel, seeing. Then he puts on him the crown of victory, which bears the strange and ill-sounding name of "numbness," for it is said "the

---

* § 20, p. 639-40. † Ἐπὶ λόγῳ θείῳ.

breadth" of prizes and proclamations and all the most admired rewards of valour "became numb."*

We need not follow him in the explanation of this numbness; it is clear that we are dealing, not with the literal facts of Jacob's history, but with the spiritual experiences of which these facts are supposed to be symbols. Let us return, then, to the original words. The divine place, we are told, is full of incorporeal Logoi. Now, the place, as we have previously learned, represents the Logos, so that the meaning of the proposition is this,—the universal Thought or highest genus or most comprehensive law is full of subordinate thoughts or species or laws. But, if this be the meaning, why does Philo add the wholly gratuitous statement that "these Logoi are immortal souls"? I conceive that he may do so because he is unable to carry out his allegory consistently. To suit his subsequent explanation he ought to have said, "these Logoi are stones," because it was one of the stones of the place that Jacob took for his pillow. But he seems unable to manufacture a stone into a Logos, partly, perhaps, owing to the intractability of the material, and partly because the Logoi are represented in the original narrative by angels. It was the presence of the angels that satisfied him that the place was full of Logoi; but if he had said that these Logoi were the angels on the ladder, the inconsistency of his interpretation would have been too obvious, and he could not have gone on to say that Jacob took one of them as a rest for his understanding. In the next section it is shown that angels are incorporeal souls living in the air, and by adopting in anticipation this term as a substitute for angels, Philo veils the incoherence of his exegesis, perhaps from his own mind as well as that of his readers. At any rate, I can see no reason why this proposition alone in the entire section is to be understood literally. Philo is describing what he conceives to be real mental processes; and if he supposed that the Logoi were really immortal souls, then he must also have believed

* Gen. xxxii. 25. § 21, p. 640.

that the human soul, in its struggle for virtue, selects one of these souls or angels on whom to rest, that the angel accepts it as a pupil, compels it to wrestle, changes its ears into eyes, and gives it a crown called numbness. But, surely, these results are rather ascribed to divine thoughts which discipline and strengthen the mind.

From the prelude to the vision, Philo passes on to the dream itself :—" Behold, a ladder fixed in the earth, the head of which reached into the heaven, and the angels of God were ascending and descending upon it." He gives different interpretations of this, according to the department of nature within which it is applied.

In the cosmos, "the air, of which the basis is earth and the head heaven, is symbolically called a ladder." The air [as we have seen in another connection] is peopled with souls, which other philosophers name demons, "but the sacred Word is accustomed to call angels, using a more appropriate name, for they announce* both the orders of the Father to the offspring, and the necessities of the offspring to the Father. Wherefore also it introduced them going up and down"; not that God requires information, "but because it was expedient for us mortals to use mediating and arbitrating Logoi," on account of our dread of the universal Ruler; for, not to speak of punishments, we cannot contain even unmixed benefits which he would offer through himself, without the use of others as ministers.†

Now, we cannot doubt that in this passage the souls in the air are represented as really existing, and are identified with the angels of Scripture ; and as these, again, presently appear as Logoi, the personality of the latter may seem to be fully established. If, however, we make sufficient allowance for Philo's loose method, I think another explanation becomes possible. So far as he accepted the stories of angelic appearances in the Old Testament literally, he probably believed that one of the souls living in the air became for that occasion visible, and acted as a divine messenger. But, though in deference to his Jewish creed he shrank from discarding the literal aspect of these ancient stories, his thought was really

* As messengers, ἀγγέλους, and διαγγέλλουσι.   † § 22, pp. 641-2.

intolerant of this materializing of a divine process, and he liked to escape as soon as possible into the universal idea which was symbolized by the temporary and local fact. Unless we are prepared to contend that he really looked upon the human soul as a scene of constant angelic visitation, and supposed that in all its thoughts of God and his will souls in the air were secretly whispering a divine message, we must resort to some such interpretation of the passage before us. So far as Jacob's dream corresponds with external facts, it points to the existence of angelic souls in the air; but since angels always symbolize Logoi, it points still more certainly to a general spiritual experience. The transition in the thought seems to be marked by the statement that Scripture "introduced" the angels going up and down; that is to say, it did not follow the hard facts of nature, but, with a view to the deeper meaning, accommodated the outward events to the spiritual lesson. It is for this reason, I conceive, that the souls or angels now change into Logoi, those universal visitors of the mind, who report to it the requirements of the divine Will, and form the link of communion between it and God. They are the ministers who bring to us the subdued light of his mercies, while they veil from us an awfulness greater than we could bear.

This interpretation is confirmed by what follows. That which was symbolically called ladder in the cosmos was something of the kind just described.

"But if we consider that which is in men, we shall find that it is the soul, of which the bodily, as it were earthly, part, sensible perception, is the basis, while the heavenly part as it were, the purest mind, is the head. Now up and down through it all the Logoi of God move incessantly—when they ascend, drawing it up with them, and disjoining it from the mortal part, and showing the vision only of things which are worth seeing; but when they descend, not casting it down, for neither God nor a divine Logos is a cause of injury, but descending with it out of humanity and compassion towards our race, for the sake of giving assistance and alliance, in order that breathing forth what is salutary they may revive the soul also, which is still borne along, as it were, in a river, the body. In the understandings, accordingly, of those that are perfectly purified the God and Sovereign of the universe walks about noiselessly, alone and invisibly,—for there is also an oracle delivered to the wise man, in which it said, 'I will walk about in you, and will be your God,'*—but in the [understandings] of those that are still undergoing cleansing, and have not yet entirely washed out the life foul and sordid with heavy bodies, angels, divine Logoi [walk], making them bright with the cleansing materials† of excellence."‡

It seems quite clear that Philo is referring in this passage to divine thoughts which visit and purify the mind, those "broken lights" of God which beam softly upon us when we cannot bear the full-orbed splendour. The juxtaposition of "angels" with "divine Logoi," so far from identifying the meaning of the two expressions, when literally understood, rather shows, in the present connection, that the latter is the symbolical meaning of the former; for otherwise the word "angels" would have been quite sufficient by itself. Philo uses the term "angels" to connect his exposition with Jacob's dream, and then adds Logoi to indicate what he conceives to be the allegorical sense. If we reject this explanation, we must ascribe to Philo the opinion that our souls are full of other souls, which, though they live in the air, are continually going up and down inside them ; but I know of no laws of exegesis which render this necessary.

Another explanation of the dream is that the ascetic saw his own life like a ladder.

For self-discipline is an irregular thing, sometimes ascending to a height, sometimes sinking to the opposite extreme. The wise have obtained the Olympian and heavenly place to live in, having learned always to go up, while the bad inhabit the recesses in the realm of Hades ; but ascetics, bordering on the two extremes, often go up and down as on a ladder, being either drawn up by the better part or dragged down by the worse, until God gives the victory to the better.||

How figuratively all this is conceived needs no remark. It is useful, however, to observe how loosely Philo attaches his allegory to the words of Scripture. He apparently did not

* Lev. xxvi. 12. † Reading, as Mangey suggests, $\dot{\rho}\dot{\nu}\mu\mu\alpha\sigma\iota\nu$ instead of $\ddot{\upsilon}\mu\mu\alpha\sigma\iota\nu$.
‡ § 23, pp. 642-3. || § 23, p. 643.

like to say that the ascetic life resembled angels, and therefore he compares it very inappropriately to the ladder. It was the angels who went up and down, while the ladder was "fixed," and ought accordingly to have been a symbol of stability. This may teach us not to insist on too great precision in Philo's manner of presenting his views.

Having got rid of the angels, and converted the ladder into a symbol of vicissitude, he proceeds to compare with it "the affairs of men" and the changes of fortune;* but on this we need not dwell.

Farther on in the same treatise some expressions occur which prove that, even if Philo fell into some momentary confusion between angels and the Logoi, he still used the latter in a sense which is absolutely impersonal. Before quitting Jacob's dream he alludes to the promises of God given through Logoi as being confirmed by works, and adds that it is the property of God to say what will come to pass, or rather his Logoi differ not from works.† In referring to another dream of Jacob's, about the sheep and the goats,‡ he refrains from immediately converting the angel who spoke to Jacob into a Logos, because it suits his purpose to say that the goat and the ram "are symbols of perfect Logoi," of which one purifies the soul, and the other nourishes it; and these presently become "the right Logoi of wisdom," which make the soul fruitful of good.|| It is evident that in these places the Logoi are not angels. A good way farther on, however, the angel who spoke to Jacob is represented as the Logos,¶ a point on which we need not now pause, since we have fully considered it in connection with Hagar.** Finally,

The ascetic having learned by continual practice that the created is movable of itself, while the unbegotten is unchangeable and immovable, sets up a pillar to God, and having set it up anoints it. But we are not to suppose that a stone was anointed, but that the dogma about the

* § 24, pp. 643-4. † § 31, p. 648. ‡ Gen. xxxi. 11 sqq.
|| § 34, pp. 650-51. ¶ § 39-41, pp. 655-6. ** Pp. 246 sqq.

stability of God alone was trained in the soul by knowledge which anoints like a teacher of gymnasts; for he who seeks after honourable pursuits, "having anointed and hammered together all the Logoi about virtue and piety, sets them as a most beautiful and strong offering to God."*

These instances may suffice to show that if we attempted to fix upon the Logoi a personal and angelic character throughout this treatise, we should be involved in hopeless absurdity. On the other hand, it is not necessary to fall back upon Philo's alleged vacillation of thought. Although we cannot acquit his exposition of the charge of uncertainty and looseness, still his general meaning is fairly satisfied if we admit nothing more than an allegorical identification of the Logoi with angels, and we are not justified by the difficulties of the passage under consideration in thrusting upon Philo a doctrine which is inconsistent with the whole scope of his philosophy.

We pass on to another event in patriarchal history, the attack of the people of Sodom upon the house of Lot, when he was entertaining "two angels."†

Do you not see [asks Philo] those who are barren of wisdom and blind in understanding, Sodomites as they are called in a foreign tongue,‡ "running round the house of the soul, in order to disgrace and corrupt those who were entertained as guests, sacred and holy Logoi, its guards and keepers, no one at all knowing how either to oppose those who would act wrongly, or to escape from doing something wrong? For it is not that some did and others did not, but 'all the people,' as [Scripture] says, 'circled the house round about together, both young and old,' having conspired against the divine works and words,§ which it is customary to call angels."||

Surely the allegory here is sufficiently plain, and there is no conceivable reason for making the angels literal when everything else is figurative. The story is turned into a parable of the war between blind and foolish thoughts on the one hand, and, on the other, words of God which the wise soul keeps as

* § 43, p. 657-8. † Gen. xix. 1 sqq. ‡ Κατὰ γλῶτταν. § Logoi.
|| Conf. Ling., 8 (I. 409). Cf. Prof., 26 (I. 567), where we hear of ἱεροὺς καὶ ἀμιάντους λόγους, which of course stand for the angels in the story, though the latter are not mentioned.

its guests and guardians. So little is Philo thinking of an historical occurrence that he immediately transfers the scene to Egypt, and, though still referring to the people of Sodom, declares that Moses will meet and stop them, even if they put forward the king Logos among them, who is most daring and formidable in speech. This Logos is the king of Egypt; for Logos is used even by the haters of virtue to introduce their false principles. And so the argument passes into a dissertation on the use of sophistical language and the way in which the virtuous must meet it. How little this has to do with a literal epiphany of angels needs no remark.

We come next to a passage on which, among others, Gfrörer particularly relies as establishing incontrovertibly the personality of the Logos. It relates to the incident of the burning bush. It is told in Exodus* that "an angel of the Lord appeared" to Moses "in a fire of flame, out of the bramble; and he sees that the bramble burns with fire, but the bramble was not burned down." In order to follow Philo's exposition we must take notice that the angel simply appears, but says nothing, and it is the Lord himself, the Self-existent,† who afterwards speaks to Moses. The following is Philo's account in his Life of Moses:‡

"When he was at a certain woody dell he sees a most astonishing spectacle. There was a bramble, a thorny and very feeble plant. This, though no one applied fire to it, suddenly burns up; and being all encompassed from root to branch with a great flame, as from a welling fountain, it continued sound, as though it were some unsusceptible substance, and not itself a fuel for fire, but using the fire as nourishment. Now in the midst of the flame was a certain very beautiful form, like nothing in the visible scene,§ a most God-like figure, flashing forth a light more brilliant than the fire, which one would have suspected to be an image of the Self-existent. But let it be called an angel,‖ because, almost, the events which were about to happen were being proclaimed¶ with a quietness clearer than a voice, by means of the magnificent vision.

* iii. 2 sqq. † 'Ο ὤν.
‡ Vita Mos., I. 12 (II. 91). § Τῶν ὁρατῶν οὐδενί.
‖ Messenger. ¶ As by a messenger: ἄγγελος . . . διηγγέλλετο.

For the burning bramble is a symbol of those who are injured; and the flaming fire, of those who injure; and the fact that the burning [substance] was not burned down, of the [truth] that those who are injured shall not be destroyed by those who assault them, but the assault will become to the latter ineffectual and profitless, and the plot harmless to the former. But the angel [is a symbol] of the providence [that issues from] God,* easing as he does, beyond the hopes of all, very terrible things with great quietness."

It will be observed that the Logos is not mentioned throughout this passage, but then, it is argued, the "image of the Self-existent" can be none other, for this is a distinctive appellation, and therefore we have here an indubitable instance of the personal activity of the Logos.† The force of this argument, however, depends in part on a mistranslation, unless, indeed, I misapprehend the precise meaning of the German. Philo's language is, ἣν [μορφὴν] ἄν τις ὑπετόπησεν εἰκόνα τοῦ Ὄντος εἶναι. This Gfrörer detaches into a separate clause, and translates, "Man möchte es wohl am besten für das Ebenbild Gottes halten."‡ By this detachment of the sentence and false rendering of the aorist, to say nothing of the gratuitous insertion of "am besten," Philo's statement of what would have been the impression on a spectator is converted into a formal interpretation of his own. Gfrörer also introduces a definite article which Philo thought proper to omit, but which seems essential to the argument about "the image," for the second person in the universe, if distinctly conceived, could not be brought upon the scene in this indeterminate manner. The passage, as Philo wrote it, does not say in effect, "the form which appeared to Moses can have been nothing less than the Logos, the image of God," but, " it was so beautiful and splendid, and so unlike any other visible thing, that anyone who saw it would have taken it for an image of God." The latter statement precisely suits the

* Προνοίας τῆς ἐκ Θεοῦ.
† Gfrörer I., p. 283-4; also Keferstein, though with more moderation, p. 122.
‡ Keferstein removes some of the errors, "Man möchte sie für ein Bild Gottes halten."

context. The appearance was an appearance only. It is true, it is called in Scripture an angel; but it is so only because it was mutely significant of coming events. It was in reality a visible symbol of the providence of God, a figure or statue of most God-like mien,* making it evident to Moses that God was really there. It is, accordingly, God, the Self-existent himself, who converses with the future legislator. Hence it is apparent that the "image" here is quite an indefinite predicate. We must add that it is used in a sense wholly inapplicable to the Logos. The latter was the image of God because it was the completest expression of the divine mind; but the image here relates only to visible form, and must therefore be figuratively understood. As the sun may suggest to our minds the thought of an archetypal intellectual light, or even of God himself,† so the splendour in the burning bush awakened in the mind of Moses the suspicion of a higher presence, and prepared him for the revelation of Him who eternally *is*.

The passage which next invites our attention has been already examined in its general bearing, and we are concerned at present only with the opening words: "To the archangel and oldest Logos, the Father who begat the universe gave a pre-eminent gift, that standing on the borders he should separate the created from the Creator."‡ This statement is made in connection with the pillar of cloud which came between the Egyptian and Israelitish armies,§ and no longer allowed the race which was temperate and dear to God to be pursued by that which was fond of the passions and godless. In the original passage, "the angel of God" is mentioned as well as the cloud; and though Philo does not quote this part of the verse, we may reasonably presume that he has it in his mind when he terms the Logos an angel rather than a cloud, for we learn from his Life of Moses that he regarded the cloud as

* Θεοειδέστατον ἄγαλμα. † See Somn., I. 13 (I. 632).
‡ Quis rer. div. her., 42 (I. 501). § Ex. xiv. 19.

the visible covering of the unseen angel,* basing his judgment, no doubt, on the proximity of the two words in the Scripture text, and the identity of action ascribed there to the angel and the cloud.† If we ask why he calls the Logos here an *archangel*, it is probably because he refers not to *a* Logos, but distinctly to *the* Logos, the oldest and universal Thought of God. This passage, accordingly, supplies us only with another instance of Philo's habit of allegorizing an angel into a Logos. If with Gfrörer‡ we insist that he regarded the Logos as personally present in the cloud, we violate all consistency of exegesis. Then we must suppose that the armies of the Israelites and the Egyptians were, in the literal sense, not only "virtuous understandings" and those "barren of science" respectively, but the Creator and the creation; for it is quite arbitrary to take strictly just what suits us, and to resolve all the rest into allegory. The inconsistency, however, becomes more glaring if we extend our view a little further. Just before the allusion to the cloud, Philo expresses his admiration of the sacred Logos running with breathless eagerness "to stand between the dead and the living,"§ so as to stop the plagues which crush our soul, by separating the holy reflections, which truly live, from the unholy, which are in reality dead. According to the history, the action referred to was performed by Aaron, so that the Logos was, after all, only a mortal man. Stranger still, he was two men, for he was not only Aaron but Moses. Just after the reference to the cloud, Philo declares that the Logos says, "I stood between the Lord and you."‖ Now it was Moses who said this; therefore, Moses was literally the Logos, and the personality of the latter is incontrovertibly established. Such are the odd results of following the

* Vita Mos., I. 29 (II. 107).
† We may notice, as a further reason, that the object with which Moses stood between the Lord and the people, according to Deut. v. 5, was ἀναγγεῖλαι ὑμῖν τὰ ῥήματα κυρίου.
‡ I., pp. 276 and 291. § Num. xvi. 48, in the Hebrew xvii. 13.
‖ Deut. v. 5.

principles of exegesis by which the Logos is identified with an angel. In the present connection the whole thought is imbedded in allegory; and we may add that far too high a position is assigned to the Logos to admit of its being confounded, except through an allegorical medium, with the souls that live in the air.

From the pillar of cloud we go on to the angel who appeared to Balaam. The journey of the soothsayer is treated historically in the Life of Moses,* and there is nothing in the narrative to suggest to an ordinary reader a manifestation of the Logos, for the Logos is not referred to from beginning to end. Gfrörer, however, has two reasons for believing that the form which opposed Balaam was supposed by Philo to be the Logos. First it is called θεία ὄψις, which is used also in connection with the burning bush and the pillar of cloud.† This argument cannot influence our judgment after what we have already said. Secondly, Philo derives from it the divine inspiration of the prophet, " which he would certainly never have ascribed to a mere angel."‡ In attributing the inspiration to the " divine vision," or angel, Philo is of course only following the text of Scripture; and though he was quite willing, as we shall see, to convert the " vision " into the Logos, yet so far as he understood the history literally he must have understood the angel literally too. It is, however, refreshing to find Gfrörer arguing that the vision must have been the Logos, because it was too great to be an angel. In another passage Philo treats this occurrence allegorically. Then Balaam becomes a representative of " the earthly Edom," who blocks the heavenly and royal way of virtue, and the angel is, as usual, turned into " the divine Logos," who blocks the way of Edom and those like him, the " conscience "§ or " the inward judge "‖ who stands against us, an angel guiding us and removing obstacles, that

---

* Vita Mos., I. 49 (II. 123-4).
† The latter I have failed to verify, and Gfrörer gives no reference.
‡ I., p. 292. § Ἔλεγχος. ‖ Τὸν ἐντὸς δικαστήν.

without stumbling we may proceed by a thoroughfare; and the lesson which we learn from the obstinacy of Balaam is this, that the diseases of the soul are incurable whenever, in the presence of conscience, we prefer our own undiscerning judgments to its suggestions, which it continually makes for our admonition and the amendment of our entire life.* The figurative character of the whole passage needs no further demonstration.

Finally, there are three passages of a more general character which call for a few remarks. In the first† it is said that

Everyone ought to repeat the words of the Psalmist, "The Lord is my shepherd,"‡ for God leads earth and water, and air and fire, and all their contents, "as a shepherd and king, in conformity with right and law, having set over them his own right Reason, first-born son, who shall receive the care of this sacred flock as a lieutenant of a great king. For also it has been said somewhere, 'Behold, I am; I will send my angel before thee, to keep thee in the way.'"§

The last clause, containing the quotation, is under some suspicion; but if we allow it to stand, it simply extends to the universe what elsewhere is limited to the imperfect mind,‖ and affords us one more proof that the "angel" of Scripture represents allegorically the Logos of philosophy.

In the next passage we read that,

In opposition to ignorant polytheists, who are described in Scripture as "the sons of men,"¶ "those who have used science are properly called sons of the one God, as Moses also confesses when he says, 'Ye are sons of the Lord God,'** and 'God who begat thee,'†† and 'Is not he himself thy Father?'‡‡ .... And if anyone, however, is not yet worthy to be called a son of God, let him be zealous to be adorned in accordance with his first-born Logos, the oldest angel, as being a many-named archangel; for he is called Beginning, and Name of God, and Logos, and the Man according to image, and Seeing Israel. Wherefore I was induced a short time ago to praise the virtues of those who say 'we all are sons of one man.'§§ For even if we have not yet become competent to be considered

---

* Quod Deus immut., 37 (I. 299).   † Agr. Noe, 12 (I. 308).
‡ Ps. xxii. [xxiii.], 1.
§ Ex. xxiii. 20. The text here is ἐγώ εἰμι, ἀποστελῶ : LXX, ἐγὼ ἀποστέλλω.
‖ See before, pp. 251 sq.   ¶ Gen. xi. 5.
** Deut. xiv. 1.   †† Ib. xxxii. 18.   ‡‡ Ib. xxxii. 6.   §§ Gen. xlii. 11.

children of God, at least we are [children] of his eternal image, the most sacred Logos; for the oldest Logos is an image of God. And in many places of the Legislation they are called again sons of Israel, those who hear [sons] of him who sees, since after seeing hearing has been honoured with the second prize, and that which is taught is always second to that which without suggestion receives clear impressions of the objects before it."*

We have here the many-named Logos of the Stoics, equipped, however, with titles derived from Hebrew, and not Hellenic thought, and pressed into the service from the language of Scripture, not devised by philosophy as the best vehicle for its own conceptions. While two of these titles, man, and Israel, are referred to their origin in the Pentateuch, the names of angel and archangel are left without comment or justification. They are, moreover, titles which Philo himself bestows, and may therefore be supposed to give some indication of his views respecting the essential nature of the Logos. Nevertheless, it seems probable that he used the term because he was accustomed to allegorizing the angels of the Old Testament into the Logos or Logoi, and there is nothing to indicate that by angel he means, in this passage, a particular order of being, personal souls in the air who acted as agents of the divine Will. The word angel has nowhere lost with Philo its primary meaning of messenger, and, even when it is applied to the souls in the air, he treats it as a descriptive epithet. He may, therefore, bestow it upon the Logos without intending to lower the divine Thought to the rank of an angel in the ordinary sense. The creative Thought which shaped the cosmos was the first messenger that issued from the solitude of God, bidding chaotic matter become clothed with ideal forms, and rational beings arise responsive to the infinite intelligence. Language of this kind does not imply individual personality. In its higher sphere the Logos is the angel of God in the same sense in which the powers of the human soul are angels of the sovereign mind.

* Conf. Ling., 28 (I. 426-7).

The last passage to which we have to refer is based upon a well-known reading of the LXX, and relates to the boundaries of virtue.

These [it is affirmed] were not set up by created beings like us, but by "the older and divine Logoi who were before us and everything earthly;" as the Law has intimated in the words, "Thou shalt not remove the boundaries of thy neighbour, which thy fathers set up,"* and again, "Ask thy father, and he will report to thee, thy elders, and they will tell thee; when the Most High divided the nations, when he distributed the sons of Adam, he set boundaries of the nations according to the number of the angels of God; and his people Jacob became the portion of the Lord, Israel the lot of his inheritance."† Fathers and elders cannot be understood literally, because, as a fact, they know no more about the original settlement of the nations than ourselves. Therefore by "father" is meant right Reason, the father of our soul, and by "elders" its companions and friends. "These were the first to fix the boundaries of virtue, to whom it is meet to resort for the sake of learning and instruction in the necessary things. Now the necessary things are these. When God distributed and walled off the nations of the soul, separating those of the same speech from those of foreign tongue, and, breaking up the dwelling of the children of earth, scattered and shot forth from himself those whom he named sons of Adam, then he set up the boundaries of the offspring of virtue equal in number to angels; for as many as are God's Logoi, so many are the nations and species of virtue. What are the shares of his angels, and what the allotted portion of the universal Ruler and Sovereign? Of the servants, therefore, the specific virtues, but of the Sovereign the select genus Israel. For he who sees God, being led by pre-eminent beauty, has been allotted and assigned as a portion to him who is seen."‡

It is evident that the Logoi are here regarded as the logical subdivisions of the universal Logos or Reason, regarded in its moral aspect as "right reason." The latter is the all-inclusive rule of virtuous conduct; the former are the several rules or laws into which it may be resolved, the divine precepts which must have severally their corresponding virtues. Can we seriously suppose that Philo looked upon these ethical laws, these ancient expressions of God's eternal Reason, as persons, real angels flitting to and fro in the air? This passage seems

---

* Deut. xix. 14.   † Deut. xxxii. 7-9.
‡ Post. Cain., 25-6 (I. 241-2).

finally to prove that the word "angels" is the accepted allegorical expression for Logoi, and that the latter are no more to be literally identified with the former than the species of virtue with the nations of the world.

This closes our long examination of Philo's doctrine of the Logos, and our original conclusions remain unimpaired by passages which are generally thought to present such a different view. From first to last the Logos is the Thought of God, dwelling subjectively in the infinite Mind, planted out and made objective in the universe. The cosmos is a tissue of rational force, which images the beauty, the power, the goodness of its primeval fountain. The reason of man is this same rational force entering into consciousness, and held by each in proportion to the truth and variety of his thoughts; and to follow it is the law of righteous living. Each form which we can differentiate as a distinct species, each rule of conduct which we can treat as an injunction of reason, is itself a Logos, one of those innumerable thoughts or laws into which the universal Thought may, through self-reflection, be resolved. Thus, wherever we turn, these Words, which are really Works, of God confront us, and lift our minds to that uniting and cosmic Thought which, though comprehending them, is itself dependent, and tells us of that impenetrable BEING from whose inexhaustible fulness it comes, of whose perfections it is the shadow, and whose splendours, too dazzling for all but the purified intuitions of the highest souls, it at once suggests and veils.

CHAPTER VII.

THE HIGHER ANTHROPOLOGY.

IN the course of the foregoing chapters we have had occasion to deal with the questions which concern creation in its more general aspects; but we have still to notice Philo's views in regard to the philosophy of man's creation, and his moral and spiritual nature and relations.

Following the order of creation given in Genesis, Philo asks why man was created last. He alleges four reasons. The first, which was put forward by those deeply versed in the Laws, declared that God having endowed man with the highest of gifts, rational kinship with himself, did not grudge him his minor blessings, but prepared everything beforehand for his use, wishing him to be in want of nothing that was conducive to life, whether in its lower or its higher needs. A second reason was the following. At the moment of his creation man found every preparation made for his subsistence, in order to teach his posterity to imitate the founder of their race, and live without toil and care in the ample supply of necessaries. This will happen when they no longer submit to the tyranny of irrational pleasures and desires; for the difficulty in procuring subsistence is intended as a punishment for guilt, and when vice is overcome by virtue, and the war in the soul is superseded by gentle peace, we may hope that God, the lover of goodness and of man, will afford spontaneous blessings to mankind, and the skill of the husbandman be no more required. The third reason is found in God's intention to adapt the beginning and end of his creation to one another. Accordingly he made heaven the beginning and man the end; the former the most perfect of incorruptible things in the sensible universe; the latter the best of things earthborn and corruptible, a tiny heaven bearing within it many starlike qualities. Finally, man came last upon the scene that by his sudden appearance he might fill the other animals with astonishment, and, subduing them to his purpose, reign as a king over the creatures in earth and air and water. Thus, though coming last, he loses nothing in rank, but, like the driver of a chariot or the pilot of a ship, he takes the last place in order to direct the whole, and to act as a kind of lieutenant of the supreme King.*

We have already noticed Philo's acceptance of the Platonic theory of ideas, and his belief that nature effects nothing in the perceptible world without an incorporeal pattern.† Agreeably to this doctrine he maintained that the generic man was created first, and subsequently the species, known as Adam.‡ The creation of the former was indicated in Scripture by the use of the word "made," the latter by the word "moulded."§ The genus was made "according to the image of God," the species was formed out of clay, into which God breathed a breath of life. Between these two there was a very wide distinction. The moulded man was an object of perception, participated in quality, consisted of body and soul, was man or woman, and naturally mortal. But "the man according to the image was an idea or genus or seal, intelligible, incorporeal, neither male nor female, by nature incorruptible."‖ We must be careful not to confound this generic man with the Logos. The Logos was, as we have seen, the archetype of human reason; and as reason is the true man within us,¶ the Logos was itself spoken

* Mundi Op., 25-29 (I. 18-21).   † Mundi Op., 44 (I. 31).
‡ Leg. All., II. 4 (I. 69).
§ Gen. i. 27, ἐποίησεν ὁ θεὸς τὸν ἄνθρωπον: ii. 7, ἔπλασεν.
‖ Mundi Op., 46 (I. 82).   ¶ See Vol. I. p. 324.

of as man.* But it was only of this higher and invisible humanity that the Logos was the idea,† whereas the generic man, in the strict sense, must have comprised not only "the idea of mind," but "the idea of sensation." This ideal or "heavenly man" was wholly immaterial, an "offspring" of God, in contrast with the "earthly moulded form" of Adam, and was "made" on the sixth day, and "stamped according to the image of God."‡ In other words, the ideal man was a thought generated within the divine Reason; and the "earthly" concrete man was an imperfect copy of this heavenly archetype.

In accordance with this distinction some things in Genesis are said of the ideal man, while some are applicable only to his concrete and imperfect representative. Thus the former is referred to when we are told that "the Lord God took the man whom he made, and set him in Paradise to work it and keep it."§ This signifies that God takes pure mind, not suffering it to go outside himself, and sets it amid the rooted and budding virtues, to work them and keep them; for many, after they have entered on the practice of virtue, have changed at the end; but he to whom God gives a secure knowledge not only *does*, but *keeps* the virtues, and never departs from them. But when in the following verses it is said that the Lord God enjoined upon Adam not to eat of the tree of the knowledge of good and evil, the moulded, earthly, corruptible man is meant; for Adam signifies "earth." It was to the latter, and not to the ideal mind, that a commandment was given, because the ideal mind, being self-taught and perfect, possesses virtue without exhortation, but the earthly requires instruction to guide it, since it occupies a medium position between the bad and good.|| The heavenly man is distinguished by the three

---

* See p. 189.   † See Quod det. pot. ins., 23 (I. 207).
‡ Leg. All., I. 9-12 (I. 47-49).
§ Gen. ii. 15, where the LXX reads ἔπλασε, not, as Philo, ἐποίησε.
|| Leg. All., I. 28-30 (I. 61-3).

constituents of good natural parts, cleverness, steadfastness, memory. The moulded mind, on the other hand, neither remembers nor practises what is good, but is only clever; and accordingly, though placed in Paradise, it is speedily ejected. Scripture marks this distinction by saying of the earthly man nothing more than that God set him in Paradise, without adding "to work it and keep it."* How completely we are moving in the world of abstract ideas is apparent from a statement found elsewhere, that the man stamped according to the image of God differs in no respect from the tree which bears the fruit of immortal life; for both are incorruptible, and have been deemed worthy of the middlemost and most sovereign portion, for it is said that "the tree of life is in the midst of Paradise."† We need not, therefore, see more than a figure of speech in an allusion to the longing of the ideal man for the archetypal image of God, founded on the words "It is not good for man to be alone."‡

When we descend to the world of actual men and women we find considerable obscurity in Philo's view owing to the presence of two unharmonized types of thought. We have seen his acceptance of the Platonic doctrine of the pre-existence of the soul; but when he speaks of the creation of man, and the communication to him of the divine Spirit, this doctrine totally disappears, and he follows the Scriptural statement that God breathed into man a breath of life. Whether he attempted to reconcile these in his own mind, or whether his adoption of the Platonic view was only a passing phase in his strangely blended speculations, must be left undetermined. If he supposed that the concrete and individual mind had descended into the body from the choir of aerial souls, he makes no use of this supposition, but proceeds as though each man began his mental history with his birth. Having pointed out this defect, we turn to Philo's account of the higher relations of mankind.

* Gen. ii. 8. Leg. All., I. 16 (I. 53 sq.).
† Gen. ii. 9. Plantat. Noe, 11 (I. 336).   ‡ Gen. ii. 18. Leg. All., II. 2 (I. 67).

The first earth-born man, the founder of our whole race, had the noblest endowments of both mind and body, and was in very ;truth beautiful and good. The fairness of his bodily form may be conjectured from three considerations. Since the earth was newly created, the material out of which things were made was unmixed and pure. Moreover God was not likely to have selected any common portion of the earth out of which to mould this statue in the human form, but to have taken from pure material the purest and best-sifted part; for the body was contrived as a house or sacred temple of rational soul, which it was to bear as the most God-like of images. And, lastly, the Creator was good, not only in other respects, but in knowledge, so that each part was both excellent in itself and exactly adapted to the entire organism. That the first man was best likewise in soul is apparent from the fact that God's own Reason was its archetype, and the imitation of an all-beautiful pattern must be itself all-beautiful. Thus equipped, he associated with rational divine natures, some incorporeal and intelligible, others, like the stars, clothed in bodies, who before him were denizens of the great cosmic city; and being, through the inflowing of the divine Spirit, related to the Sovereign of all, he was anxious to say and do everything to please the Father and King, following him in the paths of virtue. With such high communion, he naturally passed his time in unmingled blessedness. To him, in the prime of human wisdom and royalty, was entrusted the task of giving names to the subject animals, God having deemed him worthy of the second rank, and made him his own lieutenant, but sovereign of all else. Thus, he excelled in every noble quality, and reached the very limit of human bliss.*

The same happy lot was not, however, reserved for his descendants. Our birth is from men, but he was created by God, and the thing produced takes a higher rank in proportion to the superiority of the maker. The first man was the flower of

* Mundi Op., 47, 48, 50, 52 (I. 32-36). See also Nobil., 3 (II. 440).

our whole race, but those who followed him received forms and powers continually becoming more obscure through successive generations. A similar process may be seen in moulding and painting, for the copies fall short of the originals, and things painted and moulded from the copies still more so, as being farther from the beginning. Another illustration is furnished by the magnet, for of a series of iron rings the one in contact with it is most powerfully attracted, the next one less so, and at each further removal the attractive power still diminishes. Thus in generation after generation of men an increasing dimness has fallen upon the powers and qualities both of body and soul.* But Adam himself began the downward course. Though he had no mortal father, and was, in a manner, made in the image of God by virtue of the sovereign reason in his soul, he exercised a guilty choice; and when the opposites, good and evil, noble and base, true and false, were placed before him for his acceptance or rejection, he readily chose the false and base and evil, and neglected the good and noble and true, and thereby exchanged an immortal for a mortal life, and forfeited his happiness and bliss.† The beginning of his guilty life was woman, sensation, acting under the seduction of the serpent, pleasure.‡ A fuller exposition of this subject must be reserved for its proper place in the treatment of Philo's ethics.

But notwithstanding the fall and degeneracy of men they were far from having sunk into total corruption. As participating in the original idea, Adam's descendants preserved the ancient type, and, in spite of the waning of their powers through the lapse of such vast periods of time, still kept, as it were, a little torch of dominion and sovereignty handed down in succession from their founder.§ The true type of our humanity, the higher relationship of the rational soul or mind, which is the real man in each of us, was revealed

---

* Mundi Op., 49 (I. 33-4). See also Qu. et Sol. in Gen., I. 32.
† Nobil., 3 (II. 440). ‡ Mundi Op., 53 sqq. (I. 36 sqq.).
§ Mundi Op., 51, 52 (I. 35-6).

by the statement that man "was stamped according to the image of God"; that is to say, man in his higher faculties is the image of an image, and is a third impression from him who made him. The original image, "the eternal and blessed idea," which served as the archetype of human reason, was the divine Logos, which raised man into relationship with God, and endowed him with immortality.* The intermediate image, may, however, be omitted from view, and man brought into immediate connection with the Deity. "Nothing earth-born," says Philo, "is more like God than man." But this likeness or image is found, not in the body, but in the mind, which is sovereign of the soul. For the mind in each individual man has been made like that one Mind of the universe as an archetype, being in a manner a God of the body, which carries it like the statue of a Divinity. For the relation which the great Sovereign has in the whole cosmos is possessed by the human mind in man; for it is invisible, though itself seeing all things, and has an unknown essence, though apprehending the essences of all else, and it seeks for knowledge through earth and sea and sky, and presses on to the intelligible world of archetypes and ideas, till, seeking to reach the great King himself, it encounters the unmingled rays of the divine light, and the eye of the understanding turns dizzy with the brilliance.†

With this high relationship, it is not wonderful that none are wholly destitute of visitings of the divine Spirit. Who, asks Philo, is so bereft of reason or of soul as never to receive, either voluntarily or involuntarily, a notion of what is best? Even on the most abominable the conception of the noble often comes with sudden flight; but they are unable to retain it, because they harbour occupants who have departed from

---

* See Mundi Op. 7 (I. 5); § 51, p. 35; Plantat. Noe, 5 (I. 332); Quis. rer. div. her., 48 (I. 505); Vita Mos., II. 12 (II. 144); Dec. Orac., 25 (II. 202); Spec. Leg., III. 37 (II. 333); IV. 4 (II. 338); Exsecrat., 8 (II. 435).

† Mundi Op., 23 (I. 15-16).

law and right, and the higher thought serves only to convict them of choosing the base in preference to the noble.* Thus God has made no soul barren of good, though some may fail to use it; but, as he shows the superabundance of his riches and goodness by sending rain upon the sea and causing fountains to spring in the desert, he bountifully confers good things upon all, even upon the imperfect, provoking them to the zealous pursuit of virtue.† But while to those who are still defiled he allows the visits of his angel thoughts, in the minds of the perfectly purified he himself walks, noiseless and unseen; for the understanding of the wise man is in truth a palace and house of God. And hence man remains the only fitting temple. If, says Philo, we lavishly adorn our own houses for the reception of kings, that their entertainment may be graced with becoming dignity, what sort of house ought we to prepare for the King of kings, who, out of his love for man, has deigned to visit and bless our race? One of stones or timber? Absurd and impious suggestion! For not even if the whole earth were suddenly turned into gold, or something more precious than gold, and were then spent with constructive art in the preparation of porticoes and vestibules and sanctuaries, would it become a step for his feet. But a fitting soul is a worthy house.‡ This high privilege, however, is mingled with the vicissitudes of mortality, and even the greatest cannot always "carry God within them." There are fluctuations of the spirit, just as labour must be succeeded by rest, and the strings of a musical instrument must not be always on the strain.§

From such exalted language in describing the spiritual relationship of man, we might expect Philo to represent him as a son of God; but, though the expression is found, he makes little use of it, and he gives it an explanation which reduces it

* Gigant., 5 (I. 265). † Leg. All., I. 13 (I. 50).
‡ Cherub., 29 (I. 157); Somn., I. 23 (I. 643); Praem. et Poen., 20 (II. 428). See also Somn., II. 38 (I. 692).
§ Qu. et Sol. in Gen., IV. 29.

to an ordinary figure of speech. He who, like wise Abraham, is a friend of God is alone of noble birth, "as having God inscribed as his Father, and having become adopted as his only son."* Those who built the Babel tower of polytheism were called in Scripture the "sons of men," for they were ignorant of the one Maker and Father of the universe; but those who had the knowledge of him are called "sons of God"; as Moses says, "Ye are sons of the Lord God,"† and "God who begat thee,"‡ and "Is not he himself thy Father?"§ If, however, one is not yet worthy to be called a son of God, let him at least endeavour to be a son of his eternal image, the most sacred Logos.|| It is clear from these passages that the term is used as a designation of spiritual worth, and is not connected with the ontological relations of man. This is still more manifest from the remaining passage,—"Those who do what is pleasing to nature and what is noble are sons of God, for [Scripture] says, 'Ye are sons to the Lord our God,' evidently meaning that they will be deemed worthy of providence and care as from a Father."¶

Communion with God in its highest form reaches the state which is called "prophecy." This exalted condition is open to the wise and virtuous man, and to him alone. It includes, as in the case of Jacob, the power of predicting the future; but the great function of the prophet is to be the interpreter of God, and to find out through divine providence what the reflective faculties are unable to apprehend. He falls into a state of ecstasy, enthusiasm, or inspired frenzy, in which the natural reason is suspended, and he becomes a sounding organ of God, played upon invisibly by him; and when he seems to speak, he is in reality silent, and another uses his mouth and tongue to declare whatever he will. Thus he "utters nothing of his own," but speaks only what is suggested to him by

---

* Γεγονὼς εἰσποιητὸς αὐτῷ μόνος υἱός. Sobriet., 11 (I. 401).
† Deut. xiv. 1, ‡ Ib. xxxii. 18. § Ib. xxxii. 6.
|| Conf. Ling., 28 (I. 426-7). ¶ Sacrificant., 11 (II. 260).

God, by whom he is for the time possessed.* But, after all, the highest place seems to be assigned to the calm, steadfast, peaceful mind of the wise man, which, represented as it is by Moses standing between the Lord and Israel,† is superior to man, but inferior to God. The virtuous stands thus on the borders of two contrasted natures, and is neither God nor man, but touches the two extremes, the mortal genus by his humanity, the incorruptible by his virtue.‡ Here it is evident that "man" is used in its lower sense, and refers to our frailty and mortality, and in declaring that the perfect is neither God nor man Philo can allude only to that dual nature whose contrasts become most startling in the highest representatives of our race.

It is this possession of a higher and a lower nature that makes man a moral agent. Beings above man and beings below him are, as we have seen,§ alike exempt from sin; but with the possibility of following a better or a worse course of life the whole problem of ethics arises. The discussion of moral questions enters very largely into Philo's writings; but here, as elsewhere, his treatment is unsystematic, and rather aims at edification, to which his eclectic method is so well adapted, than attempts to draw the lines of ethical thought with increased precision. Still, we can clearly trace the principles which he embraced with the deepest conviction; and if we miss an Aristotelian severity, we may find some compensation in the glow of devout fervour with which his discussions are irradiated, and in the loftiness and purity of his sentiments, which made him so influential in the early ages of Christianity. As he does not himself lay out an order of investigation, we must adopt the method which seems best calculated to elucidate his thought.

* Quis rer. div. her., 52-3 (I. 510-11); Vita Mos., II. 1 (II. 135); Monarch., I. 9 (II. 222); Justit. 8 (II. 367-8); Praem. et Poen., 9 (II. 417); Qu. et Sol. in Gen., III. 9-10.
† Deut. v. 5.   ‡ Somn. II. 34 (I. 689).   § See p. 130.

The first question to which we must address ourselves is this: What is the ultimate good for man? What is the "end" of human life? If Philo does not expressly state, he evidently assumes that it is blessedness or well-being.* In speaking of hope as an incentive to action, he says, "The hope of blessedness induces those who are zealous of virtue to study philosophy, on the ground that by this means they will be able both to see the nature of things and to do what is agreeable to the perfecting of the best forms of life, the contemplative and the practical, on the attainment of which one is forthwith blessed."† If we hear elsewhere of the possibility of passing "beyond the limits of human blessedness,"‡ this can only refer to a degree of bliss greater than ordinarily falls to the lot of man, for blessedness§ is the most perfect gift that the powers of God can confer upon the soul.∥

To determine the ultimate good to be well-being, however, does little more than offer us a convenient phrase with which to start the discussion; for the well-being of any creature must depend upon its nature, and, in the case of a compound being like man, is not beyond the reach of difference of opinion. The good of the flesh is irrational pleasure; that of the soul, as of the universe, is the Mind of the universe, God. These two admit of no comparison, unless one is ready to maintain that the animate is the same as the inanimate, and the rational as the irrational, and darkness as light, and all contraries as their contraries. Nay, the case is still stronger; for these have a point of contact and affinity in the fact that they are all originated; but God, the Unbegotten and Ever-active, is not like even the best of natural objects.¶ Philosophy, however, goes a little farther in its analysis, and distinguishes three kinds of good, that which is altogether

* Εὐδαιμονία. † Praem. et Poen., 2 (II. 410).
‡ Sobriet., 11 (I. 401). § Γένος τὸ εὐδαιμον.
∥ Cherub., 31 (I. 158). See also Dec. Orac., 15 (II. 193).
¶ Gigant. 10 (I. 268).

external, that relating to the body, and that which belongs to the soul. It is possible to maintain that these are severally only the parts or elements of good, that each requires the aid of the other two, and that full and perfect good is a compound of them all. Even a lower view may be taken, and the highest good found in that which is external and sensible; but no soul in which God walks can cherish such an opinion. The former contention is more plausible; but physical and spiritual good cannot be thus blended. The so-called external and bodily goods are "advantages" only, the sphere of the "necessary and useful," but not in reality good.* This statement is not carefully reasoned out; but it follows from the whole scope of Philo's philosophy, in which the rational is separated by such an impassable interval from the irrational. And if we once admit the conception of a "sovereign principle" as the determining factor in man's nature, it seems only reasonable to assert that the true good dwells, not in anything external or in things connected with the body, or even in every part of the soul, but in the sovereign principle alone; for the mind, the temple of God, bears the good as a divine image, though some may disbelieve it who have never tasted wisdom, or tasted it only with the tips of their lips; for silver and gold, and honours and dominions, and bodily health and beauty are only appointed to the service of virtue as their queen, and true nobility belongs only to the purified understanding of the righteous.†

If in our estimate of human good we are thus confined to the highest of the faculties, it readily follows that virtue alone among created things is beautiful and good. From this sprung the Stoical maxim that the noble, or morally beautiful,‡ is alone good.§ Accordingly virtue is an end in itself; and the man of high character, as he prizes day for the sake of day, and light for the sake of light, acquires the noble for the sake

* Quod det. pot. ins., 2-4 (I. 192-3); Leg. All., III. 53 (I. 118).
† Nobil. 1 (II. 437-8).   ‡ Τὸ καλόν.   § Post. Cain., 39 (I. 251).

of the noble alone, not for the sake of something else; for this is a divine law, to honour virtue on her own account.*

We are now prepared to say that human well-being consists of good intentions, words, and deeds, bound together in indissoluble bonds of harmony.† It involves the use and enjoyment, and not merely the possession, of virtue, and accordingly may be defined as "the practice of perfect virtue in a perfect life."‡ If only men everywhere agreed with the few, and became what nature designed them to be, free from guilt, lovers of wisdom, rejoicing in the noble for the sake of the noble itself, and esteeming this only to be good, cities would be full of blessedness, released from the sources of pain and fear, and replete with what produces joy and gladness, and through all the circle of the year there would be a continual feast.§

These philosophical statements, however, can hardly satisfy the feeling of the religious man, and Philo endeavours to lift the thoughts still higher. Philosophy, he says, inculcates self-control in the indulgence of the appetites, self-control in the use of the tongue also; and it is said that these things are to be chosen on their own account, but they would appear more solemn if they were pursued for the sake of honouring and pleasing God.‖ In the lower stage of moral progress we are instructed not to neglect what is established as righteous by ordinance and universal repute, but when we have risen high enough to understand the lessons of right reason, we are taught to honour the Father of all. Thus when the Patriarch was sufficiently advanced to see clearly what before he had received by the hearing of the ears, his name was changed from Jacob to Israel, the name of perfection, signifying "the

---

* Leg. All., III. 58 (I. 120). Cf. Sobriet., 13 (I. 402).
† Mutat. Nom., 41 (I. 614); Praem. et Poen., 14 (II. 421).
‡ Quod det. pot. ins., 17 (I. 203). See also Agr. Noe, 36 (I. 324). Cf. Aristotle, Eth. Nic., I. vii. 15-16.
§ Septen., 4 (II. 279-80). ‖ Congr. erud. gr., 14 (I. 530).

vision of God"—and what could be more perfect among the things that pertain to virtue than to see the really self-existent Being?* But the power of seeing God depends on our being kindred to him through the copious inflowing of his Spirit; and accordingly our true end is likeness to God who begat us, saying and doing everything to please him, and following him in the ways which the virtues mark.† It is only another way of expressing the same thought to say that our end is "to follow God,"‡ and imitate him as far as possible.§ On this ground rests the commandment to observe the seventh day, ceasing from work, and giving it to philosophy, contemplation, and the improvement of our characters.‖ Similarly, all who are placed in authority, and have the power of doing well or ill, ought to benefit rather than injure, for this is to follow God, who, having the power to do either, wills the good alone, as is proved by the creation and government of the world.¶ Still we must never forget that the virtue of man is only an imitation and copy of the divine,** and, like other imitations, must fall far short of the original. Indeed, it is the height of ignorance to suppose that a human soul could contain the virtues of God, which are without a bias and most firmly fixed. Those of God, agreeably to the simplicity of his nature, are unmixed; but those of man, compounded as he is of the divine and the mortal, are of mingled quality. The several parts naturally pull against one another; and blessed is he who is able during the greater portion of his life to incline towards the better and diviner lot, for it is impossible to do so throughout the whole period, since the mortal weight sometimes sinks the scale, and (to use another metaphor), lying in wait, watches for an opportunity when reason is off its guard.†† But notwithstanding these

* Τὸ ὄντως ὄν. Ebriet., 20 (I. 369).
‡ Migrat. Abr., 23 (I. 456).
‖ Dec. Orac., 20 (II. 197).
** Quod. det. pot. ins., 44 (I. 222).

† Mundi Op., 50 (I. 34-5).
§ Human., 23 (II. 404).
¶ Justit., 7 (II. 367).
†† Mutat. Nom., 34 (I. 606).

drawbacks, which are incident to the weakness of mortality, we may now revise our definition, and say that the knowledge of God, or likeness to him, is the end of blessedness.* The soul that has him for its shepherd, possessing the one and only Being on whom all things depend, needs nothing further, and cares not for "blind riches."† He is "the perfect and incorruptible and true good,"‡ and refuge with him is "eternal life."§

From the foregoing account of the highest good we may easily pass to Philo's conception of the supreme evil. "He who flees from God takes refuge in himself." In our relations with God this is the simple alternative. There are only the two minds to be considered, that of the universe, which is God, and our own. These stand over against one another, and he who abandons the universal, unbegotten, and incorruptible, necessarily falls back upon the partial, begotten, and mortal, and takes a radically false view of everything in the cosmos.‖ Hence arise two antithetic opinions: one, which attributes everything to the mind as the sovereign of thought, sensation, and motion; the second, ascribing all to God. The former is symbolized by Cain, a name which means "possession;" the latter by Abel, signifying "ascribing to God." Both are the offspring of one soul; but it is impossible for them to continue to live together, and when the God-loving dogma, Abel, is brought forth, the self-loving Cain is obliged to quit.¶ The mind, then, which wishes to be the "heir of divine things," must not only, like Abraham, leave the body and sensation and speech, but must flee from itself, and rise into an ecstasy like those possessed with corybantic frenzy, and become excited and maddened with heavenly love.** Philo can hardly have supposed that this wild religious excitement could ever form

* Sacrificant, 16 (II. 264); Dec. Orac., 15 (II. 193). † Agr. Noe, 13 (I. 309).
‡ Gigant., 11 (I. 269). § Prof., 15 (I. 557).
‖ Leg. All., III. 9 (I. 93). ¶ SS. Ab. et Cain., 1 (I. 163-4).
** Quis. rer. div. her., 14 (I. 482).

the permanent and healthy condition of the pure soul, and some allowance may be made for rhetorical exaggeration, though we must not forget that he found here the genuine mark of the prophet. He speaks more soberly when he reduces the escape from self to the abandonment of the notion that we think and understand by our own autocratic judgment,* and remarks that it is not easy to believe God alone without reposing faith in anything besides, owing to our union with mortality, which draws us down to what is transient, and that to distrust the created, and believe God alone, who in truth is alone faithful, is the work of a great and Olympian understanding, enticed no more by anything on earth.† He touches a yet deeper note when he says that complete self-knowledge involves self-despair, and he who has despaired of self knows Him who eternally is.‡

From this antithesis it readily follows that the greatest evil, and the source of all evils, is self-love.§ As Philo is not very strict in his terminology, this fundamental fault sometimes receives other names. Arrogance or boastfulness,|| which we might rather describe as one of the manifestations of self-love, is referred to as "the evil most hateful to God."¶ As standing in direct antagonism to the devotion which we owe to the Creator, it becomes impiety;** and as involving a total misconception of the true relations of things, it is spoken of as ignorance.††

The last term, "ignorance," may seem to blur the boundaries of the moral and the intellectual, and either to reduce sin to a form of mistaken opinion or to clothe erroneous opinion with the attributes of guilt, and Philo is severely taken to task by Dähne for this impropriety.‡‡ It is not surprising that a Jew

---

* Ib., § 16, p. 485. † Ib., § 18, pp. 485-6. ‡ Somn., I. 10 (I. 629-30).
§ Φιλαυτία. Congr. erud. gr., 23 (I. 538); Fragments, II. 661-2.
|| Μεγαλαυχία. ¶ Somn., I. 36 (I. 652-3).
** Ἀσέβεια. Congr. erud. gr., 28 (I. 542).
†† Τῷ μεγίστῳ τῶν κακῶν, ἀμαθίᾳ, Legat. ad Cai., 1 (II. 546).
‡‡ I., pp. 354-6.

of that period was not wholly free from intolerance; but I think it is only just to remark that his works, in comparison with some of the writings of Christian fathers, are distinguished by the paucity of the odium theologicum. He undoubtedly recognized a close connection between moral self-surrender and the direction of speculative thought, and believed that absorption in self poisoned the very fountains of correct thinking; but surely it would be rash to maintain that there was no reciprocal action between these things, that wrong opinion never produced faulty conduct, and that depravity of character had no effect upon the loftiness and purity of the conceptions. It is the application of this principle that tests the charity and wisdom of the judgment, and we have seen in our Introduction that Philo was not wholly above the superstitions of bigotry. In the present connection, however, we are concerned with opinions which have their roots in the general character of the mind, and may therefore, without the reproach of intolerance, be brought into relation with that self-love which is the supreme evil. Thus he treats as an impious opinion, worthy only of Cain, the celebrated dictum of Protagoras that man or the human mind is the measure of all things; but he understands by this, not that man is precluded from objective knowledge, but that all things are the gift of the mind, by which their various powers are bestowed upon the senses, and the very exercise of thought is generated. He cannot treat this as a mere speculative error, because it is implicated with the practical fault of honouring the proximate rather than the distant cause, that is to say, man rather than God; and accordingly no success which it has obtained over the opposite opinion can make it other than impious. Cain may kill Abel; "but with me and my friends," says Philo, "death with the pious would be preferable to life with the impious: immortal life will receive the pious dead, but eternal death awaits the impious living."*

* Post. Cain., 11 (I. 232-3).

He recurs again and again to this kind of error. It is with him a fundamental truth, obvious to every pious soul that is not entangled in the sophistries of self-love, that all things are God's, and he is the only absolute Cause. He, therefore, who, like Laban, supposes everything to be his own, and honours himself before God, is blinded by self-love; he is a thief, appropriating what belongs to another, and afflicted by his own atheism and opinionativeness.* He is unable, however, while doing partial mischief, to destroy the ideas of virtue, which are imperishable; the God-loving opinion which he thinks that he has slain, lives with God, and he has succeeded only in laying violent hands upon himself.† He who is swayed by this "immeasurable ignorance," and, forgetting that it belongs to God alone to say "mine," dares to affirm that anything is his own, shall be written down a slave for all eternity.‡ It is another form of this error to attribute to oneself the causes of right actions instead of reposing one's hope upon God; and the source of such conduct is the preference of self-love to piety.§ The soul must not claim to be creative when it is only susceptible; and when it thinks that it is equal to God, and forgets that it is He who plants and builds up the virtues within it, it is self-loving and atheistical. Such opinions injure and wrong itself, not God.|| Precisely the same temper is shown in blaming God rather than ourselves for our sins. With God are the treasures of good alone; those of moral evil are in ourselves.¶ Atheism, then, which Philo treats as "the fountain of all unrighteous deeds,"** is not, in his conception, a merely speculative error, which may arise in a pure mind from the force of intellectual difficulties, but is always implicated with a selfish direction of

---

* Οἴησις.
† Leg. All., III. 10 (I. 93-4); Cherub., 19 sqq. (I. 150 sqq.); SS. Ab. et Cain., 19 (I. 176); Quod det. pot. ins., 10, 11 (I. 197-8); § 21, p. 206.
‡ Leg. All., III. 70 (I. 126).   § Praem. et Poen., 2 (II. 410).
|| Leg. All., I. 15 (I. 53).   ¶ Prof., 15 (I. 557).
** Dec. Orac., 18 (II. 196).

character, with a devotion to the interests, and a sense of the importance, of our own individuality, which induce a forgetfulness of God and of all our indebtedness to him.* At all events, the supreme evil, which ends in misery and death, is not an intellectual mistake, but the self-love which leads a man to do everything for his own sake, and to neglect the claims of parents, children, country, mankind, and God, and, instead of rendering to everyone his due, to look upon the universe as an appendage to himself, not himself as an appendage to the universe.†

Having thus ascertained Philo's theory of the highest good and its contrasted evil, we must next determine the conditions of moral responsibility.

In the first place man must have a twofold nature, the rational, directed towards the universal and eternal, the irrational, which seeks the particular and transient; for, as we have seen, creatures which are wholly rational are above the reach of moral evil, and those that are wholly irrational fall below it, while man, almost alone, with his mixed nature, admits the presence of contraries, " good and evil, noble and base, virtue and vice."‡ It follows from this that reason is by itself sufficient for the reception and practice of virtue, and, so far from deriving assistance from the body, has its chief task in holding itself aloof from the bodily desires; but for the enjoyment of vice one must have not only reason, but sensation and speech and a body, for it is only through these that the bad man can bring his vice to completion.§ The retort is sufficiently obvious that, among men at least, a good action cannot be accomplished any more than a bad one without bodily organs; but though Philo's reasoning is faulty, the thesis itself is less open to objection, that for the admission of

---

* Sacrificant., 16 (II. 264); SS. Ab. et Cain., 13 (I. 171-2).
† Quod Deus immut., 4 (I. 275).
‡ Mundi Op., 24 (I. 17); Conf. Ling., 35 (I. 432).
§ Leg. All., I. 32 (I. 64).

moral evil the presence is necessary, not only of reason, but of a lower and more limited nature, whereas pure reason may be conceived as in uninterrupted communion with the good. But though bodily tendencies are a condition without which evil would not present itself, nevertheless the home and sole receptacle, not only of virtue, but of vice, is the mind or reason, the sovereign principle itself.* This statement, however, implies that our individual, earthly reason is below the ideal; for ideal reason possesses virtue through its own self-illumination, but ours could not attain to wisdom without instruction. In its original condition, as represented by Adam, the human mind occupies a middle place, being neither bad nor good; and accordingly, in the ancient story, it received an admonition from the divine Being under both his appellations, Lord and God, in order that, if it were obedient, it might receive benefits from God, and, if it disobeyed, it might be punished by the Lord, the wielder of authority.† A choice was thus presented to a mind morally neutral; but though God called it to participate in virtue and wisdom, it chose vice, ignorance, and corruption, and preferred wretchedness, the soul's death, to blessedness, its true life.‡

This power of choice involves the freedom of the will, in which we find a second condition of responsibility. We have fully considered Philo's doctrine of the will in another connection,§ and we have now only to notice his clear recognition of the dependence of moral desert upon the voluntary character of an action. Those who have lost the eye of the soul, and turned away from God, owing to necessity, being oppressed by the force of an inexorable power, should meet with pity rather than hatred, while punishment is reserved for voluntary aberration; for as right actions which spring from a purpose

* Mundi Op., 24 (I. 17); Animal. Sacr. idon., 7 (II. 243).
† Leg. All., I. 30 (I. 62-3). See also Praem. et Poen., 11 (II. 418), where it is said that by nature all men, before the reason in them is perfected, are on the borders of vice and virtue, inclining to neither.
‡ Leg. All., III. 17 (I. 97). § Vol. I., pp. 346 sqq.

are better than the involuntary, so in the case of wrong actions the involuntary are lighter than the voluntary.* Nay, conscience, by refusing to act as accuser, testifies that involuntary offences are blameless and pure.† It is in accordance with this judgment that praise is reserved for conduct which requires some exertion of the will. Thus we do not praise old men for abstaining from youthful pleasures, to which they have no temptation. In other words, preferential choice between opposing motives is essential to moral desert.‡ But it is not only essential; it is sufficient. Many causes may interfere to prevent the attainment of our end; but a preferential judgment and endeavour has virtually attained the end, and therefore those who have begun either good or evil purposes must be considered on a par with those who have accomplished them.§

Again, in order to be responsible, man must have a knowledge of the better and the worse. Without this he might throw the blame of his wrong-doing on him who failed to inspire him with a notion of what is good, and perhaps might even maintain that he did not sin at all, since some affirm that involuntary acts and those done in ignorance have not the character of wrong-doing.‖ From this form of expression we may conclude that Philo's own opinion was that the wrongfulness of acts remained, and that actions might, in the abstract, be classified as right and wrong,¶ although, when they were done in ignorance, one could not attach merit or demerit to the individual performing them. This latter position he unequivocally maintains. Until the divine Reason has entered

* Post. Cain., 2, 3 (I. 227-8).   † Quod Deus immut., 27 (I. 291).
‡ Post. Cain., 20 (I. 238).   § Harris, Fragments, p. 71.
‖ Leg. All., I. 13 (I. 50).
¶ This is even more evidently involved in the statement that τὸ ἀκουσίως ἁμαρτάνειν καὶ κατ' ἄγνοιαν is neither δίκαιον nor ἄδικον, but on the borders of both, what some call ἀδιάφορον, ἁμάρτημα γὰρ οὐδὲν ἔργον δικαιοσύνης: Fragments II. 651, answering to Qu. et Sol. in Gen. IV. 64. Philo also perceives that the virtuous and the worthless often do τὰ αὐτὰ καθήκοντα, but from different motives: Harris, Fragm., p. 70.

the soul, all our acts are blameless, and pardon is granted to those who sin through ignorance, for they do not apprehend their actions as sinful.* Conversely, there is nothing praiseworthy in the practice of the best actions when they are not done with understanding and reason.† Man, therefore, in order that he may be responsible, has been endowed with conscience. This is a subject to which Philo recurs again and again, and on which he sometimes eloquently dilates. His main thoughts, however, may be presented in a brief compass. The mind is to each man a witness of his invisible purposes, and conscience is an impartial and most truthful conviction.‡ The true man in the soul is the rational understanding, and it is found to be sometimes a ruler and king, sometimes a judge and an umpire of life's contests; and sometimes, taking the rank of witness and accuser, it inwardly convicts, and curbs the arrogant with the reins of conscience.§ The worst men are not unconscious of this imperial claim, but they, too, receive the notions which belong to conscience, that they will not escape the notice of the Deity when they do wrong, or be able to elude punishment for ever. Conscience within convicts, and keenly goads those who follow after godlessness, so that against their will they are forced to assent to the truth that all the affairs of men are surveyed by a better Nature, and that Right stands by as an impartial avenger, detesting the unjust practices of the impious, and the words by which they defend them.‖ In its conflict with evil the conscience which dwells and has grown with each soul, exercises the twofold office of accuser and judge. In the former capacity it charges, accuses, is importunate; again, as judge, it teaches, admon-

* Quod Deus immut., 28 (I. 292). See also Flac., 2 (II. 518) — Τῷ μὲν γὰρ ἀγνοίᾳ τοῦ κρείττονος διαμαρτάνοντι συγγνώμη δίδοται· ὁ δὲ ἐξ ἐπιστήμης ἀδικῶν ἀπολογίαν οὐκ ἔχει, προεαλωκὼς ἐν τῷ τοῦ συνειδότος δικαστηρίῳ.

† Post. Cain., 24 (I. 241). ‡ Post. Cain., 17 (I. 236).

§ Quod det. pot. ins., 8 (I. 195-6). See also Mundi Op., 43 (I. 30); Quod Deus immut., 27 (I. 291); § 28, p. 292-3; Prof., 21 (I. 563); § 23, p. 565; § 37, p. 576; § 38, p. 577; Nobil., 4 (II. 441).

‖ Conf. Ling., 24 (I. 423).

ishes, advises to change, and, if it is able to persuade, it is joyfully reconciled, but, if not, it wages unceasing war, not desisting by day or night, but inflicting incurable pricks and wounds, till it snaps the miserable and accursed life.* It is clear, then, that conscience is regarded as expressing the verdict of divine Reason, and bearing witness to the presence of a higher personality than our own. God sees the things in the recesses of the understanding, and walks in its inmost sanctuaries; and, accordingly, when one wishes to offer sacrifice for sin, he must wash away the old misdeeds, and come with pure conscience to present the mind itself, cleansed with the perfect virtues, and bringing as its advocate that inward conviction of sin which has been its deliverer.†

Such, then, are the general conditions without which moral and responsible life would be impossible. We must next refer to the circumstances amid which man must fight the battle between good and evil, and the influences which draw him towards one or the other. We may notice first the sources of evil.

The most general source is found in the simple fact that man is created, and therefore belongs to the phenomenal world. In considering the nature of matter we saw how the phenomenal stood, in Philo's thought, over against the eternity of God, and was involved, by its very idea, in incurable disabilities.‡ The same law applies to man. Goodness, being divine, and therefore sharing the unchanging stability of God, cannot be received in its perfection by a changeful and mortal being. Hence it is that " not to sin at all is the property of God, perhaps also of a divine man."§ The possible exception is made on account of the mysterious proximity which one may have to the divine power and

---

* Dec. Orac., 17 (II. 195).
† Quod Deus immut., 2 (I. 274); § 6, p. 276-7; Animal. Sacr. idon., 5 (II. 241); 11, p. 247.
‡ See Vol. I. pp. 310 sqq. § Poenit., 1 (II. 405).

blessedness, if, like the all-wise Abraham, he checks by the love of knowledge the motion which is proper to everything created.* But this is only an ideal, founded upon the words of Scripture, and not supported by the experience of life. To man as we know him "the complete acquisition of the virtues is impossible."† By his very entrance on the scene of phenomena he becomes exposed to evil; for as God is the maker of good and holy things, that which is contrasted with him, by coming into existence and perishing, is the source of things evil and unhallowed,‡ and to everything generated, though it may be excellent in all other respects, sinning is naturally attached.§ Man, however, is not wholly mortal, nor is he exclusively related to the phenomenal world. He has to choose between the eternal and the transient; and if he cannot attain to absolute goodness, he prefers the worse only when he participates too largely in the mortal element.‖

This mortal element is of course found in the bodily constitution, and the body, or the flesh, is the medium in which the lower life is spent, and to which it is related. It is not because it is material that Philo regards the body as antagonistic to the soul, but because it is phenomenal, transient, mortal, and therefore antithetic to that world of eternal ideas amid which reason lives, and where alone the virtues can be won. " It is not possible," he says, "while dwelling in the body and the mortal genus, to hold communion with God."¶ The divine Spirit, accordingly, though it comes in sudden flashes of higher thought, even to him who is most destitute of soul, cannot permanently abide with our fleshly nature, which is the foundation of our ignorance, on which all the distracting cares of our ordinary life are built. Disembodied souls enjoy, without impediment, a continual feast of divine sights and sounds;

---

* Cherub., 6 (I. 142).   † Mutat. Nom., 6 (I. 585).
‡ Plantat. Noe, 12 (I. 337).   § Vita Mos., III. 17 (II. 157).
‖ Congr. erud. gr., 15 (I. 531).   ¶ Leg. All., III. 14 (I. 95).

but those that bear the burden of the flesh are unable to look up, and, being dragged down like beasts, are rooted to the earth.* In order to escape from this degrading position the souls of philosophers seek to die to the life with bodies; but this is not an end in itself; their object is "that they may participate in the incorporeal and incorruptible life with Him who is unbegotten and incorruptible."† This abandonment of the bodily life is often combined by Philo with a renunciation of the senses, the source of seductive and misleading impressions, and of speech, the organ of false opinions and sophistical reasonings. But the abandonment refers only to the emancipation of the judgment. These things are our subjects, and must never be allowed to rule; we are their kings, and must govern, but not be governed.‡ In our bodily requirements resides, not the good, but only the necessary and useful; and therefore the indulgence of them must be strictly controlled by reason, for things dissociated from reason are all disgraceful, as things combined with it are decorous.§

The body, then, with its mortal life, can only be regarded as a prison, confined by which the true man, purest mind, is unable to draw a breath of free air; and as Moses left the camp, the mind aspires to leave the body, with its irrational impulses, its strifes, battles, and quarrels, and to live with the Self-existent himself, in the contemplation of incorporeal ideas.‖ Or, changing the figure, the mortal body is a sepulchral monument in which the mind is entombed.¶ Or, again, the lover of

* Gigant., 5 and 7 (I. 265-7).

† Gigant., 3 (I. 264). The contrast between the phenomenal βίος and the timeless ζωή is lost in English. Perhaps, however, it is not intended, for we have elsewhere ἐκ θνητῆς ζωῆς εἰς ἀθάνατον βίον, Human., 4 (II. 387).

‡ See Ebriet., 16, 17 (I. 366-7); Migrat. Abr., 1-2 (I. 436-8); § 35, p. 466; Quis rer. div. her., 14 (I. 482-3); § 16, p. 485; Prof., 17 (I. 559).

§ Leg. All., III. 52-3 (I. 117 sq.).

‖ Ebriet., 25-6 (I. 372). Cf. Migrat. Abr., 2 (I. 437), where Philo goes so far as to call the body τὸ παμμίαρον δεσμωτήριον.

¶ Justit., 8 (II. 367). The play upon the words is lost in a translation, σῶμα ὃ κυρίως ἄν τις σῆμα καλέσειε.

virtue does not settle down in the body as in his own land, but is only a sojourner in it as in a foreign country; for righteousness and every virtue love the soul, unrighteousness and every vice the body, and the things which are friendly to the one are hostile to the other.* From all this it follows that the body is not neutral in the conflict between good and evil. To say the least, it must hang as a dead weight upon the soul, and, as Philo expresses it, it not only does not co-operate with us towards the attainment of virtue, but it is an active hindrance; for the work of wisdom almost consists in reaching a state of alienation from the body and its desires.† From this point of view every friend of God must recognize it as not only a dead incumbrance, but as naturally evil,‡ and a plotter against the soul.§ Nevertheless, I do not suppose that Philo meant by such language to teach a doctrine contradicting his clear statement that the reason alone is the abode of virtue and vice. The principle of moral evil is found, not in matter, or in physical organization, but in the relation which the soul assumes towards the body; and the latter is evil, not intrinsically, but because it acts as an impediment to the higher aspirations of the soul, and, through its necessities, draws off our attention, and sometimes our allegiance, from that which is spiritual. Accordingly, Philo recognizes the fact that there are other things which are more destitute of soul than the body, such as glory, wealth, dominions, honours, and all else that has been shaped or depicted, under the deceit of false opinion, by men who have not discerned what is truly beautiful.‖ Moral evil does not reside in these things themselves, for they have no meaning apart from men's regard for them, but consists in our making them rather than the reason a standard of reference, and abandoning ourselves to what is so unstable and accidental. Accordingly, in the very passage where Philo

---

* Quis rer. div. her., 54 and 50 (I. 511 and 507).
† Leg. All., I. 32 (I. 64).   ‡ Πονηρὸν φύσει, κακόν.
§ Leg. All., III. 22 (I. 100-1).   ‖ Gigant., 3 (I. 264).

uses the strongest language about the evil of the body, he declares that it was made by God,—a name which represents the goodness of the Cause,—the creation of the inferior being necessary for the manifestation of the superior.* He could hardly depart so widely from his general doctrine as to make God the creator of what was absolutely evil; and therefore we must be dealing, not with an intrinsically malignant matter, but with that which is relatively inferior, in the preference of which moral evil consists.† Indeed, the very reason why we should abandon the body, sensation, and speech, and dedicate their powers to God, is found in the fact that he is their Creator, and, accordingly, he, rather than they, is entitled to our service.‡

But we have not exhausted the subject when we have recognized in the body a mortal and material clog upon the immortal spirit. Closely connected with it are certain psychical powers, which, though intended to be helpers to men, too often lead them to their ruin. These are the senses, and their offspring, the passions. Their characteristic inferiority consists in their being irrational, and therefore unworthy guides for man, whose sovereign principle is reason.§ But notwithstanding their lower position, the powers of sense are "divine gifts, for which we ought to give thanks."|| They cannot, therefore, be evil in the proper sense of the word, and Philo expressly declares that sensation cannot be classed with things either morally bad or morally good, but, being common to the wise man and the fool, occupies an intermediate position, and becomes bad in the fool and good in the virtuous.¶ The exercise of the senses, however, brings to our notice an element of graver import. The mind and sensation are brought together by pleasure,** which is varied in its mani-

---

* Leg. All., III. 23 (I. 101).
‡ See Quis rer. div. her., 14 (I. 483).
|| Congr. erud. gr., 18 (I. 533).
** Ἡδονή.

† See note †† on p. 50.
§ Leg. All., II. 3 (I. 67-8).
¶ Leg. All., III. 21 (I. 100).

festations as the folds of a serpent, and, with all its pretended friendship, is hostile even to the senses themselves, for he who, like the drunkard and the glutton, abandons himself to pleasure, impairs his sensibility.* It is an indispensable accompaniment of our lives; for, apart from pleasure, nothing takes place among mankind, and therefore the moral difference between men consists, not in their having or not having it, but in their way of regarding it. The bad man uses it as a perfect good; the virtuous man as only a necessity.† We must interpret in accordance with this plain statement the declaration that pleasure "is not found in a virtuous man at all, but only the bad man enjoys it."‡ Philo must mean that, while the bad man makes it the chief object of pursuit, and nurses it in his consciousness, the good man does not recognize it as a principle of action, or allow his mind to dwell upon it. A contrast is here made between the senses and pleasure. The former make their appearance in all alike, and furnish no ground of moral distinction; the presence or absence of the latter, on the contrary, is a criterion of ethical value, and the ideally virtuous would have risen wholly above it.

In order to see clearly the nature of pleasure we must classify it. It is different from joy, even from the joy which breaks into the gaiety of laughter; for this, as we shall see, stands high in Philo's estimation. It is also different from well-being, or blessedness,§ for the man who is the slave of pleasure could not be blessed;|| so that hedonistic and eudaemonistic ethics would, with our philosopher, be in direct antagonism. It is one of the passions,¶ which, though as forms of consciousness they are affections of the soul, have their receptacle and seat in the body.** They are quite alien to

* Leg. All., II. 18 (I. 79 sq.); III. 64 (I. 123).
† Leg. All., II. 6 (I. 69 sq.).   ‡ Leg. All., III. 21 (I. 100).
§ Εὐδαιμονία, the highest condition affecting τὸν ἴδιον δαίμονα, λέγω δὲ τὸν ἑαυτοῦ νοῦν, Fragm., II. 635.
|| Ib.   ¶ Πάθη.   ** Post. Cain., 8 (I. 231); Congr. erud. gr., 12 (I. 528).

the understanding, and agitate the soul in contravention of its own nature; for they grow out of the flesh, in which they have their roots, and are stimulated by the various objects presented to us through the senses. They are of innumerable species, but may be summed up under four genera. Two, pleasure and desire, relate to present or future good; and two, grief and fear, are concerned with present or expected evil.* Of these, desire is the most formidable; for each of the others falls upon us from without, and appears to be involuntary, but desire alone has its source in ourselves, and is voluntary. This distinction is probably founded on the prohibition of desire in the Ten Commandments, for it is in the discussion of these that the remark is made. The prohibition implies the power of voluntary control, and accordingly Philo ascribes to it a more ideal origin than to the other passions, and traces it to the conception of an absent good. We must further notice the connection between desire and pleasure. Desire is essentially, in Philo's view, a love of absent things conducive to pleasure, and he even speaks directly of the " desire of pleasure." I think, then, we shall not misrepresent his opinion if we say that pleasure, regarded simply as the involuntary accompaniment of innocent sensation, lies outside the moral field, and that it enters it only through the attention and desire which are directed towards it with the sanction of the will.† But, though this may be true, the passions enter so largely into our life, and so imperiously attract the attention, that they must be ranked among things morally evil. They are the wild beasts and birds of the soul, which, with untamed fury, tear the mind to pieces, and fly upon the understanding with sharp and irresistible attack,‡ or, in more philosophical

---

* Ἡδονή, ἐπιθυμία, λύπη, φόβος.

† See Quis rer. div. her., 54 (I. 511-12); Congr. erud. gr., 15 (I. 531); Abr., 41 (II. 34-5); Dec. Orac., 28 (II. 204-5); Concup., 8 (II. 354); Praem. et Poen., 12 (II. 419).

‡ Leg. All., II. 4 (I. 68).

phrase, every passion is culpable, as being a boundless and excessive impulse, a movement of the soul which is irrational and in violation of its nature, and, if it be not bridled, may hurry the mind into almost irretrievable disaster.* So long as these irrational impulses are still, the mind is firm and calm; but when they call together and stir up the passions, they generate civil strife.† Reason contends with the passions, and these antagonists cannot remain together in the same place. With a change of metaphor, it is the charioteer who is set over them, to rein them in;‡ or, like Abraham marching against the confederate kings, it joins battle with them, and vanquishes them by its divine power.§

It is apparent from this account that the evil of the passions consists, not in their being forms of the sensibility, but simply in their antagonism to reason. Accordingly, though Philo is never careful to point out the distinction, we find that he really divides passions into good and bad. The disciples of Moses are to be free, not from every passion, but from "every irrational passion."‖ Are there, then, passions which are rational, and strengthen the highest element of our being? Yes; pity is a "passion the most necessary, and most akin to the rational soul."¶ Moses, in his most exalted mood, mingled with his thankful hymns to God "the genuine passions of good-will towards the nation."** His kindly passion was especially extended to Joshua, and he was, in a manner, goaded by it to disclose what he thought would be beneficial.†† We hear also of the "passion that hates evil and loves God."‡‡

It is clear, therefore, that if Philo had carefully worked

---

* Concup., 1 (II. 348). See also Agr. Noe, 7-8 (I. 304-6).
† Ebriet., 25 (I. 372).   ‡ Leg. All., III. 39-40 (I. 110 sq.).
§ Abr., 41 (II. 35).   ‖ Jud. 1 (II. 344).
¶ Human., 18 (II. 399).   ** Ib., 3 (II. 387).   †† Ib., p. 386.
‡‡ Monarch., I. 7 (II. 220). See also Spec. Leg., III. 5 (II. 304); § 12, p. 312; § 22, p. 320; IV. 2 (II. 337),—all μισοπόνηρον πάθος: Septen. 9 (II. 285), and Praem. et Poen., 13 (II. 420)—φιλοίκειον πάθος.

out the psychology of his subject, he would have divided the passions into 'good and bad according as they promoted or hindered the highest purposes of rational existence. Hence we must view desire not only as a passion, but as an irrational passion. We may, of course, in our sense of the word, desire what is really good; but the longing of the soul for the treasures of the ideal world is not included by Philo under this term. Desire was supposed to have its seat in the abdomen, the part most remote from the head, which was the seat of reason, and is defined to be the craving "for absent things which are looked upon as good, but are not truly so." Its typical example is the appetite for food and drink, which leads to gluttony and drunkenness, and delights to live, like swine, in the mire; but it includes the craving for wealth, glory, power, beauty, and all the other countless things that excite jealousy and contention in human life. And as the so-called "creeping disease" creeps over every limb from head to foot, so desire, darting through the whole soul, leaves not the smallest part of it unaffected, but spreads like a fire, till it has consumed it all. It is, then, a surpassing evil; but it is more; it is the fountain of all evils; for robberies, outrages, adulteries, murders, all public or private wrongs, have flowed from this source. It has covered land and sea with calamities, and to whatever objects it attaches itself, it changes men for the worse, like venomous animals or deadly drugs.*

It is, then, as the fruition of this lower and irrational desire that pleasure is an evil. It is not that Philo is anxious to impose a sour and gloomy life upon men. On the contrary, joy is a good affection,† and worthy of our prayers; but pleasure removes the boundaries of the soul, and takes away its love of virtue.‡ It is the good of the flesh; but the good of the soul is God; and bodily pleasure is the beginning of acts of wrong and lawlessness, because, being essentially

---

* Concup., 1-2 (II. 348-50); Praem. Sac., 3 (II. 235).
† Εὐπάθεια.   ‡ Leg. All., III. 35 (I. 103-9).

SOURCES OF EVIL: THE PASSIONS. 305

deceitful and sophistical, it blinds the mind to its true good. Its nature is most strange, for it injures by communicating its proper good, it blesses by taking it away; and hence our true wisdom is to turn away from its charms, and fix our eye upon the genuine beauty of virtue, till the love of it draws us like a magnet, and attaches us to the object of our longing.*

We conclude, then, that pleasure and the other passions are evil, not in themselves, but because, existing in beings who are capable of moral choice, they claim to be the true ends of life when they are not so. It is only in presence of an acknowledged superior that they turn into our foes. For to rejoice at pleasure, to be vexed at pain, is a purely animal instinct, which appears contemporaneously with our birth; and so far is man from being less alive to this than the irrational creatures, that he is more amply endowed with the sources of pleasure, for eye and ear minister to his gratification no less than the other senses.† During our early years, accordingly, the passions are our familiar companions, for our reason, as though buried in deep sleep, is not able to distinguish good and evil; but in progress of time, when we grow out of our childhood, virtue and vice spring from one root, for we receive an apprehension of both, and choose one or the other, the worse or the better, the mortal or the divine.‡ Thus, for the sake of sensation, the mind, when it is enslaved to it, leaves its father, the God of the universe, and the mother of all things, the virtue and wisdom of God, and makes itself one with

---

* Mundi Op., 53 (I. 36-7); Leg. All., III. 20 (I. 99 sq.); Gigant., 10 (I. 268). See also the long figurative description of pleasure and virtue in Merc. Meret., 2 sqq. (II. 265 sqq.).

† Mundi Op., 57 (I. 39). Philo can even refer to pleasure with evident approval. It is becoming, he says, in wealth to remember poverty, in peace to call to mind the dangers of war; "for there is no greater pleasure than in the midst of extreme prosperity to think of ancient misfortunes"; but in addition to the pleasure there is also a moral benefit. See Tisch., Philon., p. 67, l. 2 sqq., answering to Septen. 24 (II. 297), where the lines are omitted in Mangey's edition.

‡ Congr. erud. gr., 15 (I. 531).

sensation;* but men of God are priests and prophets, who have looked above all that belongs to the world of sense, and removed into the intelligible cosmos, where they have taken up their abode, and been enrolled in the citizenship of incorruptible and incorporeal ideas.†

We must not conclude this survey of the sources of evil without alluding to Philo's view of ignorance. Want of education, ignorance, and folly are a fruitful cause of transgression, because they blind the soul to the perception of the morally beautiful as the only real good. There are two kinds of ignorance. Simple ignorance, which consists of total want of perception, is the cause of lighter and perhaps involuntary faults. The double species includes not only a defect of knowledge, but a supposition that one knows what one does not know, lifting one up with a false conceit of wisdom; and this produces not only involuntary but intentional acts of wrong.‡ Philo does not attempt to bring this view into clear relation with his general theory of responsibility. But it is apparent from the foregoing survey of his opinions that he looked upon actions and things as morally right and wrong, or morally good and evil, independently of the merit or demerit of the person performing or affected by them, and, consequently, would regard sensuality, for instance, as no less opposed to the ideal of human life, and belonging to the domain of the morally bad, even though a man fell into it through mere brutish ignorance. But in admitting that such faults were involuntary he must intend to exempt them from guilt. In his severer condemnation of the second kind of ignorance, he may contemplate the case of a man who is sufficiently intelligent to discern the truth, but, through self-regard, allows himself to be misled into a sophistical falsehood which is flattering to his pride.

* Leg. All., II. 14 (I. 75). † Gigant., 13 (I. 271).
‡ See Ebriet., 3 (I. 358-9); §§ 39-40, pp. 381-2; Conf. Ling., 28 (I. 426); Sacrificant., 9 (II. 258); Leg. ad Cai., 1 (II. 545-6); Fragments, II. 649; 657.

From this notice of the adverse influences in the moral life of man, we must turn to those persuasives and helps which lure him on to virtue. Reason being the sovereign principle in man, by which he is distinguished from the brutes, he is conscious of a higher claim than that which is made by his bodily desires. Right reason is the father of the soul, and its companions and friends are the words of God, which determine the "nations and species of virtue." Inferior natures are under the guidance of the latter; but Israel, who sees God, is led by the full-orbed beauty.* For God is the fountain of the Logos, and hence our highest condition consists in living according to God—that is, in loving him; but he who lives irrationally is separated from the life of God,† and has gone over to brute nature, though his body retains the human form.‡ Reason, which brings man into communion with the divine Life, had for the Jew found expression in Scripture, and I cannot but think that the Scripture is occasionally in Philo's mind when he speaks of the direction of the Logos, which, in that case, passes into the sense of rational word or command. Thus he says that the perfect man, being wholly free from passion, moves spontaneously and without command towards virtuous activity, but he who is only making progress acts under command, and at the suggestion of the Logos, whose orders it is well to obey.§ He must mean, not that the perfect man has risen above the guidance of reason, but that he has become independent of positive precepts. So, walking in the steps of right reason and following God is the same as doing what God says and keeping his Law, for the Law is nothing but divine Reason (or a divine word), enjoining what is right, and forbidding what is wrong.|| To Philo the philosophical idea of the Logos and the religious conception of the Scriptures would easily, and, indeed inevitably, pass into one another. The

* Post. Cain., 25-6 (I. 241-2). † Ib., § 20, p. 238.
‡ Spec. Leg., III. 17 (II. 316). § Leg. All., III. 48-9 (I. 114-5).
|| Migrat. Abr., 23 (I. 456).

Pentateuch was simply the divine Logos resolved into Logoi, statements of philosophical truth, and precepts of the moral code. Hence he sometimes uses the "Word" in a more external sense, and, again, translates it into the highest and most universal utterance, offspring of God and his Wisdom, which comes and goes within the souls of men. So long as the latter, which is wholly unparticipant of sin, lives in the soul, no involuntary change can enter; but when it dies, in the sense of being disjoined from our soul, an entrance is immediately afforded to voluntary faults.* Reason, accordingly, is the antagonist of our most formidable foes, the senses and passions, in union with which it cannot exist, so that it is an abomination to the votaries of pleasure.† In this way nature has made the Logos a most powerful ally to man. The word of rebuke comes as a warning angel to stop us in our perversity. The divine command steals, soft and silent as the manna falling on the desert, into souls which are pure from passion and vice, and gives them light and sweetness, which they feel, but cannot at first interpret. Asking wistfully, however, what this calm and gladdening influence is, they learn from Moses that it is the bread which God showers from heaven upon souls that hunger and thirst after excellence. In different measures it comes according to the capacity of the recipient. Men like ourselves may be content if we are nourished with a portion of it, and only the soul of the more perfect feeds upon the Word in all its completeness. But we must not forget that there is a yet higher stage. The Word acts mainly the part of a physician, and saves us from evil; and it is possible to look beyond the Word, and in direct communion with God to receive from him transcendent good.‡ In more modern phrase, some are unable ever to get beyond single and detached precepts,

* Prof., 20-1 (I. 562-3).
† Leg. All., III. 39-40 (I. 110-111); § 53, p. 117-18; SS. Ab. et Cain., 12 (I. 171); Abr., 41 (II. 35); Dec. Orac., 28 (II. 205).
‡ Leg. All., III. 59-62 (I. 120-2); Cherub., 11 (I. 146); Quod Deus immut., 37 (I. 299); Prof., 25 (I. 566).

such as "Thou shalt not kill," "Thou shalt not steal,"* while others grasp the divine Law in its unity, and recognize it as the manifold expression of one informing principle, as Paul, for instance, summed up the whole Law in the single word,† "Thou shalt love thy neighbour as thyself." But even in this larger view the Word acts chiefly as a restraint upon our evil propensities, and it is only when the love changes from a command into an indwelling spirit that we become partakers of the life of God, and move spontaneously towards the divine end of our being. Philo had a glimpse of this; but he would rather say that the Word without must become a permanent Reason within, and then, in devout contemplation of the eternal, so far as created nature is capable of the vision, we pass beyond the law of commandment and restraint.

We need not spend many words on the connection between virtue and wisdom. Generic virtue, or virtue in the abstract, flows from the divine Wisdom.‡ In us, accordingly, virtue and wisdom are practically identical.§ The means and the end correspond with the source. Wisdom is the perfect way that leads to God; for guided by this the mind reaches its end, which is the knowledge and science of God, or, in other words, the great river of God's Wisdom, which overflows with joy and gladness and other blessings.|| Thus the intellectual view is more prominent than the strictly ethical, and the divine Spirit, which visits, but cannot permanently abide with man, is not the Spirit of Holiness, but of Wisdom.¶

Nevertheless Philo is quite aware of the deeper spiritual experiences of our moral struggle, of visitings of divine power, and of the ultimate dependence of our well-being on the grace of God. The changes in the direction of our thoughts are not

* Τοὺς δέκα λόγους, Dec. Orac., 9 (II. 185).
† Ἐν τῷ λόγῳ τούτῳ, Rom. xiii. 9.   ‡ Leg. All., I. 19 (I. 56).
§ See Leg. All., II. 21 (I. 81); Congr. erud. gr., 3 (I. 520); where Sarah is indifferently Wisdom or Virtue.
|| Quod Deus immut., 30 (I. 294); Quis rer. div. her., 62 (I. 518).
¶ Gigant., 7 and 11 (I. 266 and 269).

altogether under the control of the will, for often, when we wish to think of what is becoming, we are overwhelmed with an influx of what is unbecoming, and, on the other hand, when we have contracted a notion of something shameful, we have flung it off, since God by his own grace has poured into the soul a sweet stream instead of a salt.* Similarly we may have left the society of kindred and friends, and retreated into the wilderness, that we may give ourselves up to the contemplation of worthy objects; but there the mind is bitten by passion, and withdraws into thoughts directly contrary to its intention. Again, in the midst of a multitude we may have found solitude for the mind, God having dispersed the mental crowd, and taught us that it is not differences of place that work us good and ill, but God who moves and leads the chariot of the soul whithersoever he prefers.† Hence it follows that even those imperfect men who do not receive the highest good from the grace of God without trouble of their own, but have to toil for virtue, ought not to ascribe this toil to themselves, but to offer it up to God, acknowledging that it is not their own might or power that has acquired the morally beautiful, but He who graciously bestowed the love for it;‡ and he who does not thus honour the self-existent Being kills his own soul.§ Occasionally the divine grace appears to act quite unconditionally. As a husbandman sometimes, by an unexpected good fortune, hits upon a treasure as he digs a field, so at times God bestows the principles of his own Wisdom without our toil and trouble, and on a sudden we find a treasure of perfect bliss.‖

We must notice here how closely Philo approaches the problem raised in Romans ix., and how curiously he glides off from the answer which presented itself to the deeper mind of Paul. How is it, he asks, that Noah found favour before

* Leg. All., II. 9 (I. 72).   † Ib., 21 (I. 81-2).
‡ Leg. All., III. 46 (I. 114).   § Agr. Noe, 39 (I. 326).
‖ Quod Deus immut., 20 (I. 286). See also the Fragment quoted Vol. I., p. 347, Note ‖.

God,* when, so far as we know, he had not previously done anything virtuous? A similar question may be raised about Melchizedek and Abraham, and still more about Isaac and Jacob, to whom the preference was given before their birth. The preference of Ephraim to Manasseh, and the choosing of Bescleöl, are other instances in point. The thoughts which the facts might naturally suggest are dissipated in a cloud of allegorical interpretation. Certain dispositions are intrinsically praiseworthy, and have not to wait upon action before their merit can be known; and the men who have been named are all typical of virtuous dispositions. Noah is "rest" or "righteous;" Melchizedek, "king of peace," the right reason which governs the soul without tyranny; Abraham is the "high father" of the soul, who gives it what is expedient, and soars up to lofty speculations. Isaac is esteemed before his birth, because he is the joy and laughter of the soul, and joy delights us, not only when it is present, but when it is hoped for. The case of Jacob and Esau is explained partly by the foreknowledge of God, but finally resolves itself into the superiority of the virtuous and rational to the vile and irrational, a superiority which does not wait till each has become perfect in the soul, but asserts itself while there is still room for doubt about the result. Ephraim was preferred to Manasseh because "memory" is better than "recollection;" and Bescleöl was chosen because his name denotes "God in shadow," and therefore he stands for the Logos. This exposition is preceded by a reference to the serpent, which, as signifying "pleasure," was pronounced accursed, without any opportunity of defence; and to Er, whom, without any manifest cause, God knew to be wicked and slew,† for Er means "made of skin," and therefore signifies the body. The conclusion of the whole discussion is that there are two natures, made and moulded and wrought in relief by God, the one injurious in itself and blamable and

* Gen. vi. 8. † Gen. xxxviii. 7.

accursed, the other profitable and praiseworthy, the one having a spurious, the other an approved stamp.*

Though the divine grace sometimes acts in unexpected ways, there are certain conditions on man's side, in response to which it is bestowed. God becomes propitious, and propitious without waiting for supplication, to those who afflict and abase themselves, and are not puffed up with boasting and self-conceit. This is forgiveness; this, complete liberty of soul.† Again, the invisible temple of the soul ought to be duly prepared by instruction in the various branches of encyclical education, and by the practice of virtue, and then the powers of God will come with laws and ordinances from heaven to sanctify and consecrate it.‡ To our earnest desire, too, there is a response. That soul alone can spread a veil over moral evil, to which God has been made manifest, which he has deemed worthy even of the unspeakable mysteries. The Saviour shows his works to the soul that longs for the beautiful; and for this reason it is able to flee from vice, and to hide and overshadow it, and destroy injurious passion always.§ Those who love excellence become suppliants, and it is to suppliants alone that the ever-flowing fountains of God's favours are open, and permission is given, in their thirst for wisdom, to draw from the most sacred wells.‖ But God does not always wait for our prayers. He comes forth to meet and bless us; and so great is his grace that he anticipates what we are going to do, and hastens to confer his full benefit upon the soul. The very thought of God, entering the mind, instantly blesses it, and heals all its diseases.¶

But while all this is true, labour is an indispensable means of human progress. It is the enemy of indolence, and wages an implacable war against pleasure; and it may be pronounced

* Leg. All., III. 21-34 (I. 100-108). † Congr. erud. gr., 19 (I. 534).
‡ Cherub., 30-1 (I. 157-8). § Leg. All., III. 8 (I. 93).
‖ Human., 4 (II. 388). ¶ Leg. All., III. 76 (I. 130).

the first and greatest good, for God has made it the beginning of all good and of all virtue. It is not, however, a good in itself, but must be accompanied by the appropriate art. We cannot gain science unscientifically, or piety superstitiously; and so we can acquire justice and every virtue only by the deeds which are related to them. But though labour has its reward, we must not forget that it is God who has established this connection, and the fruits which we garner are no less the gifts of his grace; "for all things are anchored in the mercy of God."*

Finally, our labour in quest of virtue is happily stimulated and sustained by hope, which God has bountifully planted in the human race as one of its characteristics. Hope not only consoles us under the vexations of life, but it is a joy which anticipates the realization of joy, and is a spur to effort in all our undertakings. If hope is the fountain of their several modes of life for the merchant, the mariner, and the politician, no less is it the hope of blessedness which induces the votaries of virtue to give themselves to philosophy, in the persuasion that by this means they will be able both to see the nature of things and to do the actions which are conformable to the perfection of the best modes of life, the contemplative and the practical, in the attainment of which blessedness is found.†
Hope is most closely related to prayer, for we pray in expectation of better things, and, when we have prayed, we expect what is good; and God pours down, from the fountain of his own nature, his saving blessings on mankind.‡

These remarks naturally suggest the question, wherein precisely does virtue consist? This has already received a partial answer in treating of the highest good, and we need now only bring together in brief review Philo's leading

* SS. Ab. et Cain., 6-9 (I. 168-9); Quod det. pot. ins., 7 (I. 195).
† Quod det. pot. ins., 38 (I. 217-18); Post. Cain., 8 (I. 231); Mut. Nomat., 30 (I. 603); Abr. 2 (II. 2); Praem. et Poen., 2 (II. 410); Fragments, II. 673; Qu. et Sol. in Gen., I. 79, with the Greek in Harris, p. 17.
‡ Harris, Fragm., p. 11.

thoughts upon the subject. Moral beauty is an end in itself, and the only real good; and consequently virtue must consist in the practical acceptance of this position, so as to be really indifferent to things indifferent, so-called bodily and external goods, and to be superior to the allurements of passion. But beauty is only an expression of the divine Reason, which is above it; and hence reason is the fountain of virtue, and to live virtuously is to live rationally. As the reason of individuals is of blended quality, moral reason is frequently distinguished as "right reason;" and, as reason in its purity pervades nature, it is sometimes described as "the right reason of nature." Virtue, accordingly, consists in following the laws and ordinances of nature with voluntary judgment, or, more simply, in following nature. But this Stoical maxim admits of a more religious expression. We follow nature when we walk in the steps of right reason and follow God, remembering his commandments, and confirming them all, always and everywhere, by deeds and words.*

When Philo attempts to treat the nature of virtue more psychologically, he follows Aristotle, and defines it as a mean between two extremes of excess and defect. We may not add to or take away from what has been laid down as lawful, for to do so changes the character of virtue from the beautiful into the base. Thus, if we add to courage, we turn it into audacity; if to piety, into superstition. If we take away from the former, we have cowardice; if from the latter, impiety. But even this familiar thought is clothed by Philo in a religious garb of his own. We must walk in the royal way of wisdom, by which alone suppliant souls can come to the Unbegotten. But we must keep in the middle, turning neither to the right hand, wherein is excess, nor to the left, where there is defect;

* See especially Mundi Op., 48 (I. 33); § 50, p. 34; Leg. All., III. 25 (I. 103); Plantat. Noe, 28 (I. 347); Ebriet., 9 (I. 362); Migrat. Abr., 23 (I. 456); Somn., II. 26 (I. 682); Septen., 3-5 (II. 278-80); Human., 17 (II. 396); Quod omn. prob. lib., 10 (II. 455). For the connection between the doctrine of the Logos and following nature see before, pp. 166 sq.

CLASSIFICATION OF VIRTUES. 315

and then only can we reach our goal, the King himself, to whom the royal road belongs. There we shall recognize at once the blessedness of God and our own meanness, even as Abraham, when he drew nearest to God, knew himself to be but dust and ashes.*

The classification of virtues is treated only in a casual way, and Philo makes no attempt to work out his thoughts into a complete system. Virtues are divided into genera and species. The most generic virtue is named goodness.† This is represented by the river which watered Paradise, and flows out of the Wisdom of God. It is, therefore, in a certain sense identical with the sacred Logos, in conformity with which it has been made. As the river is said to have divided into four great streams or dominions,‡ so goodness parts itself into the four royal or generic virtues, prudence, fortitude, temperance, and justice.§ Philo, however, does not adhere consistently to this celebrated division; but, instead of saying that he regarded it as defective, he sometimes adds, without remark, piety and holiness, as though these, too, were to take their place among the leading generic virtues.‖ A Jew could not dispense with these, and they cannot be classed as species under any of the others. It is not surprising that he sometimes abandons altogether the Greek classification, and adopts one more suited to the genius of his people. Thus, he says that of the innumerable subjects of instruction appropriate to the Sabbath there are two supreme heads, the one relating to God, the other to man. Duty to God is expressed through piety and holiness, that to man through philanthropy and justice. Each of these is divided into praiseworthy ideas, which again admit of

---

* Gen. xviii. 27. Quod Deus immut., 34-5 (I. 296-7); Justit., 2 (II. 360); Creat. Princ., 4 (II. 364). See also Praem. et Poen., 9 (II. 416); and a Fragment in Harris, p. 74.   † 'Αγαθότης.   ‡ 'Αρχάς.

§ Leg. All., I. 19 (I. 56); Post. Cain., 37 (I. 250); Somn., II. 37 (I. 690); Mutat. Nom., 27 (I. 600). For the cardinal virtues, see also Vita Mos., III. 22 (II. 163); Septen., 6 (II. 282).

‖ Vita Mos., III. 27 (II. 168); Exsecrat., 7 (II. 435).

numerous subdivisions.* Elsewhere, the chief of the virtues are described as piety and philanthropy,† or as piety and justice.‡ Of these, piety of course takes the leading place, and all the other virtues follow in its train, as necessarily as in the sunshine its shadow accompanies the body.§ It requires us to love God as a benefactor, or, if we are not yet competent to do so, at least to fear him as Ruler and Lord, to serve him, not incidentally, but with the whole soul, to keep his commandments, and honour what is right. To worship the self-existent Being is the prerogative of man among the denizens of earth —a privilege which he shares with the heaven; for this, with its rhythmical movements, chants a continual melody.‖ If in one passage, justice, the offspring of equality, is said to be the sovereign of the virtues,¶ we may limit this expression to the virtues which are directed towards men.

Some of the virtues, considered singly, require a few remarks. Temperance must take a high place; for it not only, as its name implies, tempers the mind to a state of health,** but it is especially opposed to pleasure. This varied virtue is typified by the brazen serpent, which whosoever looks upon

---

* Septen., 6 (II. 282). † Human., 10 (II. 391).
‡ Praem. et Poen., 9 (II. 416), where the two are made into one presiding virtue.
§ For this statement see Poenit., 2 (II. 406).
‖ Migrat. Abr., 4 (I. 439); Sacrificant., 8 (II. 257); Somn., I. 6 (I. 625); Mundi Op., 54 (I. 37); Abr., 13 (II. 10); Dec. Orac., 23 (II. 200); Concup., 12 (II. 356); Justit., 2 (II. 360). See also Post. Cain., 35 (I. 248), and § 54, p. 261, where honouring God takes the place of piety. In Quis rer. div. her., 18 (I. 485-6), and Abr., 46 (II. 39), faith in God is said to be the most perfect, the queen, of the virtues; but this is at least closely akin to piety. The following words about faith are of interest: from the former passage, μόνῳ θεῷ χωρὶς ἑτέρου προσπαραλήψεως οὐ ῥᾴδιον πιστεῦσαι. ... Τὸ ... ἀπιστῆσαι γενέσει τῇ πάντα ἐξ ἑαυτῆς ἀπίστῳ, μόνῳ δὲ πιστεῦσαι θεῷ τῷ καὶ πρὸς ἀλήθειαν μόνῳ πιστῷ, μεγάλης καὶ ὀλυμπίου διανοίας ἔργον ἐστί: from the latter, μόνον οὖν ἀψευδὲς καὶ βέβαιον ἀγαθὸν ἡ πρὸς τὸν θεὸν πίστις, παρηγόρημα βίου, πλήρωμα χρηστῶν ἐλπίδων, ἀφορία μὲν κακῶν, ἀγαθῶν δὲ φορά, κακοδαιμονίας ἀπόγνωσις, εὐσεβείας γνῶσις, εὐδαιμονίας κλῆρος, ψυχῆς ἐν ἅπασι βελτίωσις.
¶ Plantat. Noe, 28 (I. 347).
** Σωφροσύνη, σωτηρίαν τῷ φρονοῦντι τῶν ἐν ἡμῖν ἀπεργαζομένη, Fort. 3 (II. 377-8).

shall live; for if the mind, having been bitten by pleasure, the serpent of Eve, is able to behold the beauty of temperance, the serpent of Moses, and through this to see God, it shall live. It is curious that in this connection Philo uses, not always the simple expression "temperance," but several times "the logos of temperance," as if there were some connection in his mind between the brazen serpent and the Logos, though, owing to the contrast with the serpent pleasure, he thought it best to limit this connection to one of the four cardinal virtues, which, as we have seen, are immediate divisions of the Logos.*

Closely allied to temperance is self-control,† for this also is the opponent of pleasure and desire.‡ As Philo's doctrine is so often supposed to involve asceticism, it is important to observe the moderation of his view, and his emphatic condemnation of what is generally meant by asceticism. If anyone, he says, does not take food and drink at the proper time, or avoids baths and ointments, or is negligent of covering for his body, or sleeps on the ground and keeps an uncomfortable house, he only counterfeits self-control, and is a fit object of compassion for his error; for the things which he pursues are aimless and wearisome labours, ruining soul and body with famine and other kinds of ill-treatment.§ Self-control consists in the repression of intemperance, which often produces incurable diseases, and in so governing the appetites as to maintain a healthy body and a sound understanding.‖ It requires also a proper restraint in the use of the tongue.¶

Justice, which fixes the proper limits for our conduct in regard to distribution, gives rest to the soul, and relieves it of the sorrows which arise out of our own misdirected activity, for it makes us indifferent to wealth and glory and similar things, about which the majority of mankind vex

* Leg. All., II. 20 sqq. (I. 80 sqq.). † 'Εγκράτεια.
‡ Mundi Op., 58 (I. 39); Praem. Sac., 3 (II. 235).
§ Quod det. pot. ins., 7 (I. 195). ‖ Animal. Sacr. idon., 3 (II. 239).
¶ Congr. erud. gr., 14 (I. 530).

themselves.* In all the affairs of life we must do the just thing in a just way; for the just thing is not sufficient in itself if it be done from a wrong motive. Most interesting in this connection is the high value which Philo attaches to truthful speech. He complains of the familiarity with falsehood which nurses and mothers and other members of the household produce by words and deeds from the very moment of our birth, as though it were a necessity of nature, whereas, if it really were congenital, it ought to be cut out by the practice of virtue. Nothing in life is so beautiful as truth; and it is most becoming to a rational nature not even to swear, but so to speak the truth on all occasions that the words shall have the validity of oaths. The man who swears shows thereby that he is suspected of want of veracity. If, however, the necessity for an oath should arise, we must use it circumspectly; for it is no light matter, however little it is habitually thought of. It is an appeal to God in relation to things that are called in question, and to invoke God as witness to a falsehood is in the highest degree impious.†

Fortitude does not, as most suppose, consist of martial rage, which may spring from mere bodily strength and youthful spirit. Moral courage must take precedence of physical. The latter may be the mere audacity of a savage and brutal nature which thirsts for human blood; but genuine courage may be sometimes seen in men who stay at home and never touch a weapon, who, though their bodies have been worn to a skeleton by disease and age, are yet full of youthful vigour in their soul, and by their sagacity of judgment restore the fallen fortunes of individuals and of states. Poverty and ignominy and blindness are tests of bravery to which multitudes, like tired athletes, have succumbed; but men of wise and generous spirit hold them in derision, setting wealth against poverty, not the blind wealth, but that which has sharp vision, which the soul lays up

* Leg. All., I. 19 (I. 56); Quod det. pot. ins., 32 (I. 214).
† Jud., 3 (II. 346); Dec. Orac., 17 (II. 194-5).

in its treasure-house, while wisdom, needing not the aid of spurious light, but being itself a star, guides them farther into the mysteries of nature than any sense could reach.*

Among the other virtues, we must observe that Philo attaches special importance to thanksgiving, the "eucharist," which was soon to become a term of such sacred significance. And wherein did genuine thanksgiving to God consist? Not in offerings and sacrifices, as most supposed, but in praises and hymns, not those which the audible voice would sing, but those which the invisible and pure mind would sound with inward music.† So closely did Philo approach the view that spiritual sacrifices might replace the ritual of the altar. He takes also a sober view of an ideal of human excellence which was destined to enter so largely into the aims of Christian asceticism. The perfect man loves, not moderation in the indulgence of the passions, but "apathy,"‡ the complete absence of passion. Yet there was a censurable apathy, which was akin to haughtiness and self-confidence. The nature of this is not defined; but we may presumably find it in hard and unsympathetic natures, which are as dead to the higher play of pure emotion as they are strong against the assaults of pleasure and fear. In order to understand Philo's apathy, we must remember his doctrine of the passions. It is only from these irrational impulses, which fret and mislead the soul, that he would deliver it; and this he would effect, not by self-repression, but by self-escape, through the energy of a higher love and trust. Virtue is a thing of joy, and he who has it rejoices always, and, leaving behind him the things dear to the flesh, is released from the pain of vice and passion by the gladness of inward laughter. Thus, having waited for the salvation of God, the soul becomes perfectly blessed.§

* Fort., 1-3 (II. 375-7).
† Plantat. Noe, 30 (I. 318). See also §§ 31 and 33. ‡ 'Απάθεια.
§ Leg. All., II. 25 (I. 84-5); III. 45 (I. 112-3); Mutat. Nom., 31-3 (I. 603-5); Qu. et Sol. in Gen., IV. 15.

We need not dwell at any length on the classification of sins. In contrast with the four cardinal virtues, we hear of folly, intemperance, injustice, and cowardice.* But Philo, as became a Jew, preferred the division set forth in the prohibitions of the second table, which contains the law of conduct in relation to men. Adultery, murder, theft, false witness, and desire are the genera under which the several species of transgressions must be brought. But as the first table must take precedence, and piety is the queen of the virtues, so polytheism and idolatry meet with the severest condemnation. Even a child must know that the Creator is better than the creature; and therefore idolaters are justly punished as wicked, because with voluntary judgment they have not only dimmed but cast utterly away the eye of the soul.†

Philo is fond of dwelling upon the method in which virtue, in the form of perfect wisdom, was to be attained, and of drawing instructive hints from the lives of the patriarchs. He accepts the view that virtue was acquired either by nature or by training or by learning.‡ The history of Abraham, Isaac, and Jacob relates, not to perishable men, but to the nature of things. They all pressed towards the same end, and are all enrolled among the wise; but they did not pursue their end by the same means. Abraham chose instruction as the leader of his way, and in this he has no small number of followers. This process of education takes a long time; and though with a view to civil life it is always useful to attend to the words of historians and poets, it is not necessarily followed by the highest attainment. Its reward is faith in God, the characteristic of Abraham. There is, however, the more rapid way of intuition, represented by Isaac, who is self-taught wisdom. When on a sudden the supernal light flashes in,

* Agr. Noe, 4 (I. 302).
† Quis rer. div. her., 35 (I. 496-7); Dec. Orac., 14 (II. 191-2).
‡ Cf. the saying ascribed to Aristotle, τριῶν ἔφη δεῖν παιδείᾳ, φύσεως, μαθήσεως, ἀσκήσεως (Diog. La., V. 18). The corresponding words in the Nicomachean Ethics are φύσει, ἔθει, διδαχῇ (X. ix. 6).

making us seers instead of hearers, and filling us, not with human thoughts, but with an inspired madness, it is useless, now that we are companions and disciples of God, to turn an ear to mortal suggestions. This wisdom has for its prize continual joy, joy in God and in those who do good. The third method is illustrated by Jacob, the Stoical " progressive " man, the " ascetic," who seeks for wisdom by laborious practice. This is an intermediate stage, belonging only to the immature and imperfect; and therefore those who have not passed beyond it, are not wholly exempt from the control of the passions, which, however, they experience only in a moderate degree. But earnest striving has a rich reward. Jacob changes to Israel, and God in pity gives a vision of himself, so far as mortal nature can bear it. Nor must we forget at any part of our journey the Divine pity and deliverance. As mortals we cannot be exempt from the sway of the passions, but it is the will of God to lighten the innate evils of our race; so that, even if in the beginning we are slaves of cruel lords, God will do what is appropriate to himself, and give deliverance and freedom which he has proclaimed beforehand to souls that supplicate him, not only loosening their bonds and bringing them out of their prison-house, but bestowing provisions for the way; and when we are perfect, we shall be without slavery and without war, nurtured in peace and liberty that cannot be disturbed.*

We have only to add a few words descriptive of the result of our moral discipline. Philo anticipates the final triumph of good over evil in the world. Peace and wealth and long life will bless a race which has been won to virtue, and has tamed the wild beasts in the soul.† Especially will the Israelites be blessed, being gathered together into their own land under the

* Leg. All., III. 49 (I. 115); SS. Ab. et Cain., 2 (I. 164); §§ 22-3, p. 178; Quod det. pot. ins., 9 (I. 197); § 19, p. 204; Migrat. Abr., 9 (I. 443); Quis rer. div. her., 55 (I. 512); Prof., 30 (I. 571); Somn., I. 27 (I. 645-6); Joseph., 1 (II. 41); Vita Mos., I. 14 (II. 93); Praem. et Poen., 4 sqq. (II. 412 sqq.).

† Praem. et Poen., 15-20 (II. 421-8).

leadership of a wonderful vision ;* but of a distinctly Messianic hope I still fail to discover any trace. Philo preferred moving in the region of abstract ideas, where there is more elevation of thought than warmth of personal affection; and Dähne's belief that he anticipated the identification of the Logos with the Messiah appears to me to be quite untenable.†

From these rather vague speculations about the progress of the race we must turn to the individual. The law of retribution is absolute, and administered with the strictest impartiality. A wicked man will not lose the reward of a single good deed, though accompanied by so many that are evil, nor may a good man rely upon his numerous good deeds to free him from chastisement, if in any instance he has acted wickedly; for God renders everything by balance and weight.‡ Still less may men rely upon their noble birth; for, if anyone has falsified the legal coin of his high lineage, he shall be dragged down to the lowest depth, to Tartarus itself and its deep darkness, that all men may see it and be wise.§ Certain outward ills are denounced against the wicked, poverty, disease, slavery, cowardice and fear driving them into flight when no man pursues.‖ But the unrighteous and godless soul has a more terrible doom. It is given up to its own pleasures and desires and iniquities; and this place of the impious is not that which is fabled to be in Hades; for the true Hades is the life of the wicked man, exposed to vengeance, with uncleansed guilt, obnoxious to every curse.¶ The end of these things is death.** But death is not, as men suppose, an end of punishment; in the Divine court of justice it is barely the beginning. What, then, is this death-penalty?

---

* Exsecrat., 9 (II. 436); Praem. et Poen., 16 (II. 423).

† See this point discussed at greater length in the Author's "The Jewish Messiah," pp. 271 sq., 330, 347 sqq.

‡ Fragments, II. 649. § Exsecrat., 6 (II. 433).

Ib., §§ 1 sqq. ¶ Congr. erud. gr., 11 (I. 527).

** Plantat. Noe, 9 (I. 335).

It is to live always dying, and to endure, as it were, death deathless and unending. It is to lose the very roots of pleasure and desire and hope, and to be haunted with unmingled grief and fear.*

But as only a divine man could share the property of God, and not sin at all, it is open to us to repent;† and those who do so, and confess their sins, will obtain kindness from God the Saviour and propitious,‡ and, like Enoch, they will not be found in the old blamable life, or in the crowds which bad men love, but will retreat into the quiet and solitude which are dear to the good.§ There is, however, such a thing as complete separation and expulsion from the good, and this admits of no return for ever;|| and to those who blaspheme against the Divine, and ascribe to God rather than themselves the origin of their evil, no pardon can be granted.¶

We have already seen something of both the inward and outward rewards of the good, and we need not repeat what has been already said. The former take of course the highest place; indeed the works themselves are the perfect reward.** To have the divine Spirit of wisdom abiding within;†† to share, at least where we touch the immortal, in the self-sufficingness of God, and want but little;‡‡ to draw near to the Divine power and blessedness, in the possession of a steadfast and a quiet mind;§§ to commune "alone with the Alone;"||||— these are the rewards of the virtuous, which fill the soul with a transcendent joy. And, finally, they shall leave behind them the strife and necessity and corruption of this lower world, and come to the Unbegotten and Eternal, the city of God, the mystical Jerusalem, which signifies the vision of peace;

* Praem. et Poen., 12 (II. 419 sq.).   † Poen., 1 (II. 405).
‡ Exsecrat., 8 (II. 435).   § Abr., 3-4 (II. 3-4).
|| Quod det. pot. ins., 40 (I. 219-20).   ¶ Prof., 16 (I. 558).
** Somn., II. 5 (I. 663).   †† Gigant., 11 (I. 269).
‡‡ Fort., 3 (II. 377).
§§ Cherub., 6 (I. 142); Post. Cain., 9 (I. 231).
|||| Qu. et Sol. in Gen., IV. 140.

and this is nothing less than the vision of God himself, for God alone is peace.* Thus "life and immortality" greet us at our journey's end.†

---

* Somn., II. 38 (I. 691-2); Quis rer. div. her., 58 (I. 514); Prof., 31 (I. 572); Ebriet., 18 (I. 368).
† Plantat. Noe, 9 (I. 335).

INDEX I.

Subjects and Names.

Aaron stayed the plague, I. 228
— symbolizes the Logos, I. 352; II. 227-8, 251, 268
Abba Shaül, I. 157
Abel, I. 352-3; II. 288, 290
Abiud, II. 250, 251
Abraham, appearance of God to, explained, II. 101
—, — of the Logos to, explained, II. 250-4
—, — of the Lord to, explained, II. 94
—, — of the powers to, II. 90-3, 133-8
—, change in the name of, I. 13, 264; II. 243-4, 252, 253
—, the father of the soul, II. 311
—, led by wisdom, I. 222
— symbolizes the character that seeks wisdom by instruction, II. 21, 252, 320
— — the Logos, II. 225, 303
— — the wise man, I. 22; II. 225
—, visit of the three men to, explained, II. 90-3, 133-8
—, wells of, I. 276, 279, 326
Accho, I. 238
Adam, fall of, in Philo, II. 279
— —, in Wisd. of Sol., I. 203-4
— most richly endowed, II. 278
— represents the species, II. 275
— symbolizes the mind, I. 344-5; II. 244
Agrippa, I. 8
Air, colour of, I. 272
— inhabited by souls, I. 282, 335; II. 144-5, 260
—, place of, I. 272
— produces the characteristics of natural objects, I. 281
—: see Elements, and Stoics, elements
Alabarch, I. 4, 7
Alexander Aphrodisiensis, I. 45, 87
Alexander the Great, I. 3
Alexander Jannaeus, I. 238
Alexander, Philo's brother, I7, 234
Alexandria, founding of, I. 3

Alexandria, Jewish population of, I. 3-4, 8-10
—, lectures in, I. 5
—, Library in, I. 5, 230, 234, 235
—, luxury of, I. 24
—, Museum in, I. 4, 6
Allegorical interpretation among the Egyptian Jews before Philo, I. 20-1
— — among the Stoics, I. 18, 120-4
— — before the Stoics, I. 121
— — in Aristeas, I. 239-40
— — in Aristobulus, I. 252-3
— — in the Koran, I. 18
— — in Philo, I. 18-22
— — in Plato, I. 18
— — in the Veda, I. 18
— — in Wisd. of Sol., I. 185-6, 196-7
'Αμάρτημα defined by the Stoics, I. 115
Amelius, I. 33
Anatolius, I. 242, 245
Anaxagoras, date of, I. 48
— first taught the presence of mind in the universe, I. 39
—, Philosophy of:—
Matter, I. 48
Mind, infinite, and its attributes, I. 49
— identical with the vital principle, I. 51
—, personality of, I. 49-50
—, relation of, to the universe and man, I. 50-1
Referred to, I. 121, 219
Anaximander, I. 28
Anaximenes, I. 28
Andreas, I. 230
Angel of the Lord in the Old Test., I. 136-7
Angels, Doctrine of, II. 144-7
—, fallen, in Jewish literature, I. 196
— in the Old Test., I. 135-7
— lived in the air, I. 336; II. 144
— presided over nations, I. 148-9
—, under-servants of God's powers, II. 146-7
—, wicked, I. 338; II. 145

VOL. II. 22

Antarctic circle, II. 231
Anthropology in Heraclitus, I. 39-45
— in Philo, I. 314-359
— in Plato, I. 66-67
— in the LXX, I. 102-3
— in the Sibylline Oracles, I. 173-5
— in Socrates, I. 55-7
— in the Stoical system, I. 107-120
— in Wisd. of Sol., I. 199-213
Anthropomorphism in Wisd. of Sol., I. 199
—, meaning of, according to Aristobulus, I. 252-3
— of the oldest Hebrew theism, I. 135
— rejected by Philo, II. 12-15, 41, 246
Anthropopathism rejected, II. 12-15
Antipater of Tyre, I. 83, 85
Antonia, tower of, I. 233
'Απάθεια in Philo, II. 319
— with the Stoics, I. 116
'Απαύγασμα, meaning of, I. 217
Άποιος, I. 101, 298 ; II. 23-34
Apollos possibly author of Wisd. of Sol., I. 185
Aquila, I. 157
Aratus, I. 244, 250
Arctic circle, II. 231
Areius Didymus. I. 40, 44, 89, 90, 91, 92, 94, 102, 108, 112
Aristeas (Pseudo), inventor of story about Demetrius Phalereus, I. 237, 247
— —, letter of, contents of, I. 230-1
— — —, date of, I. 232-4, 237-9
— — —, error of, about Demetrius, I. 234-7
— — —, a Jewish fabrication, I. 169, 231-2
— — —, philosophy of, I. 239-242
Aristobulus, on the Peripatetics, I. 150
—, traditional view of, I. 169, 242
—, Fragments of, arguments for genuineness of, I. 251-2
— —, arguments for late date of, I. 245-251
— — bear imposture on their face, I. 243-4, 246-7
— —, confusion about the date of, I. 245
— — defended by Valckenaer, I. 235
— —, earliest references to, I. 244-5
— —, philosophy of, I. 252-4
— —, reasons for ascription of, to Aristobulus, I. 250-1
— —, relation of, to Letter of Aristeas, I. 234, 237, 247-250
Aristocles, I. 81, 104, 106
Aristodemus, I. 51, 52

Aristotle charged Heraclitus with contradiction, I. 34
—, derivation of "ether" by, I. 276
—, Greek speculation culminated in, I. 75
—, library of, I. 5
— on a Fragment of Heraclitus, I. 32
— on Heraclitus' doctrine of the soul, I. 40
— on the presence of "Mind" in the universe, I. 39
— on the value of the oldest, II. 85
—, subordinate place of, in the philosophy of Philo, I. 27
—, theism of, not satisfactory to the Stoics, I. 77
— used allegory, I. 121
—, Works of, unclassified references to, I. 49, 50, 51, 87, 295 ; II. 286
Aristotle's Philosophy :—
Causes, theory of, I. 69
Correlative terms, II. 48
Difficulty brought to light by, I. 73-4
Distinguished inward and outward λόγος, I. 110
Five elements, I. 273
God, doctrine of, I. 72-4
Identified participation and imitation, I. 329
Ίδιον, definition of, II. 25
Immanence, doctrine of, I. 70
Knowledge pursued for its own sake, I. 264
Monotheism, I. 72 ; II. 37
Personality, vagueness in conception of, II. 127
Prime mover, I. 72-3
Teleology, I. 69-72
Transcendence, doctrine of, I. 72-3
Virtue, definition of, II. 314
Ark and its appurtenances symbolize divine powers, II. 83, 84, 161
Art the same under various manifestations, II. 97
Artapanos, I. 167
Article, use of, with θεός, II. 196
Ascalon, I. 238
Asceticism, Philo's view of, I. 23-5 ; II. 317
Astrology, I. 286-7
Astronomy cultivated at Alexandria, I. 264
— depreciated by Philo, I. 264-5, 278-9
Athanasius, II. 116
Atheism, II. 2, 220, 291
Athenagoras, I. 48, 84, 105, 122
Attributes consistent with absence of qualities, II. 25-8

SUBJECTS AND NAMES.

Attributes differently related to God and man. II. 27
— of God, II. 35-62
Augustine, I. 100; II. 44
Augustus, I. 4
Aurelius Antoninus, M., definition of the wise soul by, I. 89
— — on seeds, I. 103-4
— — on the souls of the dead, I. 107
— — unclassified references to, I. 45, 92, 94, 105, 106, 107, 108, 114
Avarice defined by the Stoics, I. 115

BABEL, tower of, I. 19-20; II. 282
Balaam, I. 22; II. 269-70
Baruch, I. 155
Bassus, I. 9
Baur on the rank of the Logos, II. 161, 201
Bear, the constellation, II. 231
Berenice, I. 235
Bernays, editor of Pseudo-Phocylides, I. 167
— on Heraclitus' view of the Logos, I. 126-9
— on the spuriousness of the *De Incor. Mundi*, I. 296
Beseleël, II. 190, 194, 215, 311
Bethuel, II. 213
Blasphemy against the Divine, unpardonable, I. 25; II. 323
Body, a burden, in Wisd. of Sol., I. 202
— made by God, II. 300
—, medium of the lower life, II. 297-300
Bretschneider, I. 213
Brutes incapable of sin, I. 348, 349; II. 139, 140, 149, 283, 292
Bywater, I. 29, 32, 44, 127

CÆSARS, deification of, I. 182
Cain, I. 203, 353; II. 288, 290
Caius Caligula, I. 8, 9, 10-11, 182-3; II. 219
Callimachus, I. 243
Campbell (L.), I. 47
Canaanites, corruption of, in Wisd. of Sol., I. 193, 203
Candlestick, golden, I. 269
Causality, distinction between principal and proximate, with the Stoics, I. 118
—, fourfold in Aristotle, I. 69
—, in Philo, I. 299, 306; II. 4-5
—, law of, as proof of the existence of God, II. 4-5
— of God, in Aristotle, I. 72-4
—, twofold in Plato, I. 61-2
Censorinus, I. 87

Chaldæans, I. 285, 286, 287; II. 2, 71, 94, 104
Charran, II. 218, 257
Cherubim, I. 21-2; II. 83, 84, 104, 119-120, 161, 189
Cheyne, I. 141
Chrysippus, argument of, for the existence of God, I. 79
— formulated Stoicism, I. 76
— made theology a sub-division of physics, I. 266
—, names given by, to the Logos, I. 90
—, on determinism, I. 117-120
—, on the essence of seeds, I. 102
—, on Nature, I. 92
—, on the use of moral evil, I. 98
—, only fragments of, survive, I. 76
— speaks of the Logos of nature and of Zeus, I. 89
— unclassified references to, I. 80, 81, 83, 91, 93, 94, 97, 104, 105, 112, 114
Cicero referred to, I. 76-122 *passim*
Cleanthes confined the sovereign principle to the sun, I. 92
— distinguished two kinds of fire, I. 84
—, Hymn of, referred to, I. 33, 87, 90, 94, 119
— —, translated, I. 88-9
—, unclassified references to, I. 40, 44, 83, 114, 305
Clemens Alex., on a disgraceful feature of Stoicism, I. 87
— —, on Gen. i. 2, I. 160
— — quotes from Heraclitus, I. 32, 37, 38
— —, unclassified references to, I. 81, 85, 236-246 *passim*, 296
Conscience, II. 124, 295-6
Consonants, II. 232
Cornutus, examples of Stoical etymology and allegory from, I. 121-4
—, other references to, I. 92, 105, 106, 107
Creation, four things needed for, I. 300; II. 198
— limited in capacity, I. 311-313
—, Mosaic account of, not literal, I. 293
— not in time, I. 19, 292-4
— "the beginning of corruption," I. 295
Cynics used allegory, I. 121

DÄHNE admits genuineness of Aristobulus, I. 243
— blames Philo for confounding error and sin, II. 289

22 *

Dähne, historical method of, I. 197
—, makes Wisdom a power of the Logos, II. 201
—, on Adam's transgression in Wisd. of Sol., I. 203-4
—, on Alexandrianism in Ecclus., I. 147-150
—, — in the LXX, I. 156-8, 160-4
—, on διάβολος in Wisd. of Sol., I. 196-7
—, on the elements in Philo, I. 307
—, on the evil of matter in Philo, I. 310
—, on the personality of the powers, II. 114
—, on the Therapeutic origin of Wisd. of Sol., I. 178
— thinks Philo identified Logos with Messiah, II. 322
—, unclassified references to, I. 6, 144, 167, 168, 236, 255, 303; II. 32, 214
Dante, II. 45
De Incorruptibilitate Mundi, possible origin of, I. 296
— — probably spurious, I. 295-6
— — —, sketch of arguments of, I. 296-7
De Providentia I., probably not genuine, I. 306
— — I. and II., Hellenic character of, II. 58
De Vita Contemplativa, I. 24, 178-9
Deane, I. 184
Death, origin of, in Wisd. of Sol., I. 194-7
Delaunay, I. 12
Demetrius, the chronicler, I. 167, 236-7
Demetrius Phalereus, I. 230, 231, 232, 234-7, 246, 247
Democracy, the best of governments, II. 199, 200
Democritus used allegory, I. 121
Demons, same as angels, I. 336; II. 144, 260
Desire, defined by the Stoics, I. 116
—, in Philo, II. 302, 304
Destiny, in Heraclitus, I. 35
—, in the Stoical system, I. 93-4
Devil, in Wisd. of Sol., I. 195-7
Diels, I. 306
Δίκη, in Heraclitus, I. 32, 35-6
—, in Philo, II. 130-2
—, in Wisd. of Sol., I. 192, 194
Diogenes Laertius, referred to, I. 28, 30, 33, 35, 80-125 *passim*, 127, 128, 235, 263; II. 320
Dion Cassius, I. 233
Divine, the, not cut, but extended, II. 115

EARTH, form and place of, in Philo, I. 267
—, —, in Plato, I. 65
—, symbolizes the idea of perception, II. 163
—, *see* Elements
Earthquakes, not sent by God, II. 60
— —, predicted, I. 286
Ecclesiasticus, authorship, country, and date of, I. 144
—, description of Wisdom in, I. 145-7, 151-3
—, not partly Alexandrian, I. 147-153
Eclecticism, I. 6, 17-18
Eclipses, signs of events, I. 286, 287; II. 60
Eden symbolizes the Logos, II. 202
— — Wisdom, II. 202, 242
Edersheim, I. 310
Eleatic philosophy, I. 28, 29
Eleazar, I. 230, 233, 239, 241, 249-50
Election, problem of, II. 310-12
Elements, in early Greek speculation, I. 28
—, in Heraclitus, I. 29-31, 33
—, in Philo, called δυνάμεις, I. 270, 308; II. 69
—, — —, character of, I. 270-3
—, — —, forms of the same matter, I. 273
—, — —, interchangeable, I. 273
—, — —, names of, I. 270
—, — —, not primitive forms of matter, I. 307-310
—, — —, only four, I. 273-9
—, in the Stoical system, I. 83, 85-6, 105
Emanation, I. 328-9; II. 105-6
Empedocles, I. 48, 70, 305
Encyclical education, I. 17, 201-2
— —, *see* Hagar
Ἔννοιαι, I. 113
Enoch, Book of, I. 195
—, type of repentance in Ecclus., I. 147-8
—, — — — in Philo, II. 323
Ephraim, II. 311
Epictetus, I. 108
Equinoctial circle, I. 270; II. 231
Er, II. 311
Eratosthenes, I. 264
Esau's inferiority to Jacob, II. 311
Eschatology, II. 321-4
Essenes, I. 23-4, 180, 181
Eternity, nature of, I. 294-5; II. 46
Ether, I. 273, 276, 279, 283
Ethics, in Philo, II. 283-321
—, in the Stoical system, I. 114-116
Eudaemonism, II. 301
Euhemerus, I. 209

Eupolemus, I. 236
Euripides, I. 296
Eurydice, I. 235
Eusebius, I. 7, 32, 37, 40, 81-112 passim, 168, 236-254 passim, 273, 305, 332 ; II. 58, 166
Euthydemus, I. 52
Eve symbolizes sensation, I. 345, 355 ; II. 279
—, tempted by the devil in Wisd. of Sol., I. 196
Evil, moral, source of, in Philo, II. 296-306
—, —, — —, in the Stoical system, I. 115-117
—, problem of, in Philo, II. 58-62
—, — —, in the Stoical system, I. 96-102
—, the supreme, II. 288-9, 292
Ewald, I. 19, 232, 243
Ezechiel, author of a tragedy, I. 168
Ezra, Fourth, I. 195

Faith, II. 316, 320
Fall, see Adam
Fear, defined by the Stoics, I. 115-116
—, in Philo, II. 302
Fire, two kinds of, distinguished by Cleanthes, I. 84
—, — —, — — Philo, I. 271
—, see Elements
Flaccus, I. 8-9
Fortitude, II. 315, 318-319
Freudenthal, I. 159, 167, 168, 169
Friedlieb, I. 171
Fritzsche, I. 148, 151

Galaxy, II. 231
Gaza, I. 238
Gellius (A.), I. 93, 97, 99, 115, 120
Gfrörer, admits genuineness of Aristobulus, I. 243
—, historical method of, I. 197
—, on Alexandrianism in Ecclus., I. 144, 147, 148, 149-50, 151-3
—, — — in the LXX, I. 156, 165
—, on allegory in Wisd. of Sol., I. 185
—, on the appearance to Balaam, II. 269
—, — — to Moses, II. 265-6
—, — — to Jacob, II. 253
—, on the body as a source of sin, in Wisd. of Sol., I. 202
—, on eschatology, in Wisd. of Sol., I. 212
—, on the essence of the mind, in Philo, I. 325, 333
—, on "the flesh," in Sib. Or., I. 174
—, on God as light, in Philo, II. 41

Gfrörer, on the incomprehensibility of God, in Wisd. of Sol., I. 198
—, on the Logos, in Wisd. of Sol., I. 228
—, on Philo's literal acceptance of stories in the Pentateuch, II. 243
—, on the pillar of cloud, II. 268
—, on πνεῦμα in Philo, II. 214, 217
—, on the powers, in Philo, II. 96, 106, 107
—, on pre-existence, in Wisd. of Sol., I. 201
—, on the primitive man, in Wisd. of Sol., I. 204
—, on the relation between Logos and Wisdom, in Philo, II. 202
—, on the Therapeutic origin of Wisd. of Sol., I. 178, 179-181
—, on the twofold Logos, in Philo, II. 172
—, on the use of " Wisdom " by Philo, II. 211-212
—, unclassified references to, I. 12, 57, 167, 168, 172, 241, 255
Gibbon, II. 95
God, above the Logos, II. 183-4
—, archetype, II. 81-2
—, — of rational nature, II. 187, 188
—, attributes of, II. 35-62
—, called " place," II. 20
—, cause only of good, II. 50, 60, 142, 291
—, compared to an architect, II. 75, 174
—, described in Scripture so as to suit the ignorant, II. 11-15
—, did not touch matter, II. 76, 113-117
—, efficiency characteristic of, II. 16, 51, 55, 148
—, essence of, unknown, II. 16-20
—, eternity of, II. 35-6
—, exempt from conditions of space, II. 41-5
—, — — — time, II. 45-6
—, existence of, argument for, from causality, II. 4-5
—, — —, — —, from conscience, II. 295-6
—, — —, — —, from intuition, II. 5-6
—, — —, — —, from nature, II. 3-4
—, fills all things, II. 29, 41, 42, 46, 108, 109
—, good, and therefore Creator, II. 54-5, 105
—, the ground of all phenomena, II. 16
—, happy, II. 52
—, the highest genus, II. 29, 160, 203
—, human analogy to, limitation of, II. 11-15

God, the husband of Wisdom, II. 206
—, intuition of, conditions of, II. 6-7, 287, 289
—, — —, variations in clearness of, II. 7-9, 281
—, — —, a vision, II. 9
—, invisible, II. 38-9
—, joy of, II. 49, 52
—, kindness of, II. 56
—, — —, limited by the capacity of the recipient, II. 56-7
—, knowledge of, affected by the human analogy, II. 10, 11
—, known through the knowledge of man, I. 315
—, light, II. 39-41, 82
— made things which were non-existent, I. 302-4
— made two natures, good and evil, II. 50, 311-312
—, manifold representation of, II. 90-6
—, Mind of the universe, II. 15, 183, 184, 288
—, name of, not to be pronounced by its own letters (according to the Mishnah), I. 157
—, namelessness of, II. 20-3
—, names applied to, II. 62-3
—, nature of, sources of knowledge of, II. 10
—, nearness of, to man, I. 14; II. 262, 280-1
—, not in human form, II. 15
—, not relative, II. 48, 141
—, omnipotent, II. 47
—, omnipresent, II. 41, 107-111
—, omniscient, II. 46-7
—, " one and the whole," II. 29
—, perfection of, II. 47-54
—, personality of, II. 15-16, 115-116, 226-7
—, pity of, older than judgment, II. 56
—, the place of ideas, II. 81, 162
—, possesses free volition, II. 15
—, providence of, II. 55-62
— punishes in proportion to the capacity of the punished, II. 57
— punishes through others, II. 135, 137, 142
—, questions about, two chief, II. 1
—, rest and peace of, II. 16, 52-4, 88
—, the " Saviour," II. 55, 102
—, seen without his powers, and manifested in them, II. 120-1
—, sinless, II. 51-2
—, solitude of, II. 182-3
—, the Soul of the universe, II. 17
—, speech of, explained, II. 179-182
—, " the good," II. 30

God, three grades in the knowledge of, II. 194-5
—, transcendent, II. 11, 41
—, unchangeable, II. 36-7
—, unity of, II. 37-8
— used to denote the creative power, II. 85-6, 109. *See* Powers
—, without participation in evil, II. 50
—, — parts, II. 38
—, — passions, II. 15, 51
—, — qualities, II. 23-34
—, — wants, II. 50
—, " wrath " of, II. 51
— : *see* Aristotle, Old Testament, Plato, Sibylline Oracles, Socrates, Stoics, Wisdom of Solomon
Good, the ultimate, II. 284-8
Grace, II. 309-310, 312, 313, 321
Grätz, on the date of the Letter of Aristeas, I. 232-4, 237
—, on *De Vita Contemplativa*, I. 24
—, on the spuriousness of Aristobulus, I. 160, 243, 247-8, 250, 252
—, on the Vathikin, I. 181
—, on Wisd. of Sol., I. 178, 182-3, 195
Grant (Sir A.), I. 76
Greek religion, nature of, I. 131-2
— thought, difference of, from Hebrew, I. 131
Grief, II. 302
Grimm, I. 177, 188, 200, 204, 212, 216, 217, 227
Grossmann, I. 304-5; II. 156, 157

" Habit " defined, I. 280
— in man, I. 315
Hades, I. 211; II. 322
Hagar symbolizes encyclical studies, I. 262; II. 243-5, 246
Halacha, relation of, to Philo's exegesis, I. 20-1
Harris (J. R.), reverence of, for Philo, I. 23
Havet, I. 23
Heaven symbolizes the idea of mind, II. 163
— — the Logos, II. 218
Heavens, form and structure of, I. 267-70
Hebrew religion, nature of, I. 132-4
Hebron, II. 241
Hedonism, II. 301
Heinichen, I. 33
Heinze, on alleged inconsistency in Philo, II. 216
—, on the " inward Logos " of the Stoics, I. 110
—, on materialism in Philo, I. 325
—, on πνεῦμα in Philo, II. 214

SUBJECTS AND NAMES. 331

Heinze, on Heraclitus, I. 32-47 *passim*, 126, 127, 128
—, on the relation of the Logos and Wisdom in Philo, II. 209-210
—, on the use of "Wisdom" by Philo, II. 211-212
—, on "Wisdom" in Wisd. of Sol., I. 221, 223-4, 225
—, unclassified references to, I. 81, 83, 89, 107, 108, 303
Heraclitus, anecdote about, I. 87
—, beginning of work "On Nature" by, I. 32-3
—, date of, I. 28
—, perhaps referred to in Wisdom of Sol., I. 229
—, physics of, adopted in the main by the Stoics, I. 77
—, system of, pantheistic materialism, I. 38
—, view of the elements, modified by the Stoics, I. 83, 85
Heraclitus's philosophy:—
  Antitheses, doctrine of, I. 33-4
  Change, principle of, I. 29
  Destiny, I. 35, 104
  Determining motive of the system, I. 29
  Δίκη, I. 32, 35-6
  Fire, changes of, I. 29-31
  —, the primitive substance, I. 29
  Law, conception of universal, I. 31-2
  —, identical with the Logos, I. 32-3
  Logos, eternal, I. 32
  —, identity of, with fire, I. 36-8
  —, not conscious, I. 39, 126-9
  —, reason for adopting the name, I. 46-7
  Sin and folly of men, I. 44-5
  Soul, an exhalation, I. 40-1
  —, fire, I 39-44
  —, mode of replenishing the, I. 42-4
  —, a portion of the Logos, I. 41
  Strife, I. 34-35
  Summary of results, I. 46
Heraclitus (author of *Alleg. Hom.*), I. 111, 121
Hereditary corruption, I. 193-4, 203
Hermes, allegorized by the Stoics, I. 122-4
—, Egyptian, I. 167
Hermippus, I. 235, 247
Herod the Great, I. 233
Heroes, same as angels, I. 336; II. 145
Hesiod, I. 243, 254
Hesychius, I. 110
Hieronymus, I. 57
High-priest symbolizes the Logos, II. 205, 210, 217, 219, 228-9.

High-priest's emeralds symbolize the sky, I. 272
— — robes symbolize the cosmos, I. 185, 277; II. 171-2, 228, 237-8
Hipparchus, I. 264
Hippolytus, I. 32, 33, 34, 81, 119, 126, 128
Hody, I. 230, 231, 232, 235, 242-3
Homer, I. 34, 123, 243, 254; II. 37
Honover, I. 46
Hope, II. 313
Huet, I. 236
Hymns, II. 236, 319

IDEAS, defined by Xenocrates, I. 59
—, in Aristotle, I. 70
—, in Philo, II. 72-82
—, in Plato, I. 57-61
Idolatry, the greatest evil, I. 206, 207; II. 320
—, origin of, in Wisd. of Sol., I. 209
Ignorance, connection of, with morals, II. 289-292, 306
Immortality, in Philo, I. 339; II. 290, 322-4
—, in Plato, I. 67
—, in Wisd. of Sol., I. 191, 209-213
—: *see* Stoics, philosophy of, soul
Impulse, defined, I. 317
Incense symbolizes the elements, I. 275
Informers, I. 233
Inspiration, I. 13-15, 134; II. 112-113
Intelligible cosmos, the older son of God, II. 45-6, 82
—, the, known only through the perceptible, I. 267, 356; II. 44
Intuition, I. 356-7. *See* God
Ionian philosophy, I. 28
Isaac, the joy and laughter of the soul, I. 261; II. 225, 311
—, symbolizes the character which gains wisdom from nature, II. 21, 254, 320-1
—, wells of, I. 276
Ishmael, II. 9, 244
Israel, the vision of God, II. 9, 206-7
Israelites, in Wisd. of Sol., called the son of God, I. 207
—, — —, a chosen people, I. 207-8
—, — —, led by Wisdom, I. 223

JACOB, change of name of, II. 252, 253, 286-7, 321
—, dream of, II. 104, 256-264
—, led by Wisdom, in Wisd. of Sol., I. 223
—, superiority of, to Esau, II. 311
—, symbolizes the character which gains wisdom from self-discipline, II. 9, 21, 252, 254, 262, 321

Jamblichus, I. 109, 110, 113
Jeremiah, mentioned by Philo, I. 16
Jerusalem, Caligula's intended outrage on, I. 10
— means "the vision of peace," I. 313; II. 53, 323
— seized by Ptolemy Lagi, I. 3
Jesus the son of Sirach, I. 144
Jewish-Alexandrian literature between LXX and Philo, I. 167-9
— — philosophy, connection of, with later Greek thought, I. 75-6
— — —, central problem of, I. 68, 74, 135
— — —, distinctive marks of, I. 150, 153
— — —, source and nature of, I. 3, 7, 154
— — —, source of vacillation of thought in, I. 135
Jews in Alexandria, Council of Elders of, I. 9
— — —, numbers of, I. 3-4
— — —, persecuted, I. 4, 8-10, 184
— — —, privileges of, I. 3
— — —, settlement of, I. 3
— — —, synagogues of, I. 9-10
Job, date of, I. 141
—, Wisdom in, I. 141-2
Joël (Dr. M.), I. 244
John, St., I. 46, 57, 68
Joppa, I. 238
Joseph, preserved by Wisdom, in Wisd. of Sol., I. 223
— symbolizes the passion-loving mind, II. 129
Josephus, I. 4, 7, 10, 160, 180, 186, 232, 234, 236, 237, 244
Jowett, I. 23
Joy, I. 26; II. 301, 304, 319, 321
Jubal, I. 351
Justice, II. 315, 317-318
Justin Martyr, I. 244

KEFERSTEIN, ascribes intercession to the Logos, II. 235, 236, 237
—, on angels in the creation of man, II. 144.
—, on the eternity of matter, I. 304
—, on the high-priest's children, II. 219
—, on natural objects as powers, II. 69
—, on "paraclete," II. 237
—, on the personality of the Logos, II. 245-9, 266
—, on πνεῦμα, II. 214, 216
Knowledge, belongs to the mind only, I. 353
—, sources of, I. 354
—, supernatural source of, I. 359

Knowledge, through contrast, I. 357
—, through intuition, I. 356-7
—, through the senses, I. 354-6
Korah, I. 210
Kuenen, I. 24

LABAN, II. 291
Labour indispensable to progress, II. 312-313
Lactantius, I. 171
Ladder, Jacob's, symbolizes the air, II. 260
—, —, — the life of self-discipline, II. 262
—, —, — the soul, II. 261
Lassalle, I. 37, 127
Laughter, a son of God, I. 26; II. 126, 230
Law, defined by Philo, II. 166, 307
—, — — the Stoics, I. 115
—, in the universe, I. 31-2, 94, 101, 108, 114, 268, 288; II. 166-8
Lepsius, I. 182
Leucippus, I. 48
Levites symbolize human speech, II. 242
— — minds of high order, II. 195
— — the suppliant word, II. 235
"Life, the, of God," II. 184, 307
" — and immortality," II. 324
Linus, I. 243, 254
Liver, I. 316
Lobeck, I. 244
Logoi, in Philo, II. 217-222
—, in the Stoical system, I. 105-7
— of God are works, II. 181, 263
Logos, meanings of, II. 156-8
Logos, represented by Hermes, I. 122-4
Logos, cosmical, doctrine of:—
  Absent from teaching of Socrates, I. 55
  Approaches to, in Plato, I. 63-5, 67-8
  In Heraclitus: see Heraclitus
  In the Stoical system: see Stoics
  In the Wisdom of Solomon, I. 226-9
  Long development of, I. 27
  Preparation for, in Old Test., I. 135-143
  — —, in the LXX, I. 137-140, 158
Logos, the Divine, philosophy of, in Philo:—
  Angel, called an, II. 239-273
  —, —, only under the influence of Scripture, II. 240
  —, general references to the Logos as an, II. 270-3
  —, meaning of the expression "called an," II. 240-2
  Appearance to Abraham, II. 250-4
  — — Balaam, II. 269-270

SUBJECTS AND NAMES.

Logos, the Divine, philosophy of, in Philo:—
Appearance in burning bush, II. 265-7
— to Hagar, II. 243-250
— — Jacob, II. 252-264
— in pillar of cloud, II. 267-9
— in Sodom, II. 264-5
Archangel, II. 267-8, 270-1
Archetypal seal, II. 164-5, 186-7
Archetype of mind, II. 165, 187-8, 193, 197, 234, 280
Bond of the universe, II. 169-170
Came into existence, in what sense, II. 194
Difficulties in inquiring into, II. 156
English equivalents of the term, II. 158-9
Eternal, II. 193-4
Generic, most, next to God, II. 29, 160-1, 189, 194, 203, 204, 242
God, a, to the imperfect, II. 195-8
Help to virtue, II. 307-9
Idea, II. 159-165
Idea of the ideas, II. 80, 164
Image of God, II. 186-190, 230-3
Instrument of creation and providence, II. 198-200
Law, the moral, II. 166-8, 200
Law of the universe, II. 165-6, 200
Many-named, II. 270
Mediates between God and the universe, II. 190-3
— — the personality of God and that of man, II. 226-7, 233-5
Mind, the, above us, II. 233-5
Not begotten, II. 192
Not unbegotten, II. 192
Oldest of things, II. 185
Personality of, discussed, II. 222-273
Personification, II. 223-4
"Place," called, II. 20, 257
Place of the intelligible cosmos, II. 162, 176
"Prophet," II. 227
Relation to God, II. 182-198
— — the Spirit, II. 214-217
— — Wisdom, II. 201-213
Shadow of God, II. 190
Shaped species, II. 168-9
Son of God, II. 185-6, 230
Source of, in the Self-existent, II. 183-4
Summary of doctrine of, II. 273
Symbolized by Aaron, II. 268
— — Abraham, II. 225
— — the book, Gen. ii. 4, II. 162-3, 41
— — the breast-plate of the high-priest, II. 172

Symbolized by city of refuge, the first, II. 83, 161
— — the covenant with Noah, II. 167
— — Eden, II. 202
— — heaven, II. 218, 241
— — the high-priest, II. 169, 205, 210, 217, 219, 228-9
— — the manna, I. 25 ; II. 29, 160, 178, 204, 242, 308
— — Melchizedek, II. 225-7, 311
— — Moses, II. 191-2, 227-8, 268
— — the river in Eden, II. 202
— — the sword that guarded paradise, II. 167-8
Twofold in the universe, II. 171-182
Unity of the intelligible cosmos, II. 161-3
Λόγος ἀΐδιος, II. 193
—, ἀνατολή, II. 188
— ἀνωτάτω, II. 186
— γεγωνός, I. 351; II. 172, 228
—, δεύτερος θεός, II. 197
—, εἰκών, II. 187
— ἐνδιάθετος, I. 110, 125, 350; II. 157, 171
— ἐπαινέτης, II. 236
— ἑρμηνεύς, I. 54, 352
— ἑρμηνευτικός, I. 353
— θεσμοθέτης, II. 228
— ἱκέτης, II. 235-7
— κοινός, I. 94, 113, 125
— ὄργανον θεοῦ, II. 198
— ὀρθός, I. 94, 113, 125, 262 ; II. 185
— παράκλητος, II. 237-9
— πολυώνυμος, II. 206 [See II. 270]
— πρεσβευτής, II. 236
— πρεσβύτατος θεοῦ υἱός, II. 185
— προφορικός, I. 110, 123, 125, 350; II. 171
— — defined by the Stoics, I. 112
— πρωτόγονος θεοῦ υἱός, II. 185
—, σκιά, II. 190
— σπερματικός, I. 102, 125
— τομεύς, II. 168, 207
Logos of man, in Philo, I. 350-3
— — —, in the Stoical system, I. 107-115
Lord, used to denote the regal power of God, II. 85-6. See Powers
Lot, delivered by Wisdom, in Wisd. of Sol., I. 223
Love to God, II. 288, 307, 316
Lucius, I. 24
Lyre, II. 232
Lysimachus, I. 234

MACCABEES, I. 184
—, 2nd and 3rd Books of, I. 167
—, 4th, I. 168
Mahaffy, I. 7, 183

334   SUBJECTS AND NAMES.

Man, all things for the good of, I. 53-4, 95-6
—, body of, nature of, I. 316
—, corrupt, not totally, II. 279-83
—, cosmical powers manifested in, I. 315
—, created last, why, II. 274-5
—, creation of, II. 138-153
—, degeneracy of, II. 278-9
—, distinguished from the brutes by reason, I. 317
—, a divine, sinless, II. 51, 296, 328
—, a duad, I. 316
—, every, has good thoughts, II. 280-1
—, fall of, II. 279
—, first, most endowed, II. 278
—, the generic, II. 275-7
—, a microcosm, I. 289, 315; II. 3, 65, 68
—, mind of, at first morally neutral, II. 293
—, most humble when nearest God, II. 315
—, questions connected with, I. 314
—, son of God, II. 188, 281-2
—, — — the Logos, II. 188-9, 271, 282
—, subject to sin through connection with phenomenal world, II. 296-7
—, the temple of God, II. 281
—, the virtuous, neither God nor man, II. 283
See Anthropology, Logos in man, Mind, Powers, Soul, &c.
Mangey, I. 12, 15, 283, 320; II. 32, 42, 133, 191, 250, 262
Manasseh, II. 311
Manna, in Wisd. of Sol., I. 179
— symbolizes the Logoi, II. 221-2
See Logos and Wisdom
Maranus, I. 173
Mariette, I. 182
Martineau (Dr. J.), I. 58
Material, the, the portal to the ideal, I. 267, 356; II. 44
Matter, in Philo, characteristics of, I. 297-8
—, common substance of the elements, I. 297
—, eternal, I. 299-307
—, feminine, I. 306
—, not actively evil, I. 310-313
—, originally formless, I. 307-310
—, predicates of, negative, I. 298
—, under necessity, II. 53
—, without qualities, I. 298; II. 24
Matter, in Anaxagoras, I. 48
—, — Aristotle, I. 69-70, 72
—, — early Greek speculation, I. 28
—, — Heraclitus, I. 38

Matter, in Plato, I. 61-5
—, — the Stoical system, I. 80-1, 86, 91, 101
—, — Wisd. of Sol., I. 188
Melchizedek symbolizes the Logos, II. 225-7, 311
Men, four classes of, according to their education, I. 262-3
Mendelssohn, I. 238
Merit, ethical, conditions of, II. 292-6
Messiah, II. 322
Metrodorus of Lampsacus used allegory, I. 121
Midrash, II. 90
Miller, I. 126
Milton, quoted, I. 203
Mind, human, connection of, with the irrational soul, I. 340
—, —, essence of, unknown, I. 325-7; II. 17
—, —, immortal, I. 339
—, —, indivisible, I. 335
—, —, Logos, archetype of, II. 165, 187-8, 193, 197, 234, 280
—, —, place of, in the body, I. 339
—, —, powers of, I. 340-353
—, —, pre-existent, I. 336
—, —, the sovereign principle, I. 323-5
—, —, substance of, I. 277, 325-335
—, in brutes, I. 322-3
—, used in different senses, II. 233-4
Moses, fast of, I. 284
—, inspired by Wisdom, in Wisd. of Sol., I, 223
—, Philo's view of, I. 15
— symbolizes the higher mind, II. 194, 283
— — the Logos, II. 191-2, 227-8, 268
Müller, I. 283; II. 32, 54, 166, 174
Mullach, I. 126
Musaeus, I. 167
Museum, I. 4, 6
Music of the spheres, I. 283-4

Nadab, II. 250-1
Nature, in the Stoical system, I. 92, 106
—, living conformably to, in Philo, II. 167, 314
—, — — —, in the Stoical system, I. 76, 114
—, order of, governed by reason, I. 280
—, powers included in, I. 280
—, used to denote the divine constitution of things, II. 62
Natures, two, in one soul, I. 317-318
Necessity, I. 35, 61, 93, 102-4
Nemesius, I. 40, 86, 110
Neo-Platonism, I. 7, 75

SUBJECTS AND NAMES. 335

Noah, II. 102, 126-7, 128, 167, 310-311
Number, learned from lapse of time,
  I. 287
—, perfect, nature of, I. 290
Numbers, male and female, I. 293

Oaths, II. 318
Old Testament, preparation for doctrine
  of the Logos in, I. 131-143
— —, relation of God to the world in,
  I. 135-143
— —, transcendence of God in, I. 133
— —, Wisdom in, I. 140-143
— : see Angel, Angels, Hebrew religion,
  Job, Proverbs, Scriptures, Word of
  the Lord.
On, I. 340
Onkelos, I. 157, 159
Opinion, with the Stoics, I. 113, 116
Or symbolizes truth, II. 228
Origen, I. 81, 83, 85, 87, 91, 105; II. 33
Orpheus, I. 243, 250, 253
Otto, I. 173
Οὐρανός, derivation of, I. 268

Panaetius, I. 112
Pantheism, in Heraclitus, I. 38
—, in the Stoical system, I. 77, 80, 84,
  92
—, involved in astrology, I. 287
—, opposed by Philo, II. 2
Paradise, I. 19; II. 207, 212, 276
Παράκλητος, not applied to the Logos,
  II. 237-9
—, not used in creation, II. 55, 183
Parmenides, I. 305
Passions, II. 301-5
Πάθος, defined by Zeno, I. 115
Patriarchs symbolize moral states, I.
  22, 147
Paul, St., on election, II. 310
— —, on the travailing of creation, II.
  53-4, 237
— —, summary of the Law by, II. 309
Peitho, I. 340
Perception, defined, I. 317
—, a source of knowledge, I. 354-6
Perfection of the universe, meaning of,
  I. 290
Personality of God, source of belief in,
  I. 133. See God.
—, notion of among the ancients, I. 50,
  56, 61; II. 127
Personification in Philo, II. 123-6,
  223-4
Petronius, I. 10; II. 125
Pfleiderer (Edm.), I. 47, 229
Pharaoh, I. 340
Pharos, I. 4, 183, 231
Philanthropy, II. 315-316

Philo accepts substantially the story in
  the Letter of Aristeas, I. 232
—, cosmopolitanism of, I. 16; II. 238
—, date of, I. 11-12
—, depreciated physics, I. 263-5
—, did not regard speculative philosophy as an end, I. 263
— does not name his predecessors in
  allegorical interpretation, I. 244
—, eclectic, Hellenizing, I. 16-18
—, eclecticism of, character of, I. 319-
  320
—, exegesis of, connection of, with
  that of the Rabbinical schools, I.
  20-1
— followed Greek models in allegorizing, I. 124
—, genius of, quality of, I. 12-13, 22,
  26, 260
—, intolerance of, I. 13, 282
—, — —, exaggerated, II. 289-292
—, life of, I. 7-11
—, moral earnestness of, I. 23-6
—, not an ascetic, I. 24
—, order of exposition of philosophy
  of, I. 266
—, an orthodox Jew, I. 13-16, 257, 359
—, place of, in the world of religious
  belief, I. 13-26
—, relation of, to the writers of the
  New Test., I. 12
— thought himself sometimes inspired,
  I. 14-15; II. 53
— visited the theatres, I. 17
—, works of, character of, I. 1, 257
—, — —, date of, I. 12
—, — —, lists of, referred to, I. 12
—, — —, source of interest in the, I. 2
Philo the elder, I. 168, 236
Philocrates, I. 230
Philoponus, I. 41
Philosophers, Greek, said to be dependent on the Hebrew Scriptures, I.
  150, 248
Philosophical investigation, incentive
  to, I. 260-1
— problems suggested by the universe,
  I. 258
— — — consciousness, I. 259
Philosophy compared to a field, I. 263
—, different principles of classifying
  branches of, I. 260
—, divisions of, I. 17, 263-6
—, motive for the study of, I. 260-1;
  II. 313
—, objects of, I. 259-260
—, order in which questions of, arose,
  I. 28
—, sources of, I, 258-9
  See Jewish-Alexandrian philosophy

336 SUBJECTS AND NAMES.

Phocylides, I. 167-8
Piety, the highest virtue, I. 205; II. 315-316
Pirqé Aboth, I. 12
Pindar, I. 220
Pity, II. 303
Plagues of Egypt, I. 275
Planets, I. 64, 65-6, 269
—, influence of, on earth, I. 286-7
Plants, how distinguished from inanimate things, I. 280
Plato, on the presence of "Mind" in the universe, I. 39
—, relation of, to Philo, I. 27, 57
—, said to have used Jewish Law, I. 246
— used "God" in a subordinate sense, I. 60, 66, 68, 91
—, unclassified references to, I. 36, 50, 263, 295, 299, 316, 329; II. 54
Plato's philosophy:—
 Anthropology, I. 66-7
 Causality, twofold, I. 61-2
 Foreshadowing of the Logos doctrine, I. 67-8
 God, doctrine of, I. 59-61, 64, 67-8
 Idea of the good, I. 59-60
 Ideas, doctrine of, I. 57-61
 —, relation between the, and phenomena, I. 62-3, 70
 Indeterminate, the, I. 61
 Necessity, I. 61, 93
 Personality, vagueness of conception of, I. 61; II. 127
 Soul, human, I. 65, 67, 318
 Soul of the universe, I. 63-5
 Speech, inward and outward, distinguished by, II. 117
 Subordinate gods helped in forming mortal creatures, I. 66-7; II. 139
 Universe, form and structure of, I. 65-6
 —, a living being, I. 65, 68
Pleasure, connection of, with desire, II. 302
—, ethical position of, II. 301, 305
—, the medium in perception, I. 345; II. 300
—, one of the passions, II. 301
—, symbolized by the serpent, I. 345; II. 279, 300-301, 311
—, used generally in a bad sense, I. 26
—, used in a good sense, II. 305
Pleiades, II. 231
Plumptre, I. 185
Plutarch, I. 30, 40, 81-119 passim, 128-9, 266, 306
Πνεῦμα, two meanings of, II. 214-215
Polytheism, II. 220, 270, 282, 320
Pope, quoted, I. 355

Poseidonius, I. 80, 87, 89, 93, 108, 113
Power (of God), creative: see regal
—, legislative, II. 83-4
—, preceptive, II. 83
—, prohibitive, II. 83
—, propitious, II. 83-4
—, punitive, II. 86-7
—, regal : see Powers, the Divine, creative
Powers, the Divine, alleged contradiction in doctrine of, II. 106-7
—, appearance of, to Abraham, II. 90-3, 133-8
—, bonds of the universe, II. 68-9
—, collectively, the intelligible cosmos, II. 79-80
—, the creative (or, beneficent) and regal, II. 83-7, 91, 92, 93, 94, 96, 102-105, 119-120, 121, 127, 128, 141
—, difficulties of inquiry about, II. 66-8
—, doctrine of, grows out of the roots of Philo's theology, II. 34
—, — —, to be kept secret, II. 89-90
—, engaged in the creation of man, what, II. 138-153
—, equivalent to the divine essence, II. 98-100
—, eternal, II. 72, 79, 85
—, God above the, II. 108-9, 119-121
—, "God and his powers," II. 117-118
—, God in his essential Being distinct from, II. 121-3
—, — omnipresent through, II. 107-111
—, — "stretches," II. 111-112
—, — surrounded by, II. 110
—, — touches things by, II. 112-117
—, — used, and did things through them, II. 118-119
—, a hierarchy, II. 82-84
—, ideas, II. 72-82
—, identified with Logoi, II. 219-220
—, illustrated by the analogy of the wise man, II. 97-8
—, immaterial, II. 71, 78
—, independent of time, II. 72
—, infinite, II. 72
—, in the highest sense, not angels, II. 147-153
—, measures, II. 74
—, mental forces, II. 70
—, natural objects called, why, II. 6 - 70
—, not independent causes, II. 70-1
—, origin of question about, II. 65-6
—, partake of the mystery and greatness of God, II. 71-2
—, personality of, discussed, II. 119-154

Powers, personification of, II. 126-133
—, physical forces, II. 69-70
—, predicates of God, II. 101-105
—, quasi relative, II. 48-9
—, relation of, to God, II. 88-155
—, τομεῖς, II. 73
—, transcendent, II. 72
—, unbegotten, II. 72
—, used interchangeably with God, II. 100-101
—, various, named, II. 87-8
—, virtues, II. 88
Powers, Human, classification of, I. 342-4
—, distribution of, I. 340-1
—, nature of, I. 341-2
—, perceptive, I. 344-6
—, preferential, I. 346-350
Prayer, II. 101, 312, 313
Pre-existence, in Philo, I. 336; II. 277
—, in Plato, I. 67
—, in Wisd. of Sol., I. 194, 200-202
Proclus, I. 106
Προλήψεις, I. 113
Property, meaning of, in Logic, II. 25
Prophecy, a state of ecstasy, I. 14; II. 282-3
Protagoras, II. 290
Proverbs, date of first part of, I. 141
—, Wisdom in, I. 141
Providence, in Philo, II. 55-62
—, in the Stoical system, I. 94-102
—, in the view of Socrates, I. 52-4
—, shown in the fate of nations, II. 199
Ψυχή, derivation of, I. 326
Ptolemaïs, I. 238
Ptolemaïs Theron, I. 238-9
Ptolemies, deification of, I. 182-3
—, generally favoured the Jews, I. 3, 184
Ptolemy Lagi, or Soter, I. 3, 4, 234, 235, 238, 245, 247
- Lathurus, I. 238
— Philadelphus, I. 4, 230, 234, 235, 237, 245, 246, 247
— Philometor, I. 242, 244, 247, 250
— Philopator, I. 184
— Physcon, I. 184, 250
Punishments, future, I. 213; II. 322-3
Pythagoras, I. 246
Pythagorean philosophy, I. 18, 28

QUAESTIONES ET SOLUTIONES, doubts about the genuineness of, I. 248, 274
Quality, meaning of, II. 24

RAMESES, I. 440

Reason acts by differentiation, I. 280-1
— and its products coincident in God, II. 176-7, 184-5
Refuge, cities of, symbolize the divine powers, II. 83
'Ρῆμα in the LXX, I. 137, 139
Repentance, II. 323
Representation, mental, how produced, I. 317
Reprobation, I. 192
Responsibility, conditions of, II. 292-6
Retribution, II. 322-3
Revelation depends on recipient as well as giver, II. 248-9
Rewards, future, I. 212-213; II. 323-4
Ritter (Bernh.), I. 10, 16, 20
Ritter (the historian of philosophy), I. 23, 123
Rock symbolizes Wisdom, II. 28, 203, 204
Rosetta stone, I. 182

SABBATH, II. 52-3, 232, 287, 315
Sacrifices, I. 26; II. 319
San, stone found at, I. 182
Sarah, change in the name of, I. 13; II. 244, 253
— symbolizes wisdom or virtue, II. 206, 243
Scepticism, I. 6, 357-9
Schleiermacher, I. 36, 127
Schürer, I. 12, 237-9, 243
Scriptures accommodate their language to the ignorant, II. 11, 41, 246
—, the basis of Philo's system, I. 13-16
—, called the Logos, II. 158, 307
— : see Old Testament
Seed, in Heraclitus, I. 104
—, in the Stoical system, I. 102-104
Seeking God may result in failure, II. 9
Self-control, II. 317
Self-love, II. 289, 291
Seneca, deviation of, from the Stoical position, I. 81-3
—, referred to, I. 79-116 passim
Sensation, morally neutral, II. 300
Senses, divided into philosophical and unphilosophical, II. 321
—, divine gifts, II. 300
—, enumerated, I. 317, 346
—, how connected with the moral life, II. 300
—, sources of knowledge, I. 354-6
Septuagint, anthropomorphism softened in, I. 158-9
—, Dähne's view of Alexandrianism of, I. 156-164
—, Gfrörer's view of, I. 165
— modified the Masoretic text, I. 156
— originated in Alexandria, I. 156

Septuagint, Philo's view of, I. 16
—, relation of, to Greek culture, I. 165-6
—, said to have been preceded by a partial translation, I. 246
—, supposed traces of doctrine of divine powers in, I. 163-4
—, supposed traces of doctrine of ideas, I. 160-2
—, traces of acquaintance with Platonism and Stoicism in, I. 162-3
—, tradition of origin of, I. 230-1
Serpent, brazen, II. 316-317
— symbolizes pleasure, I. 24, 345; II. 279, 300-1, 311
Seven, the idea impressed on the universe, II. 231-2
—, the image of God, II. 230-3
Sextus Empiricus, I. 32, 33, 34, 42, 43, 78, 85, 86, 87, 105, 110-111, 111-112, 128, 129, 263
Shakspeare quoted, I. 202, 284
Sharpe, I. 181, 182-3
Shelley quoted, I. 191
Shem, II. 254
Sibylline Oracles, Book III, anthropology of, I. 173-5
— — —, country of, I. 169-170
— — —, date of, I. 169
— — —, doctrine of God in, I. 171-3
— — —, faint indications of Jewish-Alexandrian philosophy in, I. 175-6
— — —, indicative of change of view, I. 170
— — — source of sin in, I. 174-5
Siegfried, I. 20, 299, 303; II. 90, 161
Simplicius, I. 30, 35
Sin, not found in beings above man, I. 348-9; II. 139, 149, 283, 292
—, — — — — below man : see Brutes
—, possible only to rational beings, I. 348, 349; II. 139
Sins, classification of, II. 319-320
Six, a perfect number, I. 290, 293
Socrates symbolizes self-knowledge, II. 7, 256
—, Philosophy of :—
  Divine nature, I. 55
  Gods, persons, I. 52
  Man, all things for the good of, I. 53
  —, divine care for, I. 53-4
  Monotheism mingled with polytheism, I. 54-5
  Soul, capable of knowing God, I. 56-7
  —, nature of, I. 55-6, 65
  Teleology, evidence of, I. 52-4
  —, introduced by Socrates, I. 51, 77

Sodom, II. 134-8
Sophists, I. 5, 353
Sophocles, I. 220
Soul, Anaxagoras' view of, I. 51
—, Aristotle's division of, I. 319
—, ambiguity in the word, I. 318
—, characteristics of, I. 281, 317
—, divisions of, I. 318-320
—, irrational, divisions of, I. 321-2
—, —, substance of, I. 320-1
—, rational, names of, I. 322-3
—, —, the temple of God, II. 229
— : see Heraclitus, Mind, Plato, Socrates, Stoics, Wisdom of Solomon
Soulier thinks Philo held doctrine of five elements, I. 273-8
— — — derived the soul from ether, I. 325
Souls, character and destiny of, I. 335-9
—, descent of, into bodies, I. 337
—, incorporeal, see God as he is, II. 95
— lived in the air, I. 282, 335; II. 144-5, 260
Space, origin of notion of, I. 356
Spirit, Divine, I. 327; II. 214-17
—, —, visits man inconstantly, II. 281, 297-8
—, in the Stoical system, I. 85-7
— of God, in Old Test., I. 137-9
— — —, in Wisd. of Sol., I. 214-17
Stallbaum, I. 64
Stars, fixed, I. 269
—, living beings, I. 282-3
—, unsusceptible of evil, I. 283; II. 139, 140
Stephanus, I. 127
Stoics, Philosophy of the :—
  Afflictions of the good, I. 99-102
  Allegorical interpretation, examples of, I. 122-4
  — method, I. 121
  Anthropology, I. 107-120
  Antithesis, law of, as cause of evil, I. 97-8
  Character of the, I. 75-6, 260
  Cosmos, defined, I. 91
  Concomitant results, as cause of evil, I. 98-9
  Destiny, I. 93-4
  Elements, four, I. 83, 85-7, 105
  Ethics, I. 114-16
  Etymology, I. 121-2
  Evil, problem of, I. 96-102
  —, source of moral, I. 115-17
  Fire, identified with the Logos, I. 83-5
  —, the primitive, as seed, I. 104-5
  First principles, two, I. 86

SUBJECTS AND NAMES. 339

Stoics, Philosophy of the:—
General notions, I. 106
God, identical with the Logos, I. 81
—, — — — universe, I. 90-2
"Indifferent" things, I. 99
Law, I. 94, 101, 108, 114, 115
Logoi, I. 105-7
Logos, all-penetrating, I. 87-9
—, corporeal, I. 81-3
—, identical with cause, I. 90
—, — — destiny, I. 90
—, — — fire, I. 83-5
—, — — God, I. 81
—, — — law, I. 94
—, — — nature, I. 90
—, — — necessity, I. 90
—, — — providence, I. 94
—, — — spirit, I. 85-7
—, — — truth, I. 90
—, immanent, I. 80
—, internal, I. 110-11
—, names of, various, I. 90
—, proofs of existence of, in the universe, I. 77-80
—, relation of, to man, I. 107-115
—, seminal, I. 102-7
—, uttered, I. 110, 111-12
Materialism, I. 80-1
Mind, birth and development of, I. 112-13
Nature, I. 92-3
—, living conformably to, I. 76, 114, 261
Necessity, I. 93
Order of thought, I. 76-7
Periodical cycle of change, I. 89, 104, 105
Personality, uncertain view of, II. 127
Providence, I. 94-102
Reason in man, part of universal reason, I. 107-9
—, right, I. 113, 114
Relation to future doctrine of the Logos, I. 124-5
— of part to the whole, as cause of evil, I. 98
Seed, nature of, I. 102-4
Semitic influence in the origin of, I. 76
Soul, not immortal, I. 112
—, origin of, I. 112
—, outlived the body, I. 112
—, parts of the, I. 109
Sovereign principle of man, I. 108-10
— — of the universe, I. 91-2
Spirit, I. 85-7
Suicide, I. 102
Will, problem of the, I. 117-20

Strife, I. 34-5
Stobaeus, I. 33, 35, 80-116 *passim*
Suidas, I. 83
Swearing, habit of : *see* Oaths

TABERNACLE, curtains of the, symbolize the elements, I. 275
Tacitus, I. 233
Talmud, I. 181
Targums soften anthropomorphism, I. 159
Tartarus, II. 322
Tatian, I. 87
Teleology, in Aristotle, I. 69-72
—, in Philo, II. 3-4
—, in the Stoical system, I. 77-8
—, introduced by Socrates, I. 51
Temperance, II. 315, 316-317
Ten Commandments, generic laws, II. 222, 320
— —, given by God himself, II. 130
— —, given through a voice, II. 132-3
Terah (Tharrha) symbolizes self-knowledge, II. 7, 256
Tetragrammaton, II. 22, 105
Thales, I. 28
Thamar, II. 164
Thanksgiving, II. 319
Theism, distinguished from pantheism, I. 92
—, foreshadowed by Anaxagoras, I. 49
—, in Aristotle, I. 69-74
Themistius, I. 41
Theophilus of Antioch, I. 170
Therapeutae, I. 24, 178-181
"Thirsting and hungering after excellence," I. 25
Thomson, quoted, I. 84, 218
Tiberius, I. 8, 232-3
Time, a grand-son of God, II. 45, 105
—, nature of, I. 292-3, 294-5; II. 45
—, origin of notion of, I. 356
Tischendorf, I. 16; II. 42, 109, 202
Tosiphta, I. 181
Transcendence of God in Hebrew belief, I. 133. *See* God
Treasure hid in a field, II. 310
Tropics, I. 270 ; II. 231
Truthfulness, II. 318.

UNIVERSE, arrangement of the, I. 267-270
—, composition of the, I. 270-9
— consists of body and soul, I. 315
—, created, but not in time, I. 291-4
—, a direct expression of the divine causality, II. 105-106
—, held together by law, I. 268 ; II. 165-6
—, imperishable, I. 295-6

Universe, matter the basis of the, I. 297
—, mutual dependence of the parts of the, I. 285-8
—, not eternal, I. 293-4
—, only one, I. 291
—, an organized whole, I. 285-9
—, perfect, I. 289-290
—, "perfect man," I. 288-9
—, the temple of God, I. 289; II. 146, 169, 229
—, vastness of the, I. 268
—, weariness of the, II. 53
—, a work of art, II. 4

VACHEROT, I. 22
Valckenaer, I. 235, 243, 246, 247, 250
Vathikin, I. 181
Vespasian, I. 182
Vice resides only in the reason, II. 293
Villoison, I. 123, 124
Virtue, alone good, II. 285-6
—, helps to, II. 307-313
—, the most generic, II. 315
—, nature of, II. 313-315
—, resides only in the reason, II. 293
—, species of, same in number as the Logoi, II. 221, 272
—, symbolized by Paradise, I. 19; II. 207, 276
—, — — Sarah, II. 206, 243
—, three modes of acquiring, II. 320-1
Virtues, classified, II. 315-316
—, enumerated in Wisd. of Sol., I. 205
Vowels, II. 232

WALLACE, I. 40
Water: see Elements
Well-being of man, defined, II. 286
Wellmann, I. 44
Will, in Heraclitus, I. 45
—, in Philo, I. 346-350; II. 293-4
—, in the Stoical system, I. 117-120
Winer, I. 216
Wisdom, daughter of God, II. 213
—, defined, I. 260
—, distinguished from the Logos, II. 207-208
—, explanation of distinction of, from the Logos, II. 209-211
—, identified with the Logos, II. 201-207
—, many-named, II. 206
—, mother of the Logos, II. 185, 205
—, — of the universe, II. 204, 206
—, relation of, to the Logos, II. 201-213
—, — —, to man, II. 208-209
—, same under various manifestations, II. 97
—, symbolized by Bethuel, II. 213

Wisdom, symbolized by bread, II. 212
—, — — Eden, II. 202, 242
—, — — Isaac, II. 212
—, — — manna, I. 334
—, — — Paradise, II. 212
—, — — the rock in the wilderness, II. 28, 203, 204
—, — — Sarah, II. 206
—, the way to God, II. 309
—, why Logos is generally preferred to, II. 213
—, why used instead of Logos, II. 211-213
—: see Ecclesiasticus, Old Testament, Wisdom of Solomon
Wisdom of Solomon, allegorical interpretation in, I. 185-6, 196-7
— — —, authorship of, I. 177-181
— — —, date of, I. 181-5
— — —, dogmatic character of, I. 186
— — —, prepares the way for Philo, I. 229
Wisdom of Solomon, Doctrine of :—
Anthropology, I. 199-213
Anthropomorphism, I. 199
Body, the, a burden, I. 202-203
Chosen people, I. 206-208
Creation, motive of, I. 189-190
Devil, I. 195-7
Ethics, I. 205-206
Evil not caused by God, I. 194-6
Fall, the, I. 203-205
God, I. 187-199
—, the Creator, I. 188
—, eternal, I. 187
—, knowable, I. 197
—, loving, I. 190, 206
—, one, I. 187
—, transcendent, I. 189
Hereditary corruption, I. 193-4, 203
Idolatry, I. 206, 207, 209
Immortality, I. 191, 209-213
Judgment, final, I. 211-213
Logos, I. 226-9
Man, consists of body and soul, I. 200
—, the image of God, I. 203
—, responsible for his own fate, I. 195
Necessity, I. 192-4
Providence, I. 190-7, 208-209
Revelation of God, I. 197-8
Right, avenging, I. 192, 194
Soul, pre-existence of, I. 194, 200-202
Spirit of God, everywhere, I. 214
— — —, relation of, to God, I. 215
— — —, the same as Wisdom, I. 215-217
Transcendence of God consistent with his action in the world, I. 199

SUBJECTS AND NAMES.

Wisdom of Solomon, Doctrine of:—
 Wisdom, I. 213-226
—, attributes of, I. 219-220
—, basis of morals, I. 205
—, given in answer to prayer, I. 204
—, identified with the Spirit of God, I. 215-217
—, not an attribute, I. 224
—, not essentially different from God, I. 224
—, not material, I. 225
—, origin and nature of, I. 217-218
—, personality of, I. 225-6
—, relation of, to God, I. 220-1
—, — —, to man, I. 222-3
—, — —, to the universe, I. 221
—, sources of doctrine of, I. 214
—, the source of immortality, I. 205
Word of the Lord, in Old Test., I. 137-140
Wordsworth quoted, II. 210

XENOCRATES, I. 59, 263
Xenophon, referred to, I. 52-6

YEAR, the perfect, I. 66

ZELLER admits genuineness of Aristobulus, I. 243
— admits spuriousness of *De Vita Contemplativa*, I. 24
—, on Alexandrianism in the LXX, I. 158-9, 161-2, 164-5
—, on the causality of Plato's ideas, I. 58

Zeller, on the danger of judging Philo from our modern point of view, II. 143, 222
—, on the date of Aristeas, I. 232
—, — — — of the legend about the LXX, I. 247
—, — — — of Wisd. of Sol., I. 183
—, on *De Incorrupt. Mundi*, I. 296
—, on the doctrine of Heraclitus, I. 29-31, 38
—, on the idea of the good in Plato, I. 60
—, on the identity of the powers and angels, II. 147
—, on the inward and uttered logos of the Stoics, I. 110
—, on the question whether Philo ascribed an inward Logos to God, II. 173, 174
—, on Therapeutic origin of Wisd. of Sol., I. 178
— thinks Philo necessarily contradicts himself in the doctrine of the powers, II. 106, 127, 223
Zeno, arguments of, for the existence of reason in the universe, I. 78
—, on the soul, I. 40, 44
—, only fragments of survive, I. 76
— said God was present in ditches and worms, I. 87
—, unclassified references to, I. 80, 81, 83, 84, 94, 102, 104, 114, 115, 305
Zenodotus, I. 235
Zodiac, I. 270; II. 231
Zones of the earth, I. 267.

# INDEX II.

References to passages in Philo.

Whenever a treatise is contained in Mangey's edition, the figures on the left of the column denote the section of the treatise and the page of Mangey. The Vol. of Mangey is given with the title of the treatise. References to treatises not in Mangey follow the editions from which they are taken. The figures on the right denote the volume and page where the passage is referred to.

De Abrahamo (Vita sapientis per doctrinam perfecti sive de legibus non scriptis). Vol. II.							
1, 1	I. 290		46, 39	II. 308			I. 324
2, 2	II. 313			II. 85			II. 234
3-4, 3-4	II. 323			II. 316		6, 242	II. 296
10-11, 8-9	II. 21		De Agricultura Noe. Vol. I.				I. 289
11, 9	I. 342		2, 301	I. 262			II. 54
12, 9	II. 9			II. 62			II. 55
12, 10	II. 113		3, 302	I. 17		6, 243	II. 88
13, 10	II. 316			I. 262		7, 243	II. 102
15, 11	I. 20			I. 263		7, 243-4	I. 319
	II. 2		4, 302	II. 24		7, 244-5	II. 293
15, 12	I. 289		4, 303	II. 320		11, 247	I. 339
15-16, 11-12	II. 197			I. 17			I. 316
16, 12	I. 290		5, 304	I. 262			II. 239
	II. 3		6-7, 304-5	I. 23		De Cherubim et flammeo gladio. Vol. I.	II. 296
	II. 7		7, 304	I. 324		1-3, 138-40	II. 243
	II. 39			I. 318		2, 139-40	I. 265
18, 13	I. 352		7-8, 304-6	I. 321			I. 352
	II. 157		12, 308	I. 340			II. 79
18, 14	II. 6			II. 303		2, 140	I. 261
22, 17	II. 133			II. 185		5, 141	II. 228
23, 18	II. 134		12, 308-9	II. 270		6, 142	I. 292
24, 19	II. 21		13, 309	I. 290			II. 36
	II. 119		14, 310	II. 288			II. 52
24-5, 18-20	II. 92		36, 324	I. 342			II. 56
26-28, 20-22	II. 134		38, 325-6	II. 286			II. 99
27, 21	II. 55			I. 342			II. 297
	II. 135		39, 326	I. 344			II. 323
28, 21-2	II. 135			II. 310		7, 142	I. 269
29-31, 22-24	II. 134		De Animalibus sacrificio idoneis deque victimarum speciebus. Vol. II.				I. 270
31, 24	I. 258					7-9, 142-4	I. 21
36, 29	II. 51					7-10, 142-4	I. 22
	II. 52					9, 143	I. 14
	II. 56		3, 239	I. 323		9, 143-4	II. 84
41, 34-5	II. 302			II. 165		9, 144	II. 56
41, 35	II. 224			II. 186			II. 161
	II. 303		5, 241	II. 317		11, 145	II. 168
				I. 318		11, 146	II. 200
							II. 308

DE ABRAHAMO—DE DECEM ORACULIS.

13, 147	II. 35	10, 356	I. 320	36, 432	II. 87
	II. 50		I. 321		
	II. 54	11, 356	I. 328	De Congressu quaerendae eruditionis gratia. Vol. I.	
	II. 206		I. 334		
14, 148	I. 16		I. 342		
	II. 81	12, 358	II. 316	3, 520	II. 309
	II. 162			3-4, 520-2	I. 17
	II. 206	De Confusione linguarum. Vol. I.		6, 523	I. 353
15, 148	II. 25			6, 524	I. 351
18, 149	I. 355	1 sqq., 404 sqq.		8, 524-5	I. 344
18, 150	II. 241		I. 20	9, 526	II. 2
19, 150	I. 355	7, 408	I. 319	10, 526	II. 9
19 sqq., 150 sqq.		8, 409	II. 240	10, 526-7	I. 263
	II. 291		II. 264	11, 527	II. 322
20, 151	I. 326	11, 411	II. 193	12, 528	II. 301
24, 153	I. 350	13, 412	II. 69	13, 528-9	I. 5
	II. 16	13, 413-14	II. 222	14, 529-30	I. 17
25, 154	II. 32	14, 414	II. 168		I. 262
	II. 49		II. 185	14, 530	I. 260
	II. 50		II. 188		II. 286
	II. 81	17, 416	I. 338		II. 317
26, 154-5	II. 53	17, 417	II. 221	15, 531	II. 297
26, 155	II. 16	20, 418	II. 9		II. 302
28, 156	I. 26	20, 419	I. 260		II. 305
	II. 39		I. 290	18, 533	I. 319
	II. 81		II. 195		I. 324
28-31, 156-8	II. 100	21, 419	I. 315		I. 344
29, 157	II. 281		II. 4		I. 354
30, 157-8	I. 17		II. 11		II. 300
	I. 261		II. 42	19, 534	II. 312
30-1, 157-8	II. 312	23, 422	II. 72	21, 536	I. 272
31, 158	I. 261	24, 423	II. 295		I. 275
	II. 284	25, 423	II. 4		II. 222
31, 158-9	I. 290	27, 425	II. 14	23, 537	I. 5
31, 159	I. 288		II. 41	23, 538	II. 289
32, 159	I. 319		II. 69	24, 538	II. 227
	I. 326		II. 109	25, 540	I. 259
34, 161	II. 50		II. 112		I. 318
	II. 56	28, 426	II. 306		I. 354
35, 161-2	I. 300	28, 426-7	II. 271	25-6, 539-41	I. 17
	II. 198		II. 282	28, 542	II. 289
35, 162	I. 270	28, 427	II. 185	30, 543	II. 227
	I. 289		II. 189	30, 544	II. 222
	II. 54		II. 193		
			II. 207	De Constitutione sive Creatione Principum. Vol. II.	
De Circumcisione. Vol. II.		30, 428	I. 267		
			I. 276		
1, 210	II. 222	32, 430	II. 69	4, 364	II. 315
2, 211	I. 21	33, 430	II. 158	7, 367	I. 297
		33, 431	II. 37		I. 303
De Concupiscentia. Vol. II.			II. 55		
		33-6, 430-3	II. 150	De Decem oraculis, quae sunt legum capitula. Vol. II.	
1, 348	II. 303	34, 431	II. 80		
1-2, 348-350	II. 304		II. 87		
2, 350-1	I. 319		II. 242	3, 182	II. 222
	I. 339	35, 432	I. 336	8, 185	I. 276
2, 351	I. 342		I. 348		II. 24
5, 353	I. 240		I. 349	9, 185	II. 309
8, 354	II. 302		II. 292	9, 185-6	II. 132
9, 355	I. 240	36, 432	II. 50		II. 222

23 *

INDEX II. REFERENCES TO PHILO.

10, 187	II. 35	22, 370	II. 209		I. 308
	II. 50	22, 370-1	II. 97	30, 494	I. 270
	II. 126	25, 372	II. 78		I. 296
11, 188	II. 133		II. 241		I. 307
	II. 181		II. 303		I. 308
12, 189	I. 285	25-26, 372	II. 298		I. 316
	II. 55	27, 373	I. 321	31, 494	I. 289
12, 190	I. 291		I. 341		I. 315
	I. 293		I. 346	32, 495	I. 298
	I. 295		II. 87		I. 301
13, 190	II. 2		II. 111		I. 312
14, 191	II. 35		II. 119	34, 496	I. 294
14, 191-2	II. 320		II. 214		II. 86
15, 193	II. 284	33, 378	II. 78		II. 87
	II. 288	35, 379	II. 166		II. 120
16, 194	II. 30		II. 193	35, 496	II. 222
	II. 50	39-40, 381-2	II. 306	35, 496-7	II. 320
17, 194-5	II. 318	41, 383	I. 354	38, 499	II. 170
17, 195	II. 124	41-9, 383-8	I. 359	41, 500-1	I. 275
	II. 296	43, 384	I. 17	41, 501	I. 271
18, 196	II. 291				I. 290
19, 196	II. 63	De eo: Quis rerum divin-			II. 206
20, 197	II. 124	arum heres sit.		42, 501	I. 185
	II. 232	Vol. I.			II. 236
	II. 287	1, 473	I. 351		II. 267
21, 198	I. 268	3, 474	II. 111	42, 501-2	II. 191
	I. 269	6, 476	II. 86	43, 503	I. 33
	I. 283	7, 477	II. 56	44, 503	II. 170
	II. 78		II. 57	45, 504	I. 270
	II. 231	11, 480	I. 318		I. 319
	II. 232	11, 480-1	I. 320	47, 505	I. 268
23, 200	II. 316		I. 328		II. 44
25, 202	I. 279	12, 481	II. 55	48, 505	I. 268
	I. 328	14, 482	II. 288		I. 274
	I. 335	14, 482-3	II. 298		I. 289
	II. 280	14, 483	II. 300		I. 321
28, 204	II. 243	15, 483	II. 9		II. 169
28, 204-5	II. 302	15, 484	II. 9		II. 187
28, 205	II. 308	16, 485	II. 289		II. 280
29, 205	I. 279		II. 298	48, 505-6	I. 335
	II. 222	18, 485-6	II. 289		II. 233
33, 208	II. 222		II. 316	48, 506	II. 15
33, 208-9	II. 130	20, 486	I. 287	50, 507	I. 23
De Deo (Aucher).		22, 487-8	I. 271		II. 299
3, 614-15	I. 306	22 sqq., 487 sqq.		50, 508	I. 17
6, 616	I. 306		I. 319	52, 510	I. 14
		23, 489	II. 62	52, 511	I. 15
De Ebrietate. Vol. I.		24, 489	II. 79	52-3, 510-11	II. 283
3, 358-9	II. 306	25, 490	II. 209	53, 511	I. 13
8, 362	II. 212	26, 491	I. 319	54, 511	II. 299
8-9, 361-2	II. 205	26 sq. 491 sq.	II. 168	54, 511-12	II. 302
9, 362	I. 263	27, 492	I. 270	55, 512	II. 321
	II. 57		I. 271	57, 513	I. 270
	II. 87		I. 281		I. 286
	II. 314		I. 297		II. 69
16, 367	I. 351		I. 298	57, 513-14	I. 21
16-17, 366-7	II. 298		I. 308	57, 514	I. 271
18, 368	II. 324		I. 309		I. 278
20, 369	II. 9	29, 493	I. 267		I. 331
	II. 287		I. 270	58, 514	II. 324

DE DECEM ORACULIS—DE JOSEPHO.

61-2, 518	II. 73		II. 242		II. 299
62, 518	II. 309	32, 214	I. 26	4, 265	II. 126
			I. 348	5, 265	II. 214
De eo: Quod deterius po-			II. 318		II. 281
tiori insidiari soleat.		33, 215	I. 26		II. 298
Vol. I.		34, 215	I. 352	5-7, 265-6	II. 216
2-4, 192-3	II. 285	34-5, 215-16	I. 352	7, 266	II. 309
3, 193	I. 307	37, 217	I. 26	7, 267	II. 298
4, 193	I. 349	38, 217-18	II. 313	10, 268	II. 15
6, 194	II. 241	40, 219-20	II. 323		II. 16
7, 195	I. 25	42, 220	I. 270		II. 36
	I. 26		I. 271		II. 284
	II. 313		I. 300		II. 305
	II. 317		II. 42	11, 268-9	II. 102
8, 195	I. 324	42, 220-1	I. 290	11, 269	II. 86
8, 195-6	II. 295		II. 47		II. 110
8, 196	I. 324	43, 221	II. 9		II. 118
9, 197	II. 8	43-4, 221	II. 101		II. 208
	II. 204	44, 221	I. 326		II. 216
	II. 212		II. 6		II. 229
	II. 321	44, 222	II. 287		II. 242
10, 197	I. 342	46, 223	I. 318		II. 288
	II. 291		I. 321		II. 309
11, 198	II. 291		I. 324		II. 323
12, 199	I. 351	48, 224	I. 25	11, 270	I. 351
	I. 352			12, 270	II. 216
	I. 353	De Exsecrationibus. Vol.		13, 271	II. 80
16, 201-2	II. 205	II.			II. 306
16, 202	II. 49	1, sqq. 429 sqq.	II. 322	14, 271	I. 265
17, 203	II. 286	5, 432	I. 316		I. 324
19, 204	I. 352	6, 433	II. 322		I. 333
	I. 353	7, 434	II. 62		
	II. 321	7, 435	II. 315	De Humanitate. Vol. II.	
21, 205-6	II. 79	8, 435	II. 55	2, 384	II. 47
21, 206	II. 291		II. 165	2, 385	II. 204
22, 207	I. 317		II. 280	2, 386	I. 359
	I. 343		II. 323		II. 35
	II. 33	9, 436	II. 56	3, 386	II. 303
	II. 183		II. 126	3, 387	I. 284
	II. 185		II. 239		II. 303
22-3, 206-7	I. 327		II. 322	4, 387	II. 298
23, 207	I. 317			4, 388	II. 312
	I. 320	De Fortitudine. Vol. II.		6, 389	I. 279
	I. 323	1-3, 375-7	II. 319	9, 390	II. 62
	I. 334	3, 376	II. 125	10, 391	II. 316
	I. 342	3, 377	I. 319	17, 396	II. 224
	II. 33		I. 356		II. 314
	II. 157		II. 50	18, 399	II. 303
	II. 187		II. 323	22, 403	II. 40
	II. 215	3, 377-8	II. 316	23, 404	II. 287
	II. 234	7, 381	II. 4		
	II. 276	7, 382	II. 56	De Incorruptibilitate	
24, 208	I. 339	8, 383	II. 87	mundi. Vol. II.	
	II. 6			5, 491-2	I. 296
24, 208-9	I. 330	De Gigantibus. Vol. I.		12, 498-9	I. 297
	I. 341	2, 263	I. 278	13, 499-500	I. 297
24, 209	II. 115		I. 282	19, 505-6	I. 104
25, 209	I. 351		I. 283		
31, 213-14	II. 160	2-4, 263-5	I. 338	De Josepho (Vita viri	
	II. 204		II. 145	civilis). Vol. II.	
		3, 264	II. 298	1, 41	II. 321

INDEX II. REFERENCES TO PHILO.

6, 46	I. 20		II. 15		II. 15
	I. 289		II. 194		II. 55
	II. 166		II. 199	34-5, 466-7	II. 7
40, 75	II. 47	1-2, 436-8	II. 298	35, 466	II. 11
		2, 437	II. 298		II. 15
De Judice. Vol. II.		4, 439	II. 316		II. 298
1, 344	II. 303	5, 440	II. 55	38, 470	I. 342
2, 345	I. 353		II. 228		I. 343
3, 346	II. 318	6, 440	II. 208	39, 471	I. 288
3, 347	I. 353	6, 441	II. 56		I. 289
		7, 441	I. 15		I. 314
De Justitia. Vol. II.			II. 56		I. 353
2, 360	II. 315		II. 126		II. 65
	II. 316	8, 442	II. 207		
3, 361	I. 21	9, 443	II. 218	De Monarchia. Liber I.	
7, 367	II. 74		II. 321	Vol. II.	
	II. 85	9, 443-4	II. 180	1, 213	I. 289
	II. 118	10, 444-5	II. 117	1, 213-14	I. 286
	II. 287	12, 446	I. 319	3, 216	I. 304
8, 367	II. 298		II. 224	4, 216	II. 1
8, 367-8	II. 283	13, 447	I. 351		II. 17
10, 368-9	II. 47		II. 157	4, 216-17	I. 289
14, 373-4	I. 288	13 sqq., 447 sqq.			II. 4
14, 374	I. 279		I. 353	6, 218	II. 57
		14, 448	I. 352		II. 71
De Legatione ad Caium.			II. 117	6, 218-19	II. 19
Vol. II.			II. 222		II. 74
1, 545	I. 11		II. 227		II. 117
1, 545-6	II. 306	16, 450-1	I. 20	6, 219	II. 98
1, 546	II. 9	18, 452	II. 164	7, 220	II. 303
	II. 31		II. 217	9, 222	I. 14
	II. 71		II. 229		II. 283
	II. 86		II. 242		
	II. 87	21, 454-5	II. 236	Liber II. Vol. II.	
	II. 289	22, 455	II. 55	1, 222	I. 279
8, 553	II. 219		II. 112		I. 289
16, 562	II. 119	23, 456	II. 167		II. 147
20, 566	I. 183		II. 217	5, 225	II. 186
22, 567	I. 7		II. 287		II. 199
28, 572	I. 11		II. 307	5, 225-6	I. 272
29, 573	I. 10		II. 314	5, 226	I. 287
30, 576	I. 11	27, 459	II. 158	5-6, 225-7	I. 186
31, 577	II. 125	31, 462	I. 342	6, 227	II. 238
33, 583	I. 10		II. 228		
44 sqq., 597	I. 11	31, 462-3	II. 250	De Mundi opificio secun-	
45, 598	I. 10	31, 463	II. 217	dum Moysen. Vol. I.	
46, 600	I. 10		II. 240	1, 1	I. 16
		32, 464	I. 17	2, 2	I. 290
De Mercede meretricis			I. 286		I. 299
non accipienda in			I. 287		II. 4
sacrarium. Vol. II.			I. 294		II. 15
2-4, 265-9	II. 125		II. 2		II. 31
	II. 305		II. 68		II. 54
			II. 87	2, 3	I. 292
De MigrationeAbrahami.			II. 112		I. 301
Vol. I.			II. 122	3, 2	II. 55
1, 436	I. 351		II. 157	3, 3	I. 19
1, 436-7	I. 352	33, 465	I. 259		I. 290
	II. 177		I. 265		I. 293
1, 437	I. 340		II. 3		II. 174

4, 4	I. 289		II. 292			II. 279
	I. 304		II. 293		54, 37	I. 25
	II. 118	25, 18	I. 258			II. 316
4-5, 4	II. 75	25-29, 18-21	II. 275		57, 39	II. 305
	II. 162	26, 19	I. 23		58, 39	II. 317
5, 4	II. 169		I. 302		59, 40	I. 355
5, 4-5	II. 84	27, 19	I. 296		60, 41	II. 56
	II. 87	27, 19-20	I. 289		61, 41	I. 291
5, 5	I. 297	33, 23-4	II. 231			II. 2
	I. 298	34, 24	II. 231			II. 55
	I. 299	38, 27	II. 231		61, 42	II. 54
	I. 310	38, 27-8	I. 287			
	II. 54	38, sqq., 27 sqq.			De Mutatione nominum	
6, 5	I. 311		II. 232		(quare quorundam	
	II. 55	39, 28	I. 279		in Scripturis mutata	
	II. 57	40, 28	I. 286		sint nomina). Vol. I.	
	II. 72		I. 321		1, 578-9	II. 38
	II. 77		II. 230		1, 579	I. 356
	II. 80	40, 29	I. 353			II. 39
	II. 162	43, 30	II. 295		2, 579	I. 325
	II. 164	44, 30-1	II. 78			II. 2
	II. 183	44, 31	II. 74			II. 17
	II. 187		II. 275			II. 19
	II. 239	45, 31	II. 214		2, 580	II. 21
7, 5	II. 280	46, 32	I. 316			II. 71
7, 6	I. 273		I. 328		3, 581	II. 71
	I. 279		I. 339			II. 94
	I. 283		II. 26			II. 104
	I. 309		II. 234			II. 117
7 sqq., 5 sqq.	I. 293		II. 275		3, 582	II. 222
8, 6-7	II. 165	47, 32-3	II. 278		4, 582	II. 48
9, 7	I. 272	47, 33	I. 316			II. 87
	II. 74		II. 153			II. 112
	II. 159	48, 33	I. 342		4, 582-3	II. 141
10, 7	II. 162		II. 32		4, 583	II. 119
13, 9	II. 219		II. 161		5, 584	II. 47
14, 10	II. 47		II. 165		5, 585	I. 302
	II. 71		II. 278			II. 54
	II. 151		II. 314		6, 585	II. 297
17, 11-12	I. 321	49, 33	II. 153		7, 586	I. 324
17, 12	I. 258	49, 33-4	II. 279		8, 587	I. 13
	I. 324	50, 34	I. 283			II. 69
	I. 356		I. 332			II. 234
19, 13	I. 287		II. 167		9-10, 587-9	II. 253
	I. 288		II. 314		9-10, 588-9	I. 265
	II. 166	50, 34-5	I. 26		10, 588	I. 352
20, 14	I. 317		II. 278			I. 263
21, 14	I. 280		II. 287		10, 589	I. 265
21, 15	I. 324	51, 35	I. 316		11, 590	II. 79
22, 15	I. 280		I. 321		12, 590	II. 9
	I. 321		I. 328		13, 590-1	II. 252
	I. 327		II. 165		13, 591	II. 36
	I. 339		II. 279		21, 597	II. 25
	I. 343		II. 280		23, 598	I. 26
23, 15-16	II. 280	52, 35-6	II. 278			I. 288
23, 16	I. 284	52, 36	I. 349			I. 298
	II. 3		II. 50			II. 74
	II. 157		II. 279			II. 126
24, 16, sq.	II. 139	53, 36-7	II. 305			II. 164
24, 17	I. 283	53 sqq., 36 sqq.				II. 174

INDEX II. REFERENCES TO PHILO.

25, 599	I. 21	8, 334	II. 42			II. 301
27, 600	II. 315	8-9, 334-5	I. 19			II. 313
29, 602	I. 17	9, 335	II. 322	9, 231		II. 36
30, 603	II. 313		II. 324			II. 37
31-3, 603-5	II. 319	11, 336	II. 277			II. 42
34, 606	II. 287	12, 336	II. 15			II. 99
39, 612	I. 329		II. 87			II. 323
40, 613-14	II. 110	12, 336-7	II. 130	10, 232		II. 56
41, 614	II. 286	12, 337	II. 297			II. 126
47, 619	I. 294	15, 339	I. 334			II. 202
		20, 342	II. 15	11, 232-3		II. 290
De Nobilitate.	Vol. II.		II. 56	11, 233		I. 344
1, 437-8	II. 285		II. 69	16, 236		I. 315
2, 438-9	II. 125		II. 85	17, 236		II. 295
3, 440	II. 70		II. 117	20, 238		II. 184
	II. 99	20-1, 342-3	II. 103			II. 294
	II. 153	21, 343	II. 56			II. 307
	II. 278	22, 343	II. 209	24, 241		II. 295
	II. 279	25, 345	I. 26	25-6, 241-2		II. 221
4, 441	II. 295	28, 347	I. 270			II. 272
5, 442	II. 4		I. 275			II. 307
	II. 19		II. 314	30, 244		I. 351
	II. 35		II. 316			I. 352
	II. 54	30, 348	II. 236			II. 179
5, 443	II. 126		II. 319	30-32, 244-6		I. 351
		31, 348	II. 319	31, 245		I. 324
De Parentibus colendis		31, 349	I. 290			I. 351
(*Mai*).		32, 349	I. 355	32, 246		I. 324
9, 28	II. 56	33, 349	II. 319			I. 353
				35, 248		II. 316
De Plantatione	Noe.	De Poenitentia.	Vol. II.	35, 249		II. 203
Vol. I.		1. 405	II. 51	36, 249		I. 324
1, 329	I. 267		II. 296			I. 341
	I. 297		II. 323			I. 353
	I. 300	2, 406	II. 316			II. 202
	I. 309			37, 249		I. 341
1, 330	I. 268	De Posteritate Caini sibi				I. 346
	I. 276	visi sapientis. Vol. I.				II. 202
	I. 288	1, 226-7	II. 38	37, 250		II. 211
2, 330	I. 289	1, 227	II. 50			II. 217
	I. 290	1-2, 226-7	II. 14			II. 315
	I. 297	2, 227	I. 270	38, 250		I. 262
	I. 300		I. 356	39, 251		II. 285
2, 330-1	I. 268		II. 9	41, 251-2		II. 202
	I. 288		II. 42	43, 253-4		II. 57
	II. 166		II. 294	45, 255		II. 202
3, 331	I. 278	3, 228	II. 294	48, 258		II. 18
	I. 283	4-6, 228-9	II. 20			II. 19
4, 331-2	I. 338	5, 228-9	II. 45			II. 117
	II. 145	5, 229	II. 19	54, 261		II. 316
4, 332	I. 335		II. 42			
5, 332-3	I. 333		II. 112	De Praemiis et Poenis.		
5, 332	II. 165		II. 157	Vol. II.		
	II. 193	5-6, 228-9	II. 110	2, 410		I. 260
	II. 280	6, 229	II. 87			I. 261
5, 333	II. 6		II. 115			I. 316
7, 334	I. 289		II. 218			II. 284
	I. 340	6, 230	II. 9			II. 291
	I. 344	7-9, 230-1	II. 7			II. 313
	I. 349	8, 231	II. 56	4 sqq., 412 sqq.		

DE MUTAT. NOMINUM—DE SACR. AB. ET CAINI.

	II. 321		II. 189		II. 99
5, 412-13	I. 354	20, 562	II. 170	4, 254	II. 30
5, 413	I. 290		II. 186		II. 39
	II. 59		II. 206		II. 50
6, 414	I. 276		II. 217		II. 81
	II. 31	20-1, 561-3	II. 228		II. 102
7, 414	II. 2	20-1, 562-3	II. 308	5, 254	II. 56
7, 414-15	II. 4	21, 563	II. 226	8, 257	II. 316
7, 415	II. 5		II. 295	9, 258	II. 86
	II. 55	23, 565	II. 295		II. 117
9, 416	II. 125	24, 565	I. 335		II. 124
	II. 315		II. 4		II. 306
	II. 316	25, 566	I. 25	11, 260	II. 282
9, 417	II. 167		I. 334	13, 261	I. 298
	II. 283		II. 9		I. 309
11, 418	II. 293		II. 178		II. 71
12, 419	II. 302		II. 208		II. 113
12, 419 sq.	II. 323		II. 212		II. 118
13, 420	II. 303		II. 222	13, 261-2	II. 76
14, 421	II. 209		II. 308		II. 220
	II. 222	26, 567	II. 264	14, 262-3	I. 263
	II. 286	29, 570	II. 19	15, 263	I. 322
15-20, 421-8	II. 321	30, 571	II. 321	16, 264	II. 288
16, 423	II. 322	31, 572	II. 324		II. 292
19, 427	II. 55	32, 573	I. 341		
20, 428	II. 56		I. 346	De Sacrificiis Abelis et	
	II. 281	33, 573	II. 218	Caini. Vol. I.	
		35, 575	II. 207	1, 163-4	II. 288
De Praemiis Sacerdotum.			II. 209	2, 164	II. 145
Vol. II.		36, 575	I. 298		II. 321
3, 234-5	I. 319	37, 576	II. 245	3, 165	II. 178
3, 235	I. 351		II. 295		II. 199
	II. 304	38, 577	II. 9	5, 167	II. 125
	II. 317		II. 245	6-9, 168-9	II. 313
			II. 295	8, 169	II. 16
De Profugis. Vol. I.		De Providentia ad Alex-		10, 170	I. 262
1, 546-7	II. 244	andrum. Sermo I.			I. 322
2, 547	I. 292	20-22	I. 306	12, 171	II. 200
	I. 298	59	II. 61		II. 308
	II. 4	60	II. 61	13, 171-2	II. 292
2, 547-8	II. 164			14, 173	II. 50
4-6, 549-51	I. 25	Sermo II.		15, 173	I. 274
9, 553	II. 213	3-14	II. 61		II. 72
13, 556	I. 322	16	I. 325		II. 74
	II. 56	16 sqq.	II. 62		II. 93
13-14, 556	II. 143	22	I. 316		II. 120
14, 557	II. 226	24	II. 61	15, 173-4	II. 89
15, 557	II. 288	31-2	II. 60	17, 174	II. 30
	II. 291	45-49	I. 305		II. 32
15, 557-8	II. 50	50-1	I. 305	17, 175	II. 204
16, 558	I. 25	82	II. 58	18, 175	I. 298
	II. 323	87-97	II. 58		II. 42
17, 559	I. 351	99	II. 59		II. 181
	II. 298	99-102	II. 60	18, 175-6	II. 43
18, 560	II. 195	100	I. 273	19, 176	II. 72
	II. 208	102	II. 61		II. 234
	II. 212				II. 291
18-19, 560-1	II. 84	De Sacrificantibus. Vol.		20, 177	I. 341
	II. 161	II.			I. 348
19, 561	II. 185	2, 252	I. 308		I. 349

INDEX II. REFERENCES TO PHILO.

22-3, 178	II. 8	8, 627	I. 356		II. 263
	II. 321	9, 627	I. 21	32, 648	II. 80
24-6, 179 sq.	II. 169	10, 628-9	I. 265		II. 102
26, 180	II. 178	10, 628-30	I. 259	32, 648-9	I. 267
28, 181	II. 28	10, 629	II. 256		I. 356
28-30, 181-3	II. 13	10, 629-30	II. 7	32, 649	II. 46
36, 186	II. 235		II. 289	33, 649	II. 4
	II. 242	11, 630	II. 20		II. 146
37, 188	II. 234		II. 43	34, 650-1	II. 222
	II. 241		II. 71		II. 263
38, 188-9	II. 195		II. 162	34, 651	II. 218
38, 189	II. 222		II. 184	35, 652	I. 17
39, 189	II. 90		II. 195	36, 652-3	II. 289
	II. 102		II. 208	37, 653	II. 169
De Septenario. Vol. II.		11-12, 630-1	II. 257		II. 185
3-5, 278-80	II. 314	12, 631	II. 95		II. 229
4, 279-80	II. 286		II. 120	39, 655	II. 146
5, 280	II. 30		II. 218		II. 196
	II. 49	13, 631	I. 20	39-40, 655	II. 21
	II. 50		II. 257	39-41, 655-6	II. 263
6, 282	II. 315	13, 631-2	II. 40	40, 655	II. 95
	II. 316	13, 632	I. 294		II. 146
9, 285	II. 303		I. 303	40, 655-6	II. 14
23, 296	II. 42		II. 82	40-1, 655-7	II. 246
	II. 55		II. 165	41, 656	II. 4
24, 297	II. 305	14, 632	II. 267		II. 117
			I. 340		II. 170
De Sobrietate (De his verbis: resipuit Noe). Vol. I.			I. 341		II. 196
		15, 633	II. 165	43, 657-8	II. 264
		16 sqq., 634 sqq.			
6, 396-7	I. 344		I. 20	Liber II. Vol. I.	
11, 401	II. 282	17, 636	I. 20	2, 660	I. 20
	II. 284		II. 224	5, 663	I. 26
13, 402	II. 43	19, 638	I. 21		II. 323
	II. 254		II. 8	6, 665	I. 297
	II. 286		II. 195		I. 298
			II. 240		II. 74
De Somniis (De eo quod a Deo mittantur somnia). Liber I. Vol. I.			II. 257		II. 163
		20, 639-40	II. 258		II. 164
		21, 640	II. 256		II. 186
2, 621	I. 21	22, 641	I. 272	7-9, 665-7	I. 24
3, 622	I. 276		I. 281	14, 671	II. 123
3-4, 622-3	I. 270		I. 282	16, 673	I. 270
	I. 272	22, 641-2	I. 338	20, 677	I. 20
4, 623	I. 268		II. 260	26, 681	II. 9
	I. 282	22, 642	I. 272	26, 682	II. 51
4, 623-4	I. 279		I. 279		II. 314
4, 624	I. 265		II. 57	28, 683	II. 217
5, 624	I. 319		II. 242	32, 687	II. 36
	I. 342	23, 642-3	II. 262	32 sqq., 687 sqq.	
5, 625	I. 353	23, 643	II. 218		II. 36
	II. 124		II. 262	33, 688	II. 167
6, 625	I. 279		II. 281	34, 689	II. 191
	I. 326	24, 643-4	II. 263		II. 283
	I. 328	25-6, 644-5	II. 104	36, 690	II. 167
	I. 339	26, 645	II. 87	37, 690	II. 202
	II. 214	27, 645-6	II. 321		II. 208
	II. 316	31, 648	I. 338		II. 242
6-7, 625-6	I. 284		II. 43		II. 315
8, 626-7	I. 21		II. 181	37, 691	II. 224
				38, 691-2	I. 313

DE SACR. AB. ET CAINI—FRAGMENTS.

		II. 53	20, 98	I. 276	31, 171	I. 276
		II. 324	26, 103	I. 276		II. 56
38, 692		I. 15	28, 106	II. 19		II. 102
		I. 302	29, 107	I. 185		II. 110
		II. 15		II. 268	36, 176	I. 290
		II. 88	31, 108	II. 47		I. 294
		II. 281	49, 123-4	II. 269		I. 303
39, 693		II. 256			37, 177	I. 356
43, 696		II. 2	Liber II. Vol. II.		38, 178	I. 276
			1, 134-5	I. 15	39, 179	I. 316
De Specialibus Legibus.			1, 185	I. 344		
Liber II. Vol. II.				II. 56	Fragments.	Vol. II.
4, 272		II. 222		II. 283	625	II. 33
5, 274		II. 56	3, 136	I. 15		II. 184
7, 275		II. 224	5-7, 138-40	I. 16		II. 197
				I. 232	625-6	I. 305
Liber III. Vol. II.			12, 144	II. 68	635	I. 325
1, 299-300		I. 8		II. 98		II. 301
5, 304		II. 303		II. 280	635 sqq.	II. 62
12, 312		II. 303			637	I. 316
15, 313		II. 164	Liber III. Vol. II.		638	II. 61
		II. 186	3, 146	II. 75	642	II. 59
17, 316		II. 307		II. 78		II. 60
20, 318		I. 276	6, 148-9	I. 275	643	I. 287
		I. 342	8, 150	I. 303	643-4	II. 60
		I. 356		II. 104	644	II. 61
22, 320		II. 303	9, 150	I. 267	649	II. 306
34, 330-1		I. 258	9, 150-1	I. 270		II. 322
34, 331		I. 268	9, 151	I. 284	651	II. 294
		II. 55	11, 152	II. 22	654	II. 17
		II. 65	11-14, 151-5	I. 186	655	II. 69
36, 332		II. 62		I. 277		II. 72
37, 333		II. 163	12, 153	I. 272		II. 169
		II. 186	12, 154	II. 157	656	II. 88
		II. 280	13, 154	I. 350	657	II. 306
				I. 351	658	II. 90
Liber IV. Vol. II.				I. 353	658 sq.	II. 90
2, 337		II. 303		II. 80	660	II. 88
4, 338		II. 186		II. 157	661-2	II. 289
		II. 280		II. 169	665	I. 258
8, 343		I. 14		II. 171		I. 355
		II. 52	14, 155	II. 22	668	I. 319
				II. 56		I. 320
De Vita contemplativa.				II. 105		I. 328
Vol. II				II. 170	669 sq.	II. 14
1, 472		I. 309		II. 238	673	II. 313
3, 475		I. 179	17, 157	I. 271	677	I. 290
8, 481		I. 179		I. 311		II. 55
11, 485-6		I. 179		II. 297	678	II. 234
			18, 158	I. 273	679	II. 123
De Vita Mosis, hoc est			21, 162	II. 126		
de theologia et pro-			22, 163	I. 324	Fragments of Harris not
phetia.Liber I. Vol. II.				II. 315	in Mangey.
1, 80		I. 15	23, 163-4	I. 14	p. 8	I. 347
1, 81		I. 21		I. 15		II. 310
12, 91		II. 240		II. 88	„ 11	II. 313
		II. 265	23, 164	II. 88	„ 17	II. 313
14, 92-3		II. 21	24, 164	II. 279	„ 19	II. 50
14, 93		II. 321	26, 166	II. 23	„ 23	II. 14
17, 95-6		I. 275	27, 167	I. 264	„ 26	I. 320
17, 96		I. 282	27, 168	II. 315	„ 38	I. 261

INDEX II. REFERENCES TO PHILO.

p. 63	II. 85	22	II. 88				II. 117
„ 65	II. 104	29	II. 281				II. 127
„ 66 sqq.	II. 80	64	II. 294		25, 290		II. 157
	II. 84	74	I. 338		27, 291		II. 124
„ 70	II. 294	110	I. 261				II. 294
„ 71	II. 294	115	II. 34				II. 295
„ 74	II. 315	130	II. 47		28, 292		II. 295
		140	II. 323		28, 292-3		II. 295
In Flaccum. Vol. II.					29, 293		I. 334
2, 518	II. 295	Quod Deus sit immutabilis. Vol. I.			30, 294		II. 9
6, 523	I. 4						II. 209
8, 525	I. 4	1, 272-3	II. 240				II. 309
10, 527	I. 4	1, 273	II. 117		34, 296		II. 55
		2, 274	II. 47				II. 209
Quaestiones et Solutiones in Exodum.			II. 296		34-5, 296-7		II. 315
		4, 275	II. 33		36, 298		II. 199
Sermo II.			II. 160		37, 299		II. 270
1	I. 290		II. 292				II. 308
2	II. 55	6, 276	II. 36				
40	II. 44	6, 276-7	II. 46		Quod omnis probus liber sit. Vol. II.		
45	II. 123		II. 296				
62	II. 85	6, 277	I. 293		1-2, 445-7		I. 357
66	II. 104		I. 294		10, 455		II. 314
68	II. 80		II. 82		17, 462		I. 324
	II. 84		II. 174		22, 470		I. 261
		7, 277	II. 87				
Quaestiones et Solutiones in Genesin. Sermo I.			II. 105		Sacrarum Legum allegoriarum post sex dierum opus liber I. Vol. I.		
			II. 118				
32	II. 279		II. 175				
54	II. 118	7-10, 277-9	I. 281				
55	II. 14	8, 278	II. 69		1, 43		II. 234
64	I. 271	9, 278-9	I. 317				II. 241
79	II. 313	10, 279	I. 276		2, 44		I. 19
100	II. 50		I. 324				I. 293
			I. 332				II. 231
Sermo II.			I. 339		3, 44		II. 16
34	I. 258	10, 279-80	I. 347		3, 45		I. 296
	I. 355	11, 281	II. 18		4, 45		I. 321
54	II. 14		II. 23		4-5, 45-6		II. 232
59	I. 321	11-14, 280-3	II. 14		6, 46		II. 230
62	II. 33	12, 281	II. 36		8, 47		II. 230
	II. 184		II. 199				II. 241
	II. 197	13, 282	II. 18		8-10, 47-8		II. 163
Sermo III.		15, 283	II. 51		9, 47		II. 178
3	I. 271	16, 284	II. 56				II. 234
	I. 284	17, 284	I. 311				II. 241
5	I. 322		II. 72		9, 47-8		II. 241
6	I. 274		II. 117		9-10, 47-8		II. 78
9-10	II. 283		II. 118		9-12, 47-9		II. 276
10	I. 338	17, 284-5	II. 57		10, 48		I. 318
11	I. 331	18, 285	II. 180				II. 81
19 sqq.	I. 262	19, 285-6	II. 101		11, 48-9		II. 241
45	I. 338	20, 286	II. 209		11, 49		I. 317
49	I. 271		II. 310				I. 341
		23, 288	I. 290				I. 354
Sermo IV.		23, 288-9	II. 30				II. 62
1	II. 81		II. 54		12, 49		II. 234
2	II. 92		II. 85		12, 49-50		I. 322
8	I. 274		II. 105		12-13, 50		I. 327
	II. 74	24, 289	II. 19		13, 50		I. 323
15	II. 319		II. 103				II. 23

FRAGMENTS—TISCHENDORF.

	II. 56	11, 73	I. 324	35, 108-9	II. 304
	II. 281		I. 341	35 sqq., 108 sqq.
	II. 294	13, 74	I. 343		I. 26
13, 51	I. 321	13, 74-5	I. 350	38, 110	I. 319
	I. 325	14, 75	II. 206		I. 342
	I. 340		II. 306	39-40, 110-11	II. 303
	II. 111	18, 79	I. 345		II. 308
	II. 112	18, 79 sq.	II. 301	40, 111	I. 351
14, 51-2	II. 207	20, 80-1	II. 26	40-1, 111	I. 353
	II. 212		II. 157	45, 112-13	II. 320
14, 52	II. 29	20 sqq., 80 sqq.		46, 114	II. 310
	II. 42		II. 317	48-9, 114-15	II. 307
	II. 49	21, 81	II. 309	49, 115	II. 321
15, 53	II. 23	21, 81-2	I. 24	52-3, 117 sq.	II. 298
	II. 36		II. 203	53, 117-18	II. 308
	II. 291		II. 310	53, 118	II. 285
16, 53 sq.	II. 277	21, 82	II. 29	55, 119	I. 316
18, 55	I. 21		II. 160	55-6, 119	I. 334
	II. 116	22, 82	II. 36	56, 119	I. 279
19, 56	II. 202	24, 83	I. 318		II. 56
	II. 309	25, 84-5	II. 319		II. 218
	II. 315				II. 241
	II. 318	Liber III. Vol. I.			II. 255
22, 57	I. 319	2, 88	I. 19	58, 120	I. 26
24, 58	I. 353		II. 42		II. 255
24, 59	II. 228	4, 90	II. 222		II. 286
25, 59	II. 209	8, 93	II. 312	59, 121	II. 165
28-30, 61-3	II. 276	9, 93	II. 2	59 sqq., 120 sq.	
29, 62	I. 326		II. 15		II. 255
	II. 17		II. 288	59-61, 120-1	II. 160
30, 62-3	II. 293	10, 93-4	II. 291	59-62, 120-2	II. 308
32, 64	II. 292	13, 95	I. 319	60-1, 121-2	II. 178
	II. 299	14, 95	I. 324	61, 121	II. 185
			II. 228		II. 194
Liber II. Vol. I.			II. 297	62, 122	II. 255
1, 66	II. 49	15, 96	II. 9	63, 122	II. 255
	II. 182		II. 228	63, 123	II. 50
1, 66-7	II. 38	16, 97	I. 312	64, 123	II. 301
1, 67	II. 33	17, 97	II. 43	65, 124	I. 341
2, 67	II. 187		II. 293		I. 346
	II. 277	20, 99 sq.	II. 305	66, 124	II. 9
3, 67	I. 324	21, 100	II. 300	67, 124-5	I. 346
3, 67-8	II. 301			68, 125	II. 85
3, 68	I. 355	21-34, 101-8	II. 312	70, 126	II. 291
4, 68	II. 241	22, 101	I. 23	72, 127-8	II. 222
	II. 302	22, 100-101	II. 299	73, 128	II. 18
4, 69	II. 78	23, 101	II. 105		II. 50
	II. 275		II. 300		II. 196
6, 69	II. 158	24, 102	II. 54	76, 130	II. 235
6, 69 sq.	II. 301	25, 103	II. 242		II. 312
7, 71	I. 315		II. 314	77, 130-1	II. 225
	I. 343	25-6, 102-3	II. 225		
	I. 344	31, 106-7	II. 165	Tischendorf, Philononea.
	I. 351	31-3, 106-7	II. 190	p. 20	II. 30
	II. 66		II. 195	p. 43, line 3	II. 55
	II. 233	32, 107	II. 69	p. 53	I. 16
7 sqq., 70 sqq.	I. 345	32-3, 107	II. 5	p. 64, line 1 sq.	
9, 72	I. 292	33, 108	II. 228		II. 42
	II. 36	34, 108	II. 50	p. 67, line 2 sqq.	
	II. 310		II. 218		II. 305
10, 73	I. 343		II. 241	p. 87	II. 109

INDEX III.

References to passages in the Old Testament cited by Philo.

	GENESIS.			
i. 1	I. 293		xviii.	1 sqq. II. 90-92
2	I. 299; II. 214			6 II. 89
5	II. 159			16 II. 251
11 sqq.	II. 78			22 II. 36-7
16	II. 70			27 II. 315
26	II. 138-153			33 II. 120
27	I. 333; II. 77, 142-3, 187, 197, 275		xix.	1 II. 251
				1 sqq. II. 264
ii. 1	II. 241		xxi.	6 II. 225
4	II. 162, 241			10 II. 244
5	II. 78, 241		xxii.	3-4 II. 20
6	I. 323; II. 241			7 I. 335
7	I. 322, 327; II. 275			16 II. 196
8	II. 206, 277		xxvi.	5 II. 167
9	II. 277		xxviii.	11 sqq. II. 257
10	II. 242			12 I. 336
18	I. 355; II. 183, 277			13 II. 104
21-23	I. 344-5			17 II. 102, 146,
24	II. 206			21 II. 103
iii. 9	II. 43		xxxi.	3 II. 208
22	II. 148			11-13 II. 145, 245, 263
24	II. 84, 167-8, 243			13 II. 196, 246
iv. 21	I. 351, 352		xxxii.	24 II. 252
vi. 2	I. 338			25 II. 259
3	II. 216			29 II. 21, 71
4	II. 240		xxxvii.	14 II. 241
6-7	II. 13		xxxviii.	7 II. 311
8	II. 102, 126-7, 128, 310-11		xlii. 11	II. 188, 270
			xlviii. 15-16	II. 142, 149, 255
ix. 4	I. 320			
11	II. 36			EXODUS.
27	II. 43, 254		i. 11	I. 340
xi. 5	II. 41, 108, 270		ii. 23	II. 235
7	II. 148, 150		iii. 2 sqq.	II. 265
xii. 1	II. 6, 177		9	II. 235
4	II. 167		14	II. 20
7	II. 101		ix. 29	II. 227
xiv. 7	II. 207		xiii. 11	II. 12
18	II. 225		xiv. 19	II. 267
xv. 2	II. 85		xv. 17-18	II. 129
9 sqq.	I. 271, 273, 319; II. 73, 168, 187		xvi. 4	II. 218, 241
			15	II. 29, 242
			15-16	II. 160, 178
15	I. 331		31	II. 242
xvi. 7 sqq.	II. 243		xvii. 6	II. 36
xvii. 1	II. 48, 94, 141		12	II. 227

REFERENCES TO THE OLD TESTAMENT.

xix-xx.	II. 132-3	_DEUTERONOMY._	
xx. 12	II. 205	i. 31	II. 13, 246
18	II. 133, 180	iv. 12	II. 180
19	II. 57	v. 5	II. 191, 268, 283
21	II. 19, 100	31	II. 37
xxiii. 20	II. 270	vi. 13	II. 196
20-1	II. 251-2	viii. 3	II. 178
xxiv. 1	II. 250	15	II. 28, 203
16	II. 123	x. 17	II. 149
xxv. 22	II. 119, 161, 189	xii. 23	I. 320
xxvi. 1	I. 275	xiv. 1	II. 270, 282
xxviii. 16	I. 350	xix. 14	II. 272
26 [lxx.]	I. 353; II. 172	xxi. 18-19	II. 205
30, 32	II. 229	xxx. 15-19	I. 347
xxxi. 1	II. 190	xxxii. 6	II. 270, 282
2-3	II. 215	7-9	II. 221, 272
xxxiii. 7	II. 6	13	II. 204
12 sqq.	II. 18, 74	18	II. 270, 282
17	II. 103, 127	39	II. 18
LEVITICUS.		_JOSHUA._	
ix. 24	I. 273	ii. 11	II. 121
xviii. 6	II. 102		
xxi. 11	II. 205	_PSALMS._	
xxvi. 12	II. 224, 262	xxii. 1	II. 270
NUMBERS.		xxvi. 1	II. 40
iii. 12	II. 241, 242	xlv. 4	II. 224
v. 15 sqq.	II. 228	lxi. 11	II. 179
vi. 2	II. 101	lxxvii. 49	I. 338
viii. 26	I. 352		
xi. 17	II. 215	_PROVERBS._	
23	II. 110	viii. 22-3	II. 212
xiv. 20	II. 236		
xvi. 48 [Hebrew xvii. 13]	II. 268	_ZECHARIAH._	
xx. 25	II. 228	vi. 12	II. 188
xxiii. 19	II. 12, 13, 14, 246		
xxxv. 25	II. 228		

THE END.

G. NORMAN AND SON, PRINTERS, HART STREET, COVENT GARDEN, LONDON.

www.ingramcontent.com/pod-product-compliance
Lightning Source LLC
Chambersburg PA
CBHW020241240426

43672CB00006B/604